WITHDRAWN

THE LURE OF THE LAND

By the same author

Tales of the Frontier
The Dixie Frontier
Vanguards of the Frontier
The Sod-House Frontier

THE LURE OF THE LAND

*A Social History of the Public Lands
from the Articles of Confederation
to the New Deal*

EVERETT DICK

UNIVERSITY OF NEBRASKA PRESS · LINCOLN

Publishers on the Plains

UNP

Copyright © 1970 by the University of Nebraska Press
Standard Book Number 8032–0725–5
Library of Congress Catalog Card Number 66–13015

Manufactured in the United States of America

To

Arthur Lynn Dick, M.D.

Contents

A section of illustrations follows page 178.

Preface

DURING THE course of gathering data while writing about the everyday life of the frontiersman in the different sections of the United States, I became convinced that land, before it was separated from the United States government and during the process of its actual change in ownership from the nation to the individual, was the most important single social factor in frontier history. The process of transfer to private ownership of government land or government-supervised Indian land was the woof thread on the loom of the frontier. This thread was continually interlaced with hard experiences in the struggle for existence, thus weaving the fabric of the social and economic history of the American frontier. My aim in this book is to trace this thread from government ownership of the land into private hands.

From the period of the starving time in the first colonies in Virginia and Massachusetts, which compelled the colonizing agencies to grant plots of land to individuals during the struggle for survival, land became the lure that enticed immigrants to America and settlers farther westward. The dream of many Europeans was to become landowners, but European society was so rigidly stratified that it was impossible for the landless to realize this wish. Only nobility or royalty could own land; thus, for the landless, the prospect of landownership was worth the dangerous ocean voyage and other hardships.

European immigrants wrote glowing reports of the rich land in America, so easy to possess and so abundantly productive; in the 1840's, for example, Scandinavians wrote that the orchards bore in such a bountiful manner that often the crop was not even gathered, and swine were allowed to feast upon the fallen fruit. A hog, they implied, lived better in America than a commoner in Europe. The man who farmed the rocky New England hills or the Piedmont southerner who tilled the depleted lands east of the mountains was likewise lured by the deep black soil of the Mississippi Valley.

ix

Land was the most important force that impelled the population to push across the continent. But the enticement of ever-more-bountiful agricultural production was only one strain of the siren call. Forest and mineral wealth and the speculative value of strategic locations—harbors, steamboat landings, damsites, and townsites—led to keen competition and the evolution of a class of professional land seekers—the lead miner and gold miner, the lumberman, the town developer, and more recently, the power magnate.

The movement of population across the continent, which observers around 1800 had anticipated would be snail-like, progressed with lightning swiftness. As Harold Ickes pointed out, Thomas Jefferson had reckoned that the march of population from the Appalachians to the Pacific would take one hundred generations, but Jefferson missed by ninety-five generations. Created by law in the 1780's as the "unreserved and unappropriated public domain," the western wilderness soon began to melt away, and by 1935 it had all but vanished.

It is the human side of this process of land distribution that we examine: how the land-hungry pioneer interpreted the land laws, or ignored them; his success in "handing up laws" to Congress by frontier usage when existing statutes were inadequate for his needs; his custom of illegally exploiting the natural resources; and the final end of exploitation and the coming of a policy of conservation.

It is not my purpose to play the part of the iconoclast or change the common concept of the frontiersman as a hardy, law-abiding, hardworking tiller of the soil to that of the borderer who took the law into his own hands; but it must be confessed that when it came to the public lands, far from the strong hand of authority, the frontiersman paid little heed to the laws laid down by Congress. In his defense, however, it must be said that the pioneer had an outlook concerning the natural resources of the United States different from that of the East or from that which we have today. He saw the land and its riches as unlimited, ready for exploitation by the firstcomer. To his mind there was no need to save anything since there was such an abundance that there was plenty for all, and no one should be penalized for helping himself to that which was as bountiful as atmosphere or water. His individualism, nurtured by his wild and unrestrained life, led him to seize the choicest resources for his own benefit. Such was the western attitude, but the frontier did not make the laws concerning the public lands. They were made by eastern people who were far from the scene and whose ideas were more in harmony with our present-day thinking.

Just how much illegal procedure there was is, of course, impossible to say since we have no measure with which to gauge the amount. There must have been many who obeyed the laws even though those around them did not. For example, many—perhaps the majority—of homesteaders in vast areas must have settled on their choice of land and lived there for years, fulfilling the requirements of the government that they should make their claims their homes. I well remember that when I was a lad in eastern Kansas a number of our neighbors were still living on their homesteads after forty years. It must be remembered that the unusual is newsworthy and hence is featured in the newspaper. Even in reminiscences the humdrum occurrences of everyday life are often passed over in favor of striking happenings. Inspectors in the service of the General Land Office were paid to find errors or dishonest work of surveyors and evasions of the law. Their reports, from which history is written, are silent as to the many survey contracts that were honestly executed and entries that were perfected in good faith.

Although this book deals primarily with land technically known as the "public domain," it also treats Indian territory that was opened to settlement (although never legally part of the public domain), forest reserves, and grazing lands. Even though this is a social history dealing mainly with the human side of land-acquirement procedures, as I have mentioned previously, it is built upon the foundation of political and economic histories. To writers in this field I owe a debt of gratitude. The older standard works by Thomas Donaldson, Benjamin Hibbard, Payson J. Treat, and Amelia Ford have been relied upon heavily. More recent works by William W. Robinson, Louise Peffer, Carl Coke Rister, and scores of others have been used many times. But of more help than any others have been the works of three of my good friends: Roy M. Robbins, whose distinguished work, *Our Landed Heritage*, has been a cornerstone on which this book has been built; Paul Gates, whose work on the public lands over the years has been unceasing; and Harold Dunham, whose *Government Handout* is also basic to my theme. The works of many other writers have contributed to this volume.

For the most part my primary sources are government documents or manuscript reports in the National Archives and elsewhere, although other sources of great importance are contemporary writings, articles in historical society publications, reminiscences, and newspapers. Aside from general writings upon subjects pertaining to the public lands, the greatest sources are county histories. Ordinarily—and unfortunately—little use is made of, and little credit is given to, the many master's theses and doctoral dissertations at various universities, but I have found those at the universities of Wisconsin, Illinois, Iowa, Nebraska, and California at Berkeley particularly helpful.

I am deeply indebted to a host of librarians for their courtesies, especially to those at the historical societies of Wisconsin, Kansas, Illinois, Montana, Missouri, Iowa, Minnesota, Mississippi, and Alabama. The Library of Congress and the Bancroft Library at the University of California at Berkeley were especially helpful. The librarians of my own vicinity rendered service beyond the call of duty and helped me in every possible way: those at the Nebraska State Historical Society, the Nebraska State Library, the University of Nebraska, and Union College. As for my own college—Union College—its board and administration have always been most understanding and in numerous ways have encouraged me and given me time to do research and writing.

I also wish to acknowledge my indebtedness to the Newberry Library of Chicago for a grant-in-aid that made possible the initial research and beginnings of this project.

My wife and children shared the rigors of data collection when, several years ago, we spent long months in a house trailer, traveling to Madison, Wisconsin, Washington, D.C., and through the Deep South and the Rocky Mountain West. I am especially grateful to my wife, who has labored by my side typing the manuscript, copyediting, proofreading, indexing, and giving encouragement and valuable suggestions in matters of form and style.

EVERETT DICK

Research Professor of

American History

Union College
Lincoln, Nebraska

The Lure of the Land

I

Land Precedents of the Seventeenth and Eighteenth Centuries

FREE OR CHEAP LAND was the lodestone that pulled multitudes of Europeans to America for three centuries following the first English settlement in 1607. It also was the motive that irresistibly drew the easterner to brave the danger of Indian hostilities and endure the loneliness and hardships of a life in the untamed wilderness. In contrast to many of the great migrations of world history, the steady flow of American settlers to the West was not primarily the result of political or religious oppression; it was rather an economic response to the call of opportunity. To the venturesome get-ahead individual, "out West" was the land of new beginning, and during the centuries of its existence it continued to be synonymous with opportunity. Glowing reports of rich bottomland, woodlands teeming with game, springside building locations, damsites for mills, and natural townsites where great cities would grow up to enrich the one who had the foresight to lay out the urban community—all these lured the venturesome.

When John Oldham brought back favorable reports from the Connecticut Valley in 1633, the record reads that the people of eastern Massachusetts began to have "a hankering after it." Visions of rich land continued to agitate them, and one year later the people of Newtown, under the leadership of Thomas Hooker, asked permission of the General Court to move west. As support for their request they cited the shortage of pasture for their livestock, "the fruitfulness and commodiousness of Connecticut, and the strong bent of their spirits to remove thither." Astute observers are certain that the real motives lay in the phrase "the strong bent of their spirits to remove thither." It was the same spirit which led west, ever west —not only to Connecticut but to the shores of the Pacific.

The urge to own land in colonial days was not based wholly upon economics, however. There was a political and a social basis. Just as gaining an

1

education is the surest way to rise in society today, in colonial days the acquisition of property was the key to moving upward from a low to a higher stratum. The property holder could vote and hold office, but the man with no property was practically on the same political level as the indentured servant or slave.

In Europe, because the landed person was of the nobility, landownership was the symbol of this social class. This continued to be true even into the nineteenth century; the Scottish immigrant girl who married a home-steader in Iowa illustrated this point of view when she triumphantly wrote back to her friends: "I'm a lady now. I married a Lord!"

So hungry were the people for land that it was no uncommon thing for frontier soldiers waging a campaign against the Indians to keep one eye on the Indians and the other on good country for "claim making." On John Sevier's second incursion into the Hiwassee country in eastern Tennessee, the Indians had no sooner fled than the voracious pioneers began to blaze out numerous tomahawk claims, or improvements, as they were optimisti-cally called, hoping in this way to establish prior claim to ownership by conquest rather than by purchase.

Several of the Thirteen Colonies claimed territory beyond the Appala-chian Mountains, and independence validated these claims; however, up-on the insistence of Maryland, a state with no western lands, the other states agreed to cede their claims to the national government. Ownership of this western territory posed two problems for the new nation: (1) should the new lands be governed as colonies in the manner Great Britain had governed the Thirteen; and (2) how should the land be changed from government to private ownership? In response to the first question the Confederation Congress enacted the Northwest Ordinance of 1787 pro-viding for a political apprenticeship whereby a territory could graduate into statehood on the same basis as the original states of the Union. Pro-vision for the transfer of ownership had been made when the same body had enacted the Ordinance of 1785 setting the precedent for measuring and sale of the land to the public.

Europe was just emerging from the Middle Ages when America was dis-covered; because of this it was natural that the feudal system, which had dictated the form of land tenure for so many years, should largely influence landownership in the New World. Under the feudal system, the king theoretically owned all the land in the realm but suffered the barons to possess large holdings. The barons, in turn, allowed the actual tillers of the soil to hold small plots as tenants, but no one ever thought of the little man actually owning the soil he worked. Although the feudal system was on the decline in the Old World, it was the basis for early land-tenure policies in America. The king made land grants, and although the term "baron" or "lord" was not used, the feudal idea prevailed nevertheless. Whether a man came as an employee of a trading company, as a settler upon the land of a proprietor, or as a newcomer upon the land of the king in a royal colony, there was at first no thought of the common man actually owning the soil he tilled. Gradually, however, the feudal system lost its viability under the impact of the great distance from home controls, the life-and death struggle for survival amidst primitive nature, and the proximity of unoccupied virgin land. Because of these factors the powers that controlled the unoccupied lands found it more and more difficult to keep the land-hungry from occupying the land and using it without the payment of rent. In some cases a colonial governor granted land to a number of men called "warlike Christian men," on condition that they settle on the western border and form a buffer against the Indians, thus affording protection to the population farther east.

The legislative body of the colony controlled land distribution in New England. In 1722, for example, Joseph Parsons and 176 others petitioned the General Court of Massachusetts for land for a settlement. In response they were given two townships in Hampshire County. A committee was appointed to purchase the land from the Indians, to divide the tract, and to reserve land for the ministers, the church, and the school. Each proprietor of one hundred acres was to pay thirty shillings for purchasing the land from the Indians, and the committee bought the land for £460, three barrels of cider, and thirty quarts of rum.[1]

Following the Old World feudal pattern, many of the colonial governments granted large tracts to proprietors who then rented smaller tracts to settlers. These proprietors often met great difficulty, however, in securing possession of their grants due to settlers trespassing upon the unoccupied land. The Penn family, whose head received his grant directly from the crown, had more difficulty with the Scotch-Irish squatters than any other landlords had with trespassers. In the first place, these newcomers had recently come from Ireland, where they had served a long apprenticeship in fighting landlords and turbulent neighbors. In 1724, James Logan, one of William Penn's agents, complained that these "bold and indigent strangers" had seized at least 150,000 acres of the best land in the country without authority, and when challenged concerning their illegal procedure, these "audacious and disorderly" people excused themselves saying

1 David D. Field, *A History of the County of Berkshire, Massachusetts* (Pittsfield, Mass., 1829), pp. 201, 202.

that the proprietor had invited them to come and that "it was against the laws of God and nature, that so much land should be idle while so many Christians wanted it to labor on and to raise their bread."[2]

An occasional eviction and cabin burning merely schooled the settlers in devious methods of clinging to the land despite proprietary disfavor. In Pennsylvania, in 1769, settlers along Lycoming Creek, a branch of the Susquehannah River, formed an organization which became the prototype of the claim clubs which were to reappear from time to time during the next century. Because of a dispute between the Indians and the whites over the interpretation of a treaty, the Pennsylvania government forbade settlement until this was resolved; but the impatient, greedy pioneers took matters into their own hands, moved onto the disputed land, and made their claims. To protect themselves in their illegal proceedings they formed an organization known as the Fair Play System and framed their own land laws. Each year they elected three of their members, designated as the Fair Play men, to settle boundary disputes in the unsurveyed area and to protect the members in the possession of their land. There was no appeal from their decision or resistance to its enforcement; the whole group turned out on notice, and execution of judgment or eviction of a losing claimant was certain. A newcomer was required to apply for admission to the organization, and upon a solemn oath to subscribe to the rules and submit to the laws, was permitted to possess a tract of vacant land. If an obdurate person refused to comply with the decision of the tribunal, he was placed in a canoe and paddled to the mouth of Lycoming Creek—one of the borders of the settlement—and set adrift. One of the rules of the Fair Play System provided that if a claimant left his claim for six months it was to be regarded as abandoned and another could take it. If a man joined the army, however (the Fair Play System continued during the Revolutionary War), his claim was protected.[3]

Some proprietors spent large sums of money attempting to remove illegal settlers, but the wiser ones came to agreements by which the intruders secured their land cheaper because of having illegally possessed it. Here was the origin of pre-emption, which was to become so important in the history of the public domain after the United States became a nation. Pre-

[2] *History of Franklin County, Pennsylvania* (Chicago, 1887), p. 143; Charles A. Hanna, *The Scotch-Irish* (New York: G. P. Putnam, 1902), pp. 63, 64.

[3] Sherman Day, *Historical Collections of Pennsylvania* (New Haven, Conn., 1843), p. 450; John F. Meginness (ed.), *Proceedings of the Centennial Anniversary of Lycoming County, Pennsylvania* (Williamsport, Pa., 1896), p. 172; Edwin MacMinn, *On the Frontier with Colonel Antes* (Camden, N.J.: S. Chew & Sons, 1900), pp. 249–255.

emption, which became well established by custom, simply consisted of establishing a prior claim by residence and improvement. It was widely practiced on lands owned by the colonies in the South. Erecting a cabin was the basis for a claim known as cabin rights; raising a patch of corn, even an insignificant crop, as corn rights. An observer in western Virginia noticed near a spring a number of deadened, blazed trees with initials on them and was told that this formed the basis for a type of imperfect title known as tomahawk rights, which enabled the owners to buy and sell their claims. Marking a maple grove to indicate that the trees had been used for making maple syrup and sugar indicated a sugar claim.

The Penn family were not the only proprietors who found it hard to restrain the land-hungry frontiersmen—even the name and will of the king himself failed to command the respect and obedience of his frontier subjects that it should have elicited in the heart of a loyal Briton. When George III, in his famous proclamation of 1763, decreed that his "loyal subjects" should not settle west of a line drawn along the watershed of the Appalachians, they paid not one bit of attention to His Majesty's edict. Lord Dunmore, the royal governor of Virginia, made this interesting excuse for his inability to keep the frontiersmen from scattering over the king's royal domain:

When I was removed to this Government I found the boundary line, mentioned by your Lordship . . . and My Lord I have invariably taken every Step which depended on me, to prevent any infringment of it by the people of this colony; nor, with regard to grants, has any infringment of it been made, or Settlement either that the power of this government could prevent.

But my Lord I have learnt from experience that the established Authority of any government in America, and the policy of Government at home, are both insufficient to restrain the Americans: and that they do and will remove as their avidity and restlessness incite them. They acquire no attachment to Place: But wandering about Seems engrafted in their Nature; and it is a weakness incident to it, that they Should for ever immagine the Lands further off, are still better than those upon which they are already settled. But to be more particular.

I have had, My Lord, frequent opportunities to reflect upon the emigrating Spirit of the Americans, Since my Arrival to this government. There are considerable bodies of Inhabitants Settled at greater and less distances from the regular frontiers of, I believe, all the Colonies. In this Colony Proclamations have been published from time to time to restrain them: But impressed from their earliest infancy with Sentiments and habits, very different from those acquired by persons of a Similar condition in England, they do not conceive that Government has any right to forbid their taking possession of a Vast tract of Country, either uninhabited, or which Serves only as a shelter to a few scattered tribes of Indians. Nor can they be easily brought to entertain any belief of the permanent obligation of Treaties made with those People, whom they consider, as but little removed from brute Creation.[4]

It was with this background that the new American nation started its long process of attempting to find a satisfactory method of disposing of its land.

Since the new government was practically bankrupt, its credit at a low ebb, and holders of various types of bills payable were crying for settlement, one of the first thoughts of statesmen was to sell the public land and bolster the country financially. A New England proposal was to survey the land into townships of seven miles square and auction them at a minimum of one dollar an acre to citizens who would unite, buy, and settle their tracts en masse, a common practice in that area. Southern congressmen, thinking in terms of the individualistic concept of tomahawk rights or corn-claim custom, held out for sales in smaller lots. A compromise was reached in drawing up the Ordinance of 1785, which provided that the land be sold at auction at a minimum price of one dollar an acre and that it be offered in townships of thirty-six square miles to accommodate group settlers, or in sections of 640 acres (one square mile) for individual settlers.

As it turned out, the arrangement was advantageous to no one. The states still had quantities of land within their borders to sell at a low figure, and settlers were loath to exchange residence in their home states for a tract in the remote wilderness at prices no more inviting than those at home. Hence there were few sales and income to the United States was negligible. Furthermore, the minimum tract was too large for the individual settler to handle, the price was too high for the speculator, and the New England community idea elicited no response. In its fumbling search for a better policy, the old Confederation government, by legislative act, sold several large tracts at a few cents an acre to land companies, the best known of which was the Ohio Company of Associates.

When, under the Constitution, the new government was set up in 1789, the question of the disposal of the public domain arose once more. The

[4] Lord Dunmore to the Earl of Dartmouth, Secretary of State for the Colonies, December 24, 1774, quoted in Reuben Gold Thwaites and Louise P. Kellogg (eds.), *Documentary History of Lord Dunmore's War* (Madison: Wisconsin State Historical Society, 1905), pp. 370–371.

general opinion in Congress was that the land should be sold in large lots, for cash, to retire the national war debt. Strangely enough, it was a dyed-in-the-wool Federalist, Alexander Hamilton—under whose jurisdiction the lands fell in his capacity as Secretary of the Treasury—who came to the support of the small land-buyer. In 1790, in response to an invitation by the House of Representatives for recommendations concerning the public lands, Hamilton suggested measures to accommodate three types of buyers, with the proceeds to be applied to the public debt: (1) moneyed individuals who might wish to buy land in quantity and resell after a time; (2) associations of settlers who might wish to join forces, buy a large tract, move West together, and occupy the tract as neighbors; and (3) individuals who wished to purchase an area as small as one-hundred acres at thirty cents an acre. Hamilton further recommended that a central land office be set up in the nation's capital and local land offices in the West where land business could be conducted.

Albert Gallatin, who represented the frontier area of western Pennsylvania in Congress, naturally favored selling small tracts to actual homemakers. He was convinced that such sales would bring in enough money to liquidate the public debt in ten years and would at the same time build a contented, economically happy citizenry. He said that the policy of favoring the actual settler had universally prevailed before the Revolution and

If the cause of the happiness of this country was examined . . . it would be found to arise as much from the great plenty of land in proportion to the inhabitant, which their citizens enjoyed, as from the wisdom of their political institutions. It is, in fact . . . because the poor man has been able always to obtain his portion of the land.[5]

Notwithstanding many pious expressions in favor of the settlers and the poorer classes, an amendment to sell in 160-acre plots was voted down when the land law of 1796 was passed—the first such law under the Constitution and the law that set the pace for future land policy. The law provided for the auction of land by the square mile, at a minimum price of two dollars an acre. Since there was no provision for sales in immense tracts at a few cents an acre, it may be considered a compromise measure that favored the homemaker. The financial terms provided that one-twentieth of the total price be paid at the time of application, nine-twentieths in thirty days, and the balance in one year. As a concession to the New England idea, half the townships offered for sale were left undivided, to be sold

[5] Kenneth W. Colgrove, "The Attitude of Congress Toward the Pioneers of the West," *Iowa Journal of History and Politics*, VIII (Iowa City, Ia., 1910), 12–14.

at the capital in Philadelphia in lots of quarter townships; the other half offered for sale was to be sold in sections at the land offices set up by the act —Pittsburgh and Cincinnati. The increase in the price per acre, it was thought, would discourage speculators from buying large quantities because they would have to pay just as much as the small buyers. However, Hamilton's idea of a general land office within the Treasury Department was not put into practice until 1812.

The 1796 land law brought a new element into the picture—credit. Although few western residents had the $1,280 needed to buy a section, optimism took over where money left off, and the frontiersman spent his last dollar as a down payment in the hope of making enough from the land for the second and third payments in the short space of one year. Actually he was lucky if at the end of the first year his family had sufficient food and clothes and if his stock had escaped the perils of the forest. Failure to make the second payment called for the forfeiture of the land and of the first payment. The land law of 1796 thus set a precedent for the next half century of land legislation, occupancy, and ownership in the new nation. We shall see, however, that the people entirely changed the intent of the statute by their usage, which had its precedent rooted deep in seventeenth- and eighteenth-century custom.

II

The Early Nineteenth-Century Land Program

NOT UNTIL after 1799 was there a voice in Congress from the public land area. When the second stage of territorial government was inaugurated in the Northwest Territory, William Henry Harrison was sent by that territory to speak—but was not allowed to vote—for the desires of the frontier people. The West wanted a policy that would enable the settler to purchase land on which to live and earn his livelihood, and this meant smaller lots and easier payment terms. In addition, the settlers wanted to buy at a point close to the land that was to be sold, but often the land the pioneers wished to purchase was several days' journey from Cincinnati and Pittsburgh, the only land offices at the time. This meant a long and expensive trip to see the land and select a tract, another long journey to reach the land office where the auction was to be held, and the return journeys. Albert Gallatin once more advocated land for the homemaker and aided Harrison in securing passage of a bill favorable to the settlers. The resultant land law of 1800, sometimes called the Harrison Land Law, contained all of the above points: (1) a man could purchase as little as a half section instead of 640 acres; (2) three additional land offices were established in the vicinity of the tracts to be sold; and (3) a liberal system of credit was set up. The credit feature, which proved to be unwise, allowed an individual to pay 25 per cent forty days after his purchase, 25 per cent in two years, 25 per cent in three years, and the final 25 per cent in four years—at a 6 per cent rate of interest. The auction feature was retained and also the minimum price of two dollars per acre. A cash discount of 8 per cent was allowed but this was less important than the credit feature. A pre-emption provision was urged by a Tennessean but without avail.

As early as 1803, Congress received a grist of petitions for specific changes in the land laws, such as the abolition of credit sales, a decrease in prices, and the reduction of the minimum purchase from 320 to 160 acres. Albert Gallatin, now the Secretary of the Treasury, recommended cutting the

9

minimum size of tracts to 160 acres, the minimum price to $1.25 an acre, and the abolition of credit. In the resultant land law of 1804, Congress cut the minimum to 160 acres, continued the credit system and the $2.00-an-acre minimum, but cut the cash price to $1.64 minimum per acre.[1]

The evils of the installment plan soon became evident. Not only did those who expected to live on the soil overbuy, using all of their capital for the down payment, hoping to make the money for future payments by tilling the soil, but moneyed men bought great quantities of land for speculation. Before long it was obvious that purchasers had overbought. Jacob Burnet, a settler in the Miami River country of Ohio, said it was the opinion of the newspapers, often repeated by citizens in conversation, that nine-tenths of the buyers of public land would lose everything they had put into the land unless a law was passed bringing relief to the despairing settlers.[2] This circumstance brought about an unwholesome political situation. Voters on the whole frontier were in debt to the United States government for at least four years and in most cases were unable to pay for their land by the time payment was due—which colored their thinking and molded their attitude toward the government. The settlers therefore voted for policies that would ease their indebtedness without regard to the contracts they had made. Instead of hailing the government as a benefactor for making smaller plots for homes available on easy terms, defaulters saw the government as an ogre ready to destroy them, and the law of which they had gladly taken advantage as oppressive. In case of nonpayment, the land was to revert to the government, with the buyer forfeiting the money he had paid. Because westerners were Republicans and the administration at Washington also was Republican, the party in power could scarcely be depended upon to act in the best interests of the government in this conflict. Therefore, as the number of defaulters increased, the pressure upon congressmen to alter the contract in favor of the land-buyers likewise rose.

More serious than the amount of money involved, however, was the damage done to the citizens' standards of honor. Nothing was done to enforce the terms of the contract, and those who had made their payments regularly observed that those who had not done so suffered no penalty; therefore, nonpayment of one's obligations became the rule since the man who did not pay his honest debts was actually given an advantage. In this

[1] Roy M. Robbins, *Our Landed Heritage* (Lincoln: University of Nebraska Press, 1962), pp. 24, 25, 34.

[2] Jacob Burnet, *Notes on the Early Settlement of the North-Western Territory* (Cincinnati, 1847), pp. 450, 451.

way the more unscrupulous citizens set the standard of financial morality for the entire West, and the matter tended to snowball since the more defaulters there were, the less chance there was for the Treasury Department to collect.

In 1809, Congress began to pass relief laws in behalf of the debtors; by 1812, the situation was a tremendous scandal, and law after law was passed that granted indulgences to the purchasers in the form of extending the time of payment. Wise counsel urged the abolition of the credit system; but though the scheme was undeniably bad, Congress could not bring itself to abandon credit sales. Instead, the usual relief measure was passed in 1815.[3] It was now quite obvious that men could go through the motion of buying and holding land by making a down payment; consequently, sales continued briskly after the War of 1812, reaching a peak during the boom years of 1817 and 1818.

As noted above, the most unfortunate aspect of the policy of installment buying was that speculators bought great quantities of select land, on the basis of a small down payment, for quick resale at advanced prices to later comers. Cotton-growing was rapidly expanding at this time, and Alabama in particular was caught in a vortex of wild land speculation, which sometimes resulted in running the price up to $20.00 and $25.00 an acre at free auctions. Park Walton, receiver of the land office of Pearl River, La., wrote the Commissioner of the General Land Office to urge that no more extensions of time be given to delinquent buyers. Walton cited instances of people who had been using land since 1799 but had paid only one installment, and he said it was the intention of many of the occupants never to pay any more on their holdings.[4]

Installment buying also made it possible for an occupant of public land to strip it of its wealth at the cost of a down payment. A letter writer from Shawneetown, Illinois, in 1816 complained that when the register of the land office warned an intruder against cutting timber on government land, the latter filed upon the land, made a down payment of one-twentieth the purchase price, and set a forty-man crew to work cutting pipe staves for shipment to New Orleans. The lumberman expected to cut off all the timber by the end of ninety days and had no intention of making another payment. The headlong rush for land was brought to an abrupt end by the Panic of 1819. By this time Alabama, the state worst hit by this system, had

---

[3] Payson J. Treat, *The National Land System, 1785–1820* (New York: E. B. Treat & Co., 1910), pp. 129–137.

[4] Park Walton to the Commissioner of the General Land Office, May 30, 1815, in *Territorial Papers of the United States*, VI (Washington, D.C., 1938), 532.

amassed a land debt of $11,000,000—more than half the land debt of the entire nation.[5]

The land law of 1820, which was passed in an effort to repair the twenty years of damage caused by installment selling, provided that land was to be sold in tracts as small as eighty acres, for cash, and at the reduced minimum price of $1.25 an acre. Unfortunately, this was a blow to the conscientious husbandman who had already paid for his land. He was at a disadvantage because of his honesty and his promptness in paying his obligations: he had paid a price based upon two dollars an acre.

The next year Congress came to the rescue of those in arrears by offering three plans of relief. Settlers could (1) give up part of the land they had purchased and retain the acreage that was equivalent to their payments; (2) pay the whole amount, less the 37.5 per cent discount; or (3) receive further time in which to pay the original debt. This plan was re-enacted in 1824 and 1826, and by 1832 eleven such relief acts had been passed. Unfortunately, men who, in accordance with the terms of the law of 1821, were supposed to relinquish part of the land for which they were unable to pay did not consider that they were giving up their right to it; they continued to live on it, cultivate it, and in every way treat it as their own. They expected to be able to buy it back someday under favorable arrangements that they fully expected would be enacted in their behalf and toward which they bent their political activities. In Alabama, nearly half of the land that had been sold was relinquished.[6] Whole counties were occupied by these tenants-by-common-consent, and they elected congressmen who would vote "right" on the land question. In the natural course of events, by law relinquished land would again be offered for sale at public auction, and the occupant would be obliged to compete with all comers for fields he had cleared, was still cultivating, and to which he claimed he still had vested rights. Regional public opinion, of course, was entirely with the relinquisher, and it was considered dishonorable to bid against an occupant who regarded the land as his by natural right. Schemers, however, were ready to take advantage of the situation; they would go to a relinquisher and threaten to bid against him at the auction unless he would give them hush money—perhaps a sum equivalent to that which he had to pay the government.[7]

[5] Albert B. Moore, *History of Alabama and Her People* (New York: American Historical Society, 1927), p. 87.

[6] Thomas Perkins Abernethy, *The Formative Period in Alabama, 1815–1828* (Montgomery: Brown Printing Co., 1922), pp. 54, 55.

[7] Charles Shepard Davis, *The Cotton Kingdom in Alabama* (Montgomery: Auburn Printing Co., 1939), p. 32.

Combines of speculators were formed to defraud the government at these auctions of relinquished lands. Land that had originally been purchased at thirty or forty dollars an acre at a free auction was often even more valuable at the time of resale due to the rise in cotton prices, the press of population, and improvements upon the land; but these illegal rings stifled competition, and the land was bought for little more than the minimum price. Their numbers, organization, and money power enabled these shysters to work both ends against the middle; they compelled actual settlers to pay the clique the difference between the minimum price and the actual worth—or they got the land they desired at approximately the minimum price. At times, however, the settlers also organized and made the speculators pay dearly for their land. In such instances the government benefited, in keeping with the intent of the law, but after a few episodes of this kind the two forces compromised their differences at the government's expense.[8]

In 1830 and 1831 two acts brought alleviation to relinquishers who had attempted to retain and pay for their land: occupants were allowed to buy their land at the rate of $3.50 or $1.25 an acre. Land purchased at a price of over $14.00 an acre could be reclaimed for $3.50 an acre, and at $1.25 an acre if purchased for less than $14.00. Thus, quantities of valuable land were reclaimed at a very low figure.

Interestingly enough, some occupants continued to live on land without paying the balance due—and Congress occasionally passes a private bill today that allows a man to finish paying for a tract his great-great-grandfather bought on the installment plan before 1820. When such a person is required to pay interest, it is far more than the original principal, but the heirs of William Collins were more fortunate. At the Washington, Mississippi, land office on July 21, 1819, Collins bought 490 acres for $980. He paid $49 on the date of purchase, and on August 30 of the same year paid $196, which left him owing $735. In order to secure title to the land in 1948, his heirs were successful in securing the passage of a private bill by the 80th Congress allowing them to pay the $735 without interest and to secure the patent to the land the family had been using for over a century and a quarter with the status of squatters.[9]

The transition in ownership of certain areas from the French to the British or to the American governments offered opportunity for speculation and land disputes. In 1783, when by the Treaty of Paris the United States secured possession of the territory east of the Mississippi River, several isolated areas were held as claims from foreign countries. A number of these

8 *American State Papers, Public Lands*, V (Washington, D.C., 1860), 376–379.
9 Private Law 391, H.R. 3768, passed by the 80th Congress on June 24, 1948; General Land Office Records, U.S. Archives, Washington, D.C.

lay where the French had settled—around Detroit, Mackinaw, Green
Bay, and Vincennes, or around Kaskaskia and other points along the
Mississippi. Such holdings were known as private land claims and sometimes were the occasion of controversy and fraud. An early instance of this
concerned the area around the French settlements in Illinois and Indiana.
Even during the Revolutionary War, Virginia and Kentucky patriots had
kept an eye open to their own interests as well as to saving the Northwest
for the American cause, and in 1780, before the peace treaty was signed,
Virginia established a court at Vincennes which assumed the right to grant
land to applicants. Having exercised this prerogative for some time and
concluding that they could grant land to themselves, the members of the
court divided among themselves all the land to which Indian title was presumed to have been extinguished. Each member absented himself on the
day the court voted his portion to him so that it might appear that the
grant was the sole act of his fellows. These proceedings were duly recorded
in the minutes of the court and involved twenty or thirty thousand acres
along the Wabash River; but the judges soon found that their questionable
grants were of no advantage since they could not find the expected purchasers, and they abandoned their project. In 1802, however, William
Henry Harrison, the governor of Indiana Territory, wrote that other
speculators had discovered the old grant, had gained control of part of it,
and were selling tracts to people in different parts of the United States who
were planning to settle on them. The prices, he reported, were trifling—a
thousand acres for an indifferent horse or a "rifle gun"—but some of the
buyers had resold the land to the uninformed, quoting the original action
of the court as title. Harrison forbade the use of the seal of the territory by
way of condemning such a fraud, and this, he wrote, had helped somewhat
in stopping the evil.[10]

Congress took care of the French settlements by providing that donations
of four hundred acres should be given to each head of a family who was a
citizen of the United States before 1783. These donations were to be distributed by lottery and could not be sold until the grantee had been a resident of the region for three years after the distribution.

Commissioners were appointed by Congress to investigate the whole
matter of land claims. Testimony before this body revealed that a small
clique of rich and unscrupulous speculators had secured almost a complete
monopoly of the lands of Illinois. An appalling amount of corruption was
brought to light, and even Governor Arthur St. Clair, the first governor of

[10] William Henry Harrison to James Madison, January 19, 1802, in *American State
Papers, Public Lands*, I (Washington, D.C., 1834), 123.

the Northwest Territory, did not escape unsullied. In attempting to establish claims to the land, land-grabbers had made use of a group of men whom one writer has called professional swearers. These perjurors made depositions concerning improvements made in the 1780's when actually they had not been over eight or ten years of age at the time.

One of these unscrupulous individuals, Simon Torton, after having made over two hundred depositions, repented of his ways and confessed that he had been drunk most of the time. On one occasion, he recollected having drunk a quart of liquor before he left home and having fortified himself for the work in hand by drinking another quart before he began his work. He remembered having completed twenty-two or twenty-three sworn statements by midnight; that is, he copied them from a model. In his confession he solemnly swore that all of his depositions were false, that all had been made while he was not in his "sober senses," and that he was not acquainted with the improvements of the country concerning which he had made affidavits.[11]

The commissioners had confirmed to one man nearly forty claims, for four hundred acres each, which were finally rejected in court because of perjured evidence. Commissioners also settled the question of ownership claims around Detroit and elsewhere. Congress finally passed two acts in 1812 and 1817 that allowed grants to Detroit residents who by French grant had held only narrow strips along the waterfront. The acts allowed them to enter so-called donations rights by which each such landholder was allowed to add to his old strip a tract that extended eighty arpents (roughly eighty acres) inland.

The problem of making decisions concerning claims in the Louisiana Purchase was infinitely more complicated than in the Old Northwest. In the first place, the Spanish had made large grants without paying much attention to whether the grantor terms were fulfilled. The United States government desired to recognize legitimate claims of residents of the new purchase, but when it became known that there was to be a change in sovereignty, certain granting authorities of Louisiana began to sell grants of land. These claim applications were granted by Spanish officials who antedated the grants to 1799, the last year of Spanish rule, before France took over the government. One of these men, Lieutenant Governor Zenon Trudeau, who was Spanish commandant of Upper Louisiana in 1799, was living in New Orleans at the time of the transfer of the territory from France to the United States. It was at this time that many claims were

---

[11] May Allison, "Conditions in the Illinois Country, 1787–1800" (Master's thesis, University of Illinois, 1907), p. 129.

made out and antedated 1799. By the exercise of even the clumsiest detective work, one could not help but note the unusually large number of claims that had been granted in 1799. But what was more noteworthy was that of 124 petitions for land purported to have been made by 124 different persons, the applications were in the handwriting of no more than four persons, and one investigator felt there were only two. The same words were misspelled and other identical errors permeated the whole stack of applications, although they were represented to have been made over a period of fifteen years by persons who resided at different places. Even more inculpatory was the fact that although different signatures were appended they were in the same handwriting. Equally extraordinary and conclusive evidence of forgery was that the Spanish governors in writing documents invariably misspelled the same words as the applicant.[12] By means of fraudulent grants of one kind or another, most of the valuable iron- and lead-mining areas of Missouri were claimed by speculators.

Fortunately, President Jefferson had been warned by faithful government servants of the fraudulent proceedings in Louisiana. Captain Amos Stoddard, United States army, wrote to the Secretary of War on January 10, 1804, that a rush was on to defraud the government of the United States. He stated that the Spanish custom was for an applicant to petition the commandant for a tract of land, described by the applicant, and at the bottom of the sheet or on the reverse side of the petition the commandant acceded to the request and directed the surveyor to run the lines. This document, together with the surveyor's report, entitled the settler to the land when it was presented to the proper official in New Orleans. Stoddard strongly suspected that many blank sheets had been signed and later filled in to suit the convenience of the land seeker. He stated that at the time of his writing there was great activity in surveying land and that as near as could be estimated 200,000 acres, including the best mines, had been surveyed in the past few weeks although the petitions were dated in 1799.[13]

As early as February 29, 1804, Jefferson passed this information on to Congress, and that body appointed a commission to determine the validity of Louisiana land titles. This body had an enormous task, which tried to the utmost its patience and integrity, and even required physical courage; it had to stand adamant against fraud, corruption, threats, and even violence. The commissioners even suffered bodily attacks, and so virulent, bold, lawless, and avaricious were the land-greedy that the commissioners

[12] *American State Papers, Public Lands*, VI (Washington, D.C., 1860), 5, 6.

[13] Capt. Amos Stoddard (Kaskaskia, Ill.) to the Secretary of War, January, 1804, in *American State Papers Public Lands*, I (Washington, D.C., 1834), 193–194.

had to carry arms for their own protection. This task, moreover, was extremely complicated because of the tangled network of fraud, and it was necessary to compel every holder of real estate acquired under the Spanish or French regimes—from town lots and small plots to princely domains of thousands of acres—to prove ownership. This work dragged on for more than thirty years.[14]

Unfortunately, frontiersmen were notoriously careless about paying attention to the requisites of legal procedures that accompany the march of civilization, and they tended to neglect fulfilling the conditions of their contract with the Spanish government. Although the commissioners tried to take this into consideration when separating the legitimate claims from the fraudulent, nevertheless such famous men as Daniel Boone and Moses Austin both lost their tracts in the end.

One factor that made the work of the commissioners difficult and brought much pressure upon them was that certain large holders, having secured vast areas by trickery, as mentioned above, had sold tracts to settlers. In some cases the settlers had subdivided and resold the tracts, until the whole was a tangled economic network wherein the people who would be hurt by an adverse decision were unfortunately not the ones responsible for the debacle. Large numbers were pressing for a favorable decision in such cases. James Bowie sold quantities of dubious claims to men in Arkansas, and a number of the leading early figures of the state bought 126 of these claims. In 1827 the buyers attempted to secure title to them by suit. According to one authority, all the lawyers in Arkansas—except the attorney for the United States—fought for the claimants. The first decision was in favor of the speculators and lawyers, but later the decision was reviewed and all of the fraudulent claims were turned down.[15]

This long-drawn-out process of deciding land titles was very harmful to the proper functioning of the public land system. It was impossible to survey land and open it to settlement as long as there was a question whether it had passed to private ownership under Spanish land grant or was indeed part of the public domain and open to settlement. Uncertainty created a title vacuum and thousands of squatters rushed in, hopeful that the final decision would be against the dubious claims and that the big holdings would be open to government sale. This squatter occupancy brought up the question of pre-emption. Some actual homemakers, tired of

[14] Aaron M. Sakolski, *The Great American Land Bubble* (New York: Harper & Brothers, 1932), p. 195.

[15] Josiah H. Shinn, *Pioneers and Makers of Arkansas* (Little Rock: Genealogical and Historical Publishing Co., 1908), I, 87, 88.

waiting, bought off the claimants for a nominal sum. By and large the whole country was a land of squatters, and this was a great hindrance to the administration of sales and the settlement of government lands. Another problem was the bitterness and acrimony of the settlers, who regarded the big land men as land hogs, speculators, and thieves, who were trying to rob them of their natural heritage.

III

Surveying

SECOND IN IMPORTANCE ONLY to the preservation of life on the frontier was the security of ownership of one's tract of land, which required an effective system of surveys. In the following pages I shall attempt to trace the rise and application of the surveying scheme of the national government, together with the problems incident to marking the land. No attempt will be made to follow the process chronologically.

The colonial conception had varied from the muddle in Virginia to the more efficient procedure of New England and North Carolina, but in Kentucky and in the Virginia Military Reserve in Ohio the chaos of the Old Dominion prevailed. According to this custom the land hunter ranged at will in the forest, "running out" the richest tracts according to his fancy and recording the surveys. This led to a hodgepodge of claims that were irregular in size and shape; half a dozen tracts sometimes overlapped or infringed upon one another.[1]

In New England, the land was surveyed in rectangular townships, six to ten miles square, before the land was occupied; and a variation of this system was carried to the Western Reserve by Connecticut emigrants. Each township, five miles square, was divided into quarters, known as sections, which contained about three thousand acres each.

The old decrepit Congress set up by the Articles of Confederation passed two of the most important and far-reaching laws in United States history: the Ordinance of 1785 and the Northwest Ordinance of 1787. The former ordinance adopted the system of survey thereafter used on the public lands of the United States. Thomas Jefferson, the chairman of the committee which drew up the law, is generally given credit for its merits; but Hugh Williamson of North Carolina, a member of the committee, claimed that the plan was his, and certain likenesses between the Carolina plan and the Ordinance of 1785 lend credence to his claim. The act, which was passed

[1] Burke Aaron Hinsdale, *The Old Northwest* (New York, 1888), pp. 260, 261.

19

April 26, 1785, provided that a line, to be known as a base line, should be drawn due west from a point on the north bank of the Ohio River where the river crossed the Pennsylvania boundary. Another line, some distance west, known as a principal meridian, was to be drawn north and south intersecting and perpendicular to the base line. Townships six miles square were laid out in tiers, or ranges as they were called, east and west of the principal meridian. Tiers of townships were numbered north and south of the base line and the townships were subdivided into thirty-six sections, each one a mile square. Each section, in turn, was cut up into quarter sections of 160 acres.

This rectangular survey system, established by law, was not popular in the West because the majority of the earlier settlers were from Virginia where the indiscriminate type was used. The southerner, a true frontier type, was insulted by a system that impinged upon his personal liberty in forbidding him to roam where he pleased, selecting the choicest land, and marking it according to his fancy.[2] Nevertheless, the rectangular survey was infinitely more fair and efficient than the old hit-or-miss surveys. Once the surveys had been made and the plats deposited in the land office, the chance for disputes to arise was reduced to a minimum. This made possible the orderly transfer of land from the government to the individual without the endless litigation that occurred in the indiscriminate-survey areas.

Because squatters were fairly trampling on the heels of the government in their occupancy of the Old Northwest, the first survey was of seven ranges westward from the western boundary of Pennsylvania. All of the seven columns of townships were numbered from the Ohio River northward, number one in each case being the most southerly township; and the numbers ran as high as necessary to reach the base line, or geographers' line as it was called at that time. The actual procedure of measuring, however, began at the geographers' line and proceeded southward, leaving fractional townships along the meandering river. After the seven ranges were measured, the surveying program moved to the first principal meridian and the land was measured by ranges east and west of it. Later, when Ohio was admitted to the Union, this line became the boundary between Ohio and Indiana. By the Ordinance of 1785, township sections were numbered from one to thirty-six beginning with one in the southeast corner and running from south to north in each column. In 1796 the law

---

[2] Erie Mesnard, "Surveys," *Firelands Pioneer*, V (June, 1864), 94; Payson J. Treat, "Origins of the National Land System under the Confederacy," *American Historical Association Annual Report*, I (Washington, D.C., 1905), 378.

was changed to read: "The sections shall be numbered, respectively, beginning with number 1 in the northeast section, and proceeding west and east, alternately through the township with progressive numbers till the thirty-sixth be completed." From time to time as population moved westward and there was need for measuring the public domain, other principal meridians and base lines were drawn.

There were only slight variations in the surveying program over the years. Originally, because land was considered one of the principal sources of income to the government, the land business fell within the jurisdiction of the Secretary of the Treasury. After 1812 in charge of the land under the Secretary's supervision, was the Commissioner of the General Land Office, who supervised a number of land districts, each comprising the approximate area now embraced by a state or in some instances two states. A surveyor general was in charge of each district. When the Department of the Interior was set up in 1849, the General Land Office was transferred to that department. When, from time to time, Congress appropriated funds for surveying new portions of a district, the surveyor general let contracts to deputy surveyors who went into the field and did the actual work. The deputies signed a covenant by which for a stipulated sum they agreed to follow the prescribed methods, make the plats, and record the descriptions of the land. A deputy and his men each took a solemn oath, which was recorded in the deputy's notebook, faithfully to discharge his duties, and the deputy personally furnished bonds that would be forfeited if the work was not completed or was poorly executed.[3] The actual work was widely dispersed. For example, about three hundred deputy surveyors engaged in the survey of the present state of Minnesota. Many of them held a number of contracts at different times.

It was customary to let a contract to "run" the township lines first and by a later contract subdivide them into sections and quarter sections. This system made it imperative that the contractors each do accurate work. If, for example, the surveyor who ran the township lines did not measure off a full six miles, the subdivider would not have room enough for thirty-six full sections. The township corners were established six miles apart, the section corners every eighty chains, or one mile apart. The early regulations prescribed that a tree be marked if one was on the exact spot where a corner was to be established; otherwise, a post was to be set at the "true corner," and two "witness" or "bearing" trees were to be marked and a detailed description of the kind of trees and their measurements was to be

[3] Dwight Agnew, "The Government Surveyor as a Pioneer" (Master's thesis, University of Iowa, 1938), p. 9.

recorded in the field notes. Trees were blazed and were burned with a branding iron to indicate township and subdivision corners. At a section corner, for example, the numbers of the section, township, and range were burned into the blaze. If the region abounded in stone, a township corner was marked by a pile of stones that was capped with a marked stone; all other corners were designated by a single marked stone.[4]

By 1823 the surveyor's frontier had reached the prairie lands of Indiana, and additional regulations had to be prescribed. At a section corner a post was set and a pile of earth 2.5 feet high and 2.5 feet across was thrown up around it and a trench a spade's length deep was dug to form a quadrangle. A pit was dug, and the earth from the trench and the pit was piled up around the corner post to form the mound. A township corner mound was to be six feet square and three feet high, and the sod from the excavations was used to cover the mound. The post was four inches square and emerged from the ground two feet. Regulations required that red chalk be applied to the notches and identification marks on the post to make them more readily discernible. In the prairie country it was no little task to provide these posts. In order to cut the posts for these mounds, a crew sometimes carried poles two and three inches in diameter for miles. Hervey Park, who surveyed in Iowa, said that he occasionally entered the prairie with three of these poles on his shoulder and a compass and staff in hand.[5] It was recommended that the surveyor plant the seeds of a fruit tree so that a clump of useful trees might in time mark the corner.

Farther west on the Plains, where posts were practically impossible to procure, a hole was dug at a township corner and a marked stone set, or in the absence of stones a quantity of charcoal was buried in a hole on the exact corner beneath the mound. Later regulations allowed the surveyors to drive a stake with a charred point and to build a mound around it. In an endeavor to fulfill the requirements of the law, the deputy would lay up a rick of poles, set fire to one side and burn the ends. The stakes were charred by pouring water upon the ends while they were burning. The extreme difficulty of carrying out the regulations in a barren land encouraged delinquency. The story is told that one surveyor rationalized that the entire absence of wood on the Plains made a substitution imperative.

[4] William W. Lester, *Decisions of the Interior Department in Public Land Cases* (Philadelphia, 1860), p. 708.

[5] Hervey Park, "Reminiscences," *Michigan Pioneer Collections*, III (Lansing, Mich., 1881), 590. In our own times, in cases of dispute over boundaries, these corners can be found by skimming off the sod around the outlines of the old pit and trenches; below the pit, the charcoal deposit should still be preserved.

With an extraordinary stroke of genius he stuck a burned matchstick at each corner and swore that he had set a charred stick of the best available timber.[6]

The government in Washington furnished each surveyor general with a standard chain which he kept in his office. That official furnished each deputy surveyor with three chains: a standard chain, which he carried in his baggage, and two field chains with which he made the actual measurements. Before the deputy set out to execute his contract he adjusted his standard chain with that of the surveyor general, and every morning before the deputy started on his day's work, it was his duty to adjust the chain he was going to use for the day with the standard chain which had been trued with that of the surveyor general.

On level ground a four-pole, 66-foot chain was used; in hilly country a two-pole chain had to be used because it was necessary to keep the chain level while the measurements were taken. It was the duty of two chainmen to measure the distance along the line indicated by the surveyor and to inform him when a half-mile had been measured so that the axmen, or moundmen as they were later called, might mark a corner. The forward chainman carried eleven tally pins, each rendered conspicuous by having a piece of red cloth tied in the ring at its top. He stuck a pin in the ground after he had stretched the chain for a measurement. When he had stuck the eleventh pin, he cried "Tally!" which was repeated by the other chainman, and each man registered the tally by slipping a button or leather ring on a string stretched from one of his front pockets to another. The rear chainman, who had collected the pins, now came up to the front, counted the pins to check against loss, and became the forward chainman for the next tally. Four tallies made a half-mile. With the chain taut, the exact spot where a pin had to be stuck was determined by a plumb bob. This was important when descending a hill since in order to keep the chain level the front end of the chain was held several feet above the ground while the pin was stuck.[7]

The surveyor was kept busy with his field notes; he made rough notes while on the line during the day and at night wrote them up in ink. In addition to the description of corners and the type of marker, the surveyor was required to record the location of every object on land, every body of water the line intersected, data on timberland, prairies, improvements, towns, sugar camps, mineral deposits, Indian villages, natural curiosities such as caves and mounds, the land surface—hilly, rolling or broken—and finally whether the soil was first, second, or third class.

[6] Gifford Pinchot, *Breaking New Ground* (New York: Harcourt, 1947), p. 81.

[7] Lester, *Decisions*, pp. 706, 710, 711, 713, 767.

Until 1841 no scrutiny was taken of the work of the surveyors general by the government at Washington. In that year an examiner of surveyors general was established. Possibly one reason for this innovation was that it had been discovered that the standard chain at the surveyor general's office at Cincinnati was two inches too long. At any rate, an inspector from the General Land Office was required to carry an accurate chain and to correct variations in the chains at the various offices of the surveyors general.

Exceptions to the standard rectangular survey were made by the government from time to time. For example, a law of 1824 provided that at the discretion of the President, the land along any lake, bayou, or watercourse could be surveyed in strips two acres wide and forty acres deep and could be offered for sale as eighty-acre plots. In the 1830's, bayous or oxbows in the rivers were surveyed in segments of a circle in such fashion that every landholder could have a wharf. In the Oregon country the early settlers laid out their donation claims in curious shapes in order to possess the level, fertile land nestled among the hills but adjacent to undesirable terrain. The terms of the Donation Act of 1850 allowed these irregular tracts to be surveyed without regard to the township and sectional lines.

Much inefficient and dishonest surveying was done, as might have been expected, since political appointees and men often with almost no technical training were selected without examination of any kind. If a man wanted a contract he ordinarily entered the business not by demonstrating his ability but by the recommendation of a powerful political connection who swore that the candidate could survey and was politically qualified.The following is a typical recommendation:

> We recommend to your favorable notice Mr. J. L. Cozad of East Cleveland. We know him to be an experienced, practical surveyor and engineer of high standing; and in every respect worthy of your confidence and esteem. He is a warm supporter of the administration. By letting him a contract, you will confer a favor upon a large circle of his Democratic friends, as they feel assured that through him the department will be well served.[8]

Careless or inefficient work became especially evident when lines were run subdividing a township. In one case in Nebraska a quarter section had only 52.5 acres instead of 160.

[8] This recommendation is to be found on file in the office of the Board of Educational Lands and Funds, State of Nebraska.

As has been noted, the first United States land surveys took place in Ohio. With the seven ranges completed by the early 1790's, surveyors were in the field in western Ohio running their lines. Since the Indians north of the Ohio River were still unsubdued, the greatest caution had to be taken, and one of the surveyors, Nathaniel Massie, did much of his work in the midst of winter while the redskins were in their winter quarters. Massie hired three assistant surveyors, each of whom had a six-man crew. Their tours of duty in the field were thirty days, but they carried only the most meager provisions. For the first two weeks each mess of seven men carried a ration of only a pint of flour and a small amount of salt that they mixed with the water in which they boiled their meat; after that they lived entirely on the game which the wilderness yielded. One or two men had charge of the pack horses which carried the supplies and camp equipment. At night four fires were built in proximity for cooking—one for each mess—and the entire company pleasantly spent the frosty winter evenings in song and story. When the fire burned low, Massie gave the signal, the men left the fires, carried their blankets and firearms two or three hundred yards, scraped the snow from the ground, and huddled down for the night. This removal was carried out in absolute silence in the darkness so that Indian ears and eyes might not locate them for a midnight attack. Each mess formed one bed, with half of the blankets spread on the ground and the other half used for cover. Seven men, rifles in arms, slept together spoon-fashion with the head of every other one turned in the opposite direction, each man's feet extending to about the middle of the body of his neighbor. There they lay with scarcely a whisper until sleep overtook them. At daylight Massie would send two of the best woodsmen to range about the camp in search of Indians. The party then divided, each mess forming a surveying team. Every man, including the surveyor himself, carried his rifle, blanket, and other personal articles, and each had a prescribed duty to perform. [9] John McDonald, a member of such a party in 1794, described the procedure:

> In front went the hunter, who kept in advance of the surveyor two or three hundred yards, looking for game, and prepared to give notice should any danger from Indians threaten them. Then followed, after the surveyor, two chainmen, marker, and packhorse-men with the baggage, who always kept near each other to be prepared for defense in case of an attack. Lastly, two or three hundred yards in the rear, came a man called

[9] John McDonald, *Biographical Sketches of General Nathaniel Massie* (Cincinnati, 1838), pp. 46–47.

the spy, whose duty it was to keep on the back trail and look out lest the party in advance might be pursued and attacked by surprise.[10]

Through the years, as the surveys moved westward, the surveyor had to contend with Indian hostility from time to time, especially where an area was still in the possession of the red men, who felt that the work of the land measurers was "bad medicine." Because the Indians used pegs to hold their tents and the whites were covering the country with pegs, they feared that the whites were going to cover the whole country with a great tent and take away their hunting grounds. Several surveyors were killed by the Indians, who also broke their instruments out of fear that these things meant the loss of their land and homes.[11] On the Plains in the 1870's, the Indians pulled up the stakes and scattered the mounds, threatened the surveying parties, and even attacked and drove them from the field. On August 19, 1871, E. C. Cunningham, the surveyor general for the Nebraska area, wrote to a member of Congress that except for the summer of 1870 there had not been a single season since 1863 during which the government surveyor had been allowed to do his work unmolested.[12] Most notable among the tragedies was that of Nelson Buck and his crew of eleven, who disappeared on a summer day in Nebraska in 1869. Although fragments of their instruments and equipment were found, to this day their disappearance is one of the mysteries of the Plains. As a result of these attacks, in the 1870's military escorts were sent to guard the surveyors.

As the crews moved north and west of the early Ohio surveys, the hardships of transporting supplies, equipment, and personnel through almost impenetrable forests many miles beyond the line of settlement increased. The New England crews who surveyed the Western Reserve in the summer of 1796 complained of swampy woodlands teeming with ravenous mosquitoes, oppressive heat, and rainy weather. James Backus wrote in his journal on June 6, 1789: "Nats plagued us amazingly."[13] The men, far from home and social comforts, enduring days of exposure and toil, sometimes became rebellious.

[10] W. H. Hunter, "The Pathfinders of Jefferson County," *Ohio Archeological and Historical Publications*, VI (Columbus, Ohio, 1898), 44–45, 170.

[11] McDonald, *Biographical Sketches of General Nathaniel Massie*, p. 29; James Backus, "Journal," April 1, 1789, MS, Ohio Archeological and Historical Society Library, Columbus, Ohio; Zoe A. Tilghman, *Marshal of the Last Frontier* (Glendale, Calif.: Arthur H. Clark Co., 1949), pp. 100, 105.

[12] E. C. Cunningham to John Taffe, M.C., August 19, 1871, "Surveyors' Correspondence," MS in the Office of the Commissioner of Public Lands of the State of Nebraska, I (not paged).

[13] James Backus, "Journal," June 6, 1789.

Surveying marshes and river bottoms was extremely difficult and tedious. A Michigan surveyor confided to his diary on Saturday, August 24, 1833: "While surveying this day we were most of the time waist deep in water"; and on Monday: "Worked all day on the flats in water from one and a half to three feet deep."[14] Surveyor Blair H. Matthews, running a line for a mile and a half near the Missouri River, crossed a prairie creek twenty-five times. The stream was skirted by a narrow belt of timber, a tangled underbrush of hazel, and a thick growth of vines through which the crew had to stretch the chain and set the transit.[15]

Edwin Jerome and his party left Detroit in October, 1831, to survey in present-day Wisconsin. They followed a wagon track or Indian trail much of the way to the southeastern rim of Lake Michigan where they found a cabin or Indian hut in which to lodge, but beyond that point they found neither road nor cabin. They arrived at Fort Dearborn, on the site of present-day Chicago, in a rainstorm. Twenty-three days later, after fording or swimming swollen streams and enduring exposure to rainy weather, they arrived at Galena where their survey began.[16]

In the lake country of Michigan, Wisconsin, and Minnesota, the surveyor often had to hire professional packers to carry his equipment on foot through the marshes and dense thickets to the area of operations. These bearers carried loads of fifty to seventy pounds through the forest. The *Lake Superior News*, commenting on a surveying crew which came to Mackinaw, Michigan, after running a range of townships to the north, said:

In enterprises of this sort, it is only by physical energy, and great powers of endurance that the contractor can realize anything from the prices allowed by the Government for its original surveys. They provision themselves by carrying all on their backs, from depots on the shore. The thickets through which they pursue their work, week after week, and month after month would be declared absolutely impracticable to a person not trained in that school, especially in the vicinity of the lake. No beast of burden could pass without bridges, even in case a pathway should be cut through the matted evergreens that cover the ground. To make a path for horse or mule, would consume more time and labor per

[14] Henry Hunt Snelling, "Memoirs of a Life From My note book and Journal, with additions and reflections, 1829–1867," 3 vols., MS 815, Edward E. Ayer Collection, Newberry Library, Chicago, I, 174.
[15] Everett Dick, *Vanguards of the Frontier* (New York: D. Appleton-Century Co., 1941), p. 420.
[16] Friend Palmer, *Early Days in Detroit* (Detroit: Hunt and June, 1906), p. 123.

mile than the survey itself. There is a class of Frenchmen and half breeds, cousins germain [*sic*] to the Canadian Voyageur, called "packers"; they were bred in the service of the fur companies, to carry goods from the nearest landing to the trading post, and return with a pack of furs.[17]

In 1823 a party on the northern peninsula of Michigan went ten days without a morsel of meat and had only a half-pint of rice per day. Then, fortunately, an Indian gave them a portion of a bear he had killed and the party greedily devoured it and lived on the broth from the boiled bones for three days, but after this some of the men tried to eat their buckskin clothing and shoes. They attempted to spear fish, but were too dizzy to succeed.[18] When in summer a luckless rattlesnake fell into the hands of such starving men, they wasted no time discussing proprieties but consumed its meat with gusto.

While running the fourth principal meridian and third correction line in Wisconsin in 1847, Harry Wiltse found it was impossible for a man to carry more than the provision for his own needs, and each member of the party was restricted to the clothes he was wearing and a single blanket in order that he might carry maximum provisions. For four weeks his sodden party traversed deep swamps and clambered over fallen trees amid clouds of ravenous mosquitoes, but the principal hardship resulted from the lack of sufficient provisions. Finally, worn out by fatigue, hardship, and starvation rations, the party was forced to make a three-day march to Lake Superior in search of food, during which time they had not a morsel of food. Wiltse, who had contracted to survey 175 miles at ten dollars a mile, swore that he would not take a contract for a similar survey at any price.[19]

The marshland of the northern lakes area, so difficult to traverse in summer, had to be surveyed in winter when the underfooting was frozen, but this also presented problems. While wading through snowdrifts, an unfortunate surveyor might strike an air hole and sink into the icy marsh waist deep. In the Florida Everglades, the swamps of Louisiana, and the other Gulf States, the problems were even greater because the terrain did not freeze over in winter.

The work of running lines in the mountains, although completely different, was equally exasperating. W. A. Richards, in surveying the line between Wyoming and Montana, spent several days building bridges and rafts in order to cross turbulent mountain streams, and in one instance

---

[17] *Lake Superior News* (Mackinaw, Mich.), July 11, 1846.

[18] "Ferry Letters," MS in the Michigan Historical Collection, William L. Clements Library, University of Michigan, pp. 60–61.

[19] Lowell O. Stewart, *Public Land Surveys* (Ames, Ia.: Collegiate Press, 1935), p. 84.

timbers for a raft had to be carried three-quarters of a mile. Because the current was too rapid for rafts, the party had to make canoes, and it took seven days to cross the Snake River. Surveying rugged canyons and mountain ridges involved difficult climbing, but as in the lake region, the carrying of supplies was the greatest problem. Richards recorded that a little black mare lost her footing, slid down a mountain side, and landed heels up against a fallen tree which fortunately stopped her from plunging into a canyon. Two days later he wrote: "Old Jim tipped over on a side hill but did nothing worse than smash a waterbucket which was serious enough in that wild region."[20]

But if going beyond the settlements caused much hardship, on the other hand, surveys that lagged behind occupation created difficulties. Squatters, fearful that the survey lines would not run to their advantage, sometimes threatened and even mobbed a surveyor and his crew. One can easily imagine the confusion that resulted when random claims, taken according to fancy, were later crossed by rectangular survey lines. In the Platte Purchase in northwestern Missouri in 1839, the new survey lines ran through houses, or between the house and the barn, or sometimes separated a settler from his valuable spring.[21] When Ira Cook subdivided an area on the boundary between Iowa and Minnesota in 1852, the surveys revealed that a squatter's farm was partly in Iowa and partly in Minnesota and that it was divided among four townships and six sections.[22] Another reason for hostility of settlers toward the surveyor was the fact that running the surveys was a sure forerunner of the land sales. One surveyor reported that since the people did not have money to buy the lands, they had set fire to the prairie, destroyed his camp, and obliterated the markings of his survey. To protect the surveyors a law of May 29, 1830, provided a fine and imprisonment for the interruption of a surveyor's work or for threatening his activities.

Conditions under which the contractors worked were so difficult that errors were bound to occur and conditions often provided eloquent excuses for careless work. After regulations provided for the use of mounds on the prairie, the surveyor found it difficult or impossible to make the mounds in the depth of winter; he would therefore make a temporary mark at a corner, with the intention of retracing his steps when the ground had

20 W. A. Richards, "Diary Kept by W. A. Richards the Summer of 1873," MS in Wyoming Historical Society Library, Cheyenne (not paged).

21 Charles C. Royce, *John Bidwell, Pioneer, Statesman, Philanthropist* (Chico, Calif.: C. C. Royce, 1906), p. 11.

22 Agnew, "The Government Land Surveyor as a Pioneer," p. 63.

thawed and making the mounds according to regulations. Sometimes he failed to return and fulfill his intention, or he forgot in which area he had done the work, or perhaps his temporary marker was gone and his conscience was not tender enough to require him to make the location again.

When properly made in summer, the sod corner-mark was excellent; thick prairie sod was cut and placed over the mound of loose dirt where, if there was sufficient rainfall, it continued to grow. But if a mound was piled up in winter, the excavation had to be hacked out with a pickax and the mangled sod would not grow; as a result, the mound flattened out with the spring rains.[23]

Fraudulent operations were even more vexing to the government officials than slipshod work. As early as 1815, in the region of present Gladwin County, Michigan, an infamous fraud occurred. It was said the crew surveyed that district from a hotel room. At any rate, it cost the government $50,000 to re-survey the 150 townships involved. At a later period the *Kansas City Times* declared that in Colorado and adjoining areas, surveys were made from the top of moving trains and that the survey maps were later filled in by sketches from the geological survey maps that showed ravines, gulches, ruins, etc. Even in the 1880's and 1890's in Arizona and New Mexico, conclusive evidence showed that much of the alleged surveying had not been done.[24]

In earlier times there had been no law requiring a surveyor general to inspect the work of the deputy surveyor before paying him for fulfillment of his contract, but it was suggested that the surveyor general go into the field and trace a few miles at random to learn how well the work had been done. If the surveys were too remote from the office, it was further suggested that the surveyor provide certificates from disinterested persons who lived near the surveys stating that they had examined one or more sections in each township and had found them satisfactorily executed. One need not comment on the dubious value of such documents, not only because of the would-be inspector's lack of knowledge of the technique of surveying, but also because of the ease with which sworn statements could be secured on the frontier. But by 1884 when this perfunctory method of inspection was replaced by a system of sending inspectors from the General Land Office, things began to happen. In California the surveys of the Klamath River were found to be a mile in error; as if to make up for this, there were two boundary lines between Nevada and Utah. On the north boundary of another survey district, although the surveyor's notes indicated

---

[23] Stewart, *Public Land Surveys*, pp. 48, 49, 50.

[24] *Report of the Commissioner of the General Land Office, 1896*, pp. 42–49.

that Big Muddy Creek flowed across the line at a given point, there was a dry mesa nine thousand feet high and the creek was located five miles to the west. According to settlers who were questioned, the deputy who made the survey had been accompanied by an intoxicated inspector and a saloonkeeper. A special agent who had made a trip of several hundred miles in New Mexico reported that he had not found a pit, mound, or post made by a deputy surveyor; for mile after mile there was no sign that the country had been surveyed. The settlers nevertheless stated that they had paid surveyors many dollars to tell them the correct numbers of the land on which they lived. When correct surveys were made, the settlers found that they had made entries on land many miles from the land on which they were living and had intended to enter on account of its water or other advantages.

When William A. J. Sparks became Commissioner of Public Lands in 1885, he uncovered an amazing amount of graft and administrative laxity in the land surveys. He asserted that the land office was a mere instrument in the hands of surveying rings. An example of what was going on all over the West was the activity of John Benson, who operated out of San Francisco and worked in most of the far western states, including Wyoming. In 1879, Benson was awarded seven contracts between September 9 and the close of the year. Some of the townships were not visited at all, and field notes were faked in his office. A vivid imagination was a tremendous asset in his business. A county map and Benson's fancy produced apparent evidence of fieldwork. It was estimated that his activities brought him from $150,000 to $200,000 annually by working hand in glove with banks, railroads, and other corporations that profited from his wiles. It was commonly known that railroad land he surveyed ran from 1,000 to 1,400 acres to the section instead of the honest 640. When government investigators began to close in, the influence of this politically powerful conniver caused their removal. Finally, a shrewd incorruptible special agent, under the direction of a Secretary of the Interior and a Commissioner who could not be influenced, secured the proof, but the California Central Railroad and other moneyed interests were able to quash the indictments on technical grounds. New indictments were drawn up, but after eight years of prosecution the whole thing fizzled out and it was not until later that Benson was convicted of crimes against the United States government.[25]

Fraudulent or poorly marked surveys produced a harvest of disputes and ill-feeling among neighbors when settlement came. In Garden County,

[25] Harold H. Dunham, *Government Handout* (New York: Edwards Brothers, 1941), pp. 249–253. See also *New York Times*, October 13, 26, and 28, 1889.

Nebraska, the corners were so indistinctly marked that for years this was a continual source of animosity. The valuable hayland lay in valleys, surrounded by uplands suited only for grazing, and in the scramble for the limited valleys the homesteader, who was too unbending to compromise, brought whole neighborhoods into a bitter wrangle.

In 1910, William J. Dymond decided that his homestead extended over and across a choice hay valley of Perry Yeast. Suiting action to his ideas of boundary lines, Dymond, his sons, and two neighbors moved into the valley and began putting up hay. The haying party soon found itself surrounded by a number of armed men on horseback under the command of Perry Yeast, who ordered them to get off the hayland and to repair the fence they had torn down. According to a local historian, they refused, and

> Mr. Yeast made them an oration in genuine, if not choice, cowboy language emphasizing same with ornate gesture and flourish of a six-shooter. The other men proceeded with axes, sledges and knives to break, cut, smash and demolish Mr. Dymond's haying machinery and harness. Mr. Dymond and party were not armed and did not resist.
>
> Mr. Yeast and his party were arrested and tried at the fall term of court on a charge of unlawful assembly. It being practically impossible to prove that they had planned and conspired together to commit the act, they were acquitted and discharged. They did not attempt to deny that they destroyed the machinery and cut up the harness, and offered to pay the whole damage. Mr. Dymond would not accept their money nor any part of it.
>
> Upon careful investigation, Mr. Dymond found that he was wrong in his contention concerning his boundary line and that he had been trespassing upon Mr. Yeast's land.[26]

The settlers of range 17 west in Garden County, where Oshkosh, Nebraska, is now located, wisely avoided such disputes. They took up a collection, hired a surveyor to re-survey their whole township and mark every section and quarter-section corner, thus avoiding the disputes caused by slipshod or fraudulent surveying.

In some places, especially after 1830, the surveys lagged so far behind settlement that the settlers would subdivide land that had been laid off in townships but not subdivided by the government. At times, people who had been living on unsurveyed land for years and were anxious to complete their titles, probably in order to sell, urged that their area be sur-

---

[26] Grant Lee Shumway, *History of Western Nebraska and Its People* (3 vols.; Lincoln, Nebr.: Western Publishing and Engraving Co., 1921), II, 252.

veyed. On March 3, 1879, Congress passed a law to the effect that people who wanted their land surveyed could have it done by paying for the survey; then, when they paid the surveying fee, they would be given a certificate that would be received at any land office in payment for land. This effort to oblige on the part of the government opened the door to abuses. A surveyor who wanted a contract would get his friends to request the survey of worthless but level and easily surveyed land; the pretended buyers of the undesirable land then used the certificate to buy desirable land; and the surveyor profited by a nice fat contract. This scheme was particularly useful to the schemer in the Rocky Mountain West where the surveying fee was higher than in the East; hence, a contract on a level spot there was especially desirable. An official described the law as a scheme whereby the government gave up title to valuable lands in exchange for the survey of land of no present or future worth.[27]

Although from time to time the government made a gesture of inspecting surveys, the lack of legal penalties, the mismanagement by political appointees in the General Land Office, and the failure of Congress to appropriate the necessary funds to carry out the inspection program killed the effectiveness of the plan. When Commissioner Sparks came to the General Land Office he found to his dismay that the little corporal's guard of a half-dozen deputies employed to inspect the fieldwork did not execute their inspection until after the government had accepted a surveyor's plats and field notes and had paid him in full. Sparks was further astonished and disgusted that in spite of a profusion of evidence of inefficiency and dishonesty the government had not in even a single instance collected from the bonds of a deputy surveyor whose work had been proved fraudulent. A partial reason for this, however, was that it was almost impossible to prosecute men for fraudulent work because frontier juries would not convict men for perjury.[28]

All in all, it may be said that although the United States established a magnificent plan for surveying agricultural land, the plan was inadequate for a nation of continental scope and broad diversity of topography, geological formation, and climatic conditions. A broad system of surveying

[27] Dunham, *Government Handout*, p. 79. This law was repealed in 1882.

[28] *Ibid.*, pp. 246–253. Although the government apparently had not, by legal action, collected on defective or fraudulent work, in at least one notable instance a bondsman made good the failure of a contractor. W. A. Burt, the well-known Michigan surveyor, had become a guarantor for some of his personal friends. When he was appointed an inspector in 1849, he found that the work done by his obligator was fraudulent. As an honest man, as well as a faithful public servant, he re-surveyed the contract himself, at a personal loss of some $3,000.

should have been adopted, which would have classified the different kinds of land into such categories as arable, grazing, timber, mineral, desert, and swamp. Such a program would have made it possible to have eliminated much of the fraud that accompanied the transfer of land from government to private ownership. In the administration of President Hayes, the National Academy of Science presented such a comprehensive surveying program, but the government adopted only portions of it, leaving the land department with the same old system.[29]

[29] Dunham, *Government Handout*, pp. 64, 65.

IV

Doing a Land-Office Business

AT FIRST, the official in the Treasury Department responsible for both the measurement and dispensing of the land was the Surveyor General, but as new land districts were opened from time to time a surveyor general was appointed for each district and an over-all agency was needed to handle the increasing real estate business of the nation. A law approved on April 25, 1812, established the General Land Office within the Treasury Department, and the official in charge—whose duty it was to superintend the public lands—was known as the Commissioner of the General Land Office. In 1849 the General Land Office was transferred from the Treasury Department to the newly established Home Department, or Department of the Interior as it came to be called. As previously stated, the original plan was to sell the lands at Philadelphia, but succeeding laws established land offices in the vicinity of the land to be dispensed as the frontier moved westward.

Since the land offices, in order to be near the land that was passing from public to private hands, were located on the frontier, the fixtures were in keeping with pioneer custom. In 1833 they ordinarily consisted of two plain pine tables, two bookcases, and an iron chest with a padlock. The examiner estimated the value of these fixtures at about twenty dollars for the tables and desks and fifty dollars for the iron chest. The office at Jeffersonville, Indiana, had four bookcases, but the Warren, Ohio, office used an old family bureau in lieu of a bookcase.[1]

Two officials, appointed by the President of the United States, had charge of each land office. The superior officer, known as the register of the land office, corresponded to an administrative clerk, and his associate next in rank, known as the receiver of public moneys, corresponded to a treasurer.

The register kept two books. The first was a tract book, which contained

[1] See the reports of the examiners of land offices in *American State Papers, Public Lands*, VII (Washington, D.C., 1860), 182, 189, 198, 214.

a description of the land of his district arranged by range, township, and section, and in it he kept a record of land sold, the number of acres, the names of purchasers, dates of sale, the certificate numbers, and the names of the persons to whom the land was patented. It also indicated all reservations, such as those for the use of military forces. The second book, known as the plat book, contained maps or plats of the land in each township. The plats came in loose sheets from the office of the surveyor general, but the register pasted them on canvas and arranged them in permanent book form.

It was the duty of the register to keep blanks on hand and to receive the application of any who produced a land receipt from the receiver; the register then issued a certificate of purchase, made an entry in the tract book that the land had been sold, and the entry was completed. At the end of each month, he sent to the General Land Office an abstract of the certificates he had issued. It was the receiver's duty to receive a purchaser's application and the certificate of the register that the land in question was subject to entry, to accept the buyer's payment, and to give him two receipts. The purchaser gave one of these to the register, who then consummated the purchase.[2] The receiver also acted as a government disbursing agent, paying out money on draft from the United States Treasury. Each officer sent a quarterly report to Washington.

It was intended that the register of the land office and the receiver of public moneys should work independently of each other, with the reports to the General Land Office serving as a check, but the two officers had certain duties to perform together. In the case of a dispute between two settlers, the two officers sat together on the case and rendered a joint decision. If the officers disagreed, they submitted the evidence, along with their opinions, to the Commissioner of the General Land Office, who handed down a decision. Any case could be appealed to the Secretary of the Treasury (or later, the Interior). The land officers also acted as a sort of weather bureau, recording the temperature, the direction of the wind, the aspect of the sky, precipitation, and other phenomena three times each day.[3]

Since the original idea was to offer the lands at public auction and later to sell at private sale any lands that failed to bring the minimum price, the auction was a primary function of the land office. Nevertheless, the routine business consisted of later selling by private entry at the minimum price the quantities of land that had been passed over without a bid at the auc-

[2] William W. Lester, *Decisions of the Interior Department in Public Land Cases* (Philadelphia, 1860), pp. 22–26, 311–312, 366.

[3] James Flint, *Letters from America, 1818–20* (Edinburgh, 1822), p. 154.

tion. The earlier auctions, where real competition ruled, extended over a long period, but later, as men found ways to secure land at the minimum price without much opposition, the length of auctions was curtailed. Thomas Jefferson, by proclamation, directed that the land sale at Jeffersonville, Indiana, should last six weeks; and a law of 1811 provided that land sales should be exactly three weeks in length. The rules laid down by the Commissioner of the General Land Office on May 25, 1831, were still in force in 1860:

1. The day's sale was to open at sunrise and close at sunset.

2. Two or more short intervals should be set aside for relaxation and refreshment.

3. The crier should not dwell on any tract longer than one minute for a bid.

4. The register and the receiver were to be paid $5.00 per day, but under ordinary circumstances nothing was provided for a crier or for a clerk.

If an unusually large amount of land was to be sold, however, the land officers were allowed to hire an auctioneer and extra clerical help; otherwise, the register acted as auctioneer. The tracts were put up in order of their numbers, the first in each case being the section with the lowest number in each township; and the sections were sold a quarter at a time, in a clockwise sequence that began with the northeast quarter. In boom times, when money was plentiful, just prior to the sale, hundreds of speculators and prospective homemakers combed the areas to be sold and took the section numbers of their selections. As the day of the sale approached, the drowsy little frontier hamlet, whose principal reason for existence often was the presence of the land office, began to awake.

At the sales at Cahaba, Alabama, in 1817, three to four thousand persons were scattered over the Plains, living in booths and tents. Some, while waiting for the auction to reach a plot of interest to them, basked in the sunshine or lay sprawled in the shade of the trees, discussing ways and means of obtaining the land at the lowest possible price—while a superb harvest was reaped by the merchants and liquor dealers. According to eyewitnesses, it was customary, when a moneyed man made a good investment, to buy a keg of whisky, knock out the head, and invite all to come and drink at his expense, and every man in the crowd would come with his tin cup to partake of the elixir of life.[4]

[4] A. J. Pickett, "Conversation with John Bibb," MS in the Alabama State Department of History Library, Montgomery, p. 14.

At the land sale at Ozawkie, Kansas, in July, 1857, this interior town of a dozen houses was overwhelmed with the multitude. A huge hotel had been built for the occasion, but this and every other building was crowded to suffocation, and hundreds slept in the open or in tents. Gambling and drinking booths were erected on every hand ready to serve the parched and dusty throng.

Ordinarily, a land office was closed to the public for two weeks following a sale, while the officers brought their books up to date. After the office re-opened for business, activity was again at a maximum for the next few weeks, while the books were open to private entry at the minimum price. Men were busy seeking out land, finding it already taken, coming back to look over the land-office books again, and possibly repeating the process. Sometimes a man entered land that he later found was not what he had intended, since the surveyors' marks often were indistinct. Indeed, the desired land might be a great distance from the location described in the plats. The rules allowed a man a limited time to correct such errors, but these transactions added to the work of the land officers.

The first settler in Smithfield Township, DeKalb County, Indiana, was Isaac B. Smith, who explored the area of the township and four times went on foot to Fort Wayne, some thirty-three miles away, and each time found that the quarter section he had selected had already been entered. Then, physically worn out and downhearted, he met a man who said he knew of a good place, and the land officer told Smith that the informant was reliable. "Sight unseen," Smith entered the tract and then leisurely walked out to look at his bargain—to his consternation a cottonwood swamp boot-top deep in water. Smith returned to the register, who told him he had one week to change the entry, but Smith was required to have a witness see the land and return and swear that it was unfit for cultivation. Smith did this, secured a corrected plat of the township at the land office, and—in company with two others—for the seventh time set out for the area. When the three men were ready to return to Fort Wayne, they met three others who were looking along the same lines. Smith asked if they were going to Fort Wayne, which they denied, but Smith felt that they were trying to deceive him and a race between the two parties ensued. Smith and his companions traveled at a dogtrot most of the way and arrived at the office at eleven the next day, but found that the pieces had been entered. They returned to the area—Smith for the eighth time—and found three pieces that suited them, but it was now Friday evening and there was only one more day of grace. Smith rushed back to the office in time to meet the deadline. Having traveled five or six hundred miles, and nearly worn out with fatigue and anxiety, Smith found his efforts crowned with success and his future home secured at last.[5]

If two or more persons applied at the same time for the same tract, the register was required by a law of 1800 to determine by lot who should have the tract. In later times the register was directed to hold a private auction for the interested parties. Actually, the parties would withdraw and settle the matter among themselves so that the disputed land could be bought for the minimum price. A register was not allowed to enter any land in his own name or in the name of another who would hold it in trust for him. If he wanted to purchase land, he had to make application to the General Land Office, where his application was treated the same as those of others.

In addition to a base salary, the register and the receiver each received a certain percentage of all moneys forwarded to the Treasury of the United States. They also were allowed to retain various fees—for every application or description of a plat, for an inspection of the books, and for issuing patents to the land. A maximum income was set, however, above which their total income could not rise, but the registers and receivers were provided the number of clerks requisite for the business done. On November 21, 1821, Michael Jones of Kaskaskia, Illinois, wrote that he never had less than three clerks and for some time had used four.

Often the land office was on the extreme edge of the frontier, which resulted in real hardships for the land official and his family. When John Whipple, receiver, and Samuel Clark, register, arrived at Buchanan, Minnesota—at the mouth of the Knife River on the shores of Lake Superior—they found the crudest conditions imaginable. The plats of the land had not been received from the surveyor general of the district, and their records and instructions were inadequate, but daily they were "besieged by land claimants and contestants keenly watching . . . lest somebody get the start of them." Suitable furniture could be secured no closer than Chicago or Detroit, and it was almost impossible to move their safe from the lake steamer to the land office. It would have been necessary, Whipple said, to build a plank road 275 yards long and to bring men from Superior to move the safe from the dock to the land office.

Whipple set out to trace the long-overdue mail that contained the necessary papers. In mid-October he took a ship to Chicago and from there went to Dubuque. He found that the pouches for Buchanan had gone forward from Dubuque, and thinking they had been sent to St. Paul, he proceeded to that place but found nothing. Again he went to Dubuque, where the

[5] S. W. Widney, "Pioneer Sketches of DeKalb County," *Indiana Magazine of History,* XXV (June, 1929), 160–162.

postmaster suggested that the pouches might have gone up the St. Croix River to the head of navigation, where Whipple at last found them. He still had to transport the documents across the intervening country to his station, and he and a packer, carrying the precious load, sloshed through the swamps and fought their way through the brush on a grueling journey to his post. Late in November they arrived at the office, after hardships so great that for some time Whipple was barely able to walk. He had been absent for six weeks—but the public had to be served.[6]

Since the local officers were political appointees, it is not surprising that men of all degrees of capability and honesty found their way into the service. Prior to 1816 the work of the land officers was examined by persons who lived in the vicinity, and because the examiners usually were friends and neighbors of the officers and unacquainted with the technical forms, the examination was something of a farce. After 1816 a person who was not connected with the General Land Office visited all of the offices and evaluated the work in a technical, professional way—and the work was rendered more salutary inasmuch as the land officers did not know when the examiner would appear. A comparison of the offices also proved very helpful. The inspector was directed to

> inquire, in a guarded and unsuspicious manner, into the respective characters of the registers and receivers in the vicinity of their several land offices, and report thereon as to their official conduct as Gentlemen of honor, probity, impartiality, and fidelity.[7]

A sampling of the inspectors' reports reveals the range of efficiency and honesty among the officials:

> The register at Crawfordsville, Indiana, in 1833 resided at Delphi forty miles distant and did not pretend to attend to the business personally. He refused to move his residence to Crawfordsville, but visited the office six or eight times to see how his son and the other clerks were getting on.[8]

The examiner said the register was arbitrary, overbearing, passionate, reckless, and exceedingly abusive. He felt the man was in no way qualified to win the goodwill and affection of the people to the government, which a

---

[6] Verne E. Chatelain, "The Public Land Officer on the Northwestern Frontier," *Minnesota History*, XII (December, 1931), 382–386.

[7] *American State Papers, Public Lands*, VII, 274–283, 304, 525.

[8] About 1833, after a period of scrutiny, Congress began to view the land offices with a critical eye. A congressional investigation and the reports of examiners give a view of what was going on in the land offices, and much of the story here presented comes from *American State Papers, Public Lands*, VII.

man of mildness, patience, and impartiality would do. On the other hand, of the receiver of Vincennes, the inspector wrote:

The receiver resides at his office, and gives his daily personal attention to his duties. His character stands fair as a private and public man, and his amiable and obliging disposition renders him a very popular and valuable officer.

The report of a partisan representative of a congressional committee, which was investigating alleged frauds in the land offices in 1834, made this charge against a land official:

The receiver is all the time drunk; so much so, as to incapacitate him from the discharge of his official duties . . . His situation is so notorious here, that I am of the opinion that it would be well enough, for those opposed to the present order of things to say nothing about it but let him alone; for I find it has the effect of *opening the eyes of the blind* in many instances here, and disgusting many more, and, upon the whole, I think his being retained in office has the effect of materially injuring the Administration here. [9]

It would not require much imagination to conjecture that the committeeman was not a warm supporter of Andrew Jackson.

The shortcomings of land officials ran all the way from poor or careless office and business procedures to dishonesty. For example, in 1833, the examiner found that the handwriting in the books of the Fort Wayne office was highly discreditable; moreover, the register permitted a small boy, his nephew, "to learn to write" in the journal.

The most frequent charge of unsavory conduct was that a register would sell land on credit at the expense of the government. In 1825, for example, a man might approach the register and say that he did not have the $100 purchase price but would like to buy a certain eighty-acre tract at private entry, and the register might offer to advance the money personally provided the settler would sign a note for $120 payable at the end of one year. The register and the receiver would then mark the plat sold, collect $120 one year later, send $100 to the government, and keep $20 for themselves.

Thomas Flood, the register at Zanesville, Ohio, used a third party to make his steal look more plausible. Flood arranged with a certain Charles C. Gilbert to "lend" money to Phineas Tomlinson, an impecunious land

[9] Report of G. C. Wooldridge, representative of a congressional committee to look into the frauds in the land offices, November 28, 1834, in *American State Papers, Public Lands*, VII, 525.

seeker, and Gilbert allegedly paid the money to the land office and charged Tomlinson interest. However, when the settler paid his debt at the end of the year, he found that the date of his land-office certificate was the same as the date of his repayment of the loan rather than one year before. Tomlinson concluded that if anyone had lent him money it was the United States government, although the register had written his name in the tract book at the time he had signed the note.

Sometimes for a cash fee of ten or twenty dollars a register promised to retain a settler's land for a year. The same Thomas Flood gave a receipt to Thomas Marshall for such a payment in March, 1833, which the latter, who could not read or write, accepted in good faith. When the register, pushed into a corner by someone who knew the facts, later had to sell the land, Marshall lost the land, the improvements he had made, and his down payment.[10] T. L. Sumerall testified that when he took over as register at Mount Salus, Mississippi, he found on the plats about two hundred tracts marked sold. If anyone questioned the sale of a tract, the former register claimed he had bought it himself. Later, when the country was settled and these tracts of unoccupied land rose in value, the register sold the land to purchasers for two or three times the minimum price, sent the minimum purchase price to Washington, and kept the profit.

Another abuse involved the use of land scrip. For military service, and sometimes for other reasons, the government from time to time issued negotiable scrip with a face value equal to the minimum price of land per acre. Since many who received scrip did not care to go West and use it to purchase land, they were ready to sell it at a discount. For example, when land sold for $1.25 an acre, the scrip often sold on the East Coast for as low as seventy-five cents. Capitalists bought this scrip for cash and used it to buy land at a bargain price—and here again, Thomas Flood, the receiver at Zanesville, collaborated with scrip buyers to profit at the expense of the government. When a buyer offered cash for land, Flood would hang an old black silk bonnet on a nail on the white front of the land office. His confederate in the scrip trade, upon seeing the signal, would come from down the street to the land office. After the transaction, the government held the scrip and the dealer held the cash, at perhaps a 66 per cent profit.[11] Such activity by land officers injured the reputation of the United States and was strictly forbidden.

[10] Testimony before the Senate Committee on Public Lands, 1834, *ibid.*, pp. 274–285, 304.

[11] Testimony of George H. Hilton before the Senate Committee on Public Lands, April 22 and May 7, 1834, *ibid.*, pp. 299, 302.

Closely akin to the scrip traffic was a financial maneuver known as "note shaving," which also involved some receivers. In the early nineteenth century, receivers were allowed to accept only the kind of money that could be deposited with the United States Bank, and the ordinary wildcat frontier money had to be exchanged for bankable money in order to pay the land office. At Vincennes, a bank was started where patrons could exchange their wildcat money for a 6 to 12 per cent fee. Because the receiver was president of the bank, the bankable money he received was deposited in the bank and again used for "note shaving." At Indianapolis, an unscrupulous receiver worked in conjunction with a merchant of the town who in 1833 gathered $98,000 worth of under-par money, turned it in at the land office at par for cash, and then used the cash to shave unacceptable money brought by buyers, thus coolly working both ends against the middle.[12]

Various forms of embezzlement were widely practiced by the receivers. As of September 30, 1833, thirty-five receivers had been in arrears for three years or more: one owed $52,000, one owed $30,000, six owed $20,000 to $30,000, eight owed approximately $10,000, and the others owed smaller amounts.

Another unethical land-office practice was for a receiver to lend the government's money in his care to local merchants, on call, at a high rate of interest. When the land-office inspector called to examine the receiver's books, the latter feigned illness or gave some other excuse to postpone temporarily the examination until he could collect enough money among his clientele to present the amount the records showed should be in his keeping.

A petty form of graft was the abuse of the authority to charge certain fees: unauthorized fees were charged or a larger fee than was allowable. In at least one instance, land officers demanded affidavits on every pretense, and a confederate plied the trade of notary in an adjoining store and split his fees with the land officers. Another form of petty graft was to assess a fee for serving a person out of turn. In 1854, Mary Anderson and her husband went to the land office at Minneapolis, Minnesota, to sign the necessary papers, which involved an extremely tiresome half-day of travel by oxcart. They waited hour after hour for their turn, until they feared they would have to stay over until the next day, but finally the husband seized an opportunity to tell the land officers that his wife had a baby and had to get home that night to breast feed it. The official told Anderson that

[12] Logan Esarey, *History of Indiana* (Indianapolis: W. K. Stewart Co., 1915), pp. 347–348.

for ten dollars he would process his claim immediately. Anderson paid the illegal fee and the couple started home shortly before dark.[13]

Possibly such scandals were unknown to the land officers and are chargeable to a clerk in the office, for it was charged that there was a tendency for clerks who had been in an office for a long time to become masters of chicanery. J. W. Brown, register of the Ionia, Michigan, office in 1836, wrote that he had discovered an attempt by his chief clerk and by the chief clerk of the receiver to defraud the government of $2,000. Brown, who dismissed the culprits, wrote: "My present assistants are new in the business, and we *may* make mistakes, but they have not been *long enough* in a *Land Office* to become dishonest."

The most serious scandals of the post-Civil War period occurred when moneyed interests, such as timber barons, railroads, or mining companies, secured covert control of land offices, put in "their men," and ran the public business as an auxiliary of their own. A well-known case of this kind occurred at the land office at Eau Claire, Wisconsin, in the 1860's and 1870's. Technically, the office was run by Gilbert E. Porter, register, and H. Clay Williams, receiver, but neither had more than a passing acquaintance with the office. Porter was a sawmill operator and the editor of the *Eau Claire Free Press*; Williams was too busy with his law practice to allow the land office to interfere with his movements; and for years the chief clerk, Henry C. Putnam, ran the office. Putnam, an agent for eastern investors, knew many land cruisers, whom he hired to select land for his clients in the East. As an official, he had access to the surveyors' notes and could direct the cruisers to the best prospects for pinelands. When the register and receiver were removed, a political power had two men appointed who were fully as pliant in his hands as those who had been dismissed.[14]

Other offices in Wisconsin were equally subservient to lumbering interests. Expert cruisers who located land for interests not in the ring complained that when they came to the land office with a list of tracts for entry the clerks would go into the back office, pore over the books for a time, and then claim that the lands had already been entered. The cruisers suspected that the land officials looked at the surveyors' notes, found the land to be timber, and knowing the applicant was an expert cruiser, withheld the land for a client on the strength of another man's exploration. A Duluth lumber company and associated firms secured thousands of

[13] Mary Jane Hill Anderson, *Autobiography* (Minneapolis: Agnes A. Twichell, 1934), pp. 19, 20.

[14] Paul Gates, *The Wisconsin Pine Lands of Cornell University* (Ithaca: Cornell University Press, 1943), pp. 91–93, 107, 114, 118.

acres of pinelands, under provisions of the Pre-emption Act, through the ruse of giving the land official a list of names copied from hotel registers in St. Paul and Chicago.[15]

The biggest problem of the receiver was depositing the large sums of money which flowed into the office, for transportation of these funds to the place of deposit was a matter of special concern. During a sale or on other special occasions, the register would request an armed guard from the nearest military post. The receiver's orders were to take the money by the most direct route to the place of deposit, for which, according to a law of 1831, he was allowed a compensation of six cents a mile by water and 12.5 cents a mile by land. The great weight of cash, especially after the specie circular was issued in 1836, which dictated that only hard money should be accepted for land, made necessary a special compensation for transporting specie. A hundredth part of one per cent for every ten miles was allowed. This hard cash was carried in kegs or boxes.[16]

If it was felt that an armed guard was needed, the receiver was authorized to hire one. From Fort Wayne and Crawfordsville, Indiana, the money was often transported in four-horse wagons and guarded by a score of armed men. The tremendous difficulties of transporting money in the 1850's from Buchanan, Minnesota, to the nearest depository—Chicago or Dubuque—every time $5,000 accumulated can only be imagined.

Fortunately, not all the money had to be transported to distant eastern points, for the government often used the land offices as a source of supply for the paymaster at the frontier posts or to furnish funds for other governmental purposes. In 1797, for example, John Nevil, the receiver at Pittsburgh, was directed by the Treasury Department to pay from his funds a sum to the appraisers who had been sent to estimate and pay for the damage done in western Pennsylvania by the Whisky Rebellion insurrectionists. The land officer was in a difficult position. Although a political appointee responsible to Washington, he was far away where the power of the government was weak. He had sworn to protect the interests of the United States; yet these interests often conflicted with those of the frontiersmen whom he served and with whom he brushed elbows daily. Thus placed upon the anvil of land-office regulations, he was beaten thin by the hammer blows of popular opinion. As a rule, the honest land officer, even though from the East, when thrown among the frontiersmen soon acquired

[15] Harold H. Dunham, *Government Handout* (New York: Edwards Brothers, 1941), p. 132.

[16] Circular from Commissioner, General Land Office, to Receivers, May 17, 1845, in Lester, *Decisions*, pp. 315–318.

the viewpoints of both the settler or small landowner and that of the big speculator. This dual attitude, rather than dishonest motives, accounts for much of the winking at violations of the spirit and letter of the land laws by purchasers, pre-empters, and homesteaders. Without this ambivalence, the claim clubs and speculator combines could not have existed.

At times, land officers who tried to uphold the interests of the United States when they ran counter to public opinion were placed under real duress. In 1815 and 1816, a group that the register at Washington, Mississippi, called "banditti or ruffians" threatened the register, interrupted the sale, and repeatedly caused the office to be closed. In 1824, Robert Clark, the register at Monroe, Michigan, attempted to stop timber depredations on government land, but the people called him officious, charging that there was no law authorizing him to stop such trespassing. When the government—far removed and hesitant about doing anything that might have a bad political effect—failed to back up the land officers, they had no alternative but to yield to local sentiment. Even when the land officers reported illegal auction proceedings to the Commissioner at Washington, as likely as not that worthy would not support them in the face of opposition from congressmen who wished to woo their constituents and win re-election.

In 1854 the squatters of Ramsey County, Minnesota, many of whom no doubt were speculators living in St. Paul, formed a claim club and passed a pious resolution:

> To protect our homes from the bids of wealthy and sordid speculators, the homes and improvements which have cost so many of us long years of toil and labor . . . the homes which shelter our wives and little ones, the homes doubly endeared to us by the privations, cares and anxieties . . . [and these homes] we will protect from the ruthless hands of those who would eagerly tear them from our possession.[17]

On the day of the Ramsey County sale a thousand members, dressed in red shirts, armed, and with cudgels in hand, arranged themselves in such a large but tight circle that nonmembers could scarcely have been heard had they dared bid—and only one dared, but he was soon made to see the light. In forty-five minutes the auction was over, and 4,500 acres of extremely valuable land had been sold at the minimum price of $1.25 an acre. This was not to go unchallenged, however, because one month before

---

[17] Edward D. Neill, *History of Ramsey County and the City of St. Paul* (Minneapolis: North Star Pub. Co., 1881), p. 105.

the sale Charles R. Rice, who held a tract by squatter's rights, had sold Lyman C. Dayton forty-seven acres of this same land for $1,937, or about forty dollars an acre, subject to Rice's getting a clear title from the United States government. Dayton now saw that at the sham auction, in violation of United States law, Rice had bought the entire forty-seven acres for about sixty dollars; Dayton was indignant and submitted a protest to the register and receiver that at the auction the land sold far below its worth because bidding was stifled, contrary to law. These officers reported to the Commissioner that it was their opinion that contrary to United States law there had been collusion at the recent sale. Their conclusion, they stated, was based upon public rumor and the fact that there had been the utmost harmony (that is, no competition).

The Commissioner censured the land officers for sending in a report based on mere rumor but eventually felt compelled to send an investigator. This individual, a secret agent, arrived unnoticed, mingled with the people as an ordinary squatter, and learned from them of the claim club which had completely excluded competition. He took a journey with some of the claim-club members, who gleefully told him all—with embellishments that were to cause difficulty later. The agent reported his findings to the Commissioner, stating that if the sales were confirmed the United States would lose $300,000 which rightfully belonged to the whole nation; and Dayton's protest was submitted with the report. The agent recommended an investigation and the withholding of all patents pending the results.

This report was soon made public and was referred to by the Minnesota newspapers as the "Report of the Government Spy." There were enough inaccuracies in the report to enable the claim clubbers to make a good smoke screen of them, and Dayton—no doubt under pressure—published a card denying certain statements in the report. Others, including the governor of Minnesota Territory, also published denials. Interestingly enough, Henry M. Rice, the president of the claim club, was also the delegate or representative of Minnesota in Congress. He called upon the Secretary of the Interior and in a threatening manner, with frontier gusto, demanded that the patents for the land be forthcoming at once. The Commissioner, sensing that a refusal was political dynamite, and might even result in physical violence, did not press the point. The Commissioner had thus neatly let his men down.[18]

It is no wonder that the land-office people did not risk their standing among the settlers in the interests of the United States when they were not backed by the Commissioner in Washington. Furthermore, even though

[18] *Ibid.*, pp. 195–199.

the land-office people might be certain that frauds existed, witnesses perjured themselves in furtherance of fraudulent transactions; and a register, for example, could not substantiate his knowledge because he had no means of securing evidence. Time and time again, Congress was requested to authorize officers to compel witnesses to testify in questionable cases, but without any action. Witnesses refused to testify and risk their lives when a large portion of the community was engaged in the same kind of transaction as the accused. All a register could do was report his information to the General Land Office, and these superiors, working at long range, could do little more than send an agent to investigate.

After the Civil War, fraud was so general, so little deprecated on the frontier, and the officers so few in number that the Commissioner was like a man fighting a prairie fire with its brands flying ahead and setting many little fires. While an agent was prosecuting one violation, a score of new ones was occurring. Furthermore, in this era the press of business fairly overwhelmed the land offices. Often the rush to enter land was so great that a claimant, upon arrival at the land office, had to wait for hours or even days to get into the office. At Decorah, Iowa, the land office opened in the dead of winter, but the rush was so great that the outside stairway leading to the office on the second floor was utterly jammed. Some who had stayed there all night in order to keep their places froze their toes and feet waiting for the office to open in the morning. One night, when the thermometer stood at $-35°$ F., a man took his place before the door at midnight, determined to wait it out and be the first one served. His feet were frozen, but he stuck it out, until at dawn the line behind him extended far into the street. The crowd good-naturedly urged him to hold on, and someone passed a hot breakfast and steaming coffee up to him. Meanwhile, those in the "inner circle" went up the back stairs after dark, were admitted immediately, and were allowed to enter all the land they wished. The extra— but illegal—pay for this overtime work was said to amount to hundreds of dollars for the head clerk in a single night. Finally, someone devised a plan to cut the clerk's illegitimate swollen fee: each man in line was given a number that determined when he would be served, whether an hour or a day later, and he could sit by the fire and return at the appointed time and make his entry without waiting.[19] Eyewitnesses state that at Beatrice, Nebraska, in the 1870's the crowd gathered before daybreak, shivering in the winter cold until the office opened. One of the land seekers was a woman, and when the door opened, the room was crammed full of

[19] Roscoe L. Lokken, *Iowa Public Land Disposal* (Iowa City: The State Historical Society of Iowa, 1942), pp. 121–122.

humanity in a moment, but by common consent the woman was given first chance. The *Beatrice Express* commented:

> The jam was terrible, and the poor woman was obliged to beg for more room to keep from fainting. The applications poured in as fast as they could be taken care of all day, the crowd inside and out never growing smaller for as fast as one applicant, with papers properly fixed up, would worm his way through the crowd to the door, and be cast out, panting and dripping with perspiration, another would squeeze in, and become a part of the solid surging mass within.[20]

At Garden City, Kansas, in the 1880's the press was so great that the land-office workers could not gain entrance through the front door but were obliged to erect a ladder to a second story at the back in order to avoid the throng which crowded about the office day and night. The *Yankton Press and Dakotaian* on July 16, 1874, reported that one day during the previous week the receipts of the Yankton land office had been over $1,800.

Lack of office space and an inadequate, poorly paid staff promoted inefficient procedures and encouraged the rise of a special legal practitioner, known as the land lawyer, to serve land seekers, although no legal aid should have been needed. Such conditions contributed to much fraud and favoritism in the land office itself. Thousands of disputed cases piled up, until the General Land Office sometimes was years behind in dealing with these cases. Furthermore, the General Land Office was so inadequately staffed it could not hand down consistent rulings. The editor of *Copps Land Owner*, while on a visit to Dakota Territory in 1884, found that the people continually criticized the land-office rulings with protests, ridicule, and profanity.[21]

Perhaps many of the weaknesses and shortcomings of the land office are inherent in a democracy, for the representatives of the people, politically motivated and far from the scene, overlooked the needs of the land office to the detriment of the best, long-range interest of the country.

[20] November 18, 1871.

[21] Dunham, *Government Handout*, pp. 132–137. Part of the reason for the congested condition of the land office was due to the abuse of the land laws by some of the very ones who complained; they entered, commuted, and re-entered land until it became valuable, thus multiplying the work of the land office.

V

Squatters and Pre-emption

FROM EARLY COLONIAL TIMES until the latter part of the nineteenth century
the indifference of frontiersmen to the property rights of the great landholders and the government was a real problem. In New England, New
York, and especially in Pennsylvania the immigrant paid no attention to
the landlord's demands, and the Virginia frontiersmen regarded the king's
land as lightly as Robin Hood regarded His Majesty's deer. As early as
1768 the Pennsylvania Assembly had passed an act which required all
persons who had settled illegally on western lands to remove within thirty
days or suffer death without benefit of clergy, but the intruders ignored the
threat. By 1775, in defiance of the Proclamation of 1763, there were between 25,000 and 30,000 persons beyond the Appalachians in the Fort Pitt
district.

When the colonists set up housekeeping for themselves, the new nation
found that a mere change of government did not alter the habits of its
people. Congress in 1785 felt compelled to issue a proclamation forbidding
unlawful settlement and authorized the Secretary of War to remove those
who had settled on the public domain in violation of law. Colonel Harmar,
in carrying out these orders, sent Ensign John Armstrong and a party of
soldiers down the Ohio River, destroying houses, tearing down fences, and
dispossessing settlers. Armstrong reported that every bottom between
Wheeling and the Scioto River had at least one family and that there were
at least three hundred families at the falls of the Hockhocking. In spite of
the demolitions, no sooner were the troops out of sight than the settlers
were back on the land again. In the Southwest, a similar situation existed.
In 1791 a congressman stated that 300,000 families (highly exaggerated)
had settled south of the French Broad and Big Pigeon rivers in present
eastern Tennessee.[1]

[1] Amelia C. Ford, *Colonial Precedents of our National Land System, Bulletin of the University of
Wisconsin*, History Series, II, No. 2 (Madison, Wis., 1909–1910), 117–118.

The problem became so serious that in 1796 George Washington returned to the idea of King George III, who issued the Proclamation of 1763 thirty-three years before: A line should be run between Indian Territory and the areas open for settlement, and the line should be so distinctly marked that no one in the future could plead ignorance.

The term "squatter" was first used in congressional debates in February, 1806. A member of Congress declared that on certain tracts in Indiana there were "squatters" who had already made improvements that had increased the value of the land from four to six dollars an acre. Out of these debates grew the Intrusion Act of 1807. By its terms, a settler was forbidden to settle, survey, make marks, or otherwise establish a claim on land he had not purchased. The President was authorized to use United States marshals or the military forces to remove trespassers. An intruder was to be given three months' notice, and the penalty for a violation of the law was a minimum of six months in jail or a $100 fine.

Recognizing the impossibility of enforcing such a law, Congress later passed a palliative measure, providing that those on the public domain at the time of the passage of the 1807 act could apply to the register to stay on the land until the time of the public sale as "tenants at will"—on not more than 320 acres—but the register was not to sign any such lease until an occupant had signed a declaration that he did not occupy the land by virtue of a claim or pretended claim. These leases were to be recorded in the same way as a sale, and a fee of fifty cents was levied for each application and one dollar for each permission.[2]

When the squatters learned of the government's intent to enforce the law against intrusion, they found all sorts of excuses to stay on the land they illegally occupied. The appeals to government officials in behalf of widows, orphans, and impoverished heroes who were "giving themselves" in behalf of their country's development were quite enough to wring tears from the eyes of a wooden Indian. A letter from a representative of the squatters in Mississippi Territory illustrates the point:

MISSISSIPPI TERITORY MUNROW COUNTY JANUARY 20th, 1816
DEAR SIR   in viewing our last Papers we find it very Distressing news for us to be obliged to move of of the Public lands,—which will Distress Not less than 500 families—in order for your Honour to be in possession of our Distress Situation I thought Proper to inform you we are at least

---

[2] William W. Lester, *Decisions of the Interior Department in Public Land Cases* (Philadelphia, 1860), pp. 28–30.

300 Milds from any State   the news Reached us two late to Purchase lands on the tombigbee—and all that is werth living on has been Sold—had we had Knowledg of this we would a have had land two—but genneral Jackson encouraged us to Settle on the allebarmer—there is also a Number of People from North & South Carolina & Georgia and a grate Number of them has sold there Carages waggons & &—and Now how to get back god only knows—there is also a Number of Poore widows that has lost there Husbands in the late war with the British & Indians and is Not able to Move of—there assembled also about 70 Indians on the allebarmer Near the Standing Peach tree and states that the treaty between the Amerians & British gave them there lands, and they Mean to work it—if we leave our Plantations the Indians will be shore to burn them   the People in this Cuntry are New Settlers and Mostly Poore People that has been already Ruined by the Indians—and Now to leave there Crops of wheat gardens & turnips will Compleetly Distress them over again   a grate Number of Citizens Scearcely Made bread last year oweing to the Invation with the British & Indians—I am of the opinion that there Has been Some Rong Misrepresentations made to your Honour in Regard to the Public Lands—there has been a Stop to Cutting Down timber for Several Months which was obeyed all the lands that was Improved Sold Considerably better then that was Not   it went to 6–8 & 10 Dollers Pr achre that was good and that was Not Improved went gennerally at government Price   I will also state to your Honour that if there is Not Preemptions allowd to the Citizens of this Cuntry that the Yazzoo Company will Purchase all the good land from the Head to the Mouth of the allebarmer   it will take all the good Land to Pay five Million of Dollers—if your Honour should think Proper to Let us Stay till we make a Crop it would be a Blessing to some —Particular to those widows & Children that there Husbands has been Masicreed by the Savages—it is imposible for us at this Hour to go and bui Land & build Houses and open land time Enough to make a Support—it is one of the Most Destressing News that we Ever heard of   it is worse then the Indian & British war. the feellings of our Citizens is very much Hurt Particular those who fought Brave to obtain this Cuntry and Now Cannot Injoy it   if the thing Could be Rightly Constrewd to our government I Cannot but think but what the orders would be Countermanded though I am always willing to Concur on my Part with any law that Government will adopt—if your Honour would be so good as to favour me with an an answer when Convenient and Direct your letters

to Fishers Post Office on the allebarmer Near fort Claibourne   Sir I am
with Respect your obedient and Humble servant—

Clabon Harris.[3]

The penalty of the Intrusion Act was impracticable, for the little army
could not begin to spread its handful of troops wide enough to cover the
vast spaces on which multitudes of intruders were settling. Often, moreover, the army was sympathetic to the squatters. Furthermore, the settlers
had no money to pay the fines, nor were there enough prisons for the
incarceration of all the guilty. But more fundamental, as a federal judge,
Harry Toulmin of Mississippi, pointed out in a letter to President Madison: "How can a jury be found in Monroe County to convict a man of
intrusion—where every man is an *intruder?*" The judge stated that the
legislature of Mississippi had given representation in that body to counties
in which the total population was composed of intruders. Indeed, the very
act of intrusion had multiplied the intruders' political power a hundred
times because they had moved from thickly settled areas where each vote
counted relatively little into a sparsely populated county of intruders. It is
little wonder that with such legal recognition the settlers did not regard
themselves as scoundrels.[4]

Intrusion persisted and the Act of 1807 was impossible to enforce,
although troops were called out time and time again. In July, 1827, the
federal government sent troops whose commander ordered the whites out
of Indian land in Alabama, destroyed the crops, burned houses, and dispossessed the trespassers. This was known as the Intruders' War. In 1834
and 1835 Major Henry Dodge, in command of United States Rangers, on
two different occasions drove 250 to 300 white families out of the half-
dozen Indian-owned counties of northwest Missouri. Some of the squatters
stole back secretly to keep crops growing and in other ways to maintain
evidence of occupation which would be recognized as claims by other settlers
when eventually the area was legally opened to settlement. In Iowa in the
1830's and 1840's troops removed intruders. In Kansas in the 1850's troops
should have been used, but a horde of whites settled on Indian land without molestation. Innumerable instances might be cited of trespassing by
the white population upon government and Indian territories in the

[3] Clabon Harris to the President, WD: AGO, Old Recs. Vis.: ALS, in Clarence E.
Carter (ed.), *The Territorial Papers of the United States, Mississippi Territory*, VI (Washington,
D.C.: Government Printing Office, 1938), 647–648.

[4] Judge Harry Toulmin to the President, January 20, 1816, *ibid.*, pp. 644–647.

Oregon country, California, and finally in Oklahoma where the land-hungry boomers, as they were called, had to be driven out time after time. Intrusion on their lands kept the Indians stirred up and brought protest after protest from Indian agents—or Indian chiefs, seeing the inevitable, often charged settlers hush money for occupation prior to the legal date for settlement.

In 1836, after signing the purchase papers of Keokuk's Reserve in Iowa, Henry Dodge, now governor of Wisconsin Territory (of which Iowa was a part), spoke a few fatherly words to the Indian braves and chiefs, urging them to move their families from the tract within a month. The Indians received this paternal advice with loud laughter. One of them later explained the reason for their merriment:

> My father, we have to laugh . . . we have all left the lands already, and sold our wigwams to *chemokemons* [white men]—some for one hundred, and some for two hundred dollars before we came to this Treaty. There are already four hundred *chemokemons* on the land, and several hundred more on their way moving in, and three days before we came away, one *chemokemon* sold his wigwam to another *chemokemon* for two thousand dollars, to build a great town.[5]

One of the major tasks of the army through the years was the removal of trespassers, which accounts in part for the dislike by the frontier farmer of the regular army, although the army was totally ineffectual. Many instances of squatting went unheeded, and even when troops were used, it was an extremely delicate matter to use military power in a just but thoroughgoing way. A company of dragoons stationed along the border of the Indian country in Iowa prior to the opening of a tract for settlement in 1843 was kept busy searching out stealthy settlers who hid in caves or secluded spots. Others, who were driven out, had a fortuitous pattern of "hard luck"—broken wagons, strayed cattle, and stolen oxen—and managed to move so slowly that they were still in the area at the hour the region was opened and the race for possession began.[6]

Squatters had no more respect for reservations held by the government than they had for the Indians' land. In 1835 the Commissioner of the General Land Office reported to the chairman of the Committee on Public Lands that several "bold attempts" had been made to pre-empt the site of Fort Dearborn at Chicago, which had been continuously regarded

[5] Ruth A. Gallaher, "This Iowa," *Iowa Journal of History and Politics*, XXXIX, No. 1 (January, 1941), 11.

[6] Pauline Grahame, "The Promised Land," *Palimpsest*, X, No. 5 (May, 1929), 192–195.

as a military reservation. Indeed, the land officers at Chicago allowed the tract, worth from $500,000 to $1,000,000, to be entered under the allegations of a pre-emption right. When the Commissioner of the General Land Office learned of the proceedings, he ordered the land officers to cancel the transaction and refund the small sum that had been received.

Government policy anticipated selling land on a competitive basis, assuring that it would be sold at its market value as determined by an auction, but the government's inability to control squatting led to an entirely different method of land disposal than that set forth by the original statutes. By interpretation and custom, the settlers virtually set aside the laws, and in time Congress changed the laws to conform to the usage thus established.

The squatters desired to run ahead of the Indian treaties, surveys, and land auctions in order to have the choice locations. In this connection, the professional or habitual squatter sought out and occupied strategic or ultra-valuable locations, such as millsites, townsites, rich bottomlands, mineral-rich areas (although these were supposed to be reserved by the United States), and other worthwhile locations. They argued that their living on government land was a benefit to the nation in that, by braving the dangers from the savage Indians, they set up a buffer that protected the East; that by improving the land on which they settled, they made the surrounding land more valuable; and that by taming the wilderness, making homes, and utilizing the natural resources, they made the nation richer. In view of these benefits which their lawbreaking conferred upon the nation, the squatters argued that they should be allowed to buy their claims for the minimum price at the land auction when eventually it caught up with them.[7]

Such a privilege was known as a pre-emption right. The word "pre-emption" means a preference or prior right of purchase by the occupant. Pre-emption rights had their origin in the middle and southern states, and in 1776 when the term apparently was used for the first time, the principle was recognized by the Continental Congress as related to settlers on western lands. The principle required a man to improve land for the purpose of making a home as a prerequisite for the right of buying the land at the minimum price. In spite of the plain wording of the first land laws under the new government—that the lands should be sold at auction—requests for pre-emption rights on one basis or another began to come in. Because settlement had pushed on without waiting for the new surveying system to

[7] Roy M. Robbins, *Our Landed Heritage* (Lincoln: University of Nebraska Press, 1962), p. 25.

catch up, settlers asked that they be allowed to buy their land at the minimum price, and from time to time, wavering in its determination, Congress gave in to the importuning of the citizens. Between 1799 and 1838, thirty-three special or temporary pre-emption acts were passed.[8] Naturally, these numerous exceptions virtually established a policy and led people to conclude that they could disregard the Intrusion Act as there was an excellent chance of securing the passage of a special act in behalf of intruders.

Since such laws applied to only a limited territory and for only a brief period, they did not cover all land seekers, and many squatters were unprotected; that is, they had to compete at the auction for their claims. Because some of these squatters had lived on their land for a number of years and had a house, barn, outbuildings, and part of the land under cultivation, speculators or men with money to invest in land on the frontier sometimes took advantage of the situation by threatening to bid against them at the auction. These sharpers, as the settlers called them, would agree to remain silent if the squatters paid them an amount equal to the government price, and speculators thus made great quantities of money without risk by taking advantage of the settlers' helplessness. The pioneer was usually poor, and anticipated the approach of the sale with fear and trembling. In that critical hour, bland, smooth-talking gentlemen, clad in store suits and ruffled shirts, would offer to buy a squatter's land and turn it back to him at the end of two years at a 100 per cent advance in price. The speculator then entered the land in his own name and gave bond that he would transfer it to the settler when the latter had paid double the original price, but in many instances the farmer was unable to redeem the land and the speculator simply secured an improved farm at the government price.[9] At the Burlington, Iowa, land sales in 1838, a number of rich men from the East each lent $100,000 on this condition. So many squatters lost their improvements because they were outbid at the sale by speculators, or were unable to raise the money to pay the lender his loan, that there was a tendency for them to move as far "inland" as possible and there enjoy the free use of the public domain. Many of them became habitual squatters, settling and moving a dozen times in a lifetime.

[8] Lester, *Decisions*, pp. 64, 65.
[9] In Iowa, this system of selling one's claim before the sale and buying it back at an advanced figure later was called "Barretting," after a capitalist from Springfield, Illinois, who bought many claims at the Burlington sales; Allan G. Bogue, "The Iowa Claim Clubs: Symbol and Substance," *Mississippi Valley Historical Review*, XLV (September, 1958), 241.

Rarely was an auction a free and unrigged proceeding. As early as 1805, land officers reported to President Jefferson that bidders at the land sales were agreeing among themselves not to bid more than the minimum price. In an effort to stop this practice, Jefferson instructed the registers that when they saw evidence of conniving to prevent the auction from taking its natural course, they were to buy the lands in the name of the United States. If collusion became too serious, the registers were instructed to stop the sale. This, of course, was an awkward situation for the land officers. It was difficult to know exactly how much collusion was taking place, and if a register made a mistake he was subject to the severest criticism of the community—in fact, great pressure was placed on him to allow an auction to proceed no matter what course the buyers followed. A critic of the buyers at an auction held a few days before made this contribution to the *Missouri Intelligencer* of December 16, 1823:

The . . . multitude . . . entered into their clannish compacts, by which most of them have procured their favorite tracts of land at the minimum price [$1.25] whatever may have been the intrinsic value of the public domain. Many stratagems were resorted to by purchasers for the purpose of defrauding the public treasury. For instance, when one of the most valuable tracts in the district was offered, an old man was brought forward who was said to have a claim to it from the accidental circumstance of being father of several blind children. . . . Was not the leader of the blind the agent of some purse-proud swindler? Answer me, my countrymen, and blush for your avarice! Another instance of fraud was too notorious to be passed over without comment. A widow presented herself in a conspicuous manner, offered her bids for a desirable tract of land, while some officious person begged that the purchasers would not oppose the poor woman!

It was later reported, the critic said, that the "poor woman" was the sole owner of several Negroes and had $1,500, and it was well known that she had secured a tract for a well-to-do neighbor. The correspondent complained that when the land officers had tried to stop these frauds, they had aroused the "clamorous ill will of the sovereign people," and that men with a "good horse" or "ready cash" had bribed their neighbors not to bid. They "esteem it a singular hostility if a stranger or a 'fresh emigrant' chance to bid against them."

In answer to this, another contributor, styling himself "a Bidder," denied that there was the amount of collusion charged, and he challenged the right of the register and receiver to auction the lands to the United States. He presented the viewpoint of the buyers:

The law is positive and unconditional that when an individual bids as high as $1.25 an acre and pays for the same, the right of the soil shall be vested in him, unless some other individual bids more. . . . At auctions it is the undisputed right of everyone to bid or not to bid; their wants, their convenience, and their interests will always determine the manner in which they exercise this privilege; they are under no obligation, and everyone is supposed to know his own interests, and has a right to pursue them in any manner which is not forbidden by the statutes. If one pays another for not bidding against him, their mutual interests are concerned, and probably advanced by the contract. They alone occasion it, and probably, at the time, the contracting parties do not think of any effect it may have upon a third party; there is here no sinister intention, which is always a necessary constituent of a fraud; it is a law of nature that everyone may act as he chooses, without any restraint—and a maxim of civil jurisprudence that he may do anything consistent with legislative enactment. If, therefore, I hire a man to steal ten dollars for me, I am guilty of a wrong, because it violates the law; but if I hire him not to bid against me, I am not guilty of a wrong, because the law justifies him in so doing, and declares his previous right to do it. When a quarter section is offered that is desirable, and I suspect that another means to bid against me, I can legally hire him to ride into the country, to stand, or sit or to keep his mouth shut until it is sold and he has a most unquestionable right to do it; it is what concerns us alone, and if it gratifies our feelings, or promises a mutual benefit, we may execute the terms of the contract, and any interference to prevent it is clearly wrong and unjustifiable.[10]

This argument, whether legally sound or not, was in keeping with public opinion and practice on the frontier.

In an attempt to secure fair and untrammeled auctions, Congress passed an act on March 31, 1830, providing that any person who shall

bargain, contract, or agree, or shall attempt to bargain, contract, or agree, with other person or persons, that the last named person or persons shall not bid upon or purchase the land so offered for sale, . . .

[10] "A Bidder," *Missouri Intelligencer* (Columbia, Mo.), December 16 and 23, 1823, January 15, 1824.

or shall by intimidation, or unfair management, hinder or prevent, . . . any person . . . from bidding

shall be liable to a maximum fine of $1,000, or imprisonment for two years, or both. Furthermore, the law banned as illegal all agreements or secret understandings to purchase land and sell it for more than the price at which it had been purchased from the government. Such an agreement was declared void, and an aggrieved party, according to law, could secure damages.

In spite of this law, however, feeling rose to its highest pitch when speculators bid against squatters and took their land and improvements, or threatened to do so and compelled the squatters to buy them off. In an effort to secure their land and improvements, settlers—as we have seen—organized what have popularly become known as claim clubs, although the organizations called themselves by various names. The one at Crown Point, Indiana, was known as the Squatters' Union;[11] some were called Land Leagues; and still others were called Settlers' Protective Associations. One in Nebraska was called the Riders and another the Golden Circle. While these organizations were universal in the area from Indiana west to Nebraska and Kansas and north to the states bordering Canada, they also appeared in Mississippi and Alabama. Those in Iowa have been the subject of more thorough scholarly investigation than in any other state.

As early as 1824 the claim-club device had begun to take form at Crawfordsville, Indiana. An old settler wrote:

The land sales commenced here today, and the town is full of strangers. The eastern and southern portions of the state are strongly represented, as well as Ohio, Kentucky, Tennessee, and Pennsylvania. There is but little bidding against each other. The settlers, or 'squatters,' as they are called by speculators, have arranged matters among themselves to their general satisfaction. If upon comparing numbers, it appears that two are after the same tract of land, one asks the other what he will take to not bid against him. If neither will consent to be bought off, they then retire, and cast lots, and the lucky one enters the tract at Congress price— $1.25 per acre—and the other enters the second choice of his list. If a speculator makes a bid, or shows a disposition to take a settler's claim from him, he soon sees the white of a score of eyes snapping at him, and

---

11 See the constitution of the Squatters' Union in Lake County, Indiana, in Herbert Anthony Kellar (ed.), *Solon Robinson, Pioneer and Agriculturist*, I, 1825–1845, in *Indiana Historical Collections*, XXI (Indianapolis: Indiana Historical Bureau, 1936), 69–76.

at the first opportunity he crawfishes out of the crowd. The settlers tell foreign capitalists to hold on till they enter the tracts of land they have settled upon, and that they may then pitch in—that there will be land enough—more than enough for them all.[12]

The claim clubs, while rather secretive at first, in the nature of vigilantes, in time grew so bold as to publish their constitutions in the frontier newspapers. The constitution was formed and adopted by a mass meeting of settlers in a given area. Ordinarily, the officers consisted of a chairman, a registrar or recorder, and a board of arbitration. The constitution set forth the amount of land a member could hold, the fees to be charged by the recorder, the rules for marking, registering, and transferring of claims, and the boundaries of the association. Although often the borders of the association coincided with those of the township as laid out by the government surveyor, a club more frequently took in the area of a whole county. The constitution of the Fort Dodge, Iowa, club declared that its area ran "12 miles each way from this spot." In some instances meetings occurred where a number of clubs from an area assembled as a sort of claim-club federation. All members bound themselves to stand together; to boycott claim jumpers, or to assemble as a posse at the call of the chairman to dispossess by force any man who dared challenge the "rights" of a member. The all-important duty of every member was to enforce their demands at the auction. The amount of land members could claim depended entirely upon the decision of the squatters themselves. If there was a rush of settlers in a small area of valuable land, there was, at the same time, a tendency to divvy up "the good things" among all. This resulted in smaller claims. Such was the case in the area of the twin cities of St. Paul and Minneapolis—claims were eighty acres. In Wisconsin, on the other hand, 640 acres was a common maximum, and even 640 acres of prairie and 160 acres of timber sometimes were permitted. In Iowa the usual area was 320 acres—hopefully, a quarter section of timberland to go with a quarter section of prairie, so it was stated.[13] The recorder registered the claims of all settlers and charged a fee of from 12.5 to 25 cents for the work.

The claim-club constitution clearly stated the requirements with regard to residence, improvement, and other items concerning a man's right to his claim, and conflicts among members usually resulted from disputes over

[12] Sanford C. Cox, *Recollections of the Early Settlement of the Wabash Valley* (Lafayette, Ind., 1860), pp. 17–18.

[13] *Iowa Territorial Gazette* (Burlington, Ia.), December 1, 1838; Charles A. White, "The Early Homes and Homemakers of Iowa," *Annals of Iowa*, 3d series, IV, No. 3 (October, 1899), 187–190.

these matters. When a dispute arose, the club convened a court of arbitration before which the principals and their witnesses appeared. No person was sworn, and professional lawyers were barred, but the decision of the court was final and litigants were required to pay fees for the services of the arbitrators and the witnesses. The chief reason for disputes was claim jumping: someone would come into a community and take possession of a claim or part of a claim of a member of the club, who would then call upon the club to protect him in the possession of his holding. Often the disputes were due to greediness—perhaps a man tried to hold two claims and a newcomer tried to take possession of one of them. The former, of course, could not improve each claim and meet the residence requirement on each.

Because the claim club was usually slack in enforcing its requirements, many questionable cases arose. For example, perennial squatters, as we have seen, followed the western edge of settlement, took a number of the finest locations, held them under loose, improper claim-club usage, and sold them to later comers. These professional squatters, or "claim hucksters," were a constantly reoccurring problem on the western edge of civilization. An old Iowa squatter, Simeon Crogin, overhearing a young man, recently from Illinois, remark that no man ought to own more than one claim and not even one unless he lived on it, made this counterblast:

I own *fourteen* claims, and if any man jumps one of them, I will shoot him down at once, Sir. I am a gentleman, Sir, and [a] scholar. I was educated in Bangor, have been in the United States army and served my country faithfully—am the discoverer of the Wopsey—can ride a grizzly bear, or whip any *human* that ever crossed the Mississippi; and if you dare jump one of my claims die you must.[14]

The belligerent manner and vigorous language of the old borderer so alarmed the newcomer that he made his way back to Illinois by the shortest route. Many immigrants, intimidated like the Illinois man, rather than have a fight, passed by favored locations and went into the interior to select a tract, but others who did not mind a fight would jump a questionable claim and the club would have to decide the merits of the case.

When the landlooker chose to jump a claim, the clubs usually upheld the original claimant against the claim jumper, who was one of the most detested "varmints" on the frontier. Occasionally, however, a determined jumper would refuse to be driven from his new holding and would precipitate a claim war—he would gather about him a group of relatives and

14 George F. Robeson, "Justice in Early Iowa," *Palimpsest*, V (March, 1924), 105.

friends who were as resolute as himself and defy the claim club. Sometimes blood was shed, but more often the man with the most nerve won
out. In the 1850's at Winona, Minnesota, Erwin H. Johnson, a steamboat
carpenter, tried to hold a claim for himself and another for his captain,
who continued to ply his trade on the river. One of the claims had no improvements, and W. B. Bunnell jumped it. After a fierce battle, Bunnell
finally relinquished the claim rather than have a fight to the death. Sometimes a club was split, with part trying to protect members with questionable holdings under club rules and others holding to strict interpretation
of the regulations.

Although claim clubs ordinarily forbade a man to make more than one
claim, they did permit claimants to sell their land to others, which led to
wholesale speculation. A man, in fact, could wander along the frontier,
taking select claims and selling them to others, who in turn could hold
them without residing on them. Strange though it may seem, a trespasser
on land that belonged to the United States government could sell and give
a species of title to the land although the real title rested in the United
States. Indeed, the state of Illinois passed a statute that legalized this procedure, and Iowa and Nebraska had a similar legal provision. Such a
document, executed in 1839, reads:

> Know ye all men by these presents that I, Daniel O'Bryan of the County
> of Lee and the state of Illinois have this day bargained, sold and quit
> claimed, and by these presents do bargain, sell and quit claim unto
> William Seward of the same place all the following pieces and parcels of
> land . . . on the following conditions to wit, that the said William Seward
> does deliver to me one span of black horses at $200 . . . and shall pay to
> the said Daniel O'Bryan the full sum of six hundred and twenty five
> dollars current money on or before the first day of April next. In that
> case the said Daniel O'Bryan shall deliver to the said William Seward a
> quit claim deed for the above described pieces or parcels of land (consist-
> ing of about 360 acres) *clear from all incumbrances or disputes, the General
> Government only excepted.* And shall put the said Seward in full and peace-
> able possession of the same together with the dwelling house and all
> improvements on the same.[15]

The claim clubs gave each member a title of sorts, when he registered his
claim, in the form of a claim-club certificate that showed the description

---

[15] George Winston Smith, "Problems in the Economic Development of Dixon, Illinois"
(Bachelor's thesis, University of Illinois, 1934), pp. 22–23.

of his land. An Indiana certificate is probably typical of those that were issued by the clubs:

Office of the Registrar of Claims
March 6, 1837
Range 8
Town 35
Section 5

No. 620

Be it known that the annexed numbered land is registered to Bartlett Woods of Michigan City and that his claim to the same will be duly respected if he complies with all the requisitions of the constitution adopted by the Union of settlers on the public lands, July 4, 1836.

Signed.

Solon Robinson
Registrar

In Iowa, a law of the territorial legislature made the payment of taxes prerequisite for the validation of a squatter's claim to a parcel of land, which became a rather lucrative scheme for the county in some instances. The treasurer on one occasion received tax payments on a quarter section of land adjoining Keokuk from seven different persons.

Allan Bogue, in his study of the claim clubs of Iowa, found that in many counties where claim clubs were most active the majority of the members did not purchase land at the sales, or bought only a portion of their holdings under claim-club rules, or purchased land entirely different from that which they were holding under claim-club title.[16] Bogue substantiates the findings of this writer in other states, and indicates that one of three alternatives was acted upon: since they did not have enough money to purchase their claims at the sale, squatters sold their claim-club titles to later comers before the auction and with the proceeds bought as much land as the profits from their small speculation allowed; they bought cheaper, less desirable land with their gain; or they salted away their money, went onto the fringes of settlement to repeat the process of squatting and holding land by claim-club title, and sold their new claim after it had become valuable prior to the land auction. The poor but thrifty squatter thus was able to accumulate enough from his series of minor speculations, with no cash investment, to secure free land on the frontier long before a homestead law was passed, and in so doing, substantiated Frederick Jackson Turner's contention that there was free land on the frontier.

[16] Bogue, "Iowa Claim Clubs," *Mississippi Valley Historical Review*, pp. 252–253.

The claim club's chief reason for existence, of course, was to protect the members from those who were ready to bid more than the minimum price —perhaps even to run the price up to what it was actually worth at an unrigged auction, which was often far beyond what the squatter could pay. The land covered by a claim club was sometimes occupied by towns and villages, and in some instances was worth more than $100 an acre. The supreme moment was at the auction, and every member had to be on hand to "do his duty." The squatters, each with a club in hand, formed a semicircle around the auctioneer and waited breathlessly for the bids to begin. If a nervy speculator dared to bid, it was the "duty" of the nearest man to "strike! for his altars and his fires!"—to "knock the stranger sensible! before his bid was recognized by the auctioneer."[17] So far as the settlers were concerned, all business of the day was transacted between the land-office official and the man chosen by the club—usually the recorder—to bid on the land for each member of the association. The reason for confining the bidding to a single person was to prevent any mix-up. After the system became recognized, there was seldom a bid by anyone aside from the claim-club bidder.

A few descriptions of auctions held during the period when claim-club rule was supreme have been preserved. At Dubuque, Iowa, in 1840, when the time came for the government sale to begin, the crier stepped out from the land office to a platform and invited the club bidder and his assistant to take their places beside him. He then took the plat in hand and began to sell eighty-acre tracts. When he came to a tract with a squatter's name written on it, he would strike his hammer on the table and give the name to the clerk. The sale proceeded in numerical order, and two townships (576 eighty-acre tracts) were offered in less than a half-hour, with the squatters standing in stern array in a compact half-circle in front of the platform. The deathlike silence was broken only by the crier's voice. When the bidding was over, the purchasers were admitted to the office by twos or threes to pay for their land and secure certificates.

A speculator at a sale at Ionia in the Grand Valley of Michigan had the effrontery to make a bid. According to witnesses, in a twinkling a crowd of infuriated, yelling squatters sent him in headlong retreat. He was last seen at the head of a cloud of dust, streaking away into the distance with an angry yelling mob at his heels speeding him on his way. Other speculators were present, but no matter how much their mouths watered for land,

[17] Jesse Macy, *Institutional Beginnings in a Western State* (Baltimore: The Johns Hopkins Press, 1884), pp. 12–14.

they did not feel it wise to question the irregularity of the proceedings. At the Burlington, Iowa, sale in 1839, the register stood inside a house at an open window and the club's bidder on a small stand near the window, in full view of the assembly. When the register read a description, the representative of the claim club, with his list before him, would bid. There was no hesitancy, no seeking of a higher bid. So quickly and smoothly did the mock auction glide along that the process had become monotonous when suddenly someone quickly bid higher than the claim-club figure before the register had time to cry "Sold!" Instantly a violent commotion ensued. The nearest squatters bludgeoned the bidder with their big hickory canes and he was too badly used up to interfere further with the squatter program that day. The register disregarded the higher bid and accepted that of the settler. The register said later that he did not hear a bid other than that of the squatter, and his decision was final.[18]

In certain places in the South, similar organizations were formed, although I have found no claim-club constitution or records left by them. Correspondents wrote the Commissioner of the General Land Office that in the Cahaba, Alabama, land district in April, 1830, settlers had held meetings and had entered into a written agreement to obtain the land at the minimum price by force of arms. Since speculator companies were all-powerful in that area and the competition was intense, the settlers went a step further than their contemporaries in the Upper Mississippi Valley: by threats, they were able to run off all but three men who tried to look at the land. The three men went onto the land in the morning, examined it during the day, and stayed at a private house that night, but about midnight, a company of about thirty armed men surrounded the house for the purpose of taking from the three men the numbers of the land they had selected and driving them off the public land. To save their lives, the three men were compelled to make a hurried getaway in the dead of night, without their land descriptions. The man who reported this incident informed the Commissioner that it was the general opinion that the men of this organization, one hundred strong, would shoot anyone who had the temerity to bid for the land.[19]

[18] White, "Early Homes and Homemakers of Iowa," *Annals of Iowa*, pp. 187–190. The register at Burlington at this time was Caesar Augustus Dodge, a son of Henry Dodge, governor of Wisconsin Territory (of which Iowa was a part).

[19] Jabez Curry to Commissioner of the General Land Office, April 9, 1830, and Edward Harper to the Commissioner of the General Land Office, April 22, 1830, in *American State Papers, Public Lands*, VI (Washington, D.C., 1860), 188.

The *Hawk-Eye* of Burlington, Iowa, commenting on the local sale in the 1830's, noted that several tracts had been passed over without bidding because the claimants did not have the money to enter them—which suggests another function of the squatter club. The organization often tried to hold land for an impecunious member for a period of two years after the sale. Public opinion strongly favored the settler and he was free from interference from anyone in the neighborhood. If a covetous person had the audacity to enter his neighbor's improved land, the claim club, which usually died with the land sale, was resurrected and the buyer was forced to make a deed to the squatter. Thus, as has been seen, by holding land by claim club for several years before the sale, and perhaps for a short time afterward, a settler was able to keep his selection until it became valuable.[20] At Green Bay, Wisconsin, a man who bought his claim for $1.25 per acre sold it immediately after the public auction for $8,000. Although I found no record of a formal association at Green Bay, the spirit was there, and it controlled the land sale.

A settler, in fact, was often a speculator—the same as the moneyed man. The chief difference was that the settler operated on government capital while the speculator used private funds. The settler, in the North at least, who claimed from 160 to 640 acres never hoped to utilize such a large area in that day of hand cultivation; forty to eighty acres was about as much land as the ordinary family could till. In the South, a larger area could profitably be cultivated with slave labor. Even where a settlers' association was formed by bona fide homemakers, the spirit of speculation was markedly present, and in some instances the clubs were controlled by moneyed men or speculators. At Crown Point, Indiana, one of the great landowners of the area was the registrar of the settlers' union.

Senator John Davis of Massachusetts said that a member of the House who had visited Wisconsin Territory in 1836 had observed a stretch of land skirted by furrows. Upon inquiry he found that the furrows were proof of occupancy and possession, and that they had been made by an organized band of speculators, most of whom were members of the legislature of Wisconsin Territory. They had laid out their ill-gotten holdings with the expectation that Congress, in accordance with past performance, would shortly pass a pre-emption act to accommodate them. Accordingly, they agitated and lobbied for a pre-emption law for their purpose. The congressman reported that these speculators were so well organized that if anyone crossed the furrow it would be sufficient cause for killing that

---

[20] Macy, *Institutional Beginnings*, p. 14.

person. Actual settlers, the senator complained, were deprived of the richest and best land by these land-grabbers.[21]

When moneyed speculators gained control of a club it virtually became a speculator association, and opposition to the claim club would sometimes arise. In the Kishwaukie country of northern Illinois a well-defined party, popularly known as the Claim Jumpers, sprang up in opposition to the claim club. The party was not opposed to a man holding the land on which he had settled, but it resisted his making more than one claim, buying additional claims, or holding claims solely for speculative purposes. Some of the claim clubbers in that area had rolled a few logs together in the form of a pen, had put a roof of shakes or bark on the logs to give the pen the appearance of a dwelling, and had blazed around a quarter section of timberland and staked off a square mile or more of prairie. Then, by force of a neighborhood association, they would forbid anyone from settling on their claim without paying them hundreds or even thousands of dollars for what they called their farms. In DeKalb County, even before the Indians left, actual settlers were mulched for large sums for such claims. The rise of the Claim Jumpers divided the community into two factions and caused fierce quarrels and innumerable bitter rows that ruined the spirit of community life even many years after the frontier passed. In some cases, incoming settlers called meetings of the settlers' association and forced through new regulations reducing the number of acres each member could hold, thus making room for the later claimant, but the clubs usually were well entrenched and able to withstand reforming efforts. Farmers simply had to pay the speculators for their land, and then pay the government, or move farther into the wilderness to find unoccupied land.[22]

During the 1830's the agitation for a general pre-emption act became intense. Local and limited pre-emption acts, which had been passed from time to time, had only whetted the appetite of the frontiersmen: the more they got, the more they wanted. It is true that some did not have the money to buy, but in any case the speculative spirit in big purchasers and squatters alike demanded a wide choice of land. Squatters, however, rushed across the country, taking the good land here and there, leaving millions of acres of surveyed land behind but complaining that the government did not survey and open the land fast enough. They dashed ahead of

[21] Roy M. Robbins, "A History of the Pre-emption of Public Lands" (Ph.D. dissertation, University of Wisconsin, 1928), pp. 55, 56, 58.

[22] Henry Lamson Boies, *History of DeKalb County, Illinois* (Chicago, 1868), pp. 72–73.

the surveyor, and even settled on areas where Indian titles had not been extinguished. Such men, actuated by the speculative spirit, were the ones who called most loudly for pre-emption.[23]

On the other hand, the viewpoint of the easterner was that the honest settler who wanted to obey the law should wait until the land came into the market and take his chances at an honest public auction. The intruder, they pointed out, went onto the land illegally but was rewarded by being allowed to secure the choicest land at the minimum price before it came into the market.

The Panic of 1837 pricked the bubble of speculation and brought stagnation in the sale of the public lands, but settlers shouted louder than ever for pre-emption in order that the land might be tagged and held until the occupant could secure the purchase money. Memorials from state and territorial legislatures and from groups of private citizens poured into Congress. Robert J. Walker, the well-known Mississippi land speculator, stood in the forefront of the battle, wielding mighty blows for the squatter. It was argued that if the lands came into the market in 1838, the settlers would be unable to purchase them, even at the minimum price. Senator Thomas Hart Benton, always the friend of the West, worked unremittingly, and the movement was given added impetus when Van Buren brought the prestige of the Presidency into the fight in behalf of the pre-emption bill. Henry Clay, whose state was beginning to assume the attitude of the eastern states, which had no public domain within their borders, represented the eastern viewpoint when he denounced the squatters as a "lawless rabble," stating that it was no more righteous to seize upon the public land than upon the forts, arsenals, and the Treasury. Clay inveighed against pre-emption as a violation of all law and as an encouragement to people to despoil the government of its choicest lands. The heated strife continued until finally Henry Clay, in order to secure passage of an eastern-backed distribution bill introduced a combination distribution–pre-emption bill which became law in 1841.[24]

The pre-emption law, which was to remain on the statute books for over fifty years, provided that a qualified person could pre-empt a 160-acre farm for a home on the public domain provided he fell into one of the following categories: (1) a single man at least twenty-one years of age, (2) the head of a family (any age or sex), (3) a widow. An applicant had to be a

[23] Payson J. Treat, *The National Land System, 1785–1820* (New York: E. B. Treat & Co., 1910), p. 177; Dwight Agnew, "The Government Surveyor as a Pioneer" (Master's thesis, University of Iowa, 1938), pp. 59, 60, 62.

[24] Robbins, *Our Landed Heritage*, pp. 74–76.

citizen of the United States or to have filed his intention of becoming one. Furthermore, he could not be the proprietor of more than 320 acres in any state or territory, nor could he abandon his residence on land he owned in the same state or territory. Then, in order to show his good faith in selecting the tract for a home, the settler had to make such improvements and fulfill such conditions as the General Land Office would draw up. Not later than one year after the land auction, the pre-emptor was required to give proof of having met the requirements and to pay for his tract. There were two prohibitions: pre-emptors could not settle on land to which Indian title had not been extinguished nor on land which had not been surveyed. A general provision prohibited settlement on lands set aside for special uses, such as military or Indian reservations, school lands, salt or mineral lands, areas within the limits of an incorporated town, tracts set aside for townsites, and land given to the states for canals or other internal improvement. After a half century of special limited pre-emption and agitation, a general unlimited pre-emption law was in force.[25]

[25] Robert Tudor Hill, *The Public Domain and Democracy, Studies in History, Economics and Public Law* (New York: Columbia University Press, 1910), XXXVIII, 45.

VI

Lands of the Mexican Cession

DURING THE YEARS when Spain and her successor Mexico controlled the land in what became known as the Mexican Cession—California, Arizona, New Mexico, Utah, and Nevada—three general categories of land grants had been made: to the missions, to the pueblos or towns, and to individuals. In California alone, twenty-one missions had been founded. Each controlled a large area in which it operated its Christianizing effort and taught the Indians agriculture and ranching as well as the domestic arts and handicrafts.

Missions were to operate as such for only about ten years; by that time, it was thought, the Indians would finish their apprenticeship, be ready to manage their own affairs, and become a part of the white man's social order. The mission would become a village; the mission church a parish church; and the land around the mission, which had been placed in cultivation by the labor of the Indians, would become the Indians' property. Unfortunately, the Franciscan order, which operated the missions, did not teach the Indians to be independent and economically responsible, but made all decisions for them. As a result, they never gained the ability to run their own affairs. In 1833, when the Mexican government took action to secularize the missions, the Franciscans stoutly opposed the move, and the Indians, loyal to their tutors, saw the move as another instance of white abuse of them and their protectors. In the confusion that followed, the Indians scattered, leaving the friars in the mission buildings and the title to the land in doubt, whereupon the whites rushed into this ownership vacuum and occupied the former mission lands. Between 1833 and 1846, that is, between secularization and the American occupation, more than five hundred grants of former mission holdings were made to individuals by the Mexican government.

The second class of original landholdings was made to Spanish citizens who received permission to found a town, live in it, and hold grants to the surrounding land for farming and ranching. In 1846 there were seven of

70

these grants in California, each four square leagues (a Spanish league was two and three-fifths miles).

The third class of grants was made to ranchers. Later, when the question of title arose, these allotments—some of them of immense size and vague description—presented a real problem in deciding whether the grant was genuine, whether the rancher had a firm basis for possession of all the land he claimed, and whether the grantee had fulfilled the conditions of the grant. During the Spanish period in California, at least thirty of these concessions were made, and others were made later by the Mexican authorities. A few of these were as small as twenty acres but many were gigantic. Jose de la Guerra Noriega claimed a total of 215,857 acres, laid out in four mammoth ranches; and even a comparatively modest claimant, Captain John Wilson, held 32,430 acres.

By the terms of the Treaty of Guadelupe Hidalgo, which ended the Mexican War, the United States agreed to recognize the validity of all bona fide land grants that had been made in the area which she was receiving from the Mexican government. The questions which would immediately arise were, Which claims are bona fide? Which claimants had fulfilled the legal requirements of the grant and thereby had a clear title under Mexican law? Commodore John D. Sloat took possession of California at Monterey on July 7, 1846, and this was the date arbitrarily set as the end of Mexican rule.[1]

As might be supposed when such an opportunity presented itself, speculators who were in collusion with the Mexican authorities attempted to secure grants from Mexico after the American occupation began. Soon after Colonel Stephen W. Kearney took command in California, he learned through reputable citizens that the Mexican governor, Pio Pico, just prior to his departure had made sales and grants of mission property which court records later showed had been made in return for bribes. Although these conveyances were made after the deadline of July 7, 1846, they had been antedated. Furthermore, the transactions were not recorded in the usual book but were said to have been inscribed in another book, which was never located. The speculators who had bought these claims demanded that they be placed in possession. In response to these pleas, Kearney on March 22, 1847, proclaimed that the mission land claimed by these grantees should be left in the hands of the friars until a decision had been rendered by the proper authority. In the final settlement the missions received only the area covered by the church buildings, gardens, and cemeteries, which ranged from about 7 to 280 acres.

[1] William W. Robinson, *Land in California* (Berkeley: University of California Press, 1948), pp. 28–36, 67–72.

Clearly, the settlement of titles was an important problem and needed a solution as soon as possible. Accordingly, in 1849 the Commissioner of the General Land Office at Washington sent William Carey Jones, a son-in-law of Senator Thomas Hart Benton, to classify all claims derived from the Mexican and Spanish authorities. Jones was well qualified. A lawyer with an intimate knowledge of the Spanish language, Jones made a penetrating report that strongly impressed the members of Congress, who received it from the President, and the report markedly affected later decisions. Jones was impressed by the large grants, but he felt that the American government should deal in a liberal manner with the claimants. Before any scheme could be devised for settling the land titles, however, gold was discovered and a sudden swelling of the little stream of immigrants inundated the whole region. Volatile, individualistic Americans had presumed that California was part of the public domain, but they were astonished, upon arriving, to discover that a large portion of the best land in the territory had been distributed in enormous grants by the former government. They looked upon the landholders as monopolists who were holding but not using the land which should rightfully be part of the public domain.

The aggressive, land-hungry immigrants were accustomed to small private holdings, and vast areas of unoccupied government land upon which they could intrude at will; hence trespassing upon and exploiting the vast Mexican grants was like intruding upon government land—entirely legitimate.[2] The holders of Spanish grants were regarded in the same light as speculators in the Middle West and, in fact, were referred to as speculators. The immigrants felt that as American citizens they were doubly entitled to the land since the United States had conquered it and then bought it, having paid Mexico $15,000,000 as a settlement by the terms of the peace treaty.

In 1851 Congress provided for a commission of three to be appointed by the President to decide the ownership of land claimed under Spanish or Mexican grants. All claimants were invited to present their claims, with documentary evidence or the testimony of witnesses in support of their cases. The commissioners, sitting as a board, were to decide upon the justice of each claim and to render a report within thirty days. Cases could be appealed to the courts, however, and later it became routine for all decisions to be appealed automatically. If a negative decision was rendered, the land automatically became part of the public domain, as was all land

[2] *Ibid.*, p. 93; Joseph Ellison, *California and the Nation* (Berkeley: University of California Press, 1927), pp. 8–14; Alfred N. Chandler, *Land Title Origins* (New York: Robert Schalkenbach Foundation, 1945), pp. 494, 495.

for which no claim was presented. The commission began work in January, 1852, and continued in existence until March, 1856.

The announcement of this action caused the landholders to dig into strongboxes, old leather trunks, and other hiding places for documents and to search for persons who knew of the occupancy and use of the tracts they claimed. Two difficulties that attended this proceeding were, first, that the burden of proof was placed upon the landholder, and this made it necessary for him to hire lawyers to present his case not only before the commission but through succeeding trials and appeals, even many years after the commission had finished its work; and second, there was a long period of uncertainty before a claim was settled. The average length of time an owner had to wait for a patent after filing a petition, according to J. N. Bowman in his study of the proceedings of the land commission, was seventeen years.[3]

Because of the loose customs of the Spanish era, few of the grantees had fully complied with the conditions on which the grants had been bestowed. There had been no competition over land when the grants were made, and boundaries were vague, but it had made little difference whether one owned land to the top of a mountain or to some ridge short of the summit. Many grantees had failed to draw a map that showed the boundaries of the grant and to have it approved by the proper authority. The commission, however, took a liberal attitude, and if the land was actually occupied and used, it decided in favor of the claimant. Most of the 848 claims were confirmed by the commission and by the courts. Concessions made after July 7, 1846, however, were voided, and prior mammoth grants with ill-defined boundaries were trimmed.

All in all, the commission did its duty fairly and well; had it not been for the prolonged court litigation—the joy of frontier lawyers—and the long wait for a survey, minimum injustice would have been suffered by the early grantees. As it was, however, during the drawn-out court appeals not a few had to mortgage their holdings or deed half their tracts—the customary legal fee—to lawyers in order to keep the rest of their grants.[4] Then, too, during the long interim of uncertainty American settlers and gold hunters chose to believe that the lands were part of the public domain and that in the end the questionable claims would be nullified. In any case, because the frontiersmen had never been overly respectful of the government's land regulations, an orgy of squatting and land exploitation ensued.

[3] Robinson, *Land in California*, pp. 100–106, 112.

[4] Aaron M. Sakolski, *The Great American Land Bubble* (New York: Harper & Bros., 1932), pp. 263, 264.

Colonel John C. Fremont, a prominent figure in the conquest of California, bought a tract of land known as Rancho Los Mariposas, at the southern end of the Mother Lode country, from Juan B. Alvarado. The ranch, ten leagues square, was part of a grant from a Mexican governor. In 1849, Fremont, with a party of Mexicans, prospected his land and found great quantities of gold, which his men scooped up with knives and shovels and washed in cups and pans. Their rejoicing was short-lived, however, for news of the discovery circulated quickly, and miners spread over his ranch like blackbirds in a milo field, stripping the rich mineral from the land. Fremont was powerless to prevent this intrusion since his title had not been confirmed, and it may be doubted that even a good title would have been a sufficient dike to hold back the flood of miners. In 1856, Fremont's title was upheld by the Supreme Court, which gave the explorer clear title to the unexploited lodes. However, when the final survey showed that some of the valuable lodes being worked were on his property, the area became a battleground as miners attempted to hold the land despite the fact that they were on private property.[5]

Squatters became so numerous over the state that they exerted tremendous power in California politics, and men seeking public favor began to bid for their votes. National party lines were disregarded and elections hinged on land-title and squatting issues. Settlers' associations and miners' associations were formed to act against the landholders. Robinson points out that the governor, in his 1854 message to the legislature, spoke of the squatters as "bona fide settlers" who should be compensated if they were evicted after putting up a house on land they had thought was government land. In 1856 the legislature even passed a dubious law that all lands in the state were to be regarded as public until legal processes showed that the title had passed into private hands. This astounding statute was later declared unconstitutional, after having damaged the legitimate landowners immeasurably.[6]

One of the most tragic episodes of the squatters' invasion took place at Sacramento, where Sutter gave the title to the land on which Sacramento was built to his son, who as a city promoter, sold the lots to the immigrant city builders. Later immigrants, finding that all of the desirable land had been appropriated, and arguing that the Spanish land grants had been used to defraud settlers of their heritage as American citizens, formed a squatters' association in the summer of 1850. Under the leadership of

[5] Allan Nevins, *Fremont, the West's Greatest Adventurer* (2 vols.; New York: Harper & Bros., 1928), II, 433–436.

[6] D. A. Shaw, *Eldorado, or California as Seen by a Pioneer, 1850–1900* (Los Angeles: B. R. Baumgardt & Co., 1900), p. 155; Robinson, *Land in California*, p. 116.

Dr. Charles Robinson, the organization tried to hold town lots on which no buildings had been erected. The resolution of the association, framed by the intrepid Robinson, who was to become famous in the antislavery struggle in Kansas and eventually its first governor, reads:

> WHEREAS, The land in California is presumed to be public land, therefore,
> RESOLVED, That we will protect any settler in the possession of land to the extent of one lot in the city and one hundred sixty acres in the country, till a valid title shall be shown for it.

They proceeded to erect structures on unoccupied lots which had been held by Sutter for years before the American conquest, and the squatters prepared to protect one another in holding the land. Becoming more defiant as their number increased to several thousand, the squatters settled on every bit of vacant land, despite the protests of the owners and the city officials.

The landowners, in turn, formed a law-and-order association, and the city government in self-defense passed a law that imposed a heavy fine upon anyone, other than the official city surveyor, who surveyed land within the city limits. The whole town now took sides, with many men then prominent, or to become so later, on one side or the other, including a governor, judges, and other political leaders.

The holders of deeds from Sutter for the squatter-occupied lots secured writs of ejectment, and the city officers proceeded to the squatters' homes and pulled down houses and fences. At the next squatters' meeting, James McClatchy harangued the excited squatters, asserting that the claim club had hired four lawyers, and he blustered: "Let us put up all the fences that were pulled down and also put up all the men who pulled them down."

A jail had not yet been erected, but the city had anchored a ship at the wharf for use as a prison. When the city officials again sought to eject the squatters, they arrested McClatchy and Michael Moran and threw them into the prison ship on the charge of resisting the sheriff in the execution of his duties. The following morning an armed party of thirty squatters marched toward the prison ship to release their comrades.

The mayor called upon the citizens to support law and order, and a group of citizens grabbed weapons and started for the river, where they found John Malony, sword in hand, defying the officers. In the face of official opposition, however, the squatters did not attempt to rescue the prisoners but marched back up the street, followed by the officers and a jeering crowd, and halted before the sheriff and the mayor, who had ridden up on horseback. The officers now demanded that the squatters surrender but the latter opened fire and a battle began in the street. The mayor fell from his horse, fatally wounded, and the city assessor was killed; three squatters were killed; and a number of both factions were wounded. The sheriff, who had entered a saloon, came upon eight or ten squatters, and was killed in the fight which followed, as were several others. Robinson, one of those who was wounded, recuperated in the floating jail, where he became a candidate for the legislature and was elected. Released on bond to sit in that body, he went unpunished for his part in the Squatter War. The adamant stand of the city officials thwarted a complete take-over by the squatters, however.

The Sacramento battle was more violent than those elsewhere and was condemned throughout the state, but it demonstrated the attitude of squatters generally and is an indication of the bloodshed that might have taken place if the squatters had been resisted elsewhere as forcefully and resolutely as at the capital city.[7] But they were not, and confusion reigned for years.

Two hundred squatters settled along the Russian River, near Healdsburg in Sonoma County, and organized an association for defensive and offensive action. They attacked the United States government surveyor with impunity, tore up his field notes, and advised him to be gone; he thought it good advice and acted accordingly. The squatters also compelled a Spaniard to release his title to land he was holding and get out. They also threatened to burn Healdsburg, but the citizens rallied, defended their homes, and compelled the free-land party to retire. In many localities, settlers' associations took the form of secret orders, with signs and passwords, and were not above assassination and other forms of foul play.

The constitution of the Settlers' League of Alameda County has been preserved and is similar to that of the Midwest claim club, except that a fee of five dollars a year was charged for membership and the treasurer was bonded for $5,000. The membership was 509 in 1853, and every man swore he would not privately settle a dispute over his claim but that all would settle their claims simultaneously through the league.

According to a historian of Alameda County, the disabilities that Spanish land-grant owners suffered were almost unbelievable. An old resident, because he cut down a tree whose branches overhung the house

---

[7] Frank W. Blackmar, *The Life of Charles Robinson* (Topeka: Crane Printers, 1902), pp. 59–80; Shaw, *Eldorado*, pp. 151–154; Walter G. Pigman, *The Journal of Walter Pigman* (Mexico, Mo.: W. G. Staley, 1942), p. 38; Winfield Davis, *An Illustrated History of Sacramento County* (Chicago: Lewis Publishing Company, 1890), Chapter VI; *Sacramento Transcript*, in *San Francisco Daily Journal of Commerce*, July 29, 1850.

in which he had lived for many years, was sued for trespass by a squatter, who got judgment. In execution thereof, the squatter took the resident's carriage, his only means of conveyance. The squatters would not even allow such an owner the 160 acres which certainly was allowable under the Preemption Act. Men who formerly had ranged thousands of acres without a thought of ownership were barely able to retain their actual living area and enough acres to graze a few sheep. The cattle on the big ranches were killed and the timber was cut and carried off. If an owner sought to eject the trespassers, they, having the greater manpower, intimidated the officers and prevented them from doing their duty. Growing bolder, the squatters assumed the attitude of owners and proceeded to lay out the town of Oakland upon the land of Signor Peralta, and even had a law passed by the legislature that chartered the town upon land that belonged to the objecting owner. Although they did not own a foot of soil in "their town," by means of nerve, overwhelming trespass, and hired lawyers they were able to make good on their attempt. Peralta, weary of the fight and not anticipating justice, finally sold out. It was many years later—during which time countless lawyers were enriched—before the legacy of the squatter regime was dissipated and titles were cleared.[8]

Squatters swarmed over San Francisco, occupying every vacant spot whether it was claimed or not. They even raised tents and shanties upon the government reservation, and troops had to be dispatched to remove them. One enthusiast fenced in Union Square and had to be disarmed by authorities when the street commissioner endeavored to remove the obstruction. Samuel Brannan had deeded land to the Odd Fellows Lodge for a cemetery, but this was overrun by illegal claimants. By 1854, lot owners had to hire special police to keep trespassers from building shanties upon their land. At Third and Mission streets, ten men fought a battle over land, in which five were wounded and two were killed. A number of squatters wrecked an old sailing vessel, took the heavy timbers, and built a fort at the corner of First and Howard streets—Fort Larkin, they named it—and defied all attempts of the law to dislodge them. Not content with the dry land, they staked off "water lots" by driving piles into the shallow water just offshore in the bay.

In the 1850's squatting became a trade which some felt certain would pay better dividends than digging gold in the mines a few miles away. Over a twenty-year period, men equipped with a gun and a blanket squatted for hire, as a cowhand might hire out as a herder. Finally, through

---

[8] William Holley, *Centennial Book of Alameda County* (Oakland, Calif., 1876), pp. 118–119, 449–450.

sheer exhaustion, San Francisco was forced to recognize the claims of illegal possessors in large areas of the city and to give deeds on the ground of possession.[9]

On the other hand, land which seemingly was open to the public through rejection of a Spanish claim was sometimes elusive, as in the Sukol case. Some of the residents on the tract had bought their title from the Spanish grantee, but in 1862 the grant was rejected by the Supreme Court and the land was seized by settlers who raised money, paid for the government surveys, and moved onto the land preparatory to purchasing pre-emption claims at the legal government price of $1.25 an acre. Congress, unaware of the irregular survey and the squatting, passed an act in March, 1863, that gave the parties who had lost title through no fault of their own the right to buy, at $1.25 an acre, the amount of land they had held on the basis of the Spanish claim before the government's rejection. This precipitated a battle between settlers who had bought large tracts and whose possession was validated by act of Congress and the squatters. The contest, which began before the law of 1863 was enacted, lasted until after 1870. The squatters finally were defeated by a decision that the law of Congress took precedence over the pre-emption proceedings.[10]

If the opposition was strong, squatters sometimes used guile to gain a foothold. When word got around that a certain man's title probably was doubtful, the Yankee newcomer, in anticipation that the land would shortly be legally open to settlement, schemed to secure a claim on the rancher's holdings. The favorite time for squatter operations in such a case was during the night, and Aladdin himself could not have produced a more magical change than these land-hungry squatters, who by means of tents, temporary fences, and shingle houses improvised a new vista during the hours of darkness. Their activity was carried out so silently that no one knew of the changes until daylight. It happened on occasion that two parties were attracted to the same tract but did not discover this fact until morning, in which case a two-way fight between the nocturnal schemers took place and the winner then battled the original occupant. In San Mateo County, a squatter started fencing a field during the night, and on completing his labors, discovered by the light of dawn in the center of the enclosure an occupied dwelling that had been built a few days before. The extent of the squatters' control of local government is illustrated by an incident in Santa Cruz County. A landholder—the victim of mem-

[9] Robinson, *Land in California*, pp. 113–114.

[10] Milton A. Wheaton, "Statement," MS in Bancroft Library, University of California, Berkeley, pp. 36, 37.

bers of a squatters' club who had broken into his meadow, cut the hay, and built houses—sought legal redress only to find that every one of the jurors was a member of the Squatters' League. The constable and the justice of the peace also were members and the verdict, of course, was favorable to the squatters. To digress for the moment, it is interesting to note that after the trial, the owner asked the men who had cut his hay if they were going to pay the taxes on the tract since they were in possession of it. They answered that government land could not be taxed and that they did not want to astonish the government by paying taxes on its own property.[11]

Long after titles had been perfected by court decisions, squatting and disputes over ownership persisted as a species of blackmail. The long years of uncertainty had their effect, and squatters hoped either to win a decision or to secure an advantageous settlement from a harried owner. A squatter's lawyer might try to prove that a requirement of Mexican law had been neglected by the original grantee or that a survey had been too extensive and the additional land therefore was part of the public domain and open to occupancy and claim. As late as the 1880's, squatters occupied the ranches in San Joaquin County, broke the grazing land, and sowed grain. The ranchers took legal steps to possess the grain and the sheriff went to seize it, but anticipating armed resistance, he took the Stockton and Emmet guards with him. When they arrived at the grainfields they found the Settlers' League, one hundred strong, drawn up to repel them. The troops camped on the ground for about ten days. Fortunately, the incident ended without bloodshed, with the ranchers in possession of their grants as confirmed by the courts, but the affair has gone down in history as the Mokelumne War.

As late as 1890, twelve hundred squatters attempted to file on various portions of the San Fernando Ranch and on other property of the Los Angeles Farming and Milling Company; they took possession of the land, drove off the stock, and committed other depredations. Mr. Van Nuys, who represented the company, brought suit to expel the settlers, who fought the case through the state courts, to the state supreme court, and on to the United States Supreme Court, which upheld the state courts in their rulings against the settlers. The litigation cost the company not less than $50,000 in witness fees, attorneys fees, and court costs.[12] Riverside and San Diego had their squatter problems also. Although viewed from

---

11 Edward Martin, *History of Santa Cruz County, California* (Los Angeles: Historic Record Co., 1911), pp. 94–96.

12 J. A. Graves, *My Seventy Years in California* (Los Angeles: Times-Mirror Co., 1927), pp. 141–144.

the standpoint of an old Spanish grantee the settler was an avaricious aggressor, there definitely was another side to the coin; in San Mateo County lay the Rancho Laguna de la Merced. The government had shortened its boundaries to a reasonable size. Homeseekers then settled on the land excised from the swollen claim since it was now government land. They bought it under the Pre-emption Act and for six years lived upon it in peace. The owners of the half-league ranch then decided to make another attempt by legal action to get their boundaries redrawn so as to include some better land on the basis that their tract should include the sites of the original grantees. Such a change would dispossess many settlers. The latter organized the North San Mateo Settlers' Union, obtained rifles and a brass cannon, fortified a building, surrounding it with barricades of sacks of potatoes with convenient loopholes, and prepared to battle their foes to the death. Calmer counsel prevailed, however, and they allowed the law to take its course; the sheriff dispossessed them, armed guards occupied their homes, and their foes harvested and appropriated their crops. The case wound its weary way through the courts until the Supreme Court of the United States settled it in favor of the legitimate owners, who returned to their homes after having been dispossessed for three years.[13]

In New Mexico, Arizona, and Colorado, Mexican land grants also caused real difficulty, although since gold was not immediately discovered in these areas, conflict did not develop until they had become valuable for other reasons. For example, the report of the Commissioner of the General Land Office for 1890 stated that the Surveyor General had labeled the Don Miguel de Peralta claim of five million acres in Arizona "a forgery and fraud through and through and recommended the prosecution of the fraud."[14]

According to the document used to validate the Sangre de Cristo grant in the San Luis Valley in Colorado, dated December 27, 1843, the justice of the peace in Taos had proceeded to the area in January, 1844, had surveyed the land, and had placed mounds at appropriate places as markers. According to his sworn statement, the justice even placed mounds along the crest of the mountains that bounded the grant on the west side. Professor LeRoy R. Hafen, a Colorado historian who questioned the truthfulness of this document, states that marking these mountains in January would have been impossible. Nevertheless, when the heirs presented their

[13] Frank M. Stanger, *History of San Mateo County* (San Mateo, Calif.: San Mateo Times, 1938), p. 112.

[14] *Annual Report of the Commissioner of the General Land Office, 1890* (Washington, D.C.: Govt. Printing Office, 1890), p. 24.

claim (the original grantees had been killed by the Indians), the surveyor general of New Mexico ruled that the grant of 1,038,195 acres was bona fide. Pliable congressional committees endorsed the ruling and Congress in 1860 confirmed the grant, thereby endorsing a gigantic steal. The details in connection with the securing of this grant are significant; in conformity with an old feudal custom, a grantee was required to throw earth, uprooted turf, and plucked leaves into the air as evidence that he accepted the responsibilities of ownership. As the whole matter of grants came under investigation it became apparent that much more than earth, turf, and leaves had been cast in the face of the heavens.

American penetration into New Mexico before the Mexican War prepared the way for a number of grants in which United States citizens were interested. Mountain men who spent time in Taos—some of whom married Mexican girls and formed social friendships with the Mexicans—and Santa Fe traders who made commercial contacts at Santa Fe gained the confidence of the governing Mexican officials. During John C. Fremont's second expedition in 1843 and 1844, some of his party urged sundry New Mexican merchants, traders, and officials to obtain grants from the Mexican government in their own names and to bring in others who were not Mexican citizens as joint owners. This scheme evidently anticipated the conquest of New Mexico by the Americans, and Mexicans who joined the Americans beforehand would benefit by this arrangement. Professor Harold Dunham has discovered that a member of the expedition, William Gilpin, later the first governer of Colorado and a part owner of two grants, testified in a suit in 1872 and boasted that his Mexican friends had applied for grants upon his suggestion. He indicated that other grants had a similar origin, all of which accounts for the rush of activity in securing grants during the middle 1840's. When it became apparent that the country was being taken over by the Americans, there was another flurry of grants by Mexican officers, who antedated the titles. A number of these grantees became territorial officers for New Mexico because of their earlier contacts with Americans. Manuel Armijo, who was a governor under Mexican rule, received shares of a number of grants.[15]

The practice of inflating a grant to enormous proportions was as underhanded as the methods by which grants were obtained. For example, Salvador Gonzales in 1742 humbly petitioned the governor for a spot to plant corn for the support of his wife and children; when this grant fell

[15] Harold H. Dunham, "New Mexican Land Grants with Special Reference to the Title Papers of the Maxwell Grant," *New Mexico Historical Review*, XXX (January, 1955), 4, 6, 9.

into the hands of American speculators the first survey showed that the little cornfield had expanded to encompass 103,959 acres, although a later survey deflated the distended claim to 23,661 acres, which was still quite a corn patch.[16] Indeed, various persons made a business of buying small Spanish and Mexican claims and enlarging them by falsified surveys. One of these was Senator Elkins of West Virginia, who became a member of a land ring in the Southwest. He bought Mexican grants at a low figure and then, by "stretching the surveyor's chain," swelled the grants to encompass tens of thousands of acres. Because of Elkins' influence in congressional committees, the surveys were confirmed and the senator became a millionaire landholder.

The most notorious fraud involved the famous Maxwell grant, which in 1887 involved a domain almost equal to the combined area of Delaware and Rhode Island. The original grant seems to have been manipulated after the Americans had taken New Mexico, although it was predated 1841 and supposedly marked in 1843. The original grantees were Charles Beaubien and Guadeloupe Miranda. Lucien Maxwell, a famous trapper and mountaineer, married Beaubien's daughter, inherited his father-in-law's part of the grant, and bought out the other heirs. He established the Maxwell Ranch on the Santa Fe Trail and became rich; and he presented what purported to be a copy of the original map, which instead of the 97,000 acres allowed by Mexican law, covered two million acres. After Maxwell had sold his claim rights to a company for $750,000, the Secretary of the Interior ruled that the grant contained only 97,000 acres, but the new owners refused to accept the ruling and sold the two-million-acre claim to a group of Englishmen, who later went bankrupt. A member of a land ring bought the claim, formed a new company, and kept the dispute alive. Settlers in the meantime, accepting the government's decision, with the law on their side moved in upon the grant and fought the company, which kept the territory in a state of civil war. In 1879 the Commissioner of the General Land Office issued the company a patent for the two million acres, but the settlers kept up their attack and the Attorney General attempted to cancel the patent. In 1887, after an eight-year struggle, during which time the case ran the gamut of the lower courts, the Supreme Court declared in favor of the company.

For years this struggle had kept the region in turmoil. It had caused bloodshed, corrupted the territorial government, and debased justice; witnesses mysteriously dropped out of sight, and the mails were tampered

[16] Alfred N. Chandler, *Land Title Origins* (New York: Robert Schalkenbach Foundation, 1945), p. 495.

with. Because the settlers refused to accept the final decision, troops were required to enforce what was perhaps the greatest land injustice in American history. It was a victory of moneyed interests holding their ill-gotten gains against equity, by means of influence. Even United States Justice Department officials were hampered in trying the case for the people against original fraud by friends of the swindlers in positions of power and influence in the government.[17]

It was not until 1891 that Congress set up the Court of Private Land Claims, transferring decisions pertaining to New Mexico and Arizona from congressional committees to a court of judges. The court then heard 301 cases, involving 34.5 million acres, but two-thirds of the petitions were rejected. Only about two million acres were given to the petitioners, and 32.5 million acres were reserved to the national domain.

Another problem connected with the lands of the Mexican Cession pertained to the rights of the inhabitants of towns. The original grants by the Spanish or Mexican governments permitted the people to find a suitable valley for settlement and provided for a central plaza in the town. Each family held a dwelling lot in town and a farming plot outside the town limits, and all cooperated in digging and maintaining irrigation channels and in building roads and other communal necessities. When a town was founded, the *alcalde*, or mayor, by the authority of the central government parceled the building and farming plots among the residents, who then held them as their own by virtue of occupancy and use. Some of these holdings were by formal grant and others merely by occupancy. In any case, land titles that for many generations had appeared good under Mexican rule were questionable on the basis of United States custom; indeed, United States law did not recognize a communal title, even though the Mexicans obviously were clearly entitled to the land. Furthermore, the grants sometimes extended twenty miles beyond the tilled area, and the uncultivated area was used as a commons for grazing domestic animals by all the townspeople who desired to share its use. This area also gave the village room to grow and enabled newcomers and young men who wanted a piece of land to have a parcel to cultivate.

With American rule and the coming of the land survey, the mammoth commons became desirable to outsiders. Land-hunters saw the worth of these ranges, bought rights from people whose ancestors had been mentioned in the original grants, and began to fence vast tracts. The poor people of the villages now found themselves shut off from the commons. Before, by

[17] Harold H. Dunham, *Government Handout* (New York: Edwards Brothers, 1941), p. 214.

owning some sheep or goats which they pastured on the commons, they had made a comfortable living, but now they were confined to their farm plots; and widespread suffering and distress brought about restlessness and bad feeling, threatening the peace of the community.

American custom and law were based upon occupancy and rectangular surveys, but neither was appropriate in this case. The town dweller could not enter a homestead because he did not live on the land, and this prevented him from establishing ownership in the commons. Furthermore, because the shape of the fields was dictated by the need for irrigation, they usually were long and angular and paralleled a stream. Hence United States law, which provided for homesteads or pre-emption rights in rectangular quarter sections, did not help solve the people's problem. In his report in 1890, the surveyor general of New Mexico strongly recommended that the United States government take the position that all town dwellers affected by the transfer of land from Mexican to American ownership had an interest in the outlying lands and that the lands did not belong exclusively to the heirs of the grantees. He urged, in effect, that the villagers be allowed to gain a title to land that rightly was theirs.[18]

Congress responded with admirable speed; on March 3, 1891, it passed the "small-holding claims" provision in the New Mexico Act. As amended on February 21, 1893, the act provided that those who could prove their hereditary right to possession or that they had been in possession of the land for twenty years prior to the United States land survey were entitled to 160 acres in irregular tracts. A description of each holding was to be made on the land-office records in terms of the United States survey, but claimants had to be supported by at least two creditable witnesses and such documentary proof as was available. Title was to be established by the government, without fees or cost to a claimant. The New Mexico Act extended justice to the little landholders in communal settlements, not only in New Mexico but in Arizona, Utah, Wyoming, and Colorado.[19]

[18] *Annual Report of the Commissioner of the General Land Office, 1890* (Washington, D.C.: Govt. Printing Office, 1890), pp. 26–27.

[19] *Annual Report of the Commissioner of the General Land Office, 1894* (Washington, D.C.: Govt. Printing Office, 1894), pp. 269–270.

VII

The Diggings

THE LAND ORDINANCE of 1785 and other major land acts reserved all mineral lands from sale. In early times the principal known mineral lands were those bearing salt springs where people camped for a few days to boil salt. It was natural that the lawmakers should seek to keep these deposits for the free use of the public rather than allow them to fall into the hands of speculators, but they did not visualize the problems that would be involved in surface or shallow mining as large numbers of men made digging their permanent business and worked individually or in small groups, digging lead or gold. Indeed, it was not until a quarter of a century after American independence that this problem arose. In 1803, when Louisiana was purchased by the United States, there was an area southwest of St. Louis that had been mined for lead from time to time for eighty-four years by Frenchmen and Spaniards. The land had been granted by the European nations holding the area, and hence was private property. Shortly after the purchase, however, several hundred Americans moved into the area and made a number of rich new strikes on the public lands. The question then arose as to the method of safeguarding the interests of the United States, which owned the land, and at the same time giving the miner the benefits of his discovery. How much ground could he hold? How could he mark it to prevent another from moving in and taking possession in his absence? Legally, the miner was a trespasser, but it was customary on the frontier to regard the salt springs as a sort of commons open to all to boil salt. At least one writer has offered an explanation that the development of a system of mining claims in America is traceable to the medieval German custom of free mining, which allowed all persons to search for minerals without ownership of the soil; it recognized an estate in minerals that was independent of an estate in the soil.[1] From whatever

[1] Charles Howard Shinn, *Mining Camps, A Study in American Government* (New York: Knopf, 1948), p. 24; I am indebted to Shinn's thorough study for much of the information in this chapter.

source our custom may have come, it fit in well with the frontier ideals of democracy and self-determination. The Intrusion Act of 1807, in addition to providing penalties against intruders, in harmony with the principle that all mineral land was reserved for the benefit of all the people, authorized the leasing of mineral lands for a period of three years on approval of the President. This amounted to little, however, since no agent in residence was appointed to have the oversight of the arrangement. To the register of the land office at Kaskaskia, Illinois, was delegated the responsibility of leasing the land. Since this office was seventy miles away from the seat of the mines, no attempt was made to enforce the terms of the law until 1816, when the Commissioner of the General Land Office instructed Michael Jones, the register at Kaskaskia, to hold an auction and lease the mineral land to the highest bidder. The Commissioner thought probably from one fifth to one eighth of the value of the lead produced on a given tract would be a fair figure, but he said only competitive bidding would decide the amount. This plan was unworkable, however, and was never carried out. Henry Rowe Schoolcraft, the noted Indian agent who was commissioned by the government to report on the lead-mining area in Missouri in 1819, found that the government had possession of only a small portion of the lead-bearing land to which the United States had unquestioned title. When a discovery on the public domain was made, miners flocked in from the neighboring area to stake out claims, and no one troubled himself about a lease. Each man who made a discovery dug a hole four or five feet square and claimed twelve feet in every direction. Schoolcraft reported that the squatters were so bold that one had moved onto a claim, improved it, and had instituted suit to make good his trespass. Said the Indian agent, he would not be surprised if the government's agents would be fined and imprisoned by those for whose punishment the intrusion acts were intended.

When it was obvious that the register of the land office was not the logical person to enforce the laws insuring government revenue from its mineral lands, in 1821 the supervision of the mineral exploitation of the public domain was transferred to the jurisdiction of the War Department, and an officer of the army ordnance department, Lieutenant Martin Thomas, was appointed to take charge. Under his supervision a system of collecting a 10 per cent royalty, or toll, on the lead mined on the mineral-bearing United States land was devised. Since it was impractical to collect the toll from individual miners, a licensing system was instituted. The miner was required to take out a license, or permit, subject to conditions laid down by the government. The royalty lead was stored in government warehouses. Lieutenant Thomas reported that from July 1, 1825, to September 30, 1826, the accrued value of government lead was $21,653.55. When the expense of transporting it was deducted, there still remained a net value of $17,653.55 for the United States government. Since it was impractical to collect the mineral from the miners, the government collected the royalty from the smelter and the latter deducted this amount from its payments to the producers.[2]

While lead production in Missouri was reaching a peak figure, a new mining district was coming into production on the Upper Mississippi. In 1690 the famous French explorer, Nicolas Perrot, discovered lead in what is now southern Wisconsin. In 1788 Julien Dubuque, another Frenchman, made a working arrangement with the Indians in the vicinity where the city named for him is located, and produced an annual down-Mississippi shipment of the metal until his death in 1810. In the next few years discoveries by westward migrants in the same general district along the Fever River in northwestern Illinois caused an influx of lead miners into that area. In a short time the town of Galena arose—named for the metal mined there. Within ten years the small area had expanded into southwestern Wisconsin where a much larger mining field was developed. Here another town suggestive of mining—Mineral Point—was founded, and by 1829 the output of the Fever River country surpassed that of the Missouri mines. The government, however, apparently controlled the royalty situation better in the Upper Mississippi Valley mines because its licensing organization was ready to take matters in hand when the miners came flocking into the region.

The United States regulations required that two or more miners work together, and they were permitted to stake off three hundred yards square. Cessation of work for eight successive days would forfeit the ground. Should a dispute arise over rights to mining ground, the miners were to arbitrate the matter among themselves; if the contending parties were unable to come to an agreement, they were to refer the matter to the government agent, whose decision was to be final. No one was permitted to build a cabin, cultivate land, cut timber, or settle in any manner without the express permission of the agent. Each quarter, every miner was required to report to the agent the name of the smelting firm to which he delivered his ore and the amount he had brought. The following form of permit was required of each miner.

[2] Report of Lt. Martin Thomas, U.S. Artillery, on ordnance duty, January, 1826, in *American State Papers, Public Lands*, IV (Washington, D.C., 1859), 522, 523, 555, 556, 800.

———— is hereby permitted to dig or mine on United States land which is not leased or otherwise rightfully occupied. He is not to set fire to the prairie grass or woods, and must deliver his mineral to a licensed smelter, and comply with all regulations. Fever River, ————, 1825.[3]

A man who would give a $5,000 bond to the government could have a quarter section on condition that he employ twenty laborers and agree to pay the government 10 per cent royalty on the mineral dug on his survey or that he would sell it to a licensed smelter; public smelters were required to give a $20,000 bond that they would pay the government 10 per cent royalty on all lead manufactured. During the year ending September, 1827, Galena manufactured 5,000,740 pounds of lead.

The need for timber for use in shoring up the mines and for fuel in smelting the ore made the patches of forest in the neighborhood of the mines valuable, and the government treated forest land as an adjunct of the mines requiring users to lease it in the same way as the ore-bearing land. After exploitation of the mineral-laden soil on the east side of the Mississippi was well under way, miners cast covetous eyes on the ore-rich Indian land over the river. Since an early cession was anticipated, a group of miners resolved to be on the ground beforehand and, without regard for the Indians' rights, moved across the river and took possession of the lands.

On June 17, 1830, the miners assembled on an island around an old cottonwood log and appointed a committee of five to draw up regulations for their conduct. They unanimously agreed to be governed by the rules in use on the east side of the river, except that each digger should hold only two hundred yards square and that a man had to work his ground at least one day in six. Perhaps these men were speculators who wanted to work five days a week in the established diggings and one day a week to hold their new prospects, or perhaps they feared the government might force them to give up this tenuous hold on their ill-gotten claims. Col. Zachary Taylor warned them, about July 4, to go back to Illinois because the land belonged to the Indians, but the poachers replied that they "had occupied a vacant country, had struck some valuable lodes, that the government would soon purchase from the Indians and that they intended to maintain possession." As a Dubuque historian remarks, they "generally took the law into their own hands." Taylor replied: "We shall see to that, my boys"; and the miners' bravado melted away when they heard that troops were coming. The miners moved on, and the soldiers captured only three

[3] *History of Grant County, Wisconsin* (Chicago: Western Publishing Co., 1881), pp. 407–410.

of them. When, in 1833, the government did make a treaty with the Indians whereby the area around the site of Dubuque became government property, the intruders of 1830 were on hand and made good their claims.[4] Like all frontiersmen, the Upper Mississippi Valley miners felt that the natural resources of the country were theirs for the taking. The desire to gratify their personal interests soon produced rationalizations as to why they should not pay "tribute to Caesar," as they called the royalty on lead.

A more fortuitous circumstance opened Indian lands in Wisconsin. In the summer of 1827 a military expedition was sent into that territory to capture the Winnebago chief, Red Bird, who had committed a hostile act. A number of miners, more interested in lead than in Indian-fighting, accompanied the expedition and prospected the country north of the Illinois line. When they discovered a valuable deposit near the spot where Dodgeville later was founded, they purchased from the Indians the right to mine in the area and refused to pay the government its royalty on the grounds that they had not mined the ore on government-owned land and that they had paid the Indians for the privilege of operating on Indian territory. They professed not to see anything illogical about breaking the law in trespassing on Indian land and stripping it of its riches before the government possessed it, as it was sure to do shortly. Consequently, troops were ordered from Fort Crawford, at Prairie du Chien, to remove the miners, who in the face of force consented to pay the royalty—and actually began to pay two fees: one to the Indians to quiet them and one to the government to prevent expulsion. The royalty to the government was paid more and more grudgingly, however, since the operators felt themselves abused by paying for lead dug on land on which the Indian title had not been extinguished. Moreover, a rumor circulated that the collector of lead tolls was lining his pockets at the expense of the diggers and that the government was not getting its full amount. The miners felt abused by paying the government, but enriching the collector was intolerable.

Another factor entered the picture. When lead was discovered, no one could know the extent of the deposits, and therefore a comparatively small area was set aside as mineral-reserved land. In time it was discovered that the deposits extended far beyond the areas set aside, and the crafty and unscrupulous began entering the mineral-bearing lands at the land office as agricultural tracts. Before one could enter land, however, he had to swear that he knew of no mineral having been discovered upon it and he had to

---

[4] Jesse Macy, *Institutional Beginnings in a Western State* (Baltimore: The Johns Hopkins Press, 1884), pp. 6, 7; Jacob Van der Zee, "Early History of Lead Mining in the Iowa Country," *Iowa Journal of History and Politics*, XIII (Iowa City, 1915), 44.

produce a witness who also must swear that he knew of none. Charges were made that men caused their witnesses and themselves to be blindfolded and led over valuable mineral lands, and later, in the presence of the register, all swore that they had been over the land and had seen no evidence of minerals.

John P. Sheldon, the register of the land office at Mineral Point, in violation of express instructions, permitted a large number of diggings actually being worked to be entered as agricultural lands, thereby dispossessing miners who thus lost their staked-off diggings and were defrauded of their rights. Sheldon allowed 44,117 acres of fraudulent entries and later was removed because of his failure to do his duty as a government officer.[5] This was the straw that broke the camel's back so far as paying the royalty was concerned. Those who mined on so-called agricultural land, which they had bought, naturally refused to pay a royalty on lead produced on their own land. The United States agent, of course, could not prove where ore had been dug, whether on United States-reserved mineral land, on Indian land, or on private land. In fact, it was possible for miners on government-reserved land to sell to producers on private land, and no legal questions could be asked.

The miners' refusal to pay became more general, and in 1836 the system completely broke down. The agent, Captain Weber, stayed on until 1840, but he was merely a figurehead. Officials in Washington refused to take action to protect the national interest and the government was "elbowed out" of the district by the miners. When the government toll collector ceased his efforts to collect, the diggers who held their claims by virtue of government permits were left in undisturbed possession of their diggings. Speculators, by fair means or foul, gained control of many of the mines by taking advantage of the poorer men. The historian of Grant County, Wisconsin, in commenting on this touchy matter questioned "whether these tenures were exactly honest in their origin or republican in their tendency." The avarice of the miners in refusing to pay a 10 per cent royalty backfired, for many now had to pay a 20 or 25 per cent rent in order to dig lead. At any rate the speculators displaced the government as collectors of the royalty themselves.[6]

In 1842 the government made one more halfhearted effort to revive the lapsed system of leasing the diggings to the miners. When the mineowners banded together and flatly refused to pay, the government sought to prose-

[5] Joseph Schafer, *The Wisconsin Lead Region* (Madison: State Historical Society of Wisconsin, 1932), p. 114.

[6] *History of Grant County, Wisconsin*, p. 481.

cute some of the oldest and most prominent miners and haled them before the courts as trespassers. As could be expected, the juries, composed of men of the area, awarded five cents damage; the government had spent a large sum in prosecuting the cases and had received nothing. The officials in Washington, many of whom were from the western states, sympathized with the miners and were ready to accede to them. The usual arguments urged by monopolists and exploiters were brought forth.

It was contended in Congress that the mines had been a liability rather than an asset, that over the years more money had been spent in attempting to collect the government's share than had been received. This made it easy to accede to the petitions of the miners who asked that the lands be placed upon the market. Early in the session of 1846–1847, Congress passed an act providing for the auction of mineral lands in lots of forty acres at a minimum price of twice that of agricultural land, $2.50 an acre. It was presumed by the East that auctions of rich mineral land would bring in many times the sum produced by agricultural land, rather than the small sums derived from the leasing plan over the years.

This was not the end of the story, however; the possessors of the mineral lands, many of whom had occupied them for years and felt a proprietary right, were indignant that the government was preparing to "sell them out," as they interpreted it. The danger that someone might bid up a price to the actual worth and that the holder might lose his sinecure was much more appalling than the government's former policy of asking for a small percentage of the lead. Indignation meetings were held in all of the camps and resolutions were passed protesting the new policy. Anticipating that these resolutions would be of no help in securing the repeal of the law, the miners prepared for the worst.

The meeting at British Hollow, Wisconsin, on December 19, 1846, illustrates what happened. A committee of five was appointed to hear evidence in all cases of disputed claims and to make its decisions on the basis of justice and equity; its decisions would be final and it would give a certificate of decision to the rightful owner with the appropriate value affixed. The owners of the claims on each section were to appoint one or more of their number to receive the certificate of each forty-acre plot as it was bid off at the auction. This appointee was to give bond, for double the appraised value of the claims, that he would re-deed the plots to those adjudged the rightful holders. The claimants were to secure the services of the county surveyor, who was to survey the claims and give the owners a certificate that specified the number of acres in a claim, and he was also to make a plat of the entire survey for the settlers on the mineral-reserve lands. No committeeman was allowed to investigate a claim in which he had an interest. The committee, like the Committees of Correspondence in Revolutionary War days, voted to correspond with those who held meetings in other districts, offering and soliciting cooperation.

The resolutions declared that the miners were willing to pay the minimum price of $2.50 an acre for their homes and claims but would repel by force any attempt to make them pay more. The members further agreed to be present the first day of the sale and to remain until all the reserved lands on the west side of the Big Platte had been offered for sale. The *Wisconsin Herald* expressed the feeling of all classes that the government was forcing a hardship upon them:

> Fill up the ranks, present yourselves in solid serried phalanx at the land office on the day of sale. Submit all disputes unconditionally to the arbitrament of your committee, heal all dissentions, sacrifice even what you deem your individual rights if need be, and substantial justice will be done to all. . . . Congress walks into us to the extent of ten bits per acre; that is we have to pay just twice as much for land as others who buy of the public domain.[7]

On May 24, 1847, the country around Mineral Point swarmed with grim-faced miners. Since only a comparative few could get near the land office, an inspection committee was appointed to represent the miners and to see that all went according to the plan. In only one case was there an untoward incident: a stranger who bid on a tract was instantly seized, lifted over the heads of the bystanders, put out onto the street, and told not to show his head again.[8] The auction progressed, the mineral lands on the Upper Mississippi were awarded the speculators by claim-club methods, and the matter of the lead mines was a closed chapter. Thus, due to the government's feeble efforts to guard its mineral riches for the good of all the people, a few men secured the land. Once more, frontier individualism and a spirit of exploitation had triumphed. An act of March 1, 1847, provided for the sale of the copper mines of Michigan, and Congress, mindful of what had happened in connection with the lead lands, set the minimum price at five dollars an acre.

The news of the discovery of gold in California shifted the attention of the country away from the Midwest so suddenly and unexpectedly that the United States was caught off balance, as it were. There was no legal

---

[7] *Wisconsin Herald*, quoted in *History of Grant County, Wisconsin*, p. 493.

[8] Theodore Rodolf, "Pioneering in the Wisconsin Lead Region," *Collections* of the State Historical Society of Wisconsin, XV (Madison, 1900), 382.

machinery that covered the exploitation of mineral resources over a wide expanse of the public lands or which protected a miner in his discovery. According to Spanish usage, perpetual title to all mineral lands resided in the king, who could give rights to miners to dig for the metal, but these rights were valid only during the lifetime of that monarch and had to be renewed by his successor. Now that the Mexican title had passed to the United States (been abolished), there were no applicable rules—as had been the situation in the eastern lead mines, in which some of the forty-niners had worked before going to California. Because of the disdain the miners showed for Spanish customs and rights, however, the Spanish mining usage would have made little difference to the American miner. In 1848 there seemed to be no set practice among the early California miners with regard to land. By common consent, without deliberation or discussion, the miners took it for granted that title should remain in the hands of the government and that no individual could acquire more than a possessory claim; that is, a claim was the miner's property to use as long as he worked it, but when he abandoned it, title reverted to the government. No one was allowed to obtain land and not work it; he had to use the land or get out. One lucky gold hunter would strike it rich while another would prospect for months without favorable results, but all had the same opportunity.[9]

The following examples—all of which occurred in California—indicate the attitude of the miners toward the public land during the early gold-mining period of American history. In 1848, during the early months of gold digging, after the discovery at Sutter's mill, there was no division of ground into claims; the gold hunters worked "where it was richest." One digger declared that at the Woods Creek diggings he had often seen four or five men at work in a circle only six feet in diameter. Like a group of boys in a berry patch, running here and there to pick the choicest fruit, they panned here awhile and there awhile, never thinking of marking off an individual plot. To avoid this crowding and to secure some advantage from one's industry, skill, and luck, it was common practice in those early days—when miners were few—for a prospector who made a good find to attempt to keep it a secret. Often, men would come for supplies at night in order to keep secret the place where they were working. The canyon in Georgetown was worked for a long time without this being known to outsiders. A storekeeper recorded that one night four men brought in and weighed on his platform scales three hundred pounds of gold ingots and

[9] William W. Robinson, *Land in California* (Berkeley: University of California Press, 1948), p. 137.

coarse gold that they had mined in Oregon Canyon. One piece was valued at $2,000 an ounce.

E. G. Buffum made a rich discovery that produced two dollars worth of gold per pan, and the result of his first day's work was $190. He returned to his boardinghouse determined to keep his good news to himself, but either his countenance betrayed him or someone had been watching him, for early the next morning he found himself surrounded by twenty miners equipped with pans and tools. There was nothing he could say or do about this unwelcome party. The upshot of the matter was that in three days the small ravine which he had endeavored to keep as his special preserve was turned completely upside down and picked clean of its treasure. About $10,000 in gold dust was taken from the little gulch, but Buffum realized little more than $1,000.[10]

In the latter part of 1849 and in early 1850, with the large influx of gold seekers from all parts of the world, the situation changed. Miners often formed a company and worked together. If a group of resolute men had "struck it rich" and were approached by an outsider who asked for a share, the latter was told to "vamoose the ranch," or be gone, but if a company of men equally undaunted approached, trouble was in the offing. Eventually, possibly after some fighting, the original holders were forced to share their strike with the later comers. The discovery at Rough and Ready Camp, at Nevada, California, was made in 1849 by a company of ten men who were forced or induced to share the find with another group of men, and the two parties then tried to hold the entire gulch. The leader of one of the parties went East to hire men to work for his company, but while he was gone hundreds of miners moved in and by sheer weight of numbers engulfed the two parties who were attempting to monopolize the extensive holdings. By September, 1850, there were five hundred miners at work in the gulch, who occupied it from end to end.[11]

Out of such conditions developed the idea of staking out private mining claims on government land. The claims would not be purchased at a future date but were treated as private property as long as they were worked and were abandoned when the holders found another more profitable spot. This concept of proprietorship contingent upon usage emerged from the mists of history in fairly clear detail. No master plan was handed down by nation or state; the usage seems to have evolved from clashes in the gulches. When the diggings became crowded and more men were coming in than could be accommodated, or perhaps when a dispute involved a

[10] E. Gould Buffum, *Six Months in the Gold Mines* (Philadelphia, 1850), p. 91.
[11] Shinn, *Mining Camps*, pp. 162–163.

large number of men, a meeting was convened and rules were made for the governing of landholdings. It is logical to assume that the influence of the agricultural claim clubs was felt here. As in the protective associations among the farming frontiersmen, the mining frontiersmen made their own rules, decided the size of holdings, and elected officials to carry out their program. As in the squatter clubs of the Mississippi Valley, the size of claims varied in relation to the value of the land and the competition for that land.

Once a dispute that had been accompanied by hard feelings was resolved, all worked together harmoniously. At Dead Man's Bar, in a dismal spot on the North Fork of the American River, where the sun seldom shone even on the brightest day, a party of four Oregonians discovered rich gravel and claimed two-thirds of the entire bar. For a long time, by bluster and threat, they succeeded in holding the area, and a few compatible miners from the States were working the remaining third. Matters stood thus until June, 1849, when a party from Ohio, headed by a brawny man from Cleveland, Benjamin Brown, prospected the bar and found that the Oregon men had indeed made a real find. To the minds of the newcomers, the old-timers were greedy and were trying to hold more ground than they could utilize, and the Ohioans determined to work an unoccupied deposit and force the others to divide the area with them. The Oregonians threatened and blustered, but the Buckeyes did not flinch; they left the area one Saturday night, declaring they would be back with their tools on Monday morning.

Early Monday morning Brown led his men onto the bar despite the menacing gestures of the men working there, but it was evident that the possessory party had prepared to resist. Suddenly, a heavily loaded pistol was discharged, startling the belligerent miners. The leader of the Oregonians staggered and slumped to the ground. Hastening to the spot, his comrades found blood spurting from a wound in his chest. The loaded pistol had discharged after he had accidentally dropped it from his bosom onto the ground. The ball had penetrated the man's chest and gone out his back. The strife ended, and Buckeye and Oregonian alike took turns at tenderly caring for the fallen miner, who died a week later. During the rest of the summer the bar was worked amicably by both parties.[12]

Experiences such as this made it appear much wiser to get together and accept a smaller area than to precipitate a fight in which a number of men probably would lose their lives. At first, in parts where the Spanish traditions were strong, the assembled miners elected an *alcalde*, or judge, who settled disputes, but this office was soon abolished by a California state law,

[12] "G. C. W.," in the *Sacramento Transcript* (Sacramento, Calif.), April 18, 1850.

and justices of the peace were elected in each township to serve one year. A justice was given power to try civil cases in which $500 or less was involved and all disputes in which mining property was involved, of whatever value. He was thus an important official, although the miners apparently used his services infrequently. The miners of a particular camp met and by majority vote set up rules on the size of claims, on marking them, on the procedure for registering them, on the election of a recorder, on what constituted the abandonment of a claim, on the boundaries of the camp, and on the procedure for settling disputes.[13] Their first meeting often produced adjustments in the size of claims, the earlier comers being compelled to reduce the size of their holdings in order that all might have a claim. In some places a tract two hundred feet wide and from bank to bank in a canyon was allowed; in places where there were large numbers of miners, as little as ten feet square was allowed. A typical code required that each claim had to be marked by stakes and a tool had to be displayed to show it was being worked. A notice of intention to mine would hold a claim for five to ten days, but at the end of this time the claimant had to start work or put up a new notice. Ordinarily, only one claim could be held by an individual, although sometimes this restriction was evaded by a man who would take two or three claims and hire men to work them.

As had happened in the agricultural claim clubs, a speculative spirit sometimes invaded a district. The *Grass Valley Telegraph* of Round Tent, California (November 10, 1853), called attention to this spirit: the editor stated that it was supposed that nineteen thousand claims had been staked out in the three previous days by a half-dozen Grass Valleyans. By district law, a man was allowed one claim by discovery and one by purchase, but, declared the editor, all the Joneses, Smiths, Browns, Youngs, etc., had been exhausted and a dictionary was needed to supply more names for individual claims. The claimants no doubt intended to sell their ill-gotten claims at a handsome price, but the stampeders who came rushing in must have compelled an immediate and different settlement. Because the news of a find brought an immediate response from large numbers, it must have been very difficult for claimants to hold multiple claims.

In some camps the miners were required to work on their claims one day in seven, which prevented a man from going off and staying an indefinite period. In 1850, in Nevada County, California, a young man from Maine was incapacitated by rheumatism nearly all winter. He had a valuable claim, and to hold it for him, the neighboring miners took turns

[13] Robinson, *Land in California*, pp. 136–137; *Nevada Journal* (Nevada, Calif.), November 6, 1853.

working it one day a week. They took out nearly enough to pay for his food.[14] Leaving tools at a temporarily abandoned site was very important because it indicated that an owner was not using them on another claim. One could not afford to be absent-minded. Joel Harlan, however, found a rich digging on the Middle Fork of the American River and took out $1,600 the first day, but when he returned on the next day his claim and its environs were covered with miners. Harlan had neglected to observe the universal rule of leaving a tool in the hole of the mine while absent. It was an irreparable oversight; if he had complied with the requirements, his title would have been secure by custom. A correspondent of *Blackwood's Magazine* remarked with wonder that "patches of a few feet square, teeming with gold, are as sacred as if secured by deeds."[15]

Camp rules usually provided some means of recording claims and settling disputes. Recorders, who kept written records almost from the beginning, were allowed a fee of fifty cents to one dollar for recording a claim. In time, transfers were desired, and at first these were simply verbal transactions, but later they were made a matter of record on the books of the camp recorder. The manner of settling disputes varied as widely as the size of claims. Some camps organized an assembly, elected a chairman, and the whole body listened to the disputants present their cases; then the issue was settled by vote. Other camps elected a committee of three or more to settle disputes, and still others delegated the job to one man—often to the recorder. In a Yuba County camp, all disputes were referred to the oldest man, whose decisions were so just that they were accepted as final. In some instances, as at Sawmill Flat, each disputant appointed two disinterested persons and these four men chose a fifth man. The decisions of this board of arbitration were final.

Sometimes when lines were drawn for battle an entirely different solution was found. Such was the case at Scotch Bar: early in 1851 a discovery was made in California and was claimed by two parties who had arrived on the site about the same time. Each group was wholly honest in the belief that the rich find was solely its own, and when its right was disputed, each company began to recruit fighting supporters from the region, until there were twenty or thirty armed men on each side. The bonanza in dispute was so small that it was best worked in partnership, and thirty claims of the typical size in the region would occupy all the worthwhile discovery ground. Each side was determined and certain that right was on its side so

14 Albert T. Jackson, *The Diary of a Forty-Niner and Guide* (Berkeley: University of California Press, 1947), p. 67.

15 *Blackwood's Magazine*, quoted in Shinn, *Mining Camps*, p. 146.

that the issue threatened to develop into a pitched battle. Every man who had a Bowie knife, pistol, rifle, or shotgun was asked to help defend his friends against aggression. Finally, men were obliged to decline to help, not because of their unwillingness but because there were no more deadly weapons in the whole area. The opponents took positions on the banks of the gulch and after much excited talk, many threats, and a few random shots whistled through the canyon, a truce was negotiated, and the combatants agreed to a settlement by miners' legal methods. It was not to be an ordinary mining-camp arbitration in which each side gave a bit, with the man in the wrong getting more than his share and the man in the right getting less than he deserved; this case was to be settled by a court of justice set up not by law but by the miners. The litigants sent to San Francisco and secured the services of the best lawyers they could find with the understanding that the winners would pay the costs, since they could afford to do so and the losers could not. And so the case was settled by ordinary miners' law but entirely on the basis of equity. The defeated party accepted the verdict graciously and fully without complaint or appeal.[16]

After several camps had grown up in a gulch, word would go out that there would be a meeting of the miners from the different camps in the area to form a mining district and draw up a code. Many of these codes provided that only American citizens could hold claims. The code of the Upper Yuba district, established in 1850, stated that the district consisted of "Goodyear's Bar and all above."[17] Such a district tended to develop into a township, or perhaps a county, with the principal camp becoming the county seat.

In mining areas other than in California, usage differed somewhat, but in general it was similar to that which had developed in that state over the years. When Colorado territorial laws became operative—no doubt because of the influence of United States laws governing agricultural lands—claim number 3 on each lode was left vacant for the benefit of schools and was recorded free of charge. In the Black Hills of South Dakota, the early comers established three districts in the vicinity of Deadwood, but some of the miners were not content with one claim and attempted to hold excessively large claims in each district. The discoverer held nine hundred feet across the gulch from rimrock to rimrock, and his fellows held strips three hundred feet wide. Later comers, many of them experienced miners, rebelled at this greediness and called a miners' meeting between Deadwood and Gayville, demanding that the vested ones cut down on their holdings.

16 *Ibid.*, pp. 210–212.
17 William Downie, *Hunting for Gold* (San Francisco, 1893), pp. 80–81.

The new arrivals, led by an old one-eyed veteran, threatened dire action if the greedy ones did not share with them in an equitable way, but they refused to give an inch. Since they presented a desperate front and since no one was especially anxious to die, a compromise was reached whereby every claim had to be worked or forfeited. The avaricious ones thus lost or sold at a low figure two of their claims. From the precedent set by this incident, three hundred feet became the standard size of claims in South Dakota and was so recognized by territorial law, although it was unreasonably large.[18]

In Montana and Idaho, a typical claim in a narrow gulch or canyon was one hundred feet in width and ran from bank to bank, representing in some cases an acre or more. By custom the discoverer's claim was number one; later comers took alternate claims—first on one side and then the other—until the gulch was occupied, and the claims were so entered in the district records.

The forty-niners, as they rushed into California, paid no more attention to agricultural or ranching claims held under the Mexican government than American pioneers were accustomed to pay to Indian holdings. Any spot not occupied or held by a prior mining claim was subject to being staked out and mined. Throughout the 1850's the miners were in the majority, and mining was of such overshadowing importance that custom and common law were fitted to the interests of the miner.

One of the earliest authenticated instances of miners' intrusion on fenced-in property to exploit gold deposits was in Grass Valley in the spring of 1850. Two men had staked off a natural meadow as a pre-emption claim and had counted on mowing two hay crops that year, worth eighty dollars a ton, and netting at least $400 per acre that season. Alas for their agricultural dreams and their industry. Before a month had passed, a prospector nosed his way through the brush fence, sank a shaft through the black topsoil, and struck gold-bearing gravel. Within twenty-four hours the entire hay ranch was staked off in claims fifty feet square, and it is said that neither of the two despoiled farmers even so much as secured a mining claim. The argument of a miner in such a case was that farmers should prospect the claim before they started farming and whisper the secret of their discovery to their close friends, who could share in their luck, instead of fencing the land and risk losing their labors.

A man named Holden, a burly veteran of the Mexican War, attempted to hold a large area that he called his garden; he put an enclosure around it

[18] Richard B. Hughes, *Pioneer Years in the Black Hills* (Glendale, Calif.: Arthur H. Clark Co., 1957), p. 106.

and planted vegetables. Because this land was thought to be gold-bearing soil, miners formed a party and tried to make Holden open his enclosure for inspection, but the "farmer" marshaled his friends and waged a losing battle in which several were killed. The fence was torn down, the land was cut up into claims, and the place became Holden's Garden Mining Camp; a vast amount of gold was taken from the area.[19]

As early as 1848 the mining-camp law of the Jamestown district stated that miners could dig up any farm or enter any enclosure by giving security to the owner that they would pay for all damages (but they could not dig within twelve feet of a building or obstruct an entrance). The payment for damages, however, meant only that compensation should be given for the destruction of improvements and growing crops. The job of deciding the damage done to farming land, roads, and property was assigned to arbitrators. As the authority in this field, Charles Howard Shinn, says:

> At an early date the state courts of California decided that "agricultural lands, though in possession of others, may be worked for gold"; that "the right belongs to the miner to enter on public mineral lands, although used for agricultural purposes by others, and whether enclosed, or taken up and entered under the Possessory Act." "All persons," it is held, "who settle for agricultural purposes upon any mining-lands in California, so settle at their own risk;" they do it "subject to the rights of the miner, who may at any time proceed to extract any valuable metals which he finds in such lands."[20]

We have seen that the rules regulating the size and use of claims varied in different districts, but even more interesting is the fact that in the same district the claims could be of different sizes at different times. Discoverers might push in followed by a stampede of miners, and a rich area would be divided into claims of ten or twenty feet square. The diggers, anxious to process the richest gravel in the shortest time, greedily worked here and there, hit or miss, exploiting the paydirt in a profligate manner, leaving much of the gold-bearing earth behind them, and having taken the best, moved on. Others came later and staked out claims on the worked-over diggings, using a Long Tom or sluice box, and their claims might be enlarged to perhaps one hundred to three hundred feet in width from bank to bank across a gulch. Next, several men would buy a number of claims and work them by sluicing. Finally, by means of water mains and pressure, a company would exploit a super claim of twenty to thirty acres.

[19] James Woods, *Recollections of Pioneer Work* (San Francisco, 1878), pp. 98, 99.
[20] California court decisions as quoted in Shinn, *Mining Camps*, p. 248.

By miners' custom and rule, land could be claimed at the same time by more than one claimant. The firstcomer could mark off an area for placer mining, another could discover and claim an outcropping of quartz on the same footage and lay claim to it, and a third man could stake out a claim to a spring or stream to be used in washing out gold. By means of this usage the same land could be "owned" by four parties: the federal government, the placer miner, the quartz miner, and the holder of the water rights.[21]

As late as 1863 the United States surveyor general for California reported that the state was "cut up into a thousand mining districts, each having its own laws, which are and have been respected by the courts, and which any new code would upset and throw into irremediable confusion."[22]

The discoveries in California produced a new doctrine concerning ownership of the subsoil: a man who struck a lead underground on his claim was permitted to follow this underground vein to its source, even though it led beyond the boundaries of his surface claim. This was a departure from English, Spanish, and Mexican mining laws, and was recognized only by state and territorial laws until after the Civil War, when the United States belatedly passed new laws governing mining on the public domain.[23]

[21] *Ibid.*, pp. 159, 259.
[22] *Annual Report of the Commissioner of the General Land Office*, 1863 (Washington, D.C.: Govt. Printing Office, 1863), p. 119.
[23] Harold H. Dunham, *Government Handout* (New York: Edwards Brothers, 1941), p. 10.

VIII

The Pre-emption Law in Action

It MIGHT SEEM that the victory of the settlers in securing passage of the general pre-emption law would have made claim clubs unnecessary, and that after 1841 they would have ceased to exist, but this supposition is far from the truth: claim clubs flourished in the twenty-year period prior to the Civil War. These clubs were used to supplement the Pre-emption Act. The hunger for land was difficult to appease: the more the pioneer obtained, the more he wanted.

The terms of the pre-emption law limited the amount of land one could take to 160 acres, although the standard squatter claim had come to be 320 acres, and in some areas 640 or more acres were claimed. The first reason for continuing the claim clubs after the Pre-emption Act of 1841 was to secure more land than the law permitted. After 1841 the settlers pre-empted 160 acres legally and secured another 160 acres by claim-club devices. To enable its members to hold twice the legal amount of land by pre-emption, a Boone County, Iowa, claim club about 1850 placed this bylaw on its books:

> *Resolved*, That the filing of any intention to pre-empt in contravention of the right of any member hereof, shall be regarded as an attempt to deprive one member of his rights under the eternal fitness of things, and we pledge ourselves, one to another, to meet the offender on the home-stretch with logic of life or death.[1]

The land officers had become accustomed to frontier opinion and made no objection to the claim-club program. In May, 1857, for example, before the sale at Osage, Iowa, the register urged everyone to maintain harmony and "advised that the *settlers' rights* be respected." What he had in mind we cannot be sure, but certainly it was something more than carrying out the legal plan of pre-emption. It would seem that he meant each settler

---

[1] *The History of Boone County, Iowa* (Des Moines: Union Historical Co., 1880), p. 328.

should be allowed to buy double the legal amount of land at the minimum price.

The habit of stretching the legal 160-acre pre-emption to 320 acres by the extralegal action of the claim club, which had become established in states farther east, was carried into Nebraska and Kansas in the 1850's. Both territories, following the example of Iowa, passed laws permitting the pre-emption of 320 acres. This, of course, was contrary to United States law and therefore of no legal standing; nevertheless, it expressed frontier sentiment and was backed by the claim clubs. In Cass County, Nebraska, if a man who knew his legal rights under United States law jumped a claim clubber's extra quarter section, he was warned to give up this counter-claim. If he failed to heed the warning he was beaten, "ducked" in the Missouri River, and his property was destroyed—or his life was made miserable in other ways. For unyielding disobedience, he was removed from the territory or "put over the river," which in extreme cases meant that he did not reach the other side. Few men had the hardihood or stubbornness to tempt fate to the bitter end. The Platte Valley Actual Settlers' Club started four men on the journey "over the river" who never were seen or heard of again.

According to the terms of the Pre-emption Act, within three months after settling upon a quarter section a man had to go to the land office and secure a pre-emption certificate, which was actually a declaration of intention of improving the claim and eventually buying it. Thirty days later, if he desired to do so, he could prove up on it. This consisted of returning to the land office with two witnesses who supported him on oath that he had lived upon the land the required time and had made the improvements required by the General Land Office, and paying $1.25 an acre in cash or land warrants; the land was then his without waiting for the auction in the district. In any case, he had to prove up on his claim and pay for it within twenty-one months from the date of settlement.

The provision of requiring the land seeker to secure a pre-emption certificate made it more difficult for the claim clubber to hold his extra quarter section because if a jumper established himself upon a tract, even for a short time—perhaps unobserved by a claim clubber—secured his pre-emption certificate, and hid out or left the country, and later presented evidence that he had been prevented by threats from residing on and im-proving the land, he could secure it anyway. Nevertheless, the squatters' association made every effort to enforce the rules. One man who had secured his pre-emption certificate for a tract that a club member was trying to hold was attacked by the group, knocked down, tied, thrown into a wagon, and hauled to a big cottonwood tree, where a noose was placed around his neck. He was told to say his last prayers, for he would be hanged at once unless he signed over his pre-emption certificate. Refusing to pray or to sign away his land, the man was suspended and allowed to dangle until he lost consciousness, and then chopped down. He regained his senses and once more was asked if he would give up the land, but he remained obstinate and suffered a repetition of this treatment. The committee finally decided to lock him up, put a guard over him, and starve him into submission. Finally, after suffering untold torment, the pre-emptor sent for the captain of the protective association and signified his readiness to sign over his certificate and make out a quitclaim deed. On the other hand, Jacob S. Shull jumped an unoccupied but not unclaimed tract on the present site of Omaha and secured a pre-emption certificate at the land office; upon learning that the club was after him, he hid under a counter in a store for two days to escape its vengeance. He died shortly afterward, but his heirs had no difficulty in proving that he was entitled to the land, and its illegal claimants were dispossessed.[2]

Not all communities favored a claimant's taking two quarter-sections, however, for it was argued that one of the sections would lie idle, which would hinder the development of the country. This was the thinking especially in the area around Nebraska City and in various eastern Kansas areas.

A second reason for the continued existence of the claim clubs was the need for a fair distribution of timberlands, which the clubs attempted to accomplish. By the time the general pre-emption law was enacted, settlement had reached the prairie lands. Here in many places the only timber to be found lay in narrow ribbons along the streams that traversed the broad expanse of grassland. Naturally the firstcomers measured off their claims in such a manner as to secure all of the timberland, with the thought of selling part of their trees to later settlers who would from necessity have to buy from them. Since vast areas were being settled almost simultaneously, however, those who arrived after the first claimants demanded a share of the forest lands, and claim clubs divided the timberland into small plots so that each pre-emptor could have a portion to go with his prairie land.

A third reason why the claim clubs continued to flourish after the passage of the Pre-emption Act of 1841 was that they aided settlers in an

[2] A. L. Child, *Centennial History of Plattsmouth City and Cass County, Nebraska* (Plattsmouth City, Nebr.: Herald Book and Job Printing House, 1877), pp. 6–8; Alfred Sorenson, *The Story of Omaha* (Omaha: National Printing Co., 1923), pp. 120–130.

illegal practice—the occupation of land before it had been surveyed. In an effort to ensure possession of a particular piece of land before an area was opened to occupation, settlers would dash into unopened country, singly or in companies, and mark off claims. In the Des Moines Valley in June, 1843, settlers had marked off every available tract for ninety miles along the river. Some blazed trees as a sign of possession, but the experienced settlers would date stakes and drive them into the ground so that the numbers could not be seen. In case of a dispute, the marked stakes could be used as evidence of priority.

In some instances claim clubs were formed for the purpose of earmarking Indian land even before it had been bought by the federal government. When the Kansas-Nebraska Bill became law on May 30, 1854, Indian title had not been extinguished in present-day eastern Kansas. As early as April 26, 1854, however, the *St. Joseph Gazette* announced that hundreds of settlers had gone into the territory and thousands would follow and make their claims. Many claims had been made opposite St. Joseph, which the editor predicted would soon be worth thousands of dollars. The members of the Missouri Protective Association, meeting on June 3, 1854, at West-port, declared that they would not encroach on anyone and would not allow anyone to encroach on them. Until the Kansas country had been surveyed, they warned, settlements must be at least a half-mile apart so that each person might be assured of 160 acres. They also asserted that they would defend any member of the association who staked off a claim in good faith with a view to actual settlement.[3]

A fourth reason why claim clubs flourished was to settle disputes over claims after the surveys had been made. As we noted in our discussion of surveying, settlers many times ran far ahead of the surveyor, and this brought much confusion. Sometimes the government stationed troops along the boundaries of Indian land and would not allow occupation until an appointed time, as in the new purchase in the Des Moines Valley, which opened on May 1, 1843. In the preceding weeks and days, hundreds had gathered along the line, and at the stroke of midnight on April 30, guns were fired and brush piles were ignited as a signal to occupy the land. The motionless, waiting crowd was electrified into action: a mass of humanity poured across the line, wagons lurched through the darkness, and horse-men dashed around the lumbering vehicles. Men stumbled ahead through the darkness, hatchet in hand, leaving the women to come as best they could—or a woman held a torch while her husband staked out the claim.

[3] Minutes of the Missouri Protective Association, in the *Liberty Tribune* (Liberty, Mo.), June 23, 1854.

In the wildest sort of confusion boundaries were stepped off in all directions, crossing and recrossing another's boundaries. When daylight came it was found that many claims were triangular or in other odd shapes, many claims overlapped, and broad expanses of good land had not been staked off. Much of the claiming, measuring, and marking had to be redone the next day, amid arguments and disputes. This was where the claim club came in. Disputes were brought before the association and its decisions were final.[4]

The description of a claim in Nebraska that was staked off ahead of the surveyors read:

Beginning at J. N. Enoch's southeast corner, running due east along line to B. P. Rankin's west line, thence north along said line to a stake about 200 yards north of said Rankin's northwest corner, thence west a half mile, or to J. N. Enoch's northeast corner, thence south to the place of beginning, containing 320 acres more or less, or what I suppose to be.[5]

When the surveyors ran their lines there were, of course, causes for dispute. Sometimes a man's house was on his neighbor's tract, or perhaps a survey gave a rich bottomland or a well dug at great labor to the adjoining claimant. Once more, the clubs adjudicated the disputes. When this was done the claimants were ready to enter their pre-emptions at the land office and were within the law once more. Sometimes boundary disputes were resolved by letting one claimant keep the area that most nearly coincided with that which he had originally stepped off (or possibly measured with a grapevine); if his neighbor's house or barn was on the claim, he gave the neighbor a quitclaim deed in exchange for a like amount of unimproved land. An Iowan recalled that such disputes often were settled before a club committee; five or seven witnesses were called, and although none was sworn, the decision was final.

On July 22, 1854, an act was passed amending the Pre-emption Act and allowing the settlers in Kansas and Nebraska to occupy unsurveyed land. Although their occupancy was now legalized, this did not remove the risk of one's planting an orchard and finding it on his neighbor's back eighty when the survey was made. The claim clubs continued to settle these issues. Once an area had been occupied, however, the settlers often were

[4] Jacob Van der Zee, "The Opening of the Des Moines Valley," *Iowa Journal of History and Politics*, XIV, No. 4 (October, 1916), 525.

[5] Edward L. Sayre, "Early Days in and about Bellevue," *Collections* of the Nebraska State Historical Society, XVI (Lincoln: Nebraska State Historical Society, 1911), 91.

eager for a survey, for there was a stultifying effect in the uncertainty of boundaries; a man hesitated to spend time and labor in putting out an orchard, building a good house, or fencing a large area when adjudication might later deprive him of the full benefit of his labor.

In 1839 a settler on the Platte Purchase in northwestern Missouri addressed an appeal to his senator, Thomas Hart Benton:

> A great and crying evil [exists] which Congress ought to remedy. That is[,] land is unsurveyed and title is unsettled. When it shall be surveyed there is no telling how far the survey will cut up the possessions of settlers, and interfere with the prospects which now promise so much of wealth, contentment and happiness. Yet the survey ought to be made at once. The people demand it.[6]

But the people also desired that the land sale be put off as long as possible. Another correspondent addressed Senator Benton:

> We do hope that you will use your influence to have the lands surveyed as soon as possible, that we may know with certainty where to spend our labor; but we at the same time ask you to use your influence to delay the sale of these lands until the voice of the settlers is heard proclaiming their ability to purchase and their desire that it should be brought into the market.[7]

There is some question whether the voice of an actual homemaker would have been heard proclaiming his ability and desire to pay his debt if he were left to enjoy possession of his land tax free, but the speculators were anxious to secure a clear title in order to sell at a better price.

This plea for delay in land sales brings to our attention the fifth cause for the continued existence of claim clubs: the attempt to hold land for impecunious settlers after the sale. This, as we have noticed, had been done with varying degrees of success from the 1830's. In DeKalb County, Illinois, the first claims were made in 1836, but as late as 1851 some of the settlers had not yet paid for their lands and held them solely as claims although by the 1850's the land was worth ten or fifteen dollars an acre. Such claims, as I have indicated, were frequently contested—which sometimes led to claim wars—as in northern and western Illinois. Hugh McKerg entered some land that was claimed by John Secor. Apparently the claim club had been disbanded by this time but the old spirit lingered, for the people rose in a body, chose a committee to demand that McKerg release

6 *The Missouri Argus* (St. Louis), May 14, 1839.
7 *Ibid.*, June 28, 1839.

the land, and threatened to destroy his property if he failed to yield. In the words of the local historian, "Hugh's heart was hardened and he refused to let the land go." He watched his property day and night, but finally when his vigilance slackened and he risked a night's sleep, he awakened to find his fences afire, his well filled up, and much of his movable property carried off. With the whole neighborhood against him, McKerg decided to give up the fight.[8]

It became more and more difficult to hold land after an auction, however, because a man could appear at the land office, and at private sale purchase another man's claim and never seek to occupy it. There is a note of futility in the 1843 record of Iowa's Johnson County Claim Club:

> . . . any person who does purchase another's claim, without amply compensating him for all his labor, deserves to be published in every newspaper throughout this territory, and should be held in everlasting contempt by all good men, and is no better than a horse thief or highway robber.[9]

In some places, however, the challenger of a claim association had friends who came to his assistance, or there was a rift in sentiment. In such a case there might be a local civil war with the possibility of the claim jumper winning. This was the usual course if most of the settlers had paid for their land and therefore had no personal interest in the clash—or in risking their lives. As a result, the community would not rise as one man to crush a jumper, and the struggle resolved itself into a fight between a first claimant and his friends and the jumper and his friends.

In 1843 in Dahlonega Township, Wapello County, Iowa, James Woody of Georgia staked out a claim of 320 acres and sold it for $216 cash to Martin Koontz before the land had been surveyed. As soon as the lines had been run, Woody pre-empted eighty acres of his former claim and another eighty acres on an adjoining tract claimed by Joseph Kight, to make up a full 160-acre pre-emption. He had thus taken a legal pre-emption claim excised from portions of two illegal claims of 320 acres each. Although his ethics were questionable he had the law on his side and expected to pay for his quarter section with the $216. A group of Woody's friends came in to help him raise a cabin on the jumped tracts. In the meantime, the two men whose claims had been jumped assembled their friends and, while the

[8] Henry Lamson Boies, *History of DeKalb County, Illinois* (Chicago, 1868), pp. 75, 500, 501.

[9] Roscoe L. Lokken, *Iowa Public Land Disposal* (Iowa City: The State Historical Society of Iowa, 1942), p. 110.

house-raising party was celebrating with sod-corn whisky, attacked the cabin, pulled the roof down upon the Woody party, smashed the whisky jug, and generally wreaked destruction. When the celebrators gave fight, the attackers seized the handspikes used in rolling up the logs, and other weapons, and assailed the jumpers so fiercely that they beat a hasty retreat. The Koontz party then tore down the rest of the house and held possession of the disputed claim. Woody now tried a new tack; he swore out warrants for every man in the community except his party, thinking that by arresting everyone he could prevent his opposition from appearing as witnesses. The sheriff, accompanied by local lawyers, appeared in the pursuit of his duty and arrested a number of the Koontz party. These he attempted to keep in custody in an improvised jail in the neighborhood, but one escaped by crawling up the chimney; the sheriff, seeing he could not hold the rest of the prisoners, paroled them until morning and went to bed in a local house. At midnight he was awakened by a cry: "Bring out the sheriff!" When he appeared at the door he was greeted by the sharp clicks of a score of guns being cocked. The callers informed him that they had come to accompany him to the county seat and had brought along a couple of rails on which to give the lawyers a ride. The lawyers talked the night callers out of their intention on the promise that they would leave; and out of appreciation to the sheriff for paroling the arrested men, they allowed him to return to his rest. The crowd withdrew but only to recruit and regroup, and the next morning in military formation a company called upon the sheriff and paid him their respects; he left for the county seat. Nothing more was said about the lawsuit, and the Woody claim was dropped. The military company was dismissed ready to fall in again in case of another need; and that was the end of the incident known as the Dahlonega War. The old claim club had kept its members in possession of the double-sized acreages to which they were entitled according to claim-club usage.[10]

In Kansas the slavery question was intertwined with land acquisitions, and the basic factor in the struggle between the proslavery man and the antislavery man actually was land rather than a missionary spirit dedicated to making Kansas a free or a slave state. Many of the squatters' associations were formed in Missouri and perched ready to jump across the line into Kansas the moment they dared. These clubs made slavery a cornerstone of their activities. Article 8 of the Salt Creek Valley Squatters' Association—drawn up in Missouri in June, 1854—affirmed: "We will

[10] G. D. R. Boyd, "Sketches of Wapello County [Iowa]," *Annals of Iowa*, VI, No. 1 (January, 1868), 38–44.

afford protection to no abolitionists as settlers of Kansas Territories."[11] Since the Missourians were close to Kansas pre-emption opportunities they rushed across the border by the thousands within a few weeks after the Kansas-Nebraska Act became law. Soon they had staked out almost the whole country. There was a tendency all along the frontier for those who lived in an older state to the east to move across the territorial line, locate one or more good claims, or lay out towns, and mark the claims to keep others away; in winter the pre-emptor went back to civilization. It was the same story everywhere in the 1850's. The settlers from around Duluth, Minnesota, retreated to Superior, Wisconsin; the claim-makers in South Dakota spent the winter by the fire in Sioux City, Iowa; Platte Valley pre-emptors went back to Council Bluffs; Kansas claimants returned to their homes across the line in Missouri. Albert D. Richardson, while traveling in Johnson County, Kansas, in 1857, wrote:

> We found hundreds of claims taken, chiefly by Missourians, who visited them once, made improvements—inclosing a little square with four logs or rails laid upon the ground. Yet in riding twenty-five miles we saw but one occupied dwelling.[12]

The New Englanders and other antislavery people came afterward and, finding the claims unoccupied and no other tracts available for miles, concluded that the claims were not bona fide pre-emptions and jumped them. Furthermore, since they had come from a distance they were there to stay. When the Missourians came back to visit their claims, perhaps to sell them, they found them occupied. The resultant bad blood and killings intensified the political struggle over slavery.

When the first party from New England arrived at Lawrence, Kansas, and camped on Mount Oread, where Kansas University is now located, the present townsite was unoccupied but not unclaimed. On an area of less than 320 acres, five original claimants—for 160 acres each—appeared. One man returned after the city had become a reality and claimed 160 acres of the townsite on the strength of once having laid up a log pen.

Once again the multiple claimants who were so numerous before the Pre-emption Act was passed appeared to plague Kansas. In January, 1855, the editor of the (Lawrence) *Kansas Herald* remarked that the professional

---

[11] Minutes of the Salt Creek Valley Squatters' Association meeting of June 10, 1854, in the *Liberty Tribune*, June 23, 1854; *St. Joseph Gazette* (St. Joseph, Mo.), June 14, 1854.

[12] Albert D. Richardson, *Beyond the Mississippi* (Hartford, Conn., 1869), p. 80. The same thing was happening at this time in eastern South Dakota; see Joseph R. Hanson, "Reminiscences of Yankton's Early Days," *The Monthly South Dakotan*, I (May, 1898), 12–16.

squatter—the plague of the Indian lands and of the states and territories to the east and north—had arrived in Kansas. This character, he said, habitually moved in advance of permanent settlement and civilization with no intention of contributing to the improvement of the country. He secured the fords, main gateways, and vantage points, pursued his life of hunting and trapping, and awaited the approach of settlement. The homeseeker, in a hurry to secure a location, the editor stated, paid the squatter a bonus price for land and allowed himself to be skinned rather than face a squatters' club. By means of the doubtful rights granted by the pre-emption law, which permitted a man only one pre-emption, the professional squatter repeated this routine time and again as he moved west. But this system was not to be unchallenged. The *Squatter Sovereign* of Atchison, Kansas, although a proslavery paper, zealous in its effort to make Kansas a slave state and anxious to bring in proslavery settlers, commented on the situation on February 5, 1856:

. . . the idea of going into the country, and marking and branding all the good claims, not honestly taken, and selling them to settlers at high prices as they come into the country, is too unjust and absurd to think or talk about. Since our last issue, we have heard of some sharp ones, who have at least fifty brothers and brothers-in-law, etc., in the old countries, who have squatted on one quarter, hardly doing enough to secure it, but marked and branded the whole country round about for the kin when they get here. We hope they will all be good pro-slavery men—that would not be so bad—but some of them might happen to be of the wrong stripe.

When the first farmers arrived in Colorado, in connection with the Gold Rush of 1859, and desired to occupy nonmineral land, they found themselves without the slightest legal ground for occupancy. Colorado was still a part of Kansas at this time, but whereas the Indians had sold their land in eastern Kansas, no such situation obtained in Colorado, which lay in the heart of the Indian country where all others were intruders, and no immediate prospect for legal application of the Pre-emption Act was in view. Hence, recourse was had to the device that had brought protection before the passage of the act—the claim club. The clubs in this area, while performing the old functions, also extended their authority over townsites and similar landholdings, performing the work of court, county board, and recorder of deeds.

According to the rules of the Arapahoe County Claim Club, a farmer was allowed a 160-acre tract of land, a sawmill operator was allowed up to

640 acres of timber, and a town company could have two sections. The Middle Park Claim Club made the provision that no fewer than five men could lay out a town. Other squatter associations set specific amounts of land that could be claimed for a lime kiln, a coal vein (but not gold), and a ferry or bridge claim, which could not exceed two miles along the river and could be held by erecting a good bridge or ferry before an access was built.[13]

Most prophetic of the irrigation development of Colorado was an agreement recorded by the El Paso Claim Club on August 24, 1860, among four of its members for the construction of a dam and irrigation ditch for the exclusive use of the four parties. One man was to furnish a team and plow and the other men were to work equal lengths of time. Each agreed to share in the maintenance work and each promised cooperation in making the project operate profitably. Their claims formed a 640-acre tract along Cheyenne Creek.[14] A unique feature of the club was that it allowed members to take more than one claim; forty-seven members took more than one claim and one member took four claims.[15]

The Pre-emption Act stated that "proof of the settlement and improvement thereby required shall be made to the satisfaction of the register and receiver of the district in which such lands may lie, agreeably to such rules as shall be prescribed by the Secretary of the Treasury [Interior after 1849]. . . . "[16] To enable the land officers to be certain that the law was obeyed, a set of questions was formed to be answered on oath, such as: Do you have a habitable house? Does it have a window? Does it have a plank floor? Is it twelve by fourteen? Do you swear that you are buying this land for your own use as a home and that you have no agreement to sell it? In spite of the precautions of the Commissioner of the General Land Office and the efforts of his men at the land offices, the pre-emption law occasioned all sorts of graft, misrepresentation, and perjury. J. Sterling Morton, an early settler of Nebraska and later Secretary of Agriculture under President Cleveland, said that although there were many bona fide pre-emptions, many more were "perfected" by professional perjurers who swore they were taking the pre-emption for their personal use but intended to sell it at the first opportunity.

[13] Constitution of the Middle Park Claim Club (1861), in *The Colorado Magazine*, X, No. 5 (September, 1933), 190–191.

[14] George L. Anderson, "The El Paso Claim Club, 1859–1862," *The Colorado Magazine*, XIII, No. 2 (March, 1936), 51, 52.

[15] *Ibid.*, p. 47.

[16] *Pre-emption and Homestead Laws* (Lincoln, Nebr.: Journal Co., State Printers, 1874), p. 6.

As had been mentioned, a claimant would lay up a log house to hold his claim while he went after his family or spent his time in town, but for the land-grabber this was a task entirely too rigorous, and he went through the motions of building a house by simply laying up a low log pen. Usually, the pre-emptor drove a shingle bearing his name into the ground. Another subterfuge was dropping a stone at each corner of an imaginary house, splitting a small stick, inserting a piece of glass and placing "the window" on one side of the "house." A plank would be laid on the ground inside the "house," and the sham homemaker would sleep on the plank overnight. He could then swear that he had a habitable residence with a plank floor and a glass window, and that he was buying the land for his own use.

Albert D. Richardson, the correspondent, said that while visiting a squatter's home he noticed a window sash without a pane hanging upon a nail. He had seen similar frames in other cabins and asked what it was for. "To pre-empt with," was the reply. "How?" "Why, don't you understand? To enable my witness to swear that there is *a window in my house.*"[17]

Such a man was wonderfully conscientious. The land officers were accustomed to ask if a man had a house at least twelve by fourteen, and Richardson noted that a little house, twelve by fourteen inches and whittled out with a pen knife, enabled a man to swear that his claim had a house twelve by fourteen. In Nebraska, a small frame house was built on a wagon and pulled from claim to claim by oxen, stopping at each claim for a day or two while witnesses came to look at a claimant's "dwelling." Because a woman had to be either a widow or the head of a family to qualify as a pre-emptor, a single woman sometimes borrowed a child, made out adoption papers, swore at the land office that she was the head of a family, secured her land, returned the child (with a suitable gift), and had the adoption papers annulled.

Unmitigated perjury, of course, was faster and less troublesome. Although the land officers usually were diligent in ascertaining whether a claimant was fulfilling the spirit of the law, Richardson said that applicants nimbly forswore their way through the maze of searching questions. In some cases, he related, a man who had never been within miles of the land in question and whose family was in the East would certify, under oath, that he desired to pre-empt the land for his "own exclusive use and benefit" and that he had made no agreement, directly or indirectly, to sell any part of the land. The witness would swear that the pre-emptor had settled upon the land at the time stated and had erected a "habitable dwelling" in which he and his family still lived. The pre-emptor then located a land

17 Richardson, *Beyond the Mississippi*, p. 141.

warrant upon the claim and secured it for perhaps sixty or seventy cents an acre in cash. If he had taken the time to visit the land, in three cases out of four he never saw it again, unless for the purpose of selling it. "Oaths are words and words are wind," an old Spanish proverb, was never more true than in the application of the pre-emption law in the 1850's. In 1859, according to the *Nebraska City News*, the use of land warrants to buy pre-emptions outnumbered cash transactions by about forty to one.

A correspondent of the *New York Tribune*, traveling through eastern Kansas in August, 1857, wrote:

> I believe that our Government is the only one that gives a systematic premium on lying. On paying a visit to Osawkee the other day, I found, . . . that truth was at a discount, and falsehood and badly hypothecated affidavits at a premium. Nor was this commerce in rascality carried on under even a decent cloak. It was barefaced lying.[18]

The pre-emptors of southern Minnesota seem to have been only slightly more honest than those of Kansas. David Humphrey wrote:

> This *claiming* business is rather rich. The law requires that any man to hold 160 acres must build a house on it, make it his home, but does not require any particular length of time. The way the merchants, lawyers, and speculators take up claims and reside on them is amusing. For instance last week Forward selected a location about two miles out. The law requires a house. A log cabin that had already been one home was bought for two dollars, the logs drawn onto the claim and put up in the form of a pen twelve feet square and six and a half high. A board roof and floor is required; they were borrowed of the next neighbor for a couple of days. One glass window must be had; it was lent by the landlord of the hotel. A door was necessary; it was brought two miles on our backs one evening, to be returned early next morning. The cabin must be chinked and mudded. Fifteen minutes sufficed for that operation. The pre-emptor must make it his home there; the land lady furnished provisions for two days' support. A witness to all this must needs be had; of course I accompanied him. Two nights we slept in our cabin on our prairie home, and two very comfortable nights they were. Forward thinks that be it ever so humble there is no place like home. The third morning we took up our borrowed blankets, window and all fixins and came in.[19]

[18] *New York Tribune*, August 14, 1857.

[19] Letter of David Humphrey, in Seth K. Humphrey, *Following the Prairie Frontier* (Minneapolis: University of Minnesota Press, 1931), pp. 17, 18.

Although technically not part of the pre-emption program because it dealt with Indian land, the opening to settlement of Indian lands in Kansas (in 1854), which legally had never become part of the public domain, occurred during the flush times of pre-emption and illustrates the way the claim clubs were used in easing the Indians out of their land. During the Indian-removal program of the Jackson administration, a number of tribes in the East, in order to make room for white settlement there, were moved to the area now known as Kansas and Oklahoma but were guaranteed possession of their new land for as long as the grass grew green and the waters flowed. In 1833, in arranging for their peaceful association with the tribes already on the Plains, the government signed treaties whereby each tribe was assigned an area, and the lands not assigned were to remain a common hunting ground at the pleasure of the President.

Thomas Hart Benton, however, always a spokesman for the land-hungry West, discovered a plausible argument for opening Kansas to settlement. From the Commissioner of Indian Affairs he obtained a map that showed the areas assigned to the various tribes in Nebraska Territory (as Kansas and Nebraska were then called) and had the map published in St. Louis as the "Official Map of the Indian Reservations in Nebraska Territory drawn by the Commissioner of Indian Affairs at the request of Benton and published to show the public lands in the Territory subject to settlement." The map was accompanied by the argument that the land not assigned to a particular tribe was open to settlement. The Commissioner of Indian Affairs, George W. Manypenny, objected to the title of the map, saying he had merely—upon request—drawn a map showing the land reserved to the various tribes, and that in his opinion no land in Nebraska Territory was subject to lawful settlement.[20] Benton countered by declaring that most of Nebraska and Kansas was open to settlement—that the only parts *not* open were the areas specifically reserved by treaty to particular Indian tribes. Because the "neutral ground" or common area used for hunting was the property of the United States, it therefore was open to settlement.

This was good frontier doctrine, although contrary to the laws of the United States. The *Liberty Tribune*, published just east of the Kansas border, declared that Benton had discovered that Kansas had been open to settlement for years and that he should have credit for discovering this fact. In reply to those who said that government land was not open to white occupation until settlement was authorized by proclamation of the President or by act of Congress, Benton stated:

[20] Letter of George W. Manypenny, in *Liberty Tribune*, September 16, 1853.

Although there are acts of Congress forbidding settlements or cutting timber on the United States Land, yet we all know that all such acts were passed when our land policy was less liberal than it is now and that they are a dead letter on the book; and that all such settlers get pre-emption rights in 160 acres, instead of being dragooned by military and by the Government.[21]

Such an expression from a United States senator seems to the impartial observer little short of disloyal. It encouraged the pioneers to disregard the laws, but it was just what the borderers wanted to hear, and they acted accordingly. In 1853, however, even the most ardent supporter of Benton's doctrine piously advocated that the territory of the Indians specifically named be zealously respected and that whites settle only on the neutral ground.

The Wyandotte Indians, a semicivilized tribe who lived in the vicinity of present-day Kansas City, Kansas, led by half-breeds and other informed individuals, began to advocate setting up a territorial government in the area west of the Missouri River. They knew that in time they would have to move and thought that by allowing the whites to settle near them they would get a good price for their lands. A convention in the Wyandotte council house, attended by Indian leaders and by white advocates of opening Nebraska, set up a new organization known as Nebraska Territory, elected William Walker (a mixed-blood Indian) provisional governor of the new organization, and chose Abelard Guthrie (another half-breed) to go to Washington as a territorial delegate.[22] In the meantime, mass meetings were held in the present area of Kansas, Missouri, and Iowa, urging that Nebraska be declared open to settlement and that Congress provide a territorial government. In June, 1853, Benton recommended that "the hardy pioneer—that meritorious citizen—whose enterprising courage and industry is worth so much to his country—should lose no time in commencing his pre-emption settlement."[23] Earnest sentiment for the integrity of the Indian lands was expressed by the press, declaring that the red man's land rights would be respected, but with the rush of the land-grabbers across the Missouri River, squatters began to settle on the Indian lands (not the lands held in common) or to mark off claims and lay up claim pens. A squatters' meeting that was held near the wigwam of Chief

[21] Letter of Thomas Hart Benton, in *Liberty Tribune*, August 5, 1853.

[22] William Walker, "Governor Walker's Notes on the Early History of Nebraska," *Collections* of the Nebraska State Historical Society (Lincoln, 1899), III, 32–59.

[23] *Jefferson Inquirer* (Jefferson City, Mo.), June 25, 1853.

Wathena decided that four notched logs constituted a legal claim and that the squatter's name should be placed nearby.

As early as October, 1853, the newspapers of western Missouri reported Indian complaints that whites were settling on their land, and the United States marshal, upon instructions from Washington, warned these settlers to remove themselves. The newspapers noted that the whites were settling on the Indian land but that no doubt they would not be allowed to stay there. On May 6, 1854, the government signed a treaty with the Delaware Indians whereby it was to survey the tribal reserve, sell the land at auction to the highest bidder, and hold the money in trust for the use of the tribe. Manypenny, the Commissioner of Indian Affairs, tried faithfully to see that this treaty was carried out in good faith and that his wards were treated fairly. He continued to tell the squatters that they had no right to make improvements on Indian land and he remonstrated with official Washington when it did not support him. Nevertheless, the squatters on the Delaware lands, on September 4, 1854—four months after the treaty was signed —met and formed a claim club in defiance of the treaty with the Indians, as the *New York Times* termed it.[24] Manypenny continued to object to the squatters' occupation and asked for military power to enforce the terms of the treaty, whereupon Jefferson Davis, the Secretary of War, urged President Pierce to dismiss the Commissioner for his "injustice and discourtesy" to the settlers.

An interesting sidelight on this matter is that the officers and many of the men at Fort Leavenworth (which was located on the Delaware reservation), who should have been used to protect the Indians, staked out claims on Indian land and became members of the Delaware Claim Association.

The newspapers of western Missouri and eastern Kansas, having forgotten their former talk about a fair deal for the Indians, presented the settlers' view. In July, 1854, the Parkville, Missouri, *Luminary* carried this notice of the claim club's decision:

WHEREAS THE stipulations in the treaty prevent pre-emption subjecting the settlers to competitions with speculators putting the poor at the mercy of the rich, be it resolved "that we will do justice to the Delawares and the general government by giving a fair price for the lands on which we have laid our claims, Viz., the established rate of one dollar and twenty-five cents an acre; but we also demand justice, in protection from the grasping tyranny of the rich—and to secure it, we shall unite as one man for our common benefit and welfare.

[24] *New York Times*, September 24, 1854.

In September the *Kansas Weekly Herald* reported that the settlers were singing the old frontier tune that the whites had settled "in good faith," had improved claims that were subject to pre-emption, and sought only the privilege of all other settlers on the public domain. They claimed that the best interests of the Indians demanded that the government buy the land from the Indians at a fixed price, thus making it a part of the public domain (open to pre-emption at $1.25 an acre). At the same time the settlers sanctimoniously insisted: "We disclaim all intention of prejudicing the interests of the Delawares." In October the *Herald* stated that some had settled in good faith, that pre-emption was permissible, and that others "could not as pro-slavery men, suffer these lands to remain unoccupied" (at the risk of free-state occupancy). Still another reason given—the real reason—for permitting pre-emptions was that if the lands were auctioned off, according to the agreement with the Indians, and sold at their real value at a free auction the settlers would lose their improvements.

The region now began to attack George W. Manypenny, Commissioner of Indian Affairs, for protecting his charges. The *Herald*, reflecting the views of the settlers, growled that Commissioner Manypenny

> began to be fearful the rights of his wards, the Delawares, might be disrespected and must leave his business at the capitol and come out to Kansas to see how the matter stood, and to inform the Indians they had rights they had never dreamed of; told them it was their right to have the White settlers driven off, and their houses burned to make their land more valuable, but he could not make them believe such logic. He made his way back to Washington, bellowing with rage, like a little bull in fly time swearing in his wrath the settlers should be driven off, and their houses burnt, and the land sold to the highest bidder. But it was no go. Uncle Sam's cart wheels were not greased, and his commands were not heeded.[25]

The writer then sought to appeal to the whites' latent hatred for the Indians by remarking that some of these Indians might at that very time have the scalps of white women and children, which they were keeping as trophies of their treachery against the white settlers of Ohio and Kentucky while they prided themselves upon being a terror to the frontier. Appealing to the prejudice of the public, the writer asked:

> And would you Mr. Manypenny, by your mad zeal for speculation, and to serve your masters, again incite them to deeds of perfidy and treachery, against the White settlers of Kansas? Would you rob the poor

[25] *Kansas Weekly Herald* (Leavenworth, Kan.), October 6, 1854.

White man of his all, and sink his family to beggary and want to line your pockets with gold, from their hard earnings . . . ? It is not your devotion to the Indian's rights. Because you have been deprived of a good fat share out of the public lands, and not had your hands deep enough in their pockets; does the duties of your office call upon you to leave the legitimate business pertaining to your station to look after the rights of the Indians?[26]

The article then accused the clergy of dabbling in politics because they had urged justice for the Indians and demanded that the ministry be curbed from participating in political affairs. The territorial government of Kansas was so fully identified with squatters' interests that the Attorney General and Governor Geary went so far as to prosecute, under Kansas territorial law, the Indian agent who did his duty under Manypenny's instruction and sought to protect the rights of the Indians.

The settlers, representing themselves as martyrs at the hands of the Indian Commissioner, exerted so much pressure on Washington that a compromise was reached: the President appointed a commission to appraise the lands and to set a minimum price as a partial protection to the Indians. The commission appraised the land at an exceedingly low value— $1.25 to $12.00 per acre—although Leavenworth and other towns had been built on the land. The word went out that the government wished each settler to have his tract and that for those who did not have the money the land would be reserved in their names and sold at a future sale. Furthermore, those who had been driven from their claims were to have their lands passed over if they could establish this fact. Of course, the perjury mills were started again, and nine-tenths of the land was sold at the appraised rate, but the small amount of land that was left for sale on the open market—no doubt the poorest and least valuable land—sold for three to twelve dollars an acre. It was said that a family living on a 160-acre claim ten miles from Ozawkie, for which they had not yet paid the sale price of $1.25 an acre ($200), had been offered and refused $4,000 for their land.[27]

Once more the indulgent, far away government had been bullied and importuned until it had given way to frontier pressure. The gambling, venturesome borderer who had moved onto forbidden land was rewarded for having flaunted the mandate of the national government; the law-abiding, who waited, were left in the lurch financially.

[26] *Ibid.*, October 13, 1856, November 22, 1856, and August 15, 1857.
[27] Richardson, *Beyond the Mississippi*, p. 54.

IX

The Fight for Free Land

THE VAST EXPANSE of our territory and its apparently inexhaustible riches led to a prodigal spirit even in Congress and on the part of officials entrusted to manage the land, as well as in the citizens who desired to possess it.

The first big gift by Congress was to the states when they were admitted to the Union. The Ordinance of 1785 gave ownership of section 16 in each township to the states for the support of public schools (but an attempt at the same time to set aside a like amount of land for the support of religion was narrowly defeated). After August 14, 1848—beginning with Oregon's admission—each state received section 36 as well, which doubled the amount the states received for common schools. Unfortunately, most of the states, instead of keeping this land until it became valuable, frittered it away and their schools received only a very small portion of the benefits intended. When a territory set up housekeeping for itself as a state in the Union, it was customary also for the federal government to grant a dowry in the form of land on which to build a capitol or land that could be sold to help pay for its construction. Often, land also was given for the establishment of a university or for other state institutions.

Counties and cities also came in for their share. In 1806, for example, land was given to Detroit on which to build a jail and a courthouse; Natchez received a town common along the Mississippi River; and New Orleans received land in 1806 and 1812 for a common and a pumping station. Finally, in 1824, a law gave the right of pre-emption of a quarter section to all counties in the public-land states for county seats.[1] Many and varied were the requests that came from states or towns for educational institutions. In 1826, Kentucky was given a township (less section 16, which had already been given to the state in which the land lay), for the purpose of founding the "Kentucky asylum for teaching the deaf and

[1] Payson J. Treat, *The National Land System, 1785–1820* (New York: E. B. Treat and Co., 1910), pp. 315–317.

120

dumb." Because there was no federal land in Kentucky, this gift was a Florida township, given much against the will of its squatters. Vermont also received a grant for the deaf and dumb, but other states were not as fortunate; there were many requests for land but not all were granted.

Even pressure for gifts to individuals or groups was strong. In 1817, four townships in Marengo County, Alabama, were given to French immigrants for the cultivation of vines and olives.[2] Shortly before the Civil War, Congress voted to give an area in northern Illinois to Polish exiles from Russian tyranny. Churches asked for money or pre-emptions to erect a house of worship, lay out a cemetery, or build a monastery, and some of these measures were passed by Congress but others were not. A church at Salem, Mississippi, because of the convenience of the location, had been built on the public domain, and when the land in the vicinity came up for auction the church asked for a pre-emption of 320 acres. President Monroe vetoed the measure on the grounds that aid to a religious establishment was forbidden by the Constitution, and this set a precedent that protected the government from raids on the public lands by churches. One of the most notable attempts to secure land for charitable purposes was that of Dorothea L. Dix, who, for the benefit of the indigent insane, presented a petition to Congress for five million acres, with apportionment to the states according to their population. Later, the request was raised to twelve-million acres, and Miss Dix traveled far and wide in support of the measure. After many disappointments, she was on the verge of success in 1854, when the bill passed Congress, but President Pierce vetoed it.[3]

Soldiers and others who had rendered special service to the government were granted land. Daniel Boone, having lost his early holdings because of the unfortunate title uncertainties in Kentucky and having failed to satisfy the government of his right to the grant given him by Spain, was given a section of land in Missouri as a reward for his service to the country during the Revolutionary War as an Indian fighter. The legislature of Arkansas petitioned Congress for a grant of land along the Red River to be given to Henry M. Shreve, who reclaimed it. Land also was sought for Shreve as a reward for inventing a boat that kept the various rivers free of snags and safe for navigation. Still another class of requests was for outright gifts for unfortunate individuals. Various citizens of Cumberland County, Kentucky, asked for a grant of land to Keziah Shields, a widow and mother of infant triplets. The legislature of Indiana asked for a quarter section of

[2] *American State Papers, Public Lands*, V (Washington, D.C., 1860), 466–467.
[3] George M. Stephenson, *The Political History of the Public Lands from 1840 to 1862* (Boston: R. G. Badger, 1917), pp. 177–178.

land for Margaret Nation, an aged mother with a large family of deaf and dumb children who were unable to support themselves.

The most numerous gifts of land went to individuals as rewards for military service, and the first of these grants went to enemy troops. In 1776 the Second Continental Congress voted to urge Hessians and other foreigners to leave the service of the crown and promised each of them citizenship in the states and a grant of fifty acres. The resolution, translated into German and printed on tobacco wrappers, readily found its way into the hands of the Hessian soldiers—who were fighting far away from home in a cause for which they had no enthusiasm—and was a clever bit of propaganda. Some Canadians who had taken the side of the Americans and had consequently suffered a property loss also were given grants.[4]

After the Revolutionary War, the thirteen states attempted to reward their soldiers, usually with land grants in the western parts of the original states. The best-known land reserves for soldiers in the new national domain were the Connecticut Reserve in northern Ohio and the Virginia Military Reserve in south-central Ohio. The members of the Lewis and Clark expedition received land bounties, as did Lafayette. The enlisted men of the War of 1812 were given land in Michigan, Illinois, Louisiana, and Missouri, but the warrants were not assignable; the men selected one of the four areas and drew the land by lot.

The Mexican War bounty law of February 11, 1847, granted each soldier who had served one year, or was disabled, a warrant for 160 acres; those who served less than a year received only forty acres. This broke the dike. Beginning in 1850, the government, in a benevolent mood, began a series of bounty acts which indicated (according to Professor Treat) that Congress had either become wonderfully appreciative of military service or magnificently lavish in its grants of the public domain. These acts applied to all grades and classes in the military forces who had served in the wars—from the time of the Revolution through the Mexican War, including the Indian wars. Anyone who had served for fourteen days or participated in a battle qualified, including wagonmasters, teamsters, and even chaplains, provided they had not participated in earlier bounties. These land warrants were issued with a value of $1.25 an acre and were negotiable.

We have seen that over the years the custom was for the buyers to move across the continent "hogging" over the land, selecting the best at the auctions, and leaving the inferior tracts unsold and untaxed by the state in which they were located.

---

[4] Treat, *National Land System*, pp. 231, 232.

During the second quarter of the nineteenth century there was a constantly growing demand that the government sell its poorer lands at a figure lower than the minimum set by law. The favorite proposal was for a reduction in the minimum price after land had remained unsold for a specified number of years, and for further reductions to be determined by the length of time it remained unsold—the Graduation Plan. As early as 1824, Tennessee had a state land-graduation system in force; Senator Thomas Hart Benton introduced a graduation bill in Congress the same year. As the years went on, there was more and more interest in the subject. Legislatures of the older public-land states which had large areas of government land were especially anxious for such a law. During the 1830's and especially in the 1840's, lines were drawn on the issue, with the extreme frontier unfavorable and the East reluctant, but the states that had lately been on the frontier and had the most land of graduating status were the strongest proponents. Ohio, Indiana, Illinois, Alabama, Mississippi, and Missouri, for example, had extensive tracts of land which had been culled by the auction and pre-emption systems of sale. The settlers had bought the choice parcels at the minimum price of $1.25 an acre, but when the best land was gone, the edge of the frontier had moved into new, more inviting areas. As a result, millions of acres of second- and third-rate land in the states east of the frontier remained unoccupied. This was detrimental to the national government because there was little income from the sales, but land offices had to be kept open to attend to the trickle of business which persisted. Furthermore, it was argued, idle public land was open to the spoliation of those who sought its timber and would become less valuable as it was denuded of its greatest wealth, the forests.

The state governments, moreover, felt aggrieved that the national government owned and controlled vast areas within their boundaries which lay unused and untaxable—an unwholesome situation that impeded development and progress. The citizens close to these areas favored any remedy that would transfer the unoccupied land to actual settlers and bring them neighbors who would not only be an asset socially but would help facilitate better schools, churches, and roads at a lower rate of taxation, and who—above all—would raise the value of their land. The former frontier states thought that if the vacant land was lowered in price and put on the market, many of the inhabitants who would otherwise leave the area for new settlements on the western edge of the frontier would buy the land and stay there.

The new settler in the West, on the extreme edge of the frontier, was not enthusiastic about selling public land in settled communities at a large discount when he had had to pay a much higher price and face the hardships of frontier life. If anything, he argued, the firstcomer, who bore the brunt of the hardships of settling on a new frontier, should get his land cheaper. The East, far away from frontier realities, was inclined to look upon squatters as lawbreakers and upon claim clubs as corrupt combinations for robbing the government of a fair price for its land; therefore, easterners were not inclined to lower the price in an area where the frontier had so recently passed. Horace Greeley, in New York, opposed graduation because he favored a homestead law and felt graduation was contrary to its principles.[5]

After much debate, on August 4, 1854, the Graduation Act was passed. It provided that the price for land that had remained unsold for ten years should be reduced from the minimum of $1.25 to a fixed price of $1.00 an acre. For each additional five years that land remained unsold, the price was to be reduced by twenty-five cents an acre, and at the end of the twenty-fifth year the price was to be twenty-five cents an acre. At the end of the thirtieth year, the price reached the lowest level: 12.5 cents an acre. The buyer had to become an actual settler, and at the time of his application, the entryman had to swear that he was buying the land for his own use and that he had never secured more than 320 acres from the government, including the graduation purchase.[6]

As soon as it became known that a person could buy forty acres of land for five dollars, there was a tremendous rush to the previously inactive land offices of the older states. At St. Louis the crowds were so dense the office was surrounded and the street was blocked; the police had to open the way in order that teams might pass. Many who by chance came to town, upon learning of the land bargain, remained to become the possessors of 320 acres—for only forty dollars. The regular land officers were utterly unable to handle the business, and even after auxiliary help had been secured, the office was taxed far beyond its capacity. At Jeffersonville, Indiana, twenty thousand acres were sold in one week at 12.5 cents an acre.

Many received bargains; on the other hand, the craze seized thousands of city people who, fearing the land would be gone, rushed to the land office and entered land "sight unseen." They imagined that in a large tract of land some portion was bound to be arable and that they could not lose on such a proposition, but many who bought in mountainous regions—for example, in the Ozarks—were bitterly disappointed. After the town dweller had bought his land he was unable, from the brief description on

[5] Stephenson, *Political History*, pp. 126–130, 188.

[6] William W. Lester, *Decisions of the Interior Department in Public Land Cases* (Philadelphia, 1860), p. 237.

the certificate of purchase, to find it. After considerable expense and with the aid of a hunter or settler, he might wind his way into stony hills or swampland to examine his bargain—there was no need to take a second look. His bubble burst. He turned his back on the area and never returned. Since he declined to pay taxes on a wilderness of stone or marsh, it soon reverted to the state, tenantless as before.[7] Land-wise individuals, however, often were able to select bargains; some of the finest land in Grant County, Wisconsin, was bought for fifty cents an acre.

Perhaps the unprecedented rush that swept the land officials off their feet was in large measure responsible for the confusion and looseness in administering the law. In some districts, everyone was allowed to make entries. According to a story in the press, the land office at Kaskaskia, Illinois, allowed boys of twelve and fourteen years of age to buy the full quota of acres "for immediate improvement and cultivation." Other unforeseen loopholes began to appear in the application of the law. The Commissioner of the General Land Office complained that many people took the oath prescribed by law promising to cultivate the land, with the mental qualification that they would need it for cultivation at some future time. Of course, if a buyer should offer an attractive price he could be persuaded to sell. Some purchasers who owned so much land that they were legally disqualified from buying employed others to present themselves, make affidavit, pay the expenses involved, and make the payment on the land— on the understanding that they would deed their backers a portion of the land. A pre-emption clause in the Graduation Act gave a settler the right to pre-empt at the price at which the land was valued when he settled on it; in practice, however, the law operated in such a way that pre-emptors on offered lands enjoyed perpetual credit, subject only to the chance that someone else might enter it. Speculators not resident in the community could, and did, buy such a person's land on occasion, but the squatter made a tremendous outcry.

It had been anticipated that the Graduation Act would greatly increase revenue from the sale of public lands, but the effect was just the reverse, for the sales were confined largely to lands at 12.5 and 25 cents an acre, leaving the higher-priced land less sought after by buyers. Another unforeseen problem was the difficulty of classifying the land: in some instances land in several parts of a township had been offered for sale at different times and it was difficult to arrive at the proper sale price.

When the Graduation Act went into effect, the General Land Office had sent printed instructions to the land officers to notify the purchasers at the

7 William G. Bek, "The Followers of Duden," *Missouri Historical Review*, XVII (October, 1922–July, 1923), 38, 39.

time of making their entries that cultivation was required within one year after the date of purchase. In very few cases was the land cultivated by the first buyer, and the regular postauction private-entry sales and graduation sales were not kept in separate categories but were mingled in the land-office records. Pressure then was brought in Congress for a general patent law. On March 3, 1857, nearly all of the land entries prior to that date were confirmed and patented, regardless of residence or the terms laid down by the General Land Office. In his report of 1858, the Commissioner of the General Land Office wrote:

> We have reason to believe that a very considerable portion, if not the greater portion, of the entries for settlement and cultivation have been made by unscrupulous individuals in contravention of the law, and bought up by speculators, who are relying on Congress for the confirmation of their entries, by the passage of an act similar to the act of March 3, 1857, dispensing with the proof of settlement and cultivation.[8]

Over a period of many years a campaign also had been waged for free land. As early as 1803 the settlers of the Mississippi Territory had sent a memorial to Congress asking that for a limited period of three years the government give small tracts to settlers. The proposed condition was that the grantee live on the land and cultivate it for a period of five years.[9] (This was the germ of the Homestead Act, which went into effect sixty years later.) State legislatures and groups of citizens memorialized Congress, territorial governors recommended, and congressmen over the years introduced bills for such enabling legislation. In time, for one reason or another and for limited periods and in restricted areas, land was given to those who would make it their home. These laws came to be known as donation laws. The first such law, commonly known as the Donation Law, dealt with land in Arkansas and was approved on May 24, 1828. The government, in the process of removing the Cherokees from east of the Mississippi River, signed a treaty with the tribe that gave the Indians the land beyond a north-south line in western Arkansas. While the treaty was under discussion, squatters who had already illegally settled in the area raised a great outcry, which was heard in Washington, and the so-called Donation Law was passed to pacify them for giving up the improved lands under cultivation. This Arkansas donation bill contained three conditions.

[8] *Annual Report of the Commissioner of the General Land Office, 1858* (Washington, D.C., 1859), pp. 18, 19.

[9] Memorial to Congress by Citizens of the Territory (Mississippi), in *The Territorial Papers*, V (Washington, D.C., 1937), 279–287.

1. An eligible person must be the head of a family, over twenty-one and an actual settler on the Cherokee territory at the date of passage of the act.

2. The person must move from the area granted to the Cherokees before he became eligible for free land.

3. Such a person was permitted to enter two adjoining quarter-sections of surveyed land, subject to sale at the time of entry.

The act made it the duty of the register and the receiver to take testimony of actual settlement and subsequent removal, but—as the Commissioner of the General Land Office warned the registers and receivers at Batesville and Little Rock—it would be exceedingly difficult to guard against fraud and imposition. The Commissioner charged the officials to be certain a person had moved before he was given land and to be on guard against giving two donations to one person. As an aid in carrying out these instructions, he conducted a monthly check of the two offices.[10]

In spite of this, a great deal of fraud accompanied the administration of the act. On August 15, 1828, F. Wharton wrote from Fort Smith that the government was being sadly imposed upon, and he mentioned a few pieces of legerdemain which were called into play:

Pieces of paper with 21 years marked on them are placed in the shoes of children, and witnesses innumerable can be and are found who will swear that said persons are over the age of 21 years and entitled to a donation—White men living and who have lived with the Cherokees for years, have proved up their claims. Removals are made by crossing the line with a horse, and then sworn to, when the persons return to their improvements. Boatmen, who were on the river that day (27 of March) have also proven up their claims.[11]

Wharton also complained that the land officials, without waiting for the land to be advertised, allowed persons to give notice of the numbers of the land they wished even before the provisions of the donation plan had become generally known. Speculators who hung about the land offices, he added, were taking advantage of the situation to secure some of the most valuable land in the territory.

Congress on August 4, 1842—under the general plan for donation claims and to encourage settlement in east Florida so that the United States hold

---

[10] Commissioner of the General Land Office, Papers to the Register and Receiver of Little Rock and Batesville, August 26, 1828, in *American State Papers, Public Lands*, V (Washington, D.C., 1860), 625, 626.

[11] F. Wharton to George Graham, August 15, 1828, Miscellaneous Letters Received by the General Land Office, GLO National Archives, Vol. XXXIV.

on the area might be strengthened and the area more easily defended—passed the Act for the Armed Occupation and Settlement of East Florida. The law provided that the head of a family or a single person over eighteen, able to bear arms, could make settlement and by continued residence receive title to the land he had settled on. The law, however, applied to only 200,000 acres.[12]

During the early 1840's the nation's attention was called to Oregon and the desirability of the United States occupation became evident. Since the jumping-off point of the Oregon trail was in Missouri, the citizens of that commonwealth were particularly interested in Oregon, and in response to this interest Senators Benton and Linn of Missouri introduced bills providing liberal donations of land to those who would settle in the Oregon country. As early as 1842, Senator Linn introduced a bill, which the Senate passed on January 4, 1843, that provided for grants to a man, his wife, and children. Although this bill was not passed by the House of Representatives and therefore did not become law it did lead people to believe that such a bill would become law shortly and that a large area of good land was to be had by settling in Oregon. That same year a little stream of land-hungry immigrants from the frontier of the Middle West flowed across the Plains to the Pacific Northwest, and fed by the prospect of free land, the little trickle became a flood. The census of 1850 showed a population of about thirteen thousand and by the end of 1853 there were thirty-five thousand in the territory.

Although the Donation Land Law for Oregon, as finally passed on September 27, 1850, rewarded the early immigrants with a double portion, it was not as generous to those coming after that date as had been anticipated. It provided that any male citizen who was eighteen or over, who had become a resident before December 1, 1850, and who would reside on and cultivate a tract of land for four consecutive years should, if single, receive a half section. If a single man twenty-one or over became a resident between December 1, 1850, and December 1, 1853, he was entitled to a quarter section, and married couples who became residents within the same period received two quarter-sections. Donations were to be compact in form, and where practical, the boundaries were to coincide with the lines of legal subdivisions. Where this could not be done, it was the duty of the surveyor to mark each claim at the expense of the claimant and to enter the descriptions in a book of claims to be kept by him. In case of a conflict of boundaries, it was the duty of the surveyor to settle the dispute.

[12] Thomas C. Donaldson, *The Public Domain* (Washington, D.C.: Govt. Printing Office, 1884), p. 295.

After December 1, 1850, all claims were to be bounded by lines that ran east and west and north and south.[13]

The Donation Act, which seemed eminently beneficent for the settlers and entirely satisfactory to the government, brought a world of unforeseen difficulties and entanglements. In the first place, the bill Senator Linn got through the Senate in 1843, which the early emigrants chose to think would pass, projected a grant of 640 acres to a man, 160 acres to his wife, and 160 acres for each child under eighteen and to all who might be born in Oregon within five years. Men with families, accordingly, were lured to the new land by the proposed law. Peter H. Burnett, for one, confessed that he was attracted by this arrangement; having a wife and six children, he would have been entitled to 1,760 acres.[14] Moreover, the prolific couple might expect to increase its claim by four or five more quarter sections in the next five years.

The promise of large holdings led the firstcomers to spread out and occupy all they thought they would be entitled to when the bill eventually became law. Since the inviting land lay in long narrow valleys among less desirable areas, to the mind of the later arrivals, the claims of the first-comers included all of the land worth taking. William Goulder, who arrived in the Oregon country in 1845, mourned that the choice spots for homes and farms had long since been appropriated by those who had come earlier. Here is where we missed it, he wailed, in not coming with the real Oregon pioneers who have beaten us in the race to this Eden of the West. It is not to be thought that the land was settled entirely by large families, for it was estimated there were twenty men to each woman despite the incentive to family men. The large acreages and the irregular tracts in long, narrow, odd-shaped valleys forced the scattering of settlement. Even though the settlers had much more land than they could begin to use, they wanted the excess for speculation but had to live on it and cultivate it for four years in order to secure it. Smaller claims, of course, would have permitted more compact settlement, promoted the growth of urban communities, and would have brought the blessings of civilization and culture which were denied by the unreasonably large landholdings. Six hundred and forty acres were too much for a family to till, and it could not hire help because everyone held more land than he could work. After the choicest locations had been selected and later migrants arrived, a brisk trade in claims grew up, even before the donation law was enacted. These trades

13 Lester, *Decisions*, pp. 165–169.

14 Charles Henry Carey, *A General History of Oregon* (2 vols.; Portland: Metropolitan Press, 1935–1936), I, 391.

were recognized by the provisional government, which was set up before the dispute between Great Britain and the United States over the Oregon country was settled.

In the mad scramble for the maximum amount of land, wives were in great demand. It was a common saying during the Civil War that so far as males were concerned, the government was robbing the cradle to fill the ranks of the army, but in the early 1850's in the Oregon country, the nursery was robbed for wives. Marriage of girls under fifteen was the rule. One writer said he witnessed a marriage near Salem where the bride was thirteen and the groom over three times that age. Goulder tells us of an old man who lived on Howell Prairie with his charming young daughter. A young man, a great favorite of the girl's father, had won the affection of the girl but was reluctant to marry one so young. The father urged the nuptials but the young man hesitated: "Uncle Jimmy, Sally is too young." "I know she is too young but we must save the land," the father said. The marriage was performed, but the bridegroom left his bride with her father, and she attended elementary school for three years while her husband built a cabin, fenced his land, and got it under cultivation. Then the marriage was consummated and the young couple went to live on the donation.[15]

An unfortunate feature of the donation law, equal to that of dispersing the population, was the provision for holding irregular tracts on unsurveyed land. After a man chose a piece of land, he would measure it by stepping it off and would blaze trees and drive stakes to locate the boundaries and warn other claimants away. After the United States survey was made and the pioneer plats of the donation holdings were posted, there were many odd-shaped tracts and tangled boundary lines. Some tracts of 640 acres were one-half mile wide and four miles long, and often they crossed other tracts of similar shapes. In many cases the holdings jogged and overlapped in order to take in groves or belts of timber or other valuable resources. The maps presented a labyrinth of intricacies. A portion of unclaimed land in Linn County was a few rods wide at one end and tapered down to a point at the other end—over a mile away.

The law that applied to later comers required them to lay out their claims to coincide with legal subdivisions in a compact form, and it forbade crossing section lines and dodging around to pick up choice spots—a blow to those who had already laid out their holdings the irregular way. This situation promised a reign of bitter litigation and a rich harvest for lawyers, but the people resolved it otherwise. In the manner of the claim clubs, so successfully used where they had come from, they organized the

[5] William A. Goulder, *Reminiscences in the Life of a Pioneer* (Reagin, Ore., 1909), p. 169.

machinery for straightening out the maze patiently and peaceably—in a spirit of give and take—and ironed out the wrinkles. Some lost buildings in the process, some had to give up a field in a good state of cultivation, and others had to let a neighbor have a stand of timber, but the solutions were accepted in remarkably good spirit.

Although the settlers could not cultivate all their land, they could not sell a portion and give a clear title for four years, even though later comers were desirous of buying into settled communities. The old settlers, there-fore, appealed to Congress to allow them to secure title to their land sooner than the required four years, and Congress responded on February 14, 1853, by providing a new procedure: commutation. According to the terms of the new act, a person who had lived on a donation claim for two years could receive a patent to it by paying $1.25 an acre.

The early claimants who were allowed to keep the irregular tracts were very slow about paying to have the lines run by a surveyor and to record the holdings. As a result, as late as 1862 the Commissioner of the General Land Office threatened that unless the survey fee was paid and the land patented, he would take it for granted the donee was willing to accept a compact area according to the lines of the public survey. In any case, boundaries had to be run so as not to interfere with others. The results of festering land speculation were to cripple the country for a half century, but finally a law of 1877 extended the limit by which claimants could file proof and perfect title to claims to January 1, 1896.[16]

Disputes often grew out of the provision that a wife should receive 320 acres of land in her own right, and one of the most interesting cases grew out of the activities of Dr. David S. Maynard, who staked out claims for himself and wife which form part of the townsite of Seattle. Maynard's wife did not come to Oregon, and he got a divorce from her on December 24, 1852; on January 15, 1853, he married his second wife, and taking for granted that the claim he had staked out for his wife now belonged to his second wife, he disposed of parts of it and his own to newcomers, but the first wife brought suit for her part of the land. Those who had bought parts of the increasingly valuable land fought by every legal means to save their property, but the General Land Office decided in favor of the first wife, who then sold her land to different persons, overlapping the plots already dis-posed of by Maynard. The case was appealed to the Secretary of the Interior, who ruled against both women on the grounds that the first wife was never a resident of the Oregon country and consequently was not

[16] Robert C. Clark, *History of the Willamette Valley, Oregon* (Chicago: S. J. Clarke Publishing Co., 1927), p. 409.

entitled to a donation claim and that the second woman became Maynard's wife after the time had expired according to the provisions of the act. With the two women eliminated, the claim became part of the public domain and then of the city of Seattle, according to law, as part of the townsite. A battle now ensued between those who had bought from one wife or the other and the city, which was the legal owner by government decision. The court battle dragged on for thirty years, until the cost of litigation exceeded the worth of the property.[17]

The donation principal was next extended to New Mexico. A law of July 22, 1854, gave 160 acres—after four years' residence—to every man who had lived in New Mexico prior to January 1, 1853, who resided there at the time of the passage of the bill, and who continued to reside there for four years before January 1, 1858, on the conditions of settlement and cultivation. Claims had to be laid out according to legal subdivision. This law avoided the injurious provisions of the Oregon donation law.

Settlers in the Middle West, by means of their claim clubs, had been anticipating the homestead law, and in some places—in a limited way—had already obtained free land for themselves. An incident at Osage, Iowa, in 1857 illustrates the ingenuity of the settlers in securing free land. The land office opened for the business of receiving payment for pre-emptions and for the sale of other land at auction. At this time the settlers had no gold (the only money accepted by the government for land) with which to buy the 320-acre tracts they were holding by claim club. No doubt the usual scarcity of money was accentuated by the Panic of 1857. The settlers who called themselves the Barefoot Brigade because so many of them actually were barefoot, came hatless and in tattered clothes which showed signs of near dissolution from hard use on the prairie. Despite their battered dress they were not shiftless ne'er-do-wells but the bone and sinew of the frontier, and they had come, as they expressed it, with a determination to save their claims from the land-grabbers. Under the Pre-emption Act, they could buy 160 acres, but gold was obtainable only at exorbitant rates. A few borrowed at 40 per cent per annum but most of them realized that this would never do and they devised a plan to get their land free. When the hour of opening arrived, speculators went to the office with their gold bags to make their entries but found that the settlers had gathered about the door, entirely preventing entrance to the building. They appealed to the land officers for access but were told only that the books of the office were open and ready to receive entries whenever the gentlemen saw fit to come

[17] Thomas W. Prosch, *David S. Maynard and Catherine I. Maynard* (Seattle: Lowman & Hanford Stationery and Printing Co., 1906), pp. 54–58.

and do business. The wealthy land buyers then appealed to the town's police officers, who said they had not observed any disturbance and did not perceive any cause for interference. Next they solicited the mayor, demanding that the settlers be moved out of the way, but were informed that there were not enough men in the whole county to move them and that if the speculators wanted them moved they would have to do it themselves.

The speculators then chose to seek a compromise, sent a delegation to open negotiations, and learned that each settler wanted to buy, in addition to the legal quarter section provided by law, another quarter at the pre-emption price of $1.25 an acre. The speculators grudgingly gave assent, but still the Barefoot Brigade made no move to clear the entrance of the land office for business, and when the moneyed men asked them why they did not proceed, the settlers informed their opponents:

"We have no money. You are business men enough to understand that a good quarter section that we could select near settlements is a much better buy at $2.50 an acre than anything you, not knowing the country, can catch at $1.25. So we want to sell you our extra quarter sections at the first named figure."

The speculators agreed to this arrangement, and the settlers added:

"But we have no money to enter either piece. We want you to advance each of us $400 to buy both and after we get them, we will deed you one."

"Nonsense!" cried the speculators. "That is neither law nor business. Legally you cannot sell what you do not own, and it is not business to pay for land until a deed is either delivered or placed in escrow."

The leader of the Barefoot Brigade replied: "We know that the proceedings is neither law nor business; it is more than either, it is a necessity if you buy any land at this sale."

After further negotiations legal papers were made out which guaranteed that the speculators would pay the settlers $2.50 an acre for their second quarter-section and the settlers went home with paid-up receipts for their 160-acre homes. The speculators, after paying double price for a limited number of quarter sections, bought at the minimum price and tied up from immediate settlement the land in about twelve counties.[18]

As has been noted, the claim clubs made it possible for a settler to hold a portion double that which the pre-emption law allowed, and in this way

[18] Willard A. Burnap, *What Happened During One Man's Life Time* (Fergus Falls, Minn.: privately printed, 1923), pp. 115–118.

they had a built-in homestead arrangement. The territorial legislature of Nebraska passed a law providing that a person could hold 320 acres; indeed, it legalized the entire claim-club procedure. The statute read:

> The owners of claims lying in the same vicinity may form neighborhood regulations in relation to the said claims; a copy of which regulations being filed in the office of the register of deeds of the county shall be binding as the claim law of each neighborhood. A valid claim upon the public lands shall not exceed three hundred and twenty acres, eighty acres of which may be timber . . . . Any claimant may protect and defend his possession by proper civil action.[19]

A claimant could speculate on one quarter section, holding it for a time, and by selling it for $200, could buy his other quarter section and have a homestead legally, although this procedure was contrary to federal law. Hence, the settlers had to resort to their own devices, which were only partially effective as noted before. Thus, as the settlers' claim clubs had secured pre-emption rights by extralegal means, many settlers now secured free homesteads by similar methods.

The donation laws were the legal curtain raiser for the real drama of free land. As the special pre-emption acts had opened the way for a general pre-emption law, the donation acts were the opening wedge for the homestead law. The Freesoil party spearheaded the attack in a twenty-year campaign for a homestead law.[20] In 1845, Andrew Johnson, who later became President of the United States, introduced a homestead bill in the House of Representatives; and Stephen A. Douglas introduced a similar bill in the Senate in 1849. In the early 1850's, John Hutchinson, a member of a famous troupe of traveling entertainers and singers called the Hutchinson Family, wrote and set to music the popular "hit" of the day.

Uncle Sam's Farm

The brave in every nation are joining heart and hand,
And flocking to America, the real promised land;
And Uncle Sam stands ready with a child upon each arm,
To give them all a welcome to a lot upon his farm.

[19] An Act Relative to Claims on Public Lands, approved March 6, 1855, Sections 2 and 3, *Complete Session Laws of Nebraska* (Lincoln, Nebr.: Journal Co., State Printers, 1886), I, 64.

[20] Other men had advocated free land for the homemaker long before—most notably Andrew Jackson, who advocated it in his message of 1832.

A welcome, warm and hearty, do we give the sons of toil,
To come to the West and settle and labor on free soil;
We've room enough and land enough, and they needn't feel alarm—
O! Come to the land of freedom and vote yourself a farm.

(*Chorus*)

Then come along, come along, make no delay,
Come from every nation, come from every way;
Our lands they are broad enough, don't feel alarm,
For Uncle Sam is rich enough to give us all a farm.[21]

The West, and especially the actual settlers, were the strongest advocates of the homestead principle. They argued that the hardships, privations, and the services rendered the country in taming the wilds and in developing the resources entitled the borderer to be rewarded by a gift of raw land that after long years of hard work and good management, could become a home. As it was, many settlers were obliged to use their entire capital to buy the land for a home, leaving nothing on which to live and with which to equip a farm. A second argument was that it was unjust for the government to take money out of the western states and territories, where it was so badly needed to build roads, bridges, schools, and to furnish other necessities of civilization, and send it back East, where, relatively, it was not needed. A third argument, used in the late 1850's, was that the federal government was discriminating against the Middle West in favor of Oregon, and the Middle West wanted the same rights. A fourth reason, advanced in the panic years of 1857–1860, was that thousands of preemptors in Minnesota and Nebraska were unable to pay for their land in those hard times and would lose their homes at the time of the sales.

In the East, liberals like Horace Greeley and humanitarian-minded men like Daniel Webster favored the homestead bill,[22] but the East, by and large, was against the bill. It was argued, first, that such a law would draw off the population and hurt real estate values, as had actually happened from time to time—during the migrations from New England and New York to Wisconsin in the 1830's and 1840's. Second, it would raise wages, since many laborers would go west to live. Third, some disliked giving foreigners free land, as the bill of 1860 provided. Fourth, speculators in land

[21] It is interesting to note that the Hutchinson family had more than a passing interest in the development of the West; during the course of their travels they founded Hutchinson, Minnesota.

[22] Robert Tudor Hill, *The Public Domain and Democracy, Studies in History, Economics and Public Law* (New York: Columbia University Press, 1910), XXXVIII, 48.

warrants and railroad stock, and investors and other special interests were against the bill, arguing that it was not fair to those who had bought land warrants and that the government would lose revenue. Fifth, the conservatives argued that acceptance of such charity would destroy the people's self respect and noble spirit of independence.

The South had other reasons to fight the homestead bill. The geographic features of the territory included in the public domain which would be open to homesteading were such that they did not favor the South. The territory immediately west of the slaveholding states was semiarid and would not attract the slaveholding economy, whereas the area to the west of the free states was better fitted for the kind of farming in vogue in the free states to the east. Since there was little prospect of heavy migration from the South to build up large slaveholding states to the west—and a great likelihood of building up free states—southerners did not feel like encouraging a program that would soon sink them into a hopeless minority in the Senate as well as in the House. Senator Toombs of Georgia said he was willing to allow settlers to go to new states but would not vote them a bounty to go. A Virginia representative said he had no objection to the organization of territories when this was needed, but said he objected to the government's stimulating migration by a hothouse system which would bring these territories into the Union as free states to outvote and overpower the waning relative strength of the South.[23]

After much discussion and lengthy conferences, the homestead bill passed both houses and went to President Buchanan, who vetoed it in June, 1860. The spirit of the times, on the eve of the Civil War, can be seen in a bitter editorial in the *Dubuque Herald*.

> Last Saturday the old reprobate, who now sits in the Presidential chair at Washington *vetoed the Homestead Bill*. This act fills up the measure of James Buchanan's recreancy to Democratic principles—it is one of the most infamous of his infamous administration. The Slave propagandists demanded that the Bill should be vetoed, and their pliant tool was swift to obey them. Let the pimps and hirelings of the old sinner defend this last act of his, if they dare—Let them come before the masses of the people with 'Old Buck's' veto of the Homestead Bill, on their banner. . . . They dare not advocate Breckenridge on such a platform as this.[24]

In keeping with the liberal land program of his party, Lincoln, a month

23 Stephenson, *Political History*, pp. 154, 172.
24 *Dubuque Herald* (Dubuque, Ia.), June 27, 1860, as quoted in Stephenson, *Political History*, p. 217.

before his inauguration, reiterated his stand in favor of settling the wilderness in small tracts so that every poor man might have a home. The coming of the war delayed the passage of the bill, and it did not go into effect until January 1, 1863.

The long fight was won. It was thought that the day of the speculator was past, but other forces were in motion, which tended to vitiate the usefulness of this greatest innovation in land laws up to that time.

X

Free Homes for the Millions

DANIEL FREEMAN early made the claim that he was the first homesteader in the United States. He stated that as a Union soldier stationed in eastern Nebraska on detached duty in a secret service detail, he had taken advantage of his situation to select a claim near Beatrice, Nebraska. He planned to enter his claim as a homestead at the land office in Brownville as soon as the Homestead Act became operative on January 1, 1863. He said, however, he had unfortunately been ordered to leave for St. Louis early in the morning of January 1, but he sought out the assistant register of the land office at a dance on the evening of December 31, 1862, and found he was willing to open the land office at the stroke of twelve and grant Freeman the privilege of entering his homestead. According to Freeman, after his claim was taken the office was closed until January 2, and Freeman stressed his claim as the first homesteader in the United States—January 1, of course, was a holiday and the land offices over the country would be closed on that day.

The *Beatrice Express* carried the account of Freeman's claim far and wide, and because of this publicity Nebraska historians credited him with being the first homesteader in the United States, an honor which he enjoyed the rest of his life.

One thing was overlooked, however, which the National Park Service uncovered after the government decided to designate the Freeman homestead as a national monument. There were many land offices, and if any other might also have opened at midnight to allow a man to enter "No. 1" at that office, he could contest Freeman's claim of being the first homesteader. The National Park Service historians discovered that two other men had made just that claim: William Young who made entry No. 1 at the Nebraska City land office, and Mahlon Gore who made the first entry at the Yankton, South Dakota, land office. For years each had claimed that he was the first homesteader, but Freeman's claim had been broadcast more widely than theirs. In any case, Freeman was among the first, and owing to the wide publicity and energetic efforts of Nebraska citizens, the Beatrice site was selected as typical of the early homesteads. The Beatrice homestead, upon which Freeman lived for many years, now belongs to the public as the Homestead National Monument.[1]

The Homestead Act provided that anyone who was the head of a family, had reached the age of twenty-one, or had performed military service for the nation, who was a citizen of the United States or had filed his intention of becoming one, and who had not borne arms against the United States government was entitled to 160 acres of land. (In certain areas—for example, within the limits of a railroad grant—only eighty acres could be taken.) From the date of his application, usually called filing, a man was allowed six months to move onto the land and begin his improvements. He was required to swear that the land was for his own use and not for any other person, and he had to make the land his permanent residence for five years from the date of his first application. Any time after the expiration of five years, he was entitled to take out his final papers, known as proving up, and receive a patent for the land. This proceeding, consisting of giving evidence supported by two witnesses that the conditions had been fulfilled, was required within seven years from the time of filing. A nominal charge was made for filing and for proving up. These charges were to cover the expenses of operating the land offices and for the surveying of the land, and since this was more expensive in the mountain states than on the prairie and Plains to the east, the charges were higher in that area. The division between the two regions was a line drawn north and south along the western boundaries of the Dakotas, Nebraska, and Kansas. According to the act of May 20, 1862, and the supplementary act of March 21, 1864, in the area east of this line the homesteader, upon filing, had to pay a commission of two dollars each to the register and receiver and an entry fee of ten dollars, making the total entry charges fourteen dollars. The proving-up charges consisted of the two-dollar commission to each of the two land officers, making a total of eighteen dollars, or a little over eleven cents an acre. In the mountain states, however, the entry commission for each land officer was three dollars and the filing fee was ten dollars, making the filing charges sixteen dollars. The proving-up charges consisted of a three-dollar commission to each of the officers, making a total of twenty-two dollars for the western states.[2]

---

[1] Ray H. Mattison, "Homestead National Monument," *Nebraska History*, XLIII, No. 1 (Lincoln, Nebr., March, 1962), 1–10.

[2] General Land Office Circular No. 18, U.S. Department of the Interior (Washington: General Land Office, 1867), p. 6.

The first result of the passage of the Homestead Act was a tremendous migration to the trans-Missouri region. When the Civil War broke out, the frontier line had barely crossed the eastern boundaries of Kansas, Nebraska, and the Dakotas; by 1870, the flood of settlement had begun to inundate the eastern and central portions of these states. Whole counties were settled in a season or two. The *Republican Valley Empire* of Clyde, Kansas, stated that in October, 1869, there were only four settlers on Buffalo Creek in Jewell County, but on July 12, 1870, 150 claims had been taken. On July 4, 1870, at a celebration in Buffalo County, Nebraska, five hundred children sang Sunday School hymns—where eighteen months before, Indians and buffalo had roamed the prairies.

A typical representative of the soldier-homesteader was E. D. Haney, who had served with an Indiana regiment and been discharged in Texas. For the next five or six years he alternated between attending school—high school and college—and teaching elementary school in Iowa. A reader of the *New York Tribune*, Haney then decided to heed the promotion of Horace Greeley and "go West and grow up with the country." During the winter of 1870–1871, he and two other ex-soldiers decided to go West. Haney bade his sweetheart good-by, promising to send for her in two years. Arriving on the east bank of the Missouri River in their covered wagon, then waiting for three days for a strong wind to abate before they could cross, the young men met two other ex-soldiers also on their way to homestead beyond the Missouri. There was a natural affinity among them, and the quintet traveled into Kansas, where they explored a few days and homesteaded adjoining quarter sections. After two years, Haney sent for his sweetheart. Her father, meanwhile, had sold his farm and had taken his family to the prairies, and the girl was reunited with Haney and went to live on his homestead as his bride.[3]

The rush for homesteads, so swiftly begun shortly after the Civil War, continued through the 1870's, as Hamlin Garland recalled concerning his Iowa community in the late seventies; the movement became an exodus—a veritable stampede. Every man who could sell out had gone or was planning to go to the Dakotas or other western land. Farm papers and agricultural experts pleaded with the farmers to stay and take up diversified farming, promising prosperity right there in Iowa, but the reply was that they were wheat farmers and would keep in the wheat belt. The prairie schooner was now too slow; the era of the locomotive with chartered immigrant boxcars had arrived, and free land was receding with the speed of steam.

[3] E. D. Haney, "Experiences of a Homesteader in Kansas," *Collections* of the Kansas State Historical Society, XVII (Topeka: Kansas State Historical Society, 1928), 305–307.

Sometimes a family of grown children claimed adjoining homesteads. A widow and her three adult children homesteaded four quarter-sections and built a little village of sod houses around the central survey stake so that they could be near each other and yet each could live on his own homestead.

When a settler went into a partially settled area, he had to get someone in the vicinity to help him find a place. Settlers usually were happy to have neighbors and glad to tell the newcomers the section numbers of their claims and thus help them secure the description of any land they knew to be vacant. Sometimes, however, the older settlers attempted to hold land as a future pre-emption for themselves, or as a homestead for a brother, father, cousin, or brother-in-law, or for a son who would be twenty-one and eligible to take a homestead in a year or two.[4]

A Civil War veteran, who was living on his homestead eight miles from Humboldt, Kansas, told the author that he could have had a much more valuable claim three or four miles closer to town but that the homesteads closer in were being held for minor sons or friends. Rather than make trouble, he had withdrawn to a more remote claim; but not all newcomers were as docile. When Fred Hoppe, a veteran, pitched camp in a fertile valley in Jefferson County, Nebraska, at the close of the Civil War, an old settler, Loyal Stevens, visited him and asked whether Hoppe intended to remain or was merely camping as he passed through the country. Hoppe asserted that he had every intention of staying, and Stevens, upset by this encroachment, angrily declared that the government had no land in that area and that the whole valley belonged to him. Tapping his gun suggestively, Stevens indicated it would be wiser for the newcomer to be on his way, but the ex-soldier did not scare. He replied that he had practically lived on lead for the past four years and that if Stevens wanted to try his mettle there would be a funeral. The old settler saw he could not bluff the new arrival and soon the two were the best of friends.[5]

The rush for claims in the 1870's was so heavy that it was wise for a claimant on the prairies to plow a few furrows, start to dig a well, or lay four poles in the shape of a pen to make a show of occupancy and to warn others away while he went to the land office to enter his land. If it could be established that a man had actually settled on the land, his right to it was recognized as a prior right, even though someone else might file on his quarter section before he arrived at the land office. Some delayed in

---

[4] Charles J. Ritchey, "Claim Associations and Pioneer Democracy in Early Minnesota," *Minnesota History*, IX, No. 2 (June, 1928), 94, 95; Adolph Roenigk, *Pioneer History of Kansas* (Lincoln, Kan.: Adolph Roenigk, 1933), p. 304.

[5] Everett Dick, *The Sod-House Frontier* (New York: D. Appleton-Century, 1937), p. 123.

making evidence of settlement and lost their land to other claimants. In the Dakotas it was customary in the 1880's, in lieu of improvements, to mark one's claim with a "straddle-bug"; this was composed of three boards formed into a tripod by nailing the tops together. When erected on a location it could be seen for a distance and when the name of the claimant was written on one of the legs, it was, for a thirty-day period, a recognized warning to newcomers that the quarter section had been taken.

In some areas the settlers formed claim clubs—as in prehomestead days —to protect one another in holding claims. The club at Camden, Nebraska, was called the Homesteaders' League; another was called the Riders. Once a claimant had selected his land, he could join a club, register his claim with its officers, make some indication that the land was claimed, and the club would hold it for him while he went to the land office and filed or went back East to get his family. Often a claimant had to travel a great distance from the land he had selected to the land office. S. D. Butcher of Custer County, Nebraska, had to travel ninety miles to Grand Island to file and prove up on his land.

The idyllic concept of honest, hard-working homeseekers forming an association to protect their hearths and homes from voracious speculators, while a beautiful picture, was not, unfortunately, always in keeping with the facts. An organization frequently consisted of a group of petty speculators who took claims merely to hold as an investment or to sell at a later time. Some of these settlers' unions consisted of townspeople who had made claims round about and would go out to visit their "homestead" now and then to keep up a fiction of residency. A newspaper editor sometimes explained that his issue was a little late because he had been visiting his claim, and the same paper indicated that the butcher, grocer, lawyer, blacksmith, schoolteacher, and railroad employee had occasionally spent a short time on their claims. These people had no intention of making a home on their claim but merely held it as an investment while they resided in town, engaged in other business than farming, and expected in time to have a farm to sell or rent. But the frontier condoned this common practice as altogether ethical, and Senator Preston B. Plumb of Kansas defended the practice:

A man goes out from the East; he is a tinner, a shoemaker, a blacksmith, a wagon-maker, or a tradesman of some kind. He goes West for the purpose of getting a home, and in the meantime he must live. He goes into the nearest town, follows his calling, and takes a quarter section of land outside, lives upon it between times, so to speak, having his domicile part of the time perhaps in town and part of the time on his claim. . . . Perhaps the intent and the act do not fully combine, and yet the intent is as good as that of any man ever was to make that place his home, and to all intents and purposes is his home. . . . It may be called in law a fraudulent entry, and yet so far as essential elements of fraud are concerned they are entirely lacking.[6]

If a man could live in town and visit his claim every two or three months until he proved up and found a buyer, why not live farther away and visit the claim once a year? An instance early in the twentieth century in Idaho points up this question. In 1904 in the Shoshone Forest Reserve, when the exact boundary of the reserve was still in doubt, it was permissible to take a homestead, but the homesteader had to swear that the land was valuable chiefly for agriculture, was not forest land, and was not a part of the national forest reserve. If all this was true, the land could legitimately be homesteaded. In this later period, when supervision was more rigid than formerly, officials became suspicious about a sudden spurt in homesteading activity in the timbered areas, and dispatched a special agent, H. H. Schwartz, to investigate. Schwartz reported that 180 squatter cabins had been built in the area but that one hundred of these had no land that could have been cultivated since they were on steep, rocky hillsides. Some forty or fifty squatters had perhaps five acres that would be tillable if the timber was cut. On Slate Creek, thirty men had organized the Slate Creek Settlers' Association, and an old prospector had built cabins for absentee claimants for twenty-five to thirty dollars each (these were from three to seven feet high and most of them had brush roofs). During the summer each member paid four dollars a month to hire four men to patrol the area "to prevent forest fires" (rather strange procedure for areas that allegedly were fit only for agricultural purposes) and to repair leaks in the cabins' roofs. The reader may guess that their most important function was to scare off outsiders.

The roll of claimants who were sworn Shoshone residents included J. P. O'Brien, general manager of the Oregon Railroad and Navigation Company, who resided in Portland; J. W. Graham, general superintendent of motive power on the same line, also with residence in Portland; D. McDonald, engineer for the same road, with residence in Wallace, Idaho; F. J. Damon, brakeman, of Moscow, Idaho; a newspaperman and a real estate man from Colfax, Washington; a saloonkeeper of Coeur d'Alene, Idaho; and a grocer of Tekoa, Washington. Of ninety-nine men

[6] George L. Anderson, "The Administration of Federal Land Laws in Western Kansas, 1880–1890," *Kansas Historical Quarterly*, XX, No. 4 (November, 1952), 247, 248, 250.

interviewed, almost none of them had ever lived on the land, and in almost every case they voted in the towns where they lived and not in the Shoshone area. They nevertheless, contrary to law, had claimed merchantable timberland and hoped to possess it as absentee landlords.[7]

Over the years, individuals sometimes took two or more claims, perhaps several miles apart, and attempted to hold them by living on each in turn and putting in a crop. Of course, only one claim could be entered, but the tendency on the frontier was to recognize possession as ownership, even where possession was illegal.

Eugene Ware, who had been the captain of an Iowa cavalry troop in the Civil War, staked off a claim on Lightning Creek, near the site of the present town of Oswego, Kansas, put up a cabin, and broke some land. While on his way to Fort Scott, the nearest town, some fifty miles away, he found a section he thought would be just the right location for himself, his father, and his two brothers, which he named Sun-Gold Section. Ware hired a man to haul a few logs and laid up claim pens. He then joined the claim club and sent for his father and brothers who, as he said, "had then and there, unbeknown to themselves, taken claims." Ware spent the winter working in Fort Scott, and the next spring, when he and his two brothers arrived at their land, they found that their claims had been jumped. Legally, not one of the Ware claimants was entitled to the land: Ware had another claim and could not properly hold two claims; the two brothers had visited their claims but had not established residence on them; and the father had visited the land only once. Nevertheless, since "possession was nine points in the law," the brothers, by a show of force and threats that the old soldiers in the claim club would see that the occupants were removed, forced the jumpers off the land.

The three brothers then alternately lived at Lightning Creek and Sun-Gold, in a successful effort to hold five claims. To make the fiction appear more realistic, they said that the Lightning Creek claim belonged to their mother, and claim-club custom held that a woman could own a claim. Finally, after having held the Lightning Creek claim illegally for about three years, they sold it for $1,500. Captain Ware moved to Fort Scott to edit the *Fort Scott Monitor*, and his brothers, father, and mother held the four quarters of the Sun-Gold section.[8] Some "covered" a pre-emption and a homestead in a similar manner. It was perfectly legitimate to have both a homestead and a pre-emption claim simultaneously, but it was necessary

[7] *Forest Service Bulletin* (No. 67), U.S. Department of Agriculture, pp. 79–81.

[8] Eugene F. Ware, "History of Sun-Gold Section," *Kansas Historical Quarterly*, VI, No. 3 (August, 1937), 304–313.

for them to lie contiguously, since in each case the claimant had to make his home upon the claim. When Richard Garland, who had a homestead in Brown County, South Dakota, staked out a pre-emption thirty miles to the west, he sent his wife to live on it because at the time of proving up he had to swear that the pre-emption was his home. In the meantime he lived away from home on his homestead. The pre-emption could be proved up in six months and after that his wife could join him on the homestead in Brown County; when it came time to prove up on it, he could truthfully say that he was making his home on it.

Such was the way ordinary frontier citizens looked at homesteading and the way in which the program was carried out. Complementing his multiple claim-taking, an old settler would tell a newcomer that all the good claims in the vicinity were taken and that it would be necessary to go miles to secure a good homestead. Having established this untruth, he would offer one of his claims at a high price. Often the stranger bought, only to find out later that good land could have been found near at hand. Professional locators advertised their services in local newspapers and charged a standard fee for their work; in the 1880's, $25.00 was the regular fee.

A shrewd individual would sometimes arrange his claims in such a way that large blocks of government land remained in his control, to be cropped for years without disturbance. A man in Potter County, Dakota Territory, filed upon 480 acres that were arranged in eighty-acre blocks in such a way that two eighties of government land were hidden among the other eighties within a 640-acre tract; the government land surrounded by the legally possessed land was farmed for years before even the neighbors realized what had been done. In time, someone would discover that a man was trying to "cover" too much land and would jump the government-owned plot. The jumper was wholly in the right, of course, but public opinion was usually with the firstcomer. Near Wichita, Kansas, in 1872, a man took a homestead, and in connection with it was holding a government eighty. Another man attempted to exercise his homestead right on the public land, but the illegal possessor raised a mob and compelled the newcomer to disclaim it.

A dishonest or careless locator might locate a settler on a quarter section already taken but which had as yet no improvements upon it. Or he might use a particularly valuable piece of land as bait over and over again, showing a prospective settler a quarter section with some timber on it, for example, but entering him for land of an entirely different description. Since six months was allowed for settlement, a locator could use the same piece of land a number of times, entering the unsuspecting newcomers on other land on the records at the land office. The game ended when two or more persons, so located, tried to occupy the cherished land.

Dr. E. T. Lay, a dentist, and his brother, both from Missouri, arrived in Hooker County, Nebraska, in 1908. They talked to a professional locator, named Harl, who said he knew just the place they wanted—fourteen miles south of Mullen. In talking with some of the best people, the Lays did not get a good recommendation for Harl—in fact, they were told he was a crook —but the newcomers were green as to the ways of the frontier and rose to the bait of the swindler. They were anxious to find a place and were enticed by the description, and the warning was overlooked. They engaged Harl to take them out to the place, an imposing valley a mile long and a quarter-mile wide. Said Dr. Lay:

> We drove around to a section stake. Viewed the land and thought that we might make a filing as we could get three homesteads in a body, one for myself, one for Dave and one for mother. . . .
>
> After talking for a day or two with others, I concluded to have another look. Asked Harl if he had a compass, and he said that he had, so I found that the variation was six degrees. So we took the compass, went to the known stake, set it, and sighted over the hill, then stepped off the distance, and set the compass once more and took a sight. It showed the valley just right. So with never a thought but that it was on the up and up, went to town and we made a filing. . . . [After a time] We set out for the homesteads to line things up and then the bad news—I had been took and how. The stakes showed that we had no part of the valley I had so hoped for, . . . It was quite a blow. I knew at once how it had all happened. . . . He had a compass fixt with a movable dial, that would show directions off balance. When one looked north, it would not be just right, so it would throw lines out. Well I was sure let down. This valley a mile long and a quarter wide was deeded to an old soldier named John Bunn. You can imagine how I felt, and Dave and I sat down and had a very serious talk about the way we got left. Should we go on with what we had or should we just pull out and leave the whole business? [9]

In the end, Dr. Lay bought the old soldier's claim for $450, went back to Missouri during the permitted leave time from his claim, and practiced dentistry. Fortunate indeed was the man who had a profession to fall back on to enable him to "live on" a government claim long enough to prove up

---

[9] Kathryne Lichty, "A History of the Settlement of the Nebraska Sand Hills" (Master's thesis, University of Wyoming, 1960), pp. 160–165.

on it. Between his practice in Missouri and later in Mullen, the family was able to retain its cherished domain.

Editors of the local papers felt it their duty to warn people against locator swindlers. The *Keith County News* of Ogallala, Nebraska, on March 5, 1886, informed its readers:

> William Jones, a farmer living 20 miles south of the town has proved himself to be a fraud of the first water. He has located three men on claims that were imaginary and received a locating fee from each.

A man who notified the land office that he wished to enter a quarter section that he alleged was available due to the failure of a prior claimant to fulfill the requirements, was said to contest the claim. Because of the slackness of many homesteaders in stretching the allowable absentee time beyond the legal limit, or for other reasons, contesting became quite a business. Often, contesting was entirely legitimate, but at other times it was the means of fraudulent procedure in one way or another. A piece of land could be kept out of legitimate hands in the following way: an unqualified person could make a claim and another could contest it on a friendly basis. Since it took some time to settle the contest, the land was kept from entry by a legitimate claimant—no one would attempt to enter a claim which was in litigation—until the original illegal entryman could dispose of it to advantage. Those who were desirous of saving a tract for a friend or for an underage person could work together to smuggle it away from a legitimate claimant. Claims were thus reserved or "covered" by means of the contest. Unethical registers and receivers sometimes encouraged a newcomer to contest another's claim because of the fees they would receive for trying the case. Spite contests were sometimes initiated; a jilted maiden would inveigle an acquaintance into contesting the claim of her former lover. The most common type of contest, however, involved the legitimate contest against the careless homesteader who did not live up to the rules, or the blackmail variety against the scrupulous homesteader who had to buy off the contestant.[10]

When a homesteader's claim was contested he had to do one of four things: shoot his opposition or scare him out, buy him off, relinquish to him at the best possible figure, or fight the case at a trial before the register and receiver, with the prospect of an appeal to the Commissioner of the General Land Office and possibly on up to the Secretary of the Interior. Since a contest was a technical legal matter it became customary to hire a

[10] Anderson, "Administration of Federal Land Laws," *Kansas Historical Quarterly*, XX, 247–250.

person who claimed some knowledge of the law to plead the case for the homesteader; this, together with the fees charged by the land office, made a contest expensive. Hence, even if the original claimant was clearly in the right, it was usually wiser to make the best possible terms with the jumper.

In the 1880's, every town in western Nebraska had self-styled lawyers who thrived as a result of the many disputes incident to frontier life. Some made an honest livelihood by trying the many cases which normally arose in a turbulent frontier society, but some were "contest sharks" who were regarded as rattlesnakes by the frontiersmen. They took the cases of professional contesters who retained them. Some of these pettifoggers had as many as a hundred contests at one time on claims on which settlers were legitimately living; these would-be lawyers were regarded by the homesteaders as responsible for this state of affairs. If a bona fide settler fought the contest, he could be sure of winning, but at the expense of heavy lawyer's fees. When Jules Sandoz, the father of Mari Sandoz, sent protests to Washington signed by numerous settlers, he was told that the contest abuse was common on the frontier and that there was no recourse except a civil damage suit which was uncertain and expensive. Some homesteaders who were reputed to have money had to buy themselves out several times; for a price, the contest would be dropped, but the whole thing was a swindle. Notice of a contest had to be published, and columns of the local newspapers were filled with these legal notices. If justice was thwarted, however, leaving no practical legal redress, the frontier was resourceful and thorough.

C. C. Akin, a contesting attorney at Rushville, Nebraska, who had grown rich by springing traps on homesteaders and offering to release them from the jaws for a price, lived the life of a gentleman at the hotel and thrived on his ill-gotten substance, until one day a crowd of determined men, including Jules Sandoz and Ash Parks, who had bought off four contests, assembled at the saloon at the end of Main Street. They sent one of their number up the street to the hotel as a spy while a few of the men slipped around to the back of the building to prevent Akin's escape. At a signal from the spy, a score of men entered the building, the bare boards of the lobby resounding to the tramp of heavy boots. After a brief interval they emerged, dragging Akin out of the hotel and down the street. Like magic the townspeople had gathered from every direction, but no law officers. The men took Akin into a store near the depot, and a few moments later a black and white object was hurled through the door—Akin, tarred and feathered from head to foot. The lawyer fled down the street toward the open prairie, with the mob at his heels, and out-distanced his pursuers.

A few days later the sheriff and his deputy searched out twenty-two of the tar-and-feather party and took them to the county seat, where six were fined five dollars each and sentenced to one day in jail. Since there was no jail, the prisoners were "carefully watched"—although some of the church people claimed they spent the time playing poker with the county judge. The effectiveness of the tar-and-feather procedure is indicated by the remark of "Old Jules" Sandoz who, after reading the legal notices in the *Rushville Standard*, chuckled: "Not much money changing hands in bogus contests anymore."[11]

Many settlers had crossed the Missouri River with nothing but a wagon cover and high hopes, and in order to live, it was necessary for them to leave their shanties and find employment for a few months each winter. Legal provision was made for such exigencies—a leave of absence could be secured at the land office—but even so, unscrupulous persons would sometimes contest and force an absent claimant to pay a large sum in order to avoid a lawsuit.

An interesting example of this occurred in a western Nebraska valley. A Civil War veteran, with his wife and three children, took a homestead on a beautiful stream and built a sod dwelling and a stable. Having "wagered Uncle Sam fourteen dollars against a quarter-section that he would make that his home for five years"—as the saying went—he began the eternal battle against droughts, hot winds, dust storms, blizzards, grasshoppers, and coyotes. In an attempt to escape some of the severest hardships of winter and the loneliness of life on the frontier—and possibly to earn some money that would help him improve his homestead—the veteran took advantage of the legal provision, packed up most of his possessions, and returned with his family to spend the winter with "his wife's folks" east of the Missouri River. During the winter absence, a prospector took possession of the unoccupied soddy.

The neighbors informed the prospector that the claim had not been abandoned and urged him to vacate, but the usurper contended the claim was forfeited and swore he had come to stay. About the first of April, when the settler drove back to take possession of his claim, the prospector refused to get out, and although completely in the wrong legally, he had the proverbial nine points of the law in his favor. A defiant character had entrenched himself and was confronted by a veteran who had unflinchingly faced shot and shell for his country. Strong language and threats brought no results.

[11] Mari Sandoz, *Old Jules* (Boston: Little Brown, 1935), pp. 35, 36; *Ainsworth Journal* (Ainsworth, Nebr.), June 24, 1886.

If a homesteader killed a jumper, the case was dismissed, for the "un-written law" condemned a claim-jumper, but in this instance, a less san-guinary method was used. A score of homesteaders, only too glad to rid the neighborhood of a dubious interloper, volunteered to lend assistance but feared that a direct attack might result in fatalities. Because the sod house was not combustible, the usurper could not be burned out, but a stove stood in the center of the building and the pipe extended vertically through the roof. The prospector sat near the stove with his gun across his knees, scarcely daring to peek out lest a volley of lead greet him. On a cold, stormy night, a crowd of homesteaders with a good supply of sulphur and powder surrounded the sod hut, and one of them climbed up the gable of the sod house and poured a pound of sulphur down the pipe onto the coals below. While the defender rushed about seeking fresh air, the man on the roof dropped a pound of gunpowder into the pipe, which produced a ter-rific explosion. The besiegers met the blackened and coatless prospector at the door, delivered an ultimatum to him in vigorous frontier language and displayed a lariat. The jumper agreed to leave without delay and was hustled out of the valley under escort and advised to keep on going as fast as he could travel.[12]

After a man located his land and went to the land office, perhaps fifty miles away, he often found a terrific crowd within the office and an endless number of applicants waiting outside. At Concordia, Kansas, men arriving in the early morning found a long line, two abreast, that extended across the street in front of the office. Some had slept in front of the building all night in order to be at the head of the line the next morning. Under such circumstances an understanding was reached among the waiting men to allow each one to drop out now and then to get a cup of coffee or some-thing to eat without losing his place in line.

It often happened, however, that when a claimant made no sign of resi-dence and had not gone directly to the land office, his selection was entered by another claimant. Disappointed, the unlucky chap usually withdrew and tried for another tract, or gave up homesteading.

When a special tract was opened and a large number of applications came to the land office on the same day, there might be simultaneous entries for the same tract. There was no law to cover such an occurrence but the law applicable to a land purchase at a private entry was used: the tract was put up for competitive bids and given to the one who would pay the highest price. In 1875 the Commissioner of the General Land Office

[12] Frank M. Vancil, "Jumping a Claim," in Oliver G. Swan (ed.), *Frontier Days* (Philadelphia: Macrae Smith & Co., 1928), pp. 502–505.

sent out a directive that settlers be allowed a certain time after the filing of the township plats to place their claims on record before the lands were open to general entry, for often they had made improvements on their claims before the townships were opened for settlement and could not compete on equitable terms. This was a revival of the old pre-emption principle.

As was true of other land laws, fraud crept into homesteading, even on the prairies. Many, possibly the majority (depending upon the time and place), of homesteaders never intended to live on their farms, and the habitual claim taker or perennial squatter quickly found his place in the new order. It made little difference to him that the government allowed a man to exercise his homestead right only once; such a person homesteaded under one name in Nebraska, another in Kansas, and still another in the Dakotas, or repeated the homesteading operation at different land offices in the same state. It was neither healthy nor polite to inquire too closely into a man's past in the West, despite the popular song:

> Oh, what was your name in the States:
> Was it Thompson or Johnson or Bates?
> Did you murder your wife and fly for your life?
> Say, what was your name in the States?[13]

Many, after living on a place for a year or two, would sell their rights to others; giving up one's interests in a homestead in this fashion was known as relinquishment. The buyer proved up in his own name while the seller was free to move on and file on another homestead. Relinquishment, although frowned upon by the land office, became an important business. There was no fixed sale price for relinquishments; the consideration varied from a small chattel of little consequence to several hundred dollars. The law required a man to "prove up" and thus complete the homestead procedure within seven years of the time of filing, and where the country was settling up fast, a claim became valuable before that time and could be sold for a good sum by relinquishment. In the meantime the settler had paid no taxes and his homestead was free from suit to satisfy any debt he might have incurred. Congress, in an effort to help the homeseeker, had passed a law providing that "no lands acquired under the provisions of this act should in any event become liable to the satisfaction of any debt or debts contracted prior to the issuing of patent therefor."

After the Homestead Act was passed, there was a feeling among farmers that every person was entitled to a homestead and that if he did not

[13] Bruce Nelson, *Land of the Dakotahs* (Minneapolis: University of Minnesota Press' 1946), p. 112.

exercise his right he was missing something. Jules Sandoz, of the Running Water country in northwestern Nebraska, had tried to persuade his relatives in Switzerland to come to America to take advantage of the liberal land policy, and had even "covered" some claims for them. Discouraged, he lamented: "And only one of my family [is] here to get any of it. This land is going to be valuable some day."[14] Hamlin Garland, whose father left the cornlands of Iowa to take a claim in the Jim (James) River Valley, records that there was a tremendous rush for the Dakotas. When the neighbors met, he recalled, they talked of nothing else. Even those who were in comfortable circumstances remarked that it seemed a pity to waste all their rights.

Some unique problems arose in Utah in connection with the government method of distribution of the land, inasmuch as United States law conflicted with Mormon church usage, which had been established prior to Mexican cession of Utah to the United States, and which continued after cession. When the Mormons first arrived, the church fathers parceled out to each settler a small irrigable plot which—when developed—was worth more than a whole quarter section of ordinary land. Later, when United States surveys were run and the Homestead Act became operative, several of these early settlers were found to be living on one 160-acre tract. Who then was to have the homestead? As a solution to this problem, the ward bishop made the official homestead entry at the land office for a quarter section on which several of his flock lived, and when he made final proof he subdivided the homestead, deeding to each parishioner his farm. Mormon homesteading fell short of compliance with the technical statute terms even after the surveys were made and the standard 160-acre homestead was taken in the usual way. The close-knit character of the church-oriented society caused homesteaders to live in villages and go out to work on their farms but never actually to make their residence there. To make a show of compliance, a homesteader would occasionally drive his covered wagon out to his claim and camp for a time. Since there was no attempt to defraud, the land officers cooperated in this technical evasion of the law, even as they did on other frontiers where the situation was less justifiable.

In another matter the government was not so compliant: the instance of "plural wives" taking homesteads. Since the federal government had legislated that a man could have only one legal wife, a Mormon's other wives who had children could conceivably claim to be heads of families and therefore be entitled to homesteads. That is exactly what they did;

14 Sandoz, *Old Jules*, p. 71.

and when the land was patented to them they turned the title over to their common husband. When more and more gentiles moved into the territory, however, they were even more incensed at the idea of these polygamous marriages multiplying the patriarch's landholdings than they were about the moral aspects of polygamy. As early as July, 1876, the *Salt Lake Tribune* reported that gentiles were incensed about this "Mormon land monopoly."[15] Consequently, a contest was brought against the homestead of Rachael Stevens, the second wife of John G. Holman. Since the marriage was polygamous, she was legally not his wife but she had seven children. Holman, who had three wives, built a house on the intersecting corners of four quarter-sections and used this house as a polygamous residence. When called to rule on the case, the local land office decided in favor of Rachael's contention that since she was not recognized as a wife, she was entitled to the benefits that derived from such a decision. The Commissioner of the General Land Office concurred in this decision, but the Secretary of the Interior rejected the claim, pointing out that Rachael had not renounced her marriage with Holman, that she lived in the same house with him, that the crops from her homestead were used in common with those from the rest of the farm, and that Holman controlled her acts and her land. Said he:

> If the first polygamous wife, while voluntarily retaining that illegal relation to a man, may in her own name obtain title to 160 acres of public land, the second or twentieth wife may do the same, and the so-called husband would thus obtain, in fact, for his own use and benefit the control of that number of tracts of public land. This will not be permitted under the homestead or pre-emption laws.[16]

The fundamental principle, the Secretary said, was that an entry must be made for the exclusive use and benefit of the applicant and not directly or indirectly for the use and benefit of anyone else.

The principle of commutation, which originated in an Oregon donation law, was contained in the original homestead law but was seldom used in the first twenty years of the homestead era. It provided, simply, that if a homesteader wanted to secure title to his claim before the expiration of his five-year residence, he could, after six months (later changed to one year), receive a patent for his land by paying for it at the old minimum price of $1.25 an acre. As long as a man was looking for a bona fide home, however,

---

[15] Lawrence B. Lee, "The Homestead Act: Vision and Reality," *Utah Historical Quarterly*, XXX (September, 1962), 229, 230.

[16] *Report of the Secretary of the Interior, 1879* (Washington: Govt. Printing Office, 1879), pp. 428, 429.

he was in no hurry to secure title, which immediately made his farm taxable. Prior to 1880 only 4 per cent of the homesteads were commuted; from 1881 until 1904, however, 23 per cent of these claims were separated from the government in that manner. At the time of the passage of the act this provision seemed perfectly fair and harmless, but the desire for large holdings for ranches or for speculative enterprises defeated its purpose. It was contrary to the homestead idea of placing a homemaker on every quarter section. Commutation resulted in millions of acres passing from government ownership into the hands of large landowners or corporations.

It was observed that most of the commuted homesteads remained unoccupied and that in many counties 90 per cent of them were transferred within three months after the patents had been issued. In the majority of cases the commuters immediately left the community, and many of these were women.[17] Fifty million acres were alienated from the government under the commutation provision and 75 million acres under the Preemption Act, which was not repealed until 1891. Much of this acreage found its way into the hands of ranchers, timber interests, speculators, or mining magnates. Commutation flourished until long after pre-emption ended: during the first decade of the twentieth century, when flax and other small grain crops in North Dakota increased the value of raw land from $400 to $2,600 per quarter section, commutation became a lucrative business. During that decade in North Dakota, 5,781,000 acres were commuted while only 5,614,000 acres were obtained by making final homestead proofs. When the three-year homestead law was passed, commuting decreased because it was worthwhile to stay on a claim a little longer for the extra $1.25 an acre.[18]

The principal weakness of the Homestead Act, even where the act was legitimately applied, was that it made farming seem very simple and success a certainty. Its requirement of building a shanty, breaking a mere ten acres, and living on the claim a brief time until it became the settler's property seemed simple, a "sure-fire thing." The ability of a claimant to buy the necessary equipment, his aptitude for farming, and the climatic conditions were not taken into consideration. Many who had never owned or tilled land supposed that by coming into possession of land, their fortunes were automatically made. When drought, grasshoppers, blizzards, and sandstorms came, they became utterly discouraged.

[17] Robert Tudor Hill, *The Public Domain and Democracy, Studies in History, Economics and Public Law* (New York: Columbia University Press, 1910), XXXVIII, 49–50; Benjamin Hibbard, *A History of the Public Land Policies* (New York: Macmillan, 1924), p. 386.
[18] *Ibid.*, p. 387.

Early in January, 1886, George Klein, who lived in a bleak, remote, wind-swept claim shack on Mirage Flats, Nebraska, urged his team through the snow to Pine Ridge for wood. When he arrived home late that night, he found his house dark, the fire out, and his wife and three children dead. Gopher poison and an old case knife worn to a point told the mute tale. The woman had been discouraged and moody for some time, but her husband had high hopes for bigger crops and better times when he could make his wife happier by buying her a new dress, shoes for the children, curtains for the windows, and perhaps such a luxury as sugar. These things had not come in time. Friends helped make white lawn dresses for the children—something nice for the funeral—and a neighbor woman said sorrowfully: "If she could a had even a geranium—but in that cold shell of a shack. . . . "[19]

Seth K. Humphrey, an agent for an eastern investment company, who visited many homesteaders on the Plains, made this comment:

The prairie has a solitude way beyond the mere absence of human beings. In a country of trees, whether it is peopled or not, the range of vision is circumscribed. Lift the eyes, and they meet objects; perhaps not objects of special interest, yet they do engage the eye. They furnish it with normal occupation.

But raise the eyes to the bare prairie, and they sweep the horizon. Nothing stops them. They stare, stare—and sometimes the prairie gets to staring back. Always the trembling horizon, a motionless expanse in between, and the blazing sky above. No detailed picture for the hungry eye. Beyond the grass underfoot, the blur of limitless vacuity.

How much of the exodus from this frontier of the eighties was due to the women—both the women who stayed until the prairie broke them and the many more who fled from the terror of it—nobody can know.[20]

After the homesteader had spent all his money getting started or in weathering a season or two of drought, he was often compelled to borrow money at exorbitant interest rates. In Dakota Territory until 1875, for example, the legal rate of interest was 18 per cent, and in that year it was reduced to 12 per cent. Even then, by under-the-table transactions a loan company was able to circumvent the law. A borrower signed a note for one hundred dollars at 12 per cent, but he received only ninety dollars. Loan brokers were hated by the farmers, who were compelled to borrow at

[19] Sandoz, *Old Jules*, p. 83.
[20] Seth K. Humphrey, *Following the Prairie Frontier* (Minneapolis: University of Minnesota Press, 1931), pp. 131–132.

ruinous rates; nevertheless, the economic struggle of the pioneer to establish a foothold demanded that he be allowed to mortgage his homestead
before he "proved up on it." An accommodating Congress complied.

The mortgage business was not a one-sided game, however, because
many, becoming discouraged, mortgaged their claims for all they could get
and left the country feeling that the place was well sold. Hamlin Garland
was glad to mortgage his Dakota claim for $200, leave for New York, and
use the money to get a start in work more inviting than farming. When, in
the 1880's, loan companies in the East sent inspectors to visit defaulters in
an attempt to save some of the money they had lent on dubious security, one
inspector rode for miles and reported that

> almost every vacant quarter section—the regular claim of one hundred
> and sixty acres—bore the marks of its settler: the crumbling walls of a
> sod house; a caved-in well, if one wished to look for it; and the breaking
> of ten acres as required by law for "proving up" the title.[21]

In the first four days he visited forty-one pieces of land; three were occupied by the original mortgagers and three by squatters, but on the remaining thirty-five there was not so much as a board to show that claim shacks
had existed, although he saw evidence of honest failure in a great amount
of broken ground and repeated cropping. The sheer emptiness of the
country, once filled with people, caused many of the holdouts to give up
and attempt to secure money to leave. A man who applied for a loan had a
big family and a story-and-a-half frame house. He told the loan agent he
was a Connecticut Yankee, that it had taken all his money to build the
house, and that he needed $420 to buy tools and equipment. If he had
asked for as much as the property was worth, his application would have
been rejected by loan company officials in the East. The agent found that
the man had relatives in California who had a fruit farm and he had
arrived at the figure by computing the amount necessary to buy tickets for
his large family.

It might be thought that the loan company was the gainer in such a
transaction, since, upon foreclosing, it would have secured an improved
farm with a splendid house, but this was not the case, for among the
settlers there was a peculiar ethical code akin to that held concerning the
honesty of cutting the timber on the land of the speculator. A settler might
go away for six months and leave his shack with his chattels lying about
without the least fear of theft, but once the homestead was vacated and it
was known that the loan company was the owner, the buildings vanished

[21] *Ibid.*, pp. 105, 106.

piecemeal or were placed on skids and taken away to a neighbor's place. Sometimes a man would try to sell his buildings before he left, but there was little use in buying when one could have them for the taking after a settler had left the country and the land had reverted to the mortgage company. The foreclosed properties were stripped of all lumber—even the upper sections of the well curbing and the cellar steps—as soon as the settler was out of sight. A Mrs. Masters who lived near Box Butte, Nebraska, was scheduled to leave on a certain day, but unbeknown to the neighbors, she did not get away as she intended. That very night in the dense darkness six wagons drove up to her house. Two men climbed onto the roof and started tearing off the shingles while the others attacked the doors and windows. At the first rip of the shingles, Mrs. Masters—a ghost in white nightgown—appeared at the door. The men, taken aback, apologized, and whipped their horses over the nearest hill, no doubt with every intention of returning to their salvage job when the ghostly apparition had vacated the desirable house.[22]

The extent to which the Homestead Act, as it was envisioned by those who enacted it, failed on the Great Plains is indicated by the fact that every important farm mortgage company operating in that area of Nebraska and South Dakota went bankrupt in the eighties.

The Homestead Act had the greatest social impact of all the land laws; for nearly three quarters of a century it offered land for the landless. At home and far overseas the thrilling announcement of free land was heard. The recently freed Negroes of the South heard the call, which resulted in the Exoduster Movement, in which, according to one contemporary, fifteen to twenty thousand Negroes settled in Kansas in the twelve-month period that ended in April, 1880, although most of them were too poor to take advantage of free land when they arrived.

The Sioux City and Pacific Railroad (Elkhorn Valley line), which was the recipient of only a small quantity of state land, originated the tremendously popular slogan "Free Homes for the Millions," which was heard loud and clear throughout the area east of the Missouri River and far overseas where those who had some means rejoiced to hear it. John Ross Buchanan, general passenger agent of the Elkhorn Valley line from 1881 to 1903, was responsible for the motto. A historical account of Holt County, Nebraska, quotes him:

"Free Homes for the Millions"! That was my slogan or rallying phrase. . . . It headed every circular, folder, and poster which I issued, and

[22] Sandoz, *Old Jules*, p. 173.

I issued them by the million. . . . Everywhere, and in every possible publication and newspaper, printed in black, blue and red ink, in the English and German languages, was this sentence "Free Homes for the Millions."[23]

Plains states sent immigration agents abroad, who competed in presenting the superiority of the free land within the states which they represented. With the fervor of an evangelist they distributed pamphlets, advertised in the newspapers, and gave lectures with follow-up meetings for the interested, ceaselessly preaching the message that the golden horn of plenty was available to the homeless in the western area of America. Holding out the lure of free land, these agents organized immigrating parties from Europe and the East. A letter of G. B. Neilson, Nebraska's agent for Denmark, Sweden, and Norway, in 1871, reveals the competition for immigrants in the Scandinavian countries.

DEAR SIR:

Victory! The battle is won for our state, but it was a hard fought battle. . . . The fall immigration to Nebraska of people with sufficient capital to commence work on our prairies will be very large. On Monday I go to Sweden and Norway. . . . The truth shall and must be known all over this country. . . .[24]

Neilson's letter reveals one of the weaknesses of the Homestead Act. A man, in order to succeed, needed capital, and many failures were due to the fact that settlers could not succeed with free land alone. In order to carry out the intent of the law—settling the land with families on family-sized farms that would be owned and operated by the settlers—it would have been necessary to screen the settlers and to allow only those who were qualified to homestead.

Another fault (which will be treated in Chapter 18 of this volume) was that the Homestead Act was passed with the climate of Illinois or Iowa in mind, whereas within two decades after its passage the westward-moving frontier belt in which the available land was located was destined to cross the 100th meridian beyond which lay semiarid land where the 160-acre homestead was not the appropriate size for the climatic conditions. Ranching demanded a larger area, and the need for irrigation dictated an acreage even smaller than the old 160-acre homestead. New conditions

[23] Mr. and Mrs. J. G. W. Lewis, "Holt County," in *Who's Who in Nebraska, 1940* (Lincoln: Nebraska Press Association, 1940), pp. 564–565. This slogan appears also as "Free Homes for the Million."

[24] *Nebraska Statesman* (Lincoln, Nebr.), July 29, 1871.

that were met as settlement crept westward indicated the desirability of classifying the lands and of distributing them in sizes that accorded with their potential use.

But despite its defects the act had a powerful effect on American history, for year after year over a period of six decades the storybook call of free land for the homeless drew multitudes to settle the great Trans-Mississippi West region of the United States.

XI

Internal Improvement Lands

THE UNITED STATES GOVERNMENT gave land to encourage the construction of internal improvements—roads, canals, and railroads. In earlier times such grants were made to the states to be used as the officials might direct, but later the grants were often made directly to companies to encourage the building of transportation systems which would benefit the nation. Since the land in such grants to states or companies was intended eventually to come into the hands of the people, the status of the land until the settlers secured title is discussed in this chapter.

With the admission of Ohio to the Union—the first state that contained government land—5 per cent of the money derived from the sale of public lands was allocated by the federal government for use in laying out roads in the new commonwealth; and the same policy applied when Indiana, Louisiana, and other states were admitted.[1] This policy was followed by the granting of further aid to new states in the form of land. One of the earliest such gifts was a grant to Ohio in 1832 for a wagon road that was to be laid out from Lake Erie through the Connecticut Western Reserve tract. The grant ceded a 120-foot right-of-way and the equivalent of two strips of land a mile wide on each side of the projected road.

With the second decade of the nineteenth century the fever to dig canals seized the people of the Old Northwest. The completion of the Erie Canal in 1823 reduced freight rates between Buffalo and New York City from $100 to only $15 a ton and cut the transit time from twenty-eight days to eight. The canal made a tremendous difference in the lives of the people; it was a twofold benefit in that it raised the price of settlers' farm produce but lowered the cost of their consumer goods. The success of the Erie Canal was so phenomenal and immediate that the imagination of the entire Northwest was aroused. Enthusiasts pointed out that the advantages

[1] Kenneth W. Colgrove, "The Attitude of Congress Toward the Pioneers of the West," *Iowa Journal of History and Politics*, VIII, No. 1 (January, 1910), 115.

which the Erie Canal had brought to western New York could be secured by central Ohio by means of canal construction. The price lists of local commodities in every inland neighborhood in the West argued eloquently for a means of transporting agricultural products to the Ohio River or the Great Lakes. Corn that sold in Indianapolis or Columbus for twenty cents a bushel brought fifty cents along the Ohio River, or two and one-half times the farm price, due to the high freight costs by wagons on unimproved roads. Accordingly, several canals for connecting the Great Lakes with the Ohio and Mississippi rivers were projected. For one of these—the Wabash and Lake Erie Canal—the state of Indiana, by an act of Congress on March 2, 1827, secured a grant of land for the portion of the canal between the mouth of the Tippecanoe River and Terre Haute.[2] Ohio and Illinois also were recipients of land, for the Miami Canal and the Illinois and Michigan Canal, respectively. The government donated a right-of-way and laid out a strip of land ten miles wide—five miles on each side of the right-of-way. The alternate sections in the strip were given to the state for the benefit of the canal, and the remainder of the sections were retained by the government for disposal in the normal method. The merit of making these grants for the canals was debated with ardor, but finally, to secure the required number of votes to pass the bill, the proponents urged the alternate-section scheme. It was argued that the new canals would make nearby land at least twice as valuable as before and therefore the law contained the proviso that all government land within the grant belt should be sold for not less than $2.50 an acre rather than at the regular minimum price of $1.25 an acre. The government would then lose nothing, although it was giving away half of its land within a zone along a land-grant canal.

The canals proved a blessing to the farmers of the Northwest although their construction almost bankrupted the region. In 1823 inland wheat sold for twenty cents a bushel; ten years later, after the canals were completed, the farmers received fifty cents a bushel for wheat. During the same period the prices of such imported commodities as coffee, tea, salt, and sugar were cut in half. A rise in prosperity accounted somewhat for this change, but this was only part of the story. The records show that the area in the vicinity of the Wabash and Erie Canal increased 400 per cent in population in the decade after the canal was opened, whereas the rest of Indiana increased less than 200 per cent.

When railroads became a proven success, the government gave land for their construction. As early as 1833, the government transferred an unused

2 William W. Lester, *Decisions of the Interior Department in Public Land Cases* (Philadelphia, 1860), pp. 57, 58.

grant, which had been intended for the Illinois and Michigan Canal, for the construction of a proposed railroad. The extensive grants, however, began in 1850 with a grant of 2,500,000 acres to Illinois for the Illinois Central Railroad.[3] The previously adopted alternate-section scheme was followed. Sections outside the grant belt which could be purchased for as little as $1.25 an acre were known as minimum lands, and those within the grants were known as double-minimum lands. This precedent was followed even after the government had begun to distribute free land through the Homestead Act: a homesteader within a grant area was allowed to claim only eighty acres instead of the ordinary quarter section. The Illinois Central ran from Chicago and Galena in the north, converged at Cairo, Illinois, and extended to Mobile, Alabama. The states of Illinois, Mississippi, and Alabama were given a right-of-way and a twelve-mile-wide strip of land in alternate sections (Kentucky and Tennessee had no government land within their boundaries).

Iowa then requested railroad land grants for four lines across the state from east to west, the basis for the present Burlington, Rock Island, Northwestern, and Illinois Central railroads, which still serve Iowa. A law of Congress (passed May 15, 1856), gave the land to the state of Iowa and allowed her to deal with the railroads, and the government immediately issued a proclamation that all the lands within the probable limits of the grants had been withdrawn from entry. This brought practically all land-office business in Iowa to an abrupt halt and created a leapfrog situation that gave great impetus to the settlement of Nebraska and Kansas. The Iowa legislature designated the companies that would receive the land and charged them to locate their routes and submit a map to the General Land Office so that the land outside their grants might be opened for entry at the earliest possible date in order to make government lands in Iowa available to the thousands of settlers, who on the march from farther east, were passing over the state for homes in Kansas and Nebraska.[4] Not all settlers were deterred by these withdrawals and this caused disputes later. Land-hunger and a willingness to gamble led the bold or the unscrupulous to settle on the lands designated for the railroads, which were more valuable than those elsewhere, and in frontier practice a squatter had the advantage of possession in any dispute. The venturesome could settle on land after it had been withdrawn from entry and could claim that they were actual settlers, had settled in good faith, and should not have

[3] Harold H. Dunham, *Government Handout* (New York: Edwards Brothers, 1941), p. 7.

[4] Roscoe L. Lokken, *Iowa Public Land Disposal* (Iowa City: State Historical Society of Iowa, 1942), pp. 236–245.

their homes and improvements sold out from under them (when the railroad sought to do so). A conflict of this nature between settlers and the Missouri, Kansas, and Texas Railroad and the Leavenworth, Lawrence, and Gulf Railroad in eastern Kansas lasted for nearly three decades. Congress, in the late 1860's, had voted a land grant to these railroads across Indian Territory while negotiations were under way to extinguish Indian title to the area, but for decades it had been customary for whites to settle with impunity on Indian-owned and -occupied territory.

Newt Ard, of Elsmore, Kansas, squatted on land within this railroad grant in 1866. As was customary, he did not at once make entry, but when he did, on July 14, 1866, the land office would allow him to take only eighty acres since he was located within the railroad's land grant. He nevertheless occupied the other eighty acres which under normal circumstances would have been allowed him. Other settlers who hoped to be allowed to homestead 160 acres did as Ard had done, and in time a large number of settlers squatted and used the railroad land as their own. The larger their number, the bolder they grew. They originally based their claim upon the assertion that since Indian title had not been extinguished when the grant was voted, the law was void, and hence all this land was government land and open to homesteading. The first settlers, of course, saw nothing illogical in their having been on Indian land, contrary to law, when the land was given to the railroad. The position of the government was that the railroad land had never been public domain in the sense that it had been open to settlement; it had been transferred directly from the Indians to the railroad.

A new basis for occupancy had to be found. The squatters contended that since the railroad had not completed its line according to schedule, the conditions of the contract by which it had received the grant had not been fulfilled and, by default, the grant land had reverted to the government. Therefore, the land was open to entry by the settlers. Armed with this argument, encouraged by the determined stand of the old settlers, and strong in numbers, the squatters hoped to win their case. They organized the Settlers' Protective Association of the State of Kansas, known locally as the League, and each member paid an annual fee that was used to promote the interests of the whole. The railroad, meanwhile, had sold land to buyers in the East who knew nothing of the dispute and who came West prepared to occupy the land they had bought. The leaguers attempted to drive these buyers away by intimidation and threats. The jumpers built small structures which could be pulled about by horses, moved them onto the land during the night, and in the morning stoutly held possession of their claims. In September, 1866, one hundred purchasers from abroad, who had bought land from the railroad, formed the Bona Fide Purchasers' Association with the purpose of occupying their land; they had heard that the Secretary of the Interior might yield to the squatters and cancel their patents to the land they had bought.

Members of the new organization, called the Anti-Leaguers, were assaulted by armed leaguers, who even entered the homes of antileaguers, and uproarious fights resulted. Blood was shed in these clashes and whole neighborhoods were arrayed against one another in bitter recrimination, which lasted for a generation.[5] The League hired lawyers who kept the lands in litigation for years. Buyers were kept away, and the squatters harvested the prairie hay that grew luxuriantly in the contested area. In the end, with the exception of Ard and a few others who could prove that they had settled on the land before the date it was withdrawn from settlement, the leaguers lost their land.[6]

The Pacific railroads, begun during the early part of the Civil War, also received their land directly from the United States government instead of through a state. These railroads were to run through hundreds of miles of unorganized land, land in which even the territorial status was nebulous. The Northern Pacific Railroad is typical. A 400-foot right-of-way and sufficient land for stations, shops, roundhouses, etc., was given. As a construction subsidy the odd-number sections on each side of the track (within specified limits), were granted to the company. When twenty-five consecutive miles of road had been completed, the government was to survey the adjacent area on each side of the track and patents would be issued. Mineral land, tracts occupied by settlers at the time of the act, and other reserved lands were excepted from the grant. Where a section was withheld, the company was to have the right to select as indemnity, in lieu of lands lost, an equal amount of land from odd-number sections—within defined belts—that were contiguous to the grant lands. The odd-section grants came to be called in land-grant parlance, place lands, and the limits within which they were found were called place limits; the odd-number sections selected as indemnity came to be called lieu land or indem-

[5] *Iola Register* (Iola, Kan.), July 9, September 10, 1886, and January 28, 1887; Alfred Theodore Andreas, *History of the State of Kansas* (2 vols.; Chicago, 1883), I, 671. The author grew up in that community and, as a lad, heard the old-timers recite the misdeeds of the leaguers or antileaguers of forty years before. One of the worst things that could be said about a man was to recall that he was a leaguer or an antileaguer, depending upon the sympathies of the speaker.

[6] Everett Dick, personal interview with Newt Ard, January 2, 1934; Everett Dick, personal interview with Clarence J. Norton, December 29, 1933.

nity land. The defined limits within which these were located were called indemnity limits of the grant. If government-owned land in a grant was not disposed of within three years after completion of the road, it was to be open to homestead and pre-emption, on the same basis as other government land.

Of course, when a railroad grant bill came up in Congress, shrewd men, fully alert to the advantages of homesteading near a railroad, rushed in and filed homesteads or squatted upon the land along the anticipated route, hoping to be near the railroad when it was built and thus reap the advantage of holding valuable land. They knew that a homestead near a railroad would be worth a dozen homesteads in an isolated region.

Since quantities of land in the benefit area on the eastern reaches of the Northern Pacific had been occupied, the railroad had to select indemnity land farther west, much of it beyond the rain belt and therefore less valuable, which led to various irregularities. The General Land Office withdrew the right of settlement on all land between the tentative line of the tracks and the outer bounds of the indemnity belt, pending definite location of the line. Sometimes this kept settlers off the area for long periods, and they had to homestead on land far from the railroad; or settlers illegally squatted on the indemnity area, gambling that they would be able to hold the claims despite the regulations. Due to a lack of alertness by the Secretary of the Interior, the Northern Pacific was allowed to select so much indemnity land that it overdrew its quota and held large quantities of this land for years (it was not until 1940 that this matter was entirely straightened out).[7] One of the first modifications of the land-grant law for the Northern Pacific stated that the company should receive the odd sections to a depth of twenty miles on each side of the track in the states and for forty miles on each side in the territories.

At first, of course, it was impossible to know the exact route of the railroad through the mountainous areas in the western states. Not until July 30, 1870, was the first map of the route through Washington filed and approved, but another map of the amended preliminary survey was filed on February 16, 1872, and the railroad then asked that the land along the new route be withdrawn. The register and the receiver at Walla Walla, following the directions of the Land Commissioner, withdrew from entry all land in forty-mile belts on each side of the new roadway. All of the arrangements were made by the General Land Office, from cutting the size of homesteads to eighty acres to selling pre-emption tracts on the even-number sections at $2.50 an acre. Later, on October 14, 1880, the

7 Dunham, *Government Handout*, p. 114.

Northern Pacific filed a map of the definite location—on still another route—and the withdrawal of odd-number sections for forty miles on each side in the new area was ordered by the General Land Office.

Settlers complained about the withdrawal of land from entry pending the selection of a route. Accepting in good faith that the railroad would actually run through a given area, they had bought land in the railroad belt as indicated by the preliminary or the amended surveys. Anxious to settle near the railroad, they had taken the eighty-acre homesteads or paid $2.50 an acre for pre-emptions, and when the line was finally built, they found themselves far inland from the rail line for which they had paid a double portion to be near. Furthermore, the railroad company had been able to withhold from settlement half of the land over a wide area.

The Secretary of the Interior must have heard the cry of the settlers, for in his report for 1887 he offered several criticisms of the land-grant procedure. Land-grant legislation, he stated, was not in harmony with the theory of free distribution of the land among the people in order to encourage homeownership and thrifty use of the soil. Vast quantities of land had been withdrawn for the exclusive use of the railroads, but few if any of them had constructed their lines within the time prescribed in the granting act, an express condition on which the grants were made. Maps of "probable," "general," "designated," and definite routes had been filed with the department and withdrawals had been granted until the public-land states and territories were tightly gridironed by railroad and indemnity limits. In many instances, he stated, the land limits of one road overlapped and conflicted with those of other roads, and in such a bewildering manner that a settler seeking a home could scarcely find a desirable tract that was not claimed by one, two, or three of the many roads to which Congress or a state had granted land. Even if a settler found a tract apparently not within a grant, he could hardly set up a claim before agents of the corporations would appear and declare that it was within the grant of the railroad, according to right-of-way, lieu land, or construction privileges. The settler, ignorant of law and the facts of the case, would purchase his claim from the company, and in this way—in addition to the lands granted them—the railroads claimed and sold a great deal of land to which they had neither moral nor legal right, the Secretary of the Interior asserted. Thus, confusion, hardships, and impositions upon the settlers were greatly increased by the bold schemes of the corporate agents and by the withdrawal of lands that remained unsurveyed for many years through the failure of Congress to appropriate money. Some railroads had constructed their entire line, others only portions, and still others none, the Secretary asserted, but all had created an effective barrier against the homemaker so far as land was concerned.[8]

It had not been anticipated that settlement in the territories would precede the building of the railroad, and indeed, this settlement probably would not have occurred if the coming of the railroads had not been delayed and if the settlers had not therefore anticipated the railroads and hoped to reap the benefits of accessibility. A considerable number of claimants had settled upon the Northern Pacific's land in Lincoln, Adams, and Franklin counties in Washington, which occasioned the lieu land cases. The Northern Pacific chose the instance of Guilford Miller, who in 1878 settled upon land outside the limits of the map of 1870 but within the limits of the map of 1872. Miller's land was more than forty but less than fifty miles from the track and was therefore reserved by order of the Commissioner in 1872 because it was within the final lieu or indemnity belt. The railroad had selected this tract as indemnity land and the ensuing disagreement was carried through the offices of the Land Commissioner and the Secretary of the Interior.

When the matter came to the attention of President Cleveland, Cleveland said that this withholding of millions of acres from settlement in order after order and the closing of quantities of land to free settlement was contrary to the policy of the United States government. He declared that the land was the heritage of the people and, through the Department of the Interior, decided in favor of Miller. The railroad took other cases to court and litigation dragged on—until many settlers paid dearly for their lands. The final decision was that bona fide settlement prior to 1885 on odd-number sections within indemnity limits gave right to the land; if a settler located after 1885, he lost this land. The railroad did not suffer in the long run, however, for Congress passed a bill that allowed it—if indemnity land had been settled upon—to select land elsewhere. This was a boon to the railroad and the settlers; it saved further litigation, and the railroad chose valuable timberlands that were worth far more than the original grants along the tracks.[9]

The Northern Pacific, although it complained of losing much good land to settlers, was accused of using settlers to secure choice land. According to the charges, the corporation would hire "friends of the company" to file on quantities of worthless land within the place strip in a desert area and

[8] *Report of the Secretary of the Interior, 1887*, I, 89.

[9] Richard F. Steele, *An Illustrated History of the Big Bend Country* [Washington] (Place of publication unknown: Western Historical Publishing Co., 1904), p. 1024.

date their occupancy before 1885, or before the land was withdrawn. Because this land had been "taken," the company was entitled to select lieu tracts within the indemnity area—in a valuable timber region or a good agricultural area.[10] As has been noted, in many cases the railroads failed to complete their commitments in time to meet the requirements of the law, and technically their land grant was forfeited. Settlers would claim this land, which they interpreted as having been restored to the public domain, but unfortunately for them another act of Congress would extend the time allowed the company to complete its lines before it lost the land.

Sometimes disputes arose over the interpretation of a grant, and the settlers, eager to occupy the land and secure the benefit of land on the railroad, did not wait until a decision was handed down. In some cases the settlers lived on contested land for many years before a decision was reached, and every year of occupancy strengthened their claim. Such a situation arose in eastern North Dakota, where a grant was given to the St. Paul, Minneapolis, and Manitoba Railroad, which later became a portion of the Great Northern Railroad.

The grant, in 1857, gave land in Minnesota Territory for the construction of the railroad (at that time what is now North and South Dakota was part of Minnesota). Shortly thereafter, Minnesota was sheared off at the Red River, admitted to the Union as a state, and Dakota Territory was established. The settlers maintained that the admission of Minnesota precluded any grant west of the Red River because that area was no longer Minnesota and the grant was restricted to Minnesota. Hoping to profit from their settlement on lands near the coming railroad and disregarding the railroad claim, they pushed into the Dakota area and occupied both the odd and the even sections. They felt that possession would be in their favor when the matter of ownership was settled. The railroad, of course, maintained that the mere technicality of a change in name did not alter the intent of the grant.

The dispute dragged on for thirty years, with the settlers gaining confidence as their years of occupancy increased. Finally, after decades of litigation, the Supreme Court rendered a decision against the settlers, and the general secretary of the railroad ordered them to move by December 15, 1891. By this time the land was worth twenty to thirty dollars an acre, and some thirty thousand acres of the richest land in the Red River Valley were involved; even some towns were located on railroad land. The settlers declared that the railroad would possess the land over their dead bodies

[10] Dunham, *Government Handout*, p. 285.

and there was talk of taking up arms against the railroad;[11] but finally the matter was compromised.

In a number of cases the United States government extinguished an Indian land title by treaty, usually for a monetary consideration, and sold the tracts to various companies at the per-acre figure that had been given the Indians. The treaties were made by the Department of the Interior and the sale of the lands to the companies was by act of Congress, on the recommendation of the Department of the Interior. Under such an arrangement, the land never technically became part of the government domain, but all disputes were settled by the federal courts.[12]

In southeastern Kansas such a transaction—involving the Missouri River, Fort Scott, and Gulf Railroad (now the Frisco Lines)—caused serious strife. The railroad bought land at a low price per acre, with the thought that when the road was built it would enhance the value of adjacent land and that this increase would be equivalent to a land grant. The land involved was known as the Cherokee Neutral Strip and extended roughly from Fort Scott to the present Oklahoma boundary, along the Frisco Railroad as it is known today. Frontiersmen, as usual, were poised upon the boundary of the Indian reservation, hungering for the land. They presumed that the Indian title would be extinguished and that the area would be opened to homesteaders. Some had squatted upon the tract illegally prior to the railroad's purchase. Then came the unwelcome news that a corporation had bought the strip, and unlike the ordinary land grant—in which half of the land was available for homesteading—the railroad owned every section and anyone who wanted land would have to buy it from the railroad at the company price. Newcomers, seeing the original settlers on the area and sensing that land near a railroad would be very valuable, swarmed over the tract like locusts, hoping by possession and sheer nerve to gain claims.

Illegal though it was, settlers had been getting away with such a practice against the government for years. With the railroad, it was different; no politics was involved—only economics. The settlers nevertheless attempted to use the tactics that had been used against the Indians and the government. When it was learned that the railroad company was taking steps to evict them, they organized to resist. They held mass meetings where inflammatory speeches were made; at one such meeting four

[11] *Omaha Weekly Bee* (Omaha, Nebr.), December 3, 1891, p. 4; *Lincoln Evening News* (Lincoln, Nebr.), December 3, 1891.

[12] Paul Gates, *Fifty Million Acres* (Ithaca: Cornell University Press, 1954), pp. 26, 62–64, 140–150.

thousand people were reported in attendance. The Cherokee Neutral Land League was organized—though there was nothing neutral about its intentions. The settlers organized for war, placing themselves on a military footing; a regiment with battalions and companies was formed and drilled. They carried the war to the enemy and attacked the railroad workers, stopped construction, destroyed equipment, stormed the railroad's land office, burned the prorailroad newspaper at Girard, Kansas, and killed two men because they had bought land from the railroad. Pitched battles took place between railroad forces and the leaguers.

The railroad persuaded the law-abiding citizens to petition the governor for help, and he called upon the President for federal troops to put down the armed resistance to government. In response, President Grant in 1869 sent troops into the tract to restore order. The railroad then proceeded with construction, but when the company attempted to eject those who were occupying railroad land for which they refused to pay, widespread excitement and violence again resulted and all land business came to a standstill. President Grant then sent four companies of soldiers into the region to restore order, and the railroad and the squatters rested on their arms while they awaited the decision of the Supreme Court on the matter.

Eventually the troops were withdrawn and the Court handed down its decision. Only those on the tract when the treaty was signed were protected; they obtained their land for the appraised price of two dollars an acre, but all others had to pay from four to six dollars an acre. The railroad was conciliatory and arranged compromise terms and agreements, cutting the cost below the market price.[13] It is interesting to note that the settlers were not antagonistic to the railroad as a transportation agency; they wanted the land free, as homesteads or at the price paid to the Indians; at the same time they wanted the railroad near them. The fact that the railroad was building in that area made settlement adjacent to the proposed route more attractive. At this very time, tens of thousands of citizens on free land secured by homesteading were voting for county or city bonds to secure a railroad through their areas.

A dispute involving a Spanish land claim arose along the Western Pacific's line in San Joaquin County, California. The company had fixed

[13] Lulu Lemon Brown, *Cherokee Neutral Lands Controversy* (Girard, Kan.: privately printed, 1931), pp. 8–46; *Fort Scott Monitor* (Fort Scott, Kan.), January 20, February 24, April 7, May 19, 26, June 2, 9, 1869; *Cherokee Sentinel* (Baxter Springs, Kan.), November 27, 1868, October 26, 1871; Eugene F. Ware, "The Neutral Lands," *Transactions* of the Kansas State Historical Society, VI (Topeka: Kansas State Historical Society, 1900), 147–149.

its line across the Spanish grant, Moquelemos, whose ownership was in litigation. It was not known whether the tract would be declared public domain and subject to a railroad grant or private property and therefore not eligible for a railroad grant. Probably the settlers reasoned that since the land was under litigation and the situation uncertain, a settler could retain the land he had occupied. At any rate, as was customary in California, settlers chose to squat on the land. If the land was declared a bona fide Spanish grant and not public domain, they would be illegal occupants; if it was declared public domain, the railroad company would secure its grant. In the latter case, however, there was one bright prospect: those on even-number sections that had been surveyed would be entitled to land. While the Spanish claim was under litigation, the General Land Office, unaware of the uncertainty of title or feeling certain the claims were fraudulent, issued patents for the odd-number sections to the Western Pacific, and the company then sold the land to disinterested persons. In the end, after much litigation, the railroad won the case and the settlers on the odd-number sections lost the land and their improvements.[14]

In Oregon a dispute arose as the result of fraud by state officials. In the 1860's the state of Oregon was given three sections per mile of road for the construction of the Oregon Central and the Willamette Valley and Cascade Mountain wagon roads. When people learned that the roads were not being constructed according to the terms of the grants, squatters moved in and occupied the granted lands. The members of Congress, upon being apprised that neither road had been built, graded, or even cleared—that only an old Indian trail had been surveyed—declared by joint resolution that if any of the grants had been patented, the patents were fraudulent. The government thereupon authorized suits to vacate such lands as had been patented and directed that they be placed in the public domain once more. It seemed that the settlers had won their land from the United States government, but when suit was instituted to vacate the land, evidence showed that of the land allotted to the Oregon Central, forty thousand acres had been patented on certification of the governor that the road had been built, and that was conclusive. The settlers on the land grant to the state of Oregon lost their land, road or no road.

To facilitate construction, railroad companies were allowed to take materials from the public lands adjacent to the line, and Secretary of the Interior Henry M. Teller broadened the interpretation of "adjacent" to

[14] (No author), *History of San Joaquin County* [California] (Chicago, 1890), p. 97.

mean anywhere within fifty miles of the track. In this way he allowed the railroads to turn a limited privilege into an abuse. A flagrant abuse was that of the Union River Logging Company, which purported to be an adjunct of railroad building in the state of Washington. It applied to the General Land Office for right-of-way privileges, built a five-mile track into dense stands of timber, and proceeded to carry on a logging business for years, denuding an entire forest area.

Although the railroads were not always directly responsible for the reckless exploitation of natural resources because they often secured materials through contractors, those who procured stone, ties, piling, and fuel ranged far and wide in their exploitation of government forest lands. In Colorado and Wyoming tie hacks followed the headwaters of the North Platte, along the Laramie River and the Cache la Poudre, and floated their ties down the swollen streams in the flood tide of spring. In 1879 a tie contractor secured a contract to deliver 100,000 ties at Fort Collins, Colorado, for construction purposes.

The terms of a land grant ordinarily provided that when a railroad had completed a specified number of consecutive miles it could pay for its surveys and the government would then survey the land and grant a patent, but this enabled the railroads to postpone the surveys and hold the land until it was convenient to sell. If the title did not rest in the company, railroad land could not be taxed by the states. In the meantime its land increased in value and time was allowed to sell it advantageously. Nebraska attempted to tax Union Pacific lands, claiming that since the company could sell or mortgage them at will, the lands were taxable. When suit was carried to the United States Supreme Court, however, that body ruled in favor of the railroad, with the result that it continued its policy of applying for patents only insofar as this was convenient.[15] The Kansas Pacific Railroad in this manner withheld ten million acres from the tax rolls in a strip fifty miles wide through the heart of Kansas. The company was not anxious to patent its lands until the country was settled.

One thing worked in favor of those who bought railroad land, however. Not only was the railroad tax-exempt but purchasers of its land likewise were untaxed until the end of their contract (often ten years) and all payments had been made. The railroad then patented the land and turned it over to the purchaser, without any taxes having been paid by either railroad or settler during the years the land had been increasing in value. On the other hand, the homesteader's land was assessed for taxes on the first day of March following his final proof, even before his patent had been

15 Nelson Trottman, *History of the Union Pacific* (New York: Ronald Press, 1923), p. 116.

issued. It is small wonder, then, that during the farmers' revolt in the 1880's and 1890's these hard-pressed taxpayers had a special hatred for the railroads. Later on, in President Coolidge's administration, when the Northern Pacific was charged with taking more land than it was entitled to, the company's legal staff pleaded that the government's neglect in surveying had caused confusion over the amount of land to which the company was entitled.

Sometimes, after a railroad had built through the country and was holding a large grant, a second line through the same general area was given a grant of like dimensions. In that case the second railroad had to be given land farther west or there was an overlapping of the two grants. The latter was the case when the Burlington Railroad was granted land along its east-west line from Plattsmouth to Fort Kearney, Nebraska, where it was to make a junction with the Union Pacific line. The two lines ran somewhat parallel, and since much of the land had been given to the Union Pacific and a considerable amount had been settled, the Burlington was granted a vast area north of the Union Pacific's. This created a divided Burlington grant, with one area lying along the Burlington line south of the Platte River and one far north of the Platte and the Union Pacific lands, many miles away from the Burlington Railroad but subject to the same conditions as if it lay along the track. A correspondent of the *Nebraska Statesman* voiced the objection of the settlers on Burlington lands north of the Union Pacific grant: they would be no more benefited by the Burlington than by a railroad in China, and because the lands taken by the Burlington might have been used as a grant to coax another railroad to build a line through their area, they were doubly penalized. Furthermore, they were surrounded by land on which no taxes were paid, which meant higher taxes for them, and at the same time they were deprived of transportation.[16]

Railroad land was disposed of in various ways, depending upon the ethics of the directors and the needs of the road. The Burlington set up a land commission and sold its own land, and its organization included a corps of agents in the East, each in charge of a county or more. The agents worked on a commission, held passes for their own use, and were authorized

---

[16] Richard C. Overton, *Burlington West, A Colonization History of the Burlington Railroad* (Cambridge: Harvard University Press, 1941), pp. 331–332. The transcontinental Western Union telegraph line, as an internal improvement, received 160 acres for every fifteen miles of line strung from Omaha to California in 1861, in addition to an annual cash subsidy for twenty years; Alfred N. Chandler, *Land Title Origins* (New York: Robert Schalkenbach Foundation, 1928), p. 503.

to issue half-fare tickets to prospective buyers who would travel west and look over the land.[17] The records show that a Burlington representative received five dollars for advertising Nebraska land at the Republican Convention of 1880. In the 1870's the company had a policy of offering selected newspaper editors a trip over the line, together with a pass for a friend or member of the family, in exchange for publishing an occasional article of general interest concerning Iowa or Nebraska. A Chicago, Milwaukee, or Indianapolis editor could thus take a trip west and at the same time gather news. Naturally, he wrote about the glowing prospects of the country along the Burlington's lines. This kept the West and railroad land before the people and was a constant encouragement for settlement.

Agents also were sent to various countries abroad to lecture on land in America. In the early 1870's the competition between the Santa Fe, Burlington, Union Pacific, and Northern Pacific was keen in Europe. Agents distributed lithographed pictures, maps, and flowery descriptions of the territory through which their particular roads ran. Probably an attempt was made to give a fairly accurate picture, and yet it was human under the circumstances to depict the favorable side, making little mention of the hardships and more unfortunate aspects of frontier life on the Plains. Alluring offers were made. Reduced fares were offered for passengers and reduced rates on baggage and freight. Free seed was sometimes given. Houses were furnished for immigrants where the families of landlookers could stay while the head of the family went ahead to prepare a home. Immigrant trains were equipped with stoves for cooking and booths where the passengers could use their own bedding in a makeshift sleeper. Moreover, the railroads tried to help the settlers succeed. In 1873, during the financial panic, they reduced the price of land, and during the "grasshopper years" in Nebraska and Kansas they organized relief programs. At times, they lowered freight rates or provided free carriage of relief goods and the seed for the next year's sowing.

The Santa Fe Railroad sent C. R. Schmidt to Russia to urge the German Mennonites, a conscientious objector sect persecuted in Russia and Germany, to move to America. The company at one time carried seventeen cars of immigrants free of charge from Pennsylvania to Kansas, and gave free tickets good for three months to the Mennonites. In 1874 about nineteen hundred Mennonites arrived at Topeka and attracted much attention by their unusual dress and manners, but they brought with them

[17] "Burlington Railroad, Letter Book of the Land Commissioner, 1880–1881," MS in the Newberry Library, Chicago, pp. 581 ff.

a quarter of a million dollars in gold. The railroad housed them in empty car shops in Topeka for about a month. Later, the Mennonites purchased sixty thousand acres of land.[18]

When the railroads advertised "Free Homes for the Millions" they did not exaggerate, for alternate sections within the grants were government land and consequently free, and all land outside the grants was free. The companies were not badly disappointed if an immigrant chose government land inasmuch as settlement along a railroad meant increased traffic and raised the value of unsold railroad land. The Northern Pacific, however, was concerned about the possibility that Santa Fe or Burlington agents would meet their immigrant parties in Chicago and persuade them to go to Kansas or Nebraska, where they would be lost to the Northern Pacific.

An example of late nineteenth-century pioneering is that of a Dunker colony that in 1894 left Walkertown, Indiana, in a special train of thirty immigrant coaches, each equipped with stoves and crude sleeping accommodations. Large banners were strung upon the coaches: "From Indiana to the Rich Free Government Lands in North Dakota, via the Famous Red River Valley, the Bread Basket of America." To whip up enthusiasm, the agent who accompanied the train made sure that it traveled through Indiana, Illinois, and Wisconsin in the daytime. The western states aided in these attempts to settle the railroad lands; a number of them maintained immigration commissions and sent agents to Europe to influence homeseekers to settle in their states. Although many immigrants took homesteads, much land was bought from the railroads.[19]

State or territorial laws were passed to create a more favorable climate for settling the area along the railroads. A law of 1873 organized twenty-seven counties wholly within the limits of present-day North Dakota and five counties partly within its boundaries. These counties were organized to facilitate the sale of bonds for the Northern Pacific Railroad inasmuch as maps could be drawn that showed the counties and gave the effect of a well-settled, prosperous region that supplied heavy traffic, which also was an enticement to immigrants. Edwin A. Curley, a British agricultural observer, noted that in Nebraska, prior to bringing their land into the market, the railroad land experts re-examined their tracts quarter section by quarter section and classified and appraised them. He said he had

---

[18] Abraham Albrecht, "Mennonite Settlement in Kansas" (Master's thesis, University of Kansas, 1925), pp. 29–38.

[19] Everett Dick, *The Sod-House Frontier* (New York: D. Appleton-Century, 1937), Chapter XIV.

examined several hundred square miles of these tracts without finding a single misrepresentation or intentional error.

The terms of sale seem easy or lenient, viewed from our time. The Union Pacific offered eleven years' credit with 10 per cent down payment, and interest at 6 or 7 per cent. For the first three years, until the home-maker became established, the Burlington required him to pay the interest only. Often, a 25 per cent discount of the original price was allowed for cash. The average price at which the Burlington sold its entire Nebraska tract was $5.14 per acre, but great quantities of it were sold at twenty-five cents an acre. Figures may be misleading in this matter, however, since directors of the railroad companies sometimes formed a land company and sold the land to themselves at a low price, which stands on the records as the selling price. The railroad books thus showed only a small profit, or even a deficit, but the same men sold this land at a much higher figure, making a handsome profit for themselves at the expense of the stockholders of the railroads. Correspondence between the settlers and the land commissioners of the railroads indicates that the roads were lenient with those who were delinquent if they gave evidence of trying to make their payments. Misfortune, loss of crops from drought, hail, and grasshoppers, or other reasons for inability to make prompt payment were taken into consideration and eviction came only as the last resort, when a settler had shown no intention of living up to his obligation.[20]

Some roads allowed a holder of stocks or bonds to exchange them for land. Since the public's faith in a railroad often was at low ebb, the stocks and bonds frequently sold for almost nothing and such an exchange would procure land at a cheap rate. At one time such an exchange of Northern Pacific stock would have secured the choice lands in the Red River Valley, for which $2.50 an acre was asked, for fifty to sixty cents an acre.

After the bankruptcy of Jay Cook in the 1870's, the reputation of the Northern Pacific struck rock bottom. The press spoke of the line as a bankrupt enterprise, with no prospect of resurrection; there was nothing, it said, to support the road because the country through which it was projected—with the exception of a few miles in Minnesota and the Red River Valley in Dakota—was worthless. With half-breed scrip, military scrip, and homesteads available, it was difficult to get anyone to buy railroad stock.

In the winter of 1873 the land commissioner of the Northern Pacific

[20] See the correspondence of the land commissioner with land purchasers, "Burlington Railroad, Letter Book of the Land Commissioner, 1880–1881," Newberry Library, Chicago.

conceived the idea of setting up proof of the value of the land offered. He persuaded some of the reluctant directors to form a pool, buy a quantity of land, and prove its worth by actual farming. The directors acquiesced, bought sixteen sections in the Red River Valley, and hired Oliver Dalrymple, a Minnesota farmer, to manage the enterprise. This was the origin of what came to be known as bonanza farming in eastern North Dakota, and the scheme was a success from the start. Dalrymple also acquired land in his own right and managed at least two other concerns, until by 1880 he was in command of 55,000 acres. A brigade of seven or eight plows moved down the field, and a twenty-plow brigade would turn a section in a week. Dalrymple was able to raise twenty bushels of wheat to the acre. This method proved not only profitable for the farmer-directors, but when the agents broadcast the news, it started another boom in railroad real estate.[21]

When James J. Hill came into control of the railroad fragments that he welded into the Great Northern, he adopted a policy of encouraging settlers to buy land; and his plan was known as the rebate system. It had been discovered that the cost of breaking ground was $2.50 an acre and that the cost of putting in a crop and harvesting it was fifty cents an acre (if three-fourths of the tract was cropped). The company deducted these items from the price of the land, provided that it was cultivated for three years. Since, in 1885, land was offered at six to eight dollars an acre, this meant an approximate reduction of 50 per cent.[22]

During the 1870's the farmers' lack of prosperity culminated in the Granger movement, and during the late 1880's in the Farmers' Alliance, and finally in the 1890's the Populist movement. The West, which had wanted railroads more than any other thing except land, now saw the roads as the incarnation of all the evils that had wrecked the prospect of frontier prosperity. The multiplicity of litigation in which the railroads had engaged in order to secure their land, together with the fact that tens of thousands owed money to the railroads, left a bitter feeling toward the corporations. On top of this, low crop prices, depression years, and droughts made it most difficult for settlers to pay for their land, and all of this led to widespread condemnation of the railroads as the number one enemy of the settlers. After the great orgy of land giveaways, the people began to consider how they might recover some of the land that had been

---

[21] Owen G. Libby (ed.), "Bonanza Farms and the One Crop System of Agriculture," *Collections* of the State Historical Society of North Dakota (Bismarck: North Dakota State Historical Society, 1910), III, 344, 569–580.

[22] *Ibid.*, pp. 587, 588.

178   THE LURE OF THE LAND

handed out in such a prodigal fashion. Laws between 1885 and 1890 demanded the forfeiture of unearned or surplus railroad lands, but these were largely gestures since the railroads successfully resisted the efforts in the courts.[23] In a few instances the attempts succeeded; for example, as early as 1870 Congress revoked all grants to Louisiana for railroads, and two railroads lost all of their grants in 1872.

By 1905, the great "government handout," as Professor Harold Dunham calls it, was over. The United States government had given away seventy-nine land grants, consisting of 155 million acres, to encourage railroad construction.[24] During the late nineteenth century, due to reaction against the land grant for internal improvements, farmers and conservationists came to feel that it was a tragic error for the United States government to have given the land—the heritage of the people—to giant corporations, which they charged were the worst enemies of the public on account of their monopolistic practices and their political hold upon state governments. And yet in spite of the weaknesses and inefficient management of the land-grant program, it was not entirely evil by any means. A tourist has only to travel in some of the underdeveloped countries and observe their limited transportation facilities to understand why they are backward. Certainly these land subsidies made it possible for the United States to spread a network of railroads across the country such as is not found in any other country in the world, and this was a paramount factor in making the United States the dominant economic power on earth.

Another factor to the credit of the railroads, often entirely overlooked, is that, as W. W. Robinson points out, the railroad grants were not outright unconditional gifts. In part payment for its help in giving this land for railroad construction, the government required the railroads to haul the mail and handle government traffic at less than the regular charges; this has been a reduction of tremendous importance to the public. The Southern Pacific Railroad estimated that by the close of World War II the land-grant reductions for all railroads in the United States reached a total of over a billion dollars, or more than eight times the value of the lands at the time they were given to the railroads—estimated by the Southern Pacific at 123 million dollars.[25]

[23] Roy M. Robbins, *Our Landed Heritage* (Lincoln: University of Nebraska Press, 1962), p. 279.
[24] *Report of the Public Lands Commission, 1905*, S. Doc. 189, 58th Cong., 3d Sess., Appendix, p. 134.
[25] William W. Robinson, *Land in California* (Berkeley: University of California Press, 1948), p. 157.

The first settlement of the Ohio Associates at Marietta. It was to accommodate this company that the surveying system of the public lands was developed in 1785. [See Chap. 2.]

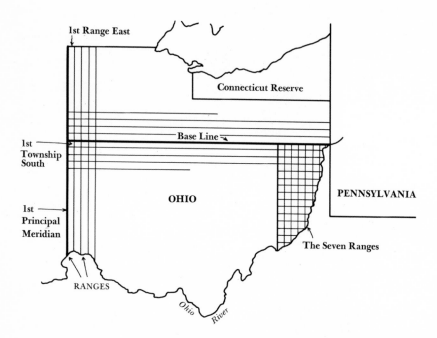

1st Range East

Connecticut Reserve

Base Line

1st
Township
South

OHIO

PENNSYLVANIA

1st
Principal
Meridian

The Seven Ranges

RANGES

Ohio River

An Ordinance of 1785 providing for the national surveying system established the base line, or geographer's line, due west from the point at which the Ohio River intersects the western boundary of Pennsylvania. The first principal meridian later became the boundary between Ohio and Indiana. To accommodate settlers who were streaming into the area, the seven ranges were marked off in an exception to the normal surveying procedures.

6 Miles

36	30	24	18	12	6
35	29	23	17	11	5
34	28	22	16	10	4
33	27	21	15	9	3
32	26	20	14	8	2
31	25	19	13	7	1

6 Miles

The methods of numbering sections as provided for in the Ordinance of 1785 (left) and the act of 1796 (below, left). The latter system has remained in effect to the present day.

6 Miles

6	5	4	3	2	1
7	8	9	10	11	12
18	17	16	15	14	13
19	20	21	22	23	24
30	29	28	27	26	25
31	32	33	34	35	36

6 Miles

Township

640 Acres–1 Mile Square

Half-Section
320 acres

Quarter-Section
160 acres

Half-Quarter Section
80 acres

Qtr-Qtr Sect
40 acres

1 Mile

Whole Section

SYSTEM OF PUBIC LANDS SURVEY—1796

DIAGRAM C

Illustrating mode of establishing Stone, Post and Mound Corners

Township Corner Stone with mound of Stone

Section Corner Stone with pits and mound of earth

Quarter Section Corner with mound of earth

From Instructions of the Commissioner of the General
Land Office to the Surveyors General *(1881)*

Types of mounds used to mark corners of townships, sections, and quarter sections. Posts and stones (upper diagram) were used where stones were available. If stones were not to be had, the township corner was to be made of earth, as were the section (center diagram) and quarter section (lower diagram) corner markers. [See p. 22 for a description of markers.]

W. H. Jackson Photograph, Courtesy Department of Interior

Surveyors' camp, Cache Valley, Utah. [See Chap. 3.]

Front and rear of the United States land office at Garden City, Kansas, in 1885. Fifty thousand acres were taken daily, and when crowds blockaded the halls and stairway, the land attorneys accommodated their clients through back windows. [See Chap. 4.]

A California vaquero at work in 1841 near San Jose Mission. [See Chap. 6.]

A lithograph of Sacramento in 1850, about the time of the squatter war. Within one year after its founding the city had 10,000 residents. [See Chap. 7.]

Montana Historical Society

Panning for gold. [See Chap. 7.]

Lead miners at work. [See Chap. 7.]

State Historical Society of Wisconsin

Mining with a rocker in Bear Gulch in the Black Hills. [See Chap. 7.]

A miners' meeting in the Black Hills. [See Chap. 7.]

A HABITABLE DWELLING

A HOUSE "TWELVE BY FOURTEEN"

A BONA FIDE RESIDENCE

From Albert D. Richardson, Beyond the Mississippi *(1867)*

To prevent preemption frauds, the Commissioner of the U.S. General Land Office directed land officers to examine the claimant as to the kind of improvements the preemptor had on his claim. The preemptor had to swear that he had a habitable dwelling at least twelve by fourteen with a glass window in it and that this was his bona fide residence. [See Chap. 8.]

Nebraska State Historical Society

On the road to Oregon was the crossing of the South Platte River near Julesburg, Colorado, sketched above by W. H. Jackson on July 25, 1866. The yokes of eight oxen were double-teamed to pull the wagons over, and then returned for another haul. [See Chap. 9.]

United States Department of Interior

Making improvements on the prairies in fulfillment of the requirement of the Homestead Act. [See Chap. 10.]

The crackerbox board and tarpaper cabin was commonly used as a claim shack in parts of the Dakotas, Montana, and Wyoming in the latter part of the homestead period. This one is being walled up with sod to ensure warmth. [See Chap. 10.]

These immigrants arriving in the Flathead Valley of Montana in the first quarter of the twentieth century came mostly from eastern states. They brought their implements and livestock in box cars. Arriving at destination, the box cars were opened and wagons were reassembled and equipment and household goods were hauled to the claims. [See Chap. 10.]

——THE——

Sioux City & Pacific Railroad

IS THE ONLY LINE OF RAILAWY RUNNING UP THE

BEAUTIFUL ELKHORN VALLEY

——WHICH IS——

The Garden Spot of Nebraska!

IN CONNECTION WITH THE

CHICAGO, ST. PAUL. MINNEAPOLIS & OMAHA RY.

This line runs from OMAHA up this entire Valley to its source, thence through the vast well noted

HOMESTEAD COUNTY

KNOWN AS THE

Free Homes for the Million

—— TO ——

FORT NIOBRARA ON THE NIOBRARA RIVER,

AND FORMS THE

SHORT LINE TO THE BLACK HILLS.

THE SIOUX CITY & PACIFIC RAILROAD,
(IOWA DIVISION.)

With its connections, constitutes the celebrated

"Sioux City Route,"

——OR THE——

KANSAS CITY, OMAHA & ST. PAUL SHORT LINE,

Which is the ONLY LINE running solid trains between COUNCIL BLUFFS and St. PAUL, and the ONLY LINE which runs

Pullman Palace Sleeping Cars,

BETWEEN

KANSAS CITY and ST. PAUL WITHOUT CHANGE.

☞ Be sure your tickets read via the SIOUX CITY & PACIFIC R. R.

P. E. HALL, General Manager,   J. R. BUCHANAN, Gen'l Pass. Agt.
            Cedar Rapids, Iowa.   Missouri Valley, Iowa.

Free homes for the million (or millions, as it was sometimes stated) appeared in advertisements such as this, which were widely distributed in America and overseas by the railroads to lure the land hungry to the railroad land and free land adjacent to the rail line. This advertisement appeared in the *Nebraska State Gazeteer and Business Directory* for 1882–1883. [See Chap. 10.]

In 1827 a land grant to the Wabash and Lake Erie Canal (shown above) set the precedent for the alternate section land grant system used extensively in land grants to railroads. [See Chap. 11.]

When the Northern Pacific failed to sell its land in small lots, some of the members of the company bought many sections and hired them farmed to prove productivity. It became known as Bonanza Farming. [See Chap. 11.]

Union Pacific Railroad

Dale Creek bridge was built entirely of wood to span Dale Creek in Wyoming. It was 125 feet high and 500 feet long and almost all the timber used was transported from Chicago. The bridge was completed in thirty working days. [See Chap. 11.]

Union Pacific Railroad

The Narrows began about four miles west of Echo, Utah, and 995 miles west of Omaha. This was some of the most difficult grading in the building of the Union Pacific. Successive shelves were hacked in rock, then pick-axed and blasted down to grade. Rough temporary tracks were laid to haul rubble away. On higher levels two-wheeled mule carts and wheelbarrows did the job. [See Chap. 11.]

Harper's Weekly

Rafting logs through the Dells on the Wisconsin River. [See Chap. 12.]

National Archives

This Montana Territory ranch in 1872 is indicative of the primitive facilities, as evidenced by chinked logs and dirt roof of the bunkhouse, which is conveniently located near the corrals. [See Chap. 14.]

WAITING FOR A CHINOOK

The Last of 5000.

Montana Historical Society

Blizzards raised havoc with western cattle herds. The painting above, "Waiting for a Chinook," or "The Last of 5,000," is a water color Charles Russell made at a cow camp on an old collar box and sent to his employer as a report of the condition of the herd in the winter of 1886–1887. [See Chap. 14.]

Masked cattlemen—Gunnysackers—killing sheep and driving away their herders. [See Chap. 15.]

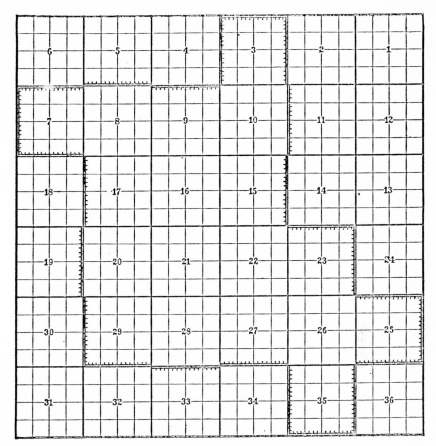

A, having purchased the odd-numbered sections from the railroad in the township represented, starts his fence at the northeast corner of section 9 and builds along the north line of that section. Arriving at the northwest corner of section 9, he puts in a post on the southeast side of the corner-stone between sections 9 and 5, and his fence stops at that post. He then puts in a similar post on section 5 on the northwest side of the north corner-stone, and from 12 to 13 inches from the post in the northwest corner of section 9. Being now on section 5, which he owns by purchase from the railroad, he runs his fence along on section 5, and diagonally opposite to the northeast corner of section 7, where a similar gap of from 12 to 18 inches is made. This he jumps across to section 7; and so on around the entire inclosure. Precisely the same method is resorted to in Arizona.

Secretary of Interior Report, 1887

How to buy railroad land and enclose the public domain, as practiced in Wyoming in the late 1880's.

Voting for the first mayor of Guthrie, Oklahoma, 1889. [See Chap. 16.]

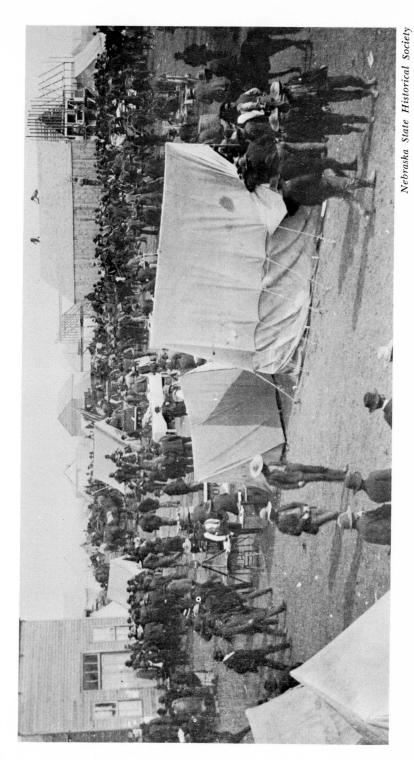

Guthrie, Oklahoma, ten days old. [See Chap. 16.]

The booths at Orlando where 36,000 registered for the race into the Cherokee Strip, Sept. 1893. [See Chap. 17.]

The first train leaving the line for Perry, Sept. 16, 1893. [See Chap. 17.]

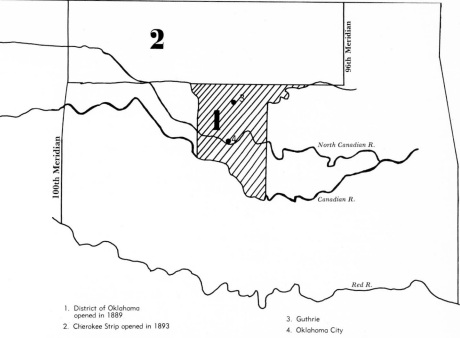

1. District of Oklahoma opened in 1889
2. Cherokee Strip opened in 1893
3. Guthrie
4. Oklahoma City

Oklahoma at the time of the land openings. [See Chap. 17.]

Harper's Weekly

Troops of the 9th Cavalry (Colored) escorting Boomers out of Indian Territory in 1885. [See Chap. 17.]

General Robert G. Dyrenforth conducted rain-making experiments in Texas during the drought of the 1890's. He used dynamite and oxy-hydrogen balloons. [See Chap. 18.]

Courtesy of Vernon Carner

Another type of rain-making device which was used in Nebraska. [See Chap. 18.]

The drought of the 1890's, especially west of the 100th meridian, gave great impetus to irrigation. One method advocated for small acreages was with the windmill and home storage reservoir. [See Chap. 18.]

The drought of the 1930's far exceeded in severity all previous weather calamities, as this Kansas farm home half buried in drifting sand so eloquently testifies. [See Chap. 18.]

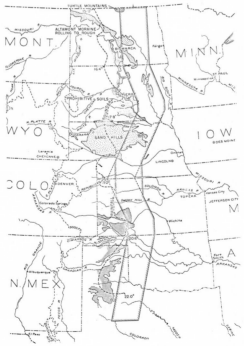

The dusty thirties required new soil and vegetation management techniques. Among these was the shelterbelt to slow the erosive forces of Great Plains winds and protect the growing crops from the hot summer blasts. [See Chap. 18.]

Despite increased prevention by lookout towers such as the one at Squaw Mountain, Colorado, at the left, countless acres of forest succumb annually to fire. [See Chap. 19.]

Forest ranger in Santa Fe National Forest, July 27, 1907. [See Chap. 19.]

Theodore Roosevelt Dam and Reservoir on Salt River, Arizona. [See Chap. 19.]

eedbeds in Bessey Nursery, Nebraska National Forest. [See Chap. 19.]

.and drawing held at Broken Bow, Nebraska, probably in 1913. [See Chap. 19.]

Counting sheep into Wasatch National Forest, Utah. [See Chap. 19.]

KILLING THE PROLIFIC GOOSE.

Public sentiment for conservation was aroused by Theodore Roosevelt. [See Chap. 19.]

XII

Timber and the Public Domain

THE FRONTIER ATTITUDE toward timber on public lands was based on the pioneers' belief that government land belonged to the people as much as the sunshine and air; moreover, during the first quarter of the nineteenth century the settled areas were so densely wooded that the great problem was to clear the land and burn the logs in preparation for farming. As settlement reached the lightly timbered region, the early settler felt it was not wrong "to visit Uncle Sam," as it was called, for wood or rails. As a result, later settlers would often find that their claims had been stripped of their valuable timber; then, when they were ready to fence their fields, they might have to buy rails from the intact oak groves of the identical persons who had denuded their claims. It was only one step from this custom of domestic use to exploitation of the timber resources.

Timberlands were denuded even before the land of "oak openings" and prairies were reached in the westward march of settlement. One of the earliest recorded instances occurred in 1811, near the mouth of the Homochitto River, where the citizens cut cypress trees, made rafts of the logs, and floated them down the Mississippi.[1] People also sought bark for the tannery trade. John Badollet, on April 25, 1814, wrote to Edward Tiffin, Commissioner of the General Land Office, that persons holding Virginia treasury warrants were cutting timber in Illinois and Indiana territories near the Ohio River. They defended their trespass on the pretense that the lowlands in these territories, which occasionally were flooded, were islands in the Ohio River that belonged to Kentucky and that the land was subject to entry with the warrants they held. On May 4, Badollet wrote:

Large speculations in oak and other bark for tanneries are, I am told, going on under colour of those pretended titles, and the great devasta-

[1] Governor David Holmes to Mr. Taylor, in Clarence Edwin Carter (ed.), *The Territorial Papers of the United States*, VII (Washington, D.C.: Govt. Printing Office, 1938), 224.

tion which is already or will be made in consequence thereof along the
Ohio on the United States lands, is an object which calls for an immediate remedy. The allarm [sic] along the Ohio is general.[2]

Another abuse occurred in Vigo County, Indiana, in 1816. During the
era of the sale of lands on the installment plan, and to accommodate those
who did not have the money or who were unprepared to make the full payment, buyers were allowed to make entry upon payment of sixteen dollars
or 5 per cent of the full amount. This payment held the land for forty days,
and during this time every valuable tree could be removed. If no other
purchaser appeared, the occupier was allowed ninety days to complete the
process of looting the quarter section.

The *Missouri Gazette* of February 6, 1818, noted that squatters were despoiling the old Spanish claims that had not been confirmed. In Alabama
in 1814, people were settling on school lands and despoiling them of their
trees. About the same time, at Vincennes, Indiana, a steam sawmill was
erected and a contract was made with an individual, who owned only an
acre of land within reach of the mill, to furnish two thousand saw logs. The
register furnished this information to the General Land Office and asked
that a United States attorney be appointed to prosecute such cases, but
nothing was done to back the register in his efforts to save the nation's
timber. Probably the Commissioner was unable to convince the Treasury
Department and the President of the need to take direct action to prosecute
the depredators.

In 1817, however, Congress provided a penalty for cutting trees of use to
the navy (oak and red cedar) on the public lands. Under the stimulus of
that act and under the general laws against intrusion, the government
warned all intruders of its intention to prosecute if the devastation of its
forests continued, but attempts to halt the use of the timber ran contrary to
the best immediate interests of the frontier. Indeed, a law of 1800 gave pre-
emption rights to anyone who had erected a sawmill or gristmill upon public land—and what was a sawmill for if not to saw logs? And if the mill was
on government land, from whence would the logs be likely to come?

When, about 1820, the government warned intruders to cease cutting
trees on United States land, the Lower Mississippi Valley residents replied
that if cutting timber on the public domain ceased, steamboats would have
to go out of business because the government owned all of the trees for

[2] John Badollet to Edward Tiffin, Commissioner of the General Land Office, April 25
and May 4, 1814, in "Letters Received from Vincennes, Ind.," Vol. 20, General Land
Office, MS, Department of Interior, National Archives.

three hundred miles on the west side of the Mississippi. It would be impossible, they argued, to furnish needed fuel without securing it from government-owned land. It never occurred to the frontiersman that the land might be bought and the trees cut from privately owned land.

M. Lyon, shortly before he ran for election as a representative from Arkansas, wrote to the Commissioner of the General Land Office to give the frontier viewpoint. He argued that the land would be more valuable to the farmer-settler after it was partially cleared and that the government would not be able to secure convictions. If a jury was patriotic, Lyon said, it would judge that where there was no damage there was no trespass. By way of emphasizing that the trees were of little value, he claimed that Louisiana and Mississippi owners wanted to sell the wood on their land but had more than could be sold on the market in a hundred years.[3]

A meeting of the grand jury of the district court of Michigan Territory at Detroit on May 24, 1830, sent a signed report to the Commissioner of the General Land Office informing him that serious depredations were being committed upon the public lands. The document stated that the loss was very heavy because the land being cut over was valuable chiefly for its, timber—it having been passed over by settlers as unfit for agriculture. The jury was incensed especially by the fact that the principal offenders came from across the international boundary. The report stated that the district attorney had prosecuted cases of depredation, but it was difficult to obtain witnesses who would testify to the exact tracts where the acts took place, and although the general fact of timber-cutting was well known, invariably the culprits had been released. The jury called the attention of the Commissioner to the fact that the Attorney General had given his opinion that there was no act of Congress against cutting timber on the public domain, except oak and red cedar, which were reserved for naval purposes, and they suggested that it would be wise for Congress to provide a penalty for timber depredation.[4] A law was enacted in 1831—perhaps in response to this appeal—which forbade the removal of timber from all lands of the United States, but enforcement was sporadic and fruitless during the next twenty years. In the meantime, the lumber industry had entered a new epoch. During the first two decades of the nineteenth century the great majority of settlers considered trees a nuisance. Aside from firewood a

[3] M. Lyon to the Commissioner of the General Land Office, *Arkansas Gazette*, May 21, 1822.

[4] Report of the Grand Jury of the District Court, Detroit, Mich., May 24, 1830, in "Miscellaneous Letters to Commissioner of Public Lands," MS in the National Archives, XXV, 227.

farmer had no use for timber beyond constructing fences and a few buildings, and since everyone had plenty of trees to erect his own buildings, there was almost no local market for lumber. However, as settlement crept out onto the prairies in the 1830's and 1840's, a new market for lumber opened up. The great treeless area of western Indiana, central Illinois, southern Wisconsin, and Iowa furnished a tremendous market. For the first time in the history of the public lands the wood products of a vast portion of government-owned land were needed in quantity for export to neighboring communities. As early as 1836, long wagon trains of lumber from the Wabash country traveled into northern Illinois, where the lumber was sold for as much as $100 per thousand feet. When the first capitol of the Wisconsin Territory was built at Belmont in 1836, the pine lumber for its construction was secured on the headwaters of the Allegheny River. It was brought down the Ohio and up the Mississippi to Galena, Illinois, where it was unloaded and hauled overland by wagon.

Because vast forest resources in Michigan, Wisconsin, and Minnesota were located near lakes and rivers and were convenient for transportation, farseeing persons soon seized the golden opportunity of exploiting the rich pine forests and marketing lumber in the needy adjacent treeless areas. From a small start in Michigan in the 1820's and 1830's, the industry grew to major status in the 1840's. In 1839 a sawmill was erected at Black River Falls, Wisconsin, and rafts of lumber were floated down the rivers to towns in Iowa and Illinois. Other squatter sawmills were soon erected, and in 1853 an authority declared that the course of the lumber industry had been permanently changed; he prophesied that the pineries of Wisconsin would soon hold exclusive possession of the markets of the Mississippi Valley and its tributary valleys. Had he foreseen the development of the lumber industry in Minnesota and the huge markets which were to open up shortly on the "sod-house frontier," he could have painted an even more rosy picture of the immense lumber business soon to develop in the Upper Mississippi Valley.

As early as November 10, 1841, the register and the receiver at the Muskoda, Wisconsin, land office recommended that the land be brought into the market as quickly as feasible since it was being cut over by the settlers. Sawmill operators also would build two or three cabins to be used as shops, warehouses, and a dwelling for the purpose of establishing the rights of settlers to unrestricted quantities of government land. Word reached the General Land Office in the late 1840's that in addition to a great deal of scattered cutting by small millowners, large companies were being organized to operate in the pineries along the Wisconsin River, the

St. Croix River, and Green Bay. Alexander Montgomery wrote that a most destructive and wasteful program had been carried on around Beaver Dam in that period. Great sections had been slashed, the trunks of the trees trimmed, and the tall stumps and tops left to clutter the land and prevent occupancy. Harry F. Brown, register of the Green Bay land office, reported that nearly fifteen million feet of pine were manufactured annually in the Green Bay watershed—every foot of which, he complained, was plundered from the lands of the United States. Brown also believed that plans were afoot for wider and more extensive depredations during the coming season.[5]

The newly instituted Home Department (Department of the Interior) handled the situation in a businesslike way, determined to save the national resources under its care. In 1850, special agents were sent to investigate the logging areas and, if cutting was being done on government land, to seize the logs and hold them until the loggers bought the land. If they refused to buy the land, the agents were to sell the logs. It was soon found that practically every lumberman in Wisconsin and Michigan was cutting trees on government land, and immediately the western newspapers unleashed a storm of abuse and criticism upon the government. For years the home-maker had been freely using the government timber, and the West could see no difference between the settlers helping themselves and the lumbermen doing the same. It was argued, rather, that this exploitation of the nation's resources was a blessing to the country.

At Milwaukee and Chicago, when the government sought to sell the seized lumber at auction, no one would bid on it, and an agent in western Michigan had to call on United States sailors to help him make arrests in carrying out his duties. Since logs had been cut on government land and were the property of the United States, the agent ordered them seized and sold. In Manistee County, Michigan, the United States marshal, a man named Durkee, shut down a sawmill, seized the logs and shingles, went to the booms, put the mark of the United States on the logs, and forbade sawing until settlement was made. The marshal, thinking he had done a good day's work, retired, but the loggers and millhands decided to give him a display of fireworks. They prepared large balls of wicking, saturated them with turpentine, lighted them, and tossed them through the window into the marshal's room—giving him, as they said, a grand illumination. A vessel he owned was sunk in the lake. Some of the transgressors were arrested but escaped. The whole incident was reminiscent of the Whisky

[5] Paul Gates, *The Wisconsin Pine Lands of Cornell University* (Ithaca: Cornell University Press, 1943), pp. 70–72.

Rebellion, and Chicago papers urged forcible prevention of the execution of the laws.

In McDonald County, Missouri, several local citizens—together with men from Arkansas—had been engaged for months with circular saws in cutting all the pine and other valuable timber on the public land. When the United States marshal for the district tried to execute the proper writs and apprehend the culprits, they and their friends, numbering 150, compelled him to leave the county and the state. Seventeen of the law-resisting party followed the marshal to Bentonville, Arkansas, surrounded his hotel, and demanded that he surrender himself.

The war raged even to the western fringe of settlement, where loggers had been denuding the banks of the Mississippi River in Minnesota. The *Omaha Nebraskan* of June 25, 1856, reported the results of a government effort to sell the logs cut on the public domain:

> The Government had a large sale of sawlogs at Sauk Rapids the other day. These logs were cut by trespassers on the public lands during the past winter and contained 31,850,000 feet of timber.
>
> Of course, the loggers attended the sale, and had everything their way. At the hour appointed the Register opened the matter by stating that the logs would be sold in lots, according to their mark and locality, and that nothing less than twelve and a half cents would be received as a bid. Lot No. 1 being offered, no bids were made; lot No. 2 the same, and so on to the end of the catalogue. It was then announced that no sale had been effected, and that the timber was still the property of the highest bidder. One cent per thousand was thereupon offered, and each lot was sold separately to one man—the person selected by the loggers as 'bidder'—and thus Uncle Samuel, the kind, (biddy?) parted with 31,850,000 feet of first rate pine timber for the sum of three hundred and eighteen dollars and fifty cents. There was a good attendance at the sale, but no outsiders interfered to bid.
>
> Had they done so, they would probably have made the acquaintance of a piece of cutlery known as a Bowie knife. Great farce, those saw-log sales!

The newspapers stormed and the western senators and representatives in Congress, led by those from Wisconsin, Minnesota, and Iowa, brought heavy pressure upon the administration. It was politically inexpedient to resist the West, and in 1856 the lumber interests were victorious. The agents were dismissed, and John W. Wilson, the Commissioner who had vigorously prosecuted the timber looters, was discharged for his devotion to the duty of preserving the natural resources of the nation—an unholy sacrifice to the god of politics. Thus ended the Timber War of 1854, in abject surrender by the national government.

The new policy, a face-saving device, assigned to the land officers the duty of preventing the plunder of timber on the public domain, but under their supervision there arose a policy of compromising with the loggers, which in 1860 became the recognized policy of the Department of the Interior. Proceedings against trespassers were dismissed if they paid for the stumpage—market value of the standing trees—and the cost of the seizure. In 1860 the Secretary of the Interior authorized a compromise on these terms: entry of the land upon which timber was cut, payment of fifty cents per thousand feet of timber, and payment of all costs incurred in the event of seizure. Since it developed later that much timber was cut on land that was not on the market, the decision was made to accept a reasonable stumpage as dictated by the market price, but in no case was it to be less than $2.50 per thousand feet. After 1864 it became customary to charge one-sixth the value of the manufactured lumber at the mill. In 1862 the Commissioner of the General Land Office said the main object was to secure the regular price of $1.25 an acre, and three years later he declared that the plan was highly successful. He remarked that a policy that is contrary to public opinion is impossible to enforce by legal means.[6]

Now came another "dodge." An operator would enter a forty "to make a show," and in a winter's logging devastate all the surrounding government land. When timber was en route to market, or even cut and piled, it was difficult to prove whether the logs were cut on the public domain or on a man's own forty, although it was evident that all of the winters' logs could not have come from the small area owned by the logger. It was in connection with this usage that the term "round forty" originated. A boss would send his crew into a location, tell the foreman to "log around the forty acres" (approximately forty acres), and the crew would cut a round forty—forty acres to the north and a like amount to the east, the south, and the west. There was many a chuckle about the round forties. If this cutting of two hundred acres instead of forty was detected, the trespasser was required to pay "its estimated value, in any case not less than $1.25 an acre."[7] Another scheme was "throwing the chain," which involved the simple operation of moving a section line a few rods east, west, north, or south of the true line and by this maneuver making a quarter section or

[6] Robert F. Fries, "A History of the Lumber Industry in Wisconsin" (Ph.D. Dissertation, University of Wisconsin, 1939), pp. 322–331.

[7] Stewart H. Holbrook, *Holy Old Mackinaw* (New York: Macmillan, 1938), p. 93.

even a forty include an exceptionally fine streak of pine lying just beyond the true line. When a logger was caught at this, it was explained as a topographical error or a compass aberration.

When, shortly after the Timber War of the 1850's, it was seen that it would be necessary for a lumber company to possess land in order to exploit it of timber, competition among the interests became keen. In the early times, some of the biggest operators adopted the claim-club technique. At a sale where a number of tracts of good pineland were to be sold by the government, a lumber magnate would send a platoon of trusty, strong-arm lumberjacks. At the auctioneer's shout, "How much is offered for this valuable land?" a lumberjack would bid $1.25. If someone bid $1.50, this was the signal for the strong-arm boys, in wedge formation, to place the impertinent bidder at the apex of their formation and rush him off the scene into the woods, where he would not interfere with the decorum of a land sale conducted in harmony with the desires of the big lumbermen. The land officers, of course, had to be a party to this high-handed theft if it was to succeed.[8] Another way in which the register and the receiver helped special interests secure valuable land at the minimum price (while other buyers had to pay the full price) was by collusion with an agent who would bid the land above the reach of competitors. The land would be knocked down to him at the high figure, but by the end of the day the agent had disappeared. The register treated the matter as if the land had been paid for, but when the office was opened for the private entry of land, a confederate of the agent secretly entered the land at $1.25 an acre.

Speculators and investment companies in the East amassed vast landholdings by collusion at the auctions through purchases at the minimum price and by buying with military warrants and later with land-grant scrip. Many planned to keep their purchases for a number of years, until the scarcity of timber and the increased demand for lumber enhanced the value of their holdings, but when the homestead law was projected they were seized by alarm. How could they, with heavy investments, survive if the free-land craze succeeded? When President Buchanan vetoed the first homestead bill, the speculators breathed a sigh of relief.

One of the most important agents in the transfer of timberlands from government to private ownership was the timber explorer or "landlooker," more popularly known as a "timber cruiser." Many times these expert woodsmen were permanently employed by a land or timber company; some, however, were independent businessmen who capitalized on their

[8] Charles Edward Russell, *A-Raftin' on the Mississip'* (New York: The Century Company, 1928), pp. 48–49.

skill and sold information. Often they combined landlooking in the summer with running a logging crew in the winter, or perhaps scaling lumber, or guiding sportsmen or prospective settlers. Sometimes a United States surveyor capitalized on the information he had secured while running the lines to start a cruising career. Cruising developed into an important business, which dealt more with trees and lumber than with exploring. There was a common saying in the great woods that a real cruiser was born to his job.

By using government surveyors' field notes, a cruiser located areas where pine was to be found in quantity, and by use of the field notes again he found at least one corner of a section; then he paced off the boundaries. Five hundred paces equal eighty rods, or the distance along one side of a forty; and two thousand paces make a mile, that is, one side of a section. Having established the boundaries of a section, the cruiser stepped off a two-hundred-foot square in average timber; then he counted the number of trees in the square, scaled a few, and estimated the average number of board feet per tree. This was then multiplied by the average number of trees per acre, and the result was multiplied by 640 to get the approximate number of board feet per section. The cruiser, after much experience, became very accurate. After a glance at a giant pine tree he could judge that it would scale so many hundred board feet; or with the help of an improvised ladder made from a small tree by trimming off the branches and leaving the spikes, he could climb a tree and estimate the amount of timber in a given area with a remarkable degree of accuracy.[9] The cruiser was the axis of the timber industry: his word stood, and transactions turned on this basis. If he said an area had one million feet of pine and it later developed that it had ten million feet, the buyer was that much ahead. Many cruisers were honest men who took pride in their integrity; others with easy consciences were not to be trusted. One retired lumberman recounted that he had got his start by taking advantage of his employers. Employed as a cruiser for the Sturgeon Bay Lumber Company, of which Senator Philetus Sawyer of Wisconsin was the principal owner, one day while he was plying his trade in the depths of the forest he decided that he was a fool to locate all this timberland for a company rather than for himself. He marked a tract of good pineland "swamp" and at the public sale bought it for $600, which he had borrowed. On part of the land, he said, he cut nine million feet that year and sold the rest for $7,500. Said he: "I didn't work for the company after that."[10]

[9] John Emmett Nelligan, *The Life of a Lumberman* (Place of publication unknown, 1929), pp. 50, 51.
[10] *Chicago Times*, May 26, 1894.

Sometimes rival companies would bribe dishonest cruisers to give false reports in order that worthless land might be mistakenly entered for timberland and pineland by the other company. By and large, however, cruisers were honest with their companies and hence remained poor. Some cruisers prospected on their own, entered timberland for a company, and received a percentage of the land for their work—ordinarily one-fourth to one-sixth of the entry. If cruisers met in the woods after they had compiled a list of valuable lands they hoped to secure when they reached the land office, each man knew that the other probably had the same descriptions, and the question then was which could outwit or out-travel the other and secure the spoils by being the first to enter the lands.

George H. Warren and a companion, who were cruising in Wisconsin, became separated one day and Warren called out to locate his companion. Shortly afterward, however, he found a pigeon that had been stripped of its feathers but was still warm. He knew that other landlookers had been in the area and guessed that they had discovered his presence by his shout to his companion. Warren, with his descriptions of more than four thousand acres of United States and Wisconsin state pinelands, immediately took the most direct route for the Stevens Point land office, sixty-five miles to the south, hoping to beat the rival claimant. Twenty-five miles was through the woods, which had to be traveled on foot, and for part of this distance Warren followed the tracks of his competitor, whom he identified by the marks of hobnail boots he had seen beside the pigeon. Some twenty-four hours later he stopped to eat at an isolated house and learned that his rival was an hour ahead of him. Warren arrived at Wausau late at night, but the stagecoach, the only public conveyance, did not leave for Stevens Point until four the next morning. Warren hired a livery team, drove to Stevens Point during the night, and immediately went to the home of the register before eating to tell him he wanted to enter some land as soon as he opened the office and thus assure himself of being served first. Warren was served at nine o'clock but was told to return at eleven to see whether any of the land had been entered and, if not, to pay for it. (This would give the clerk time to search the records.)

While Warren was still in the land office, the stage arrived from Wausau and a man wearing hobnail boots hurried in and called for the same township plat that Warren had used. As the man read the descriptions of the lands he wished to enter, Warren noted that they were in most instances the same as he had already entered, and the land officer told the newcomer the land had been entered. In his agitation, the latecomer had also read the descriptions of some of the state land he wished to enter at Madison, and Warren, noting that they had made the same choices, immediately wired the land office at Madison to enter both men's descriptions. Warren kept a deposit with the state treasurer to cover such an exigency.[11]

Sometimes an independent cruiser would look up valuable logging land and give the descriptions to a company on the condition that it would buy the land and give the cruiser a royalty on one-fourth of the land for his discovery. The dishonest officials, however, might take the descriptions but tell the cruiser that they could not buy the land, perhaps claiming that it was inaccessible. When the woodsman had gone away, the lumber company would enter the land by wire and send the money to the land office by express. Cruisers complained that some of the land officers also took advantage of them in this way. Some land officials were agents of speculating companies or silent partners of big operators.

It was charged that John H. Knight, register of the land office at Bayfield, Wisconsin, formed a partnership with William F. Vilas, a lumberman and land speculator, and later a senator from Wisconsin and the Secretary of the Interior. Knight and Vilas worked various schemes on the landlookers. An exhausted cruiser might enter the Bayfield land office and ask to enter certain designated tracts, but Knight, knowing the cruiser was an expert woodsman and had a find, would reply: "I'll have to look at the records and see if that is taken. Come around tomorrow." After the woodsman had gone, it took only a few minutes to enter the land in the name of Vilas and draw on his account for the amount. When the applicant called next day, he found that the rich timberland had already been entered.[12]

After the Homestead Act became operative, auctions were held only in special cases; sometimes, however, a tract that had been withheld from entry was sold to the highest bidder, and in such cases the buyers made arrangements among themselves to buy the land cheaply. In 1869 a strip in the Chippewa Valley in Wisconsin, which contained 247,680 acres and had been withdrawn from entry for railroad purposes, was put up at auction. By this time much of the desirable land had passed from the government into private hands and there was considerable competition among the buyers. At the beginning of the sale the land sold for two to six dollars an acre, but after a time, and at the suggestion of the clerk of the land office, a ring or pool was formed to prevent competitive bidding. Competition was eliminated and the remaining acreage was divided among the "big interests" at a very low price.

11 George Henry Warren, *The Pioneer Woodsman* (Minneapolis: Hahn & Harmon, 1914), pp. 26, 50–54.
12 *Chicago Times*, May 26, 1894.

Four years later, in the same state, a similar auction was held and loggers, pine dealers, speculators, and moneyed men flocked to buy land. A "machine" was organized to prevent competition, but by some slip, the one hundred buyers became confused and began competitive bidding. The bids forced the land as high as $19.75 an acre. The buyers considered the matter that night and the next morning high-priced tracts were forfeited. When the tracts were offered again, they were purchased for about three dollars an acre. Once the combine started to work, it functioned smoothly throughout the sale. The *Eau Claire Free Press* of August 23, 1873, speaking of the combines that were formed to secure the land at the sale, said of the buyers: "They all feel and express themselves, that the excitement of the hour has led them into operations, which has not added to their respectability."

The sale of the lands given to Wisconsin by the United States was attended by the same abuses. At a sale of state school lands in September, 1883, a pool bid land at the state's minimum price of three dollars an acre. Some of the same lands at the private auction among the bidders brought as high as fifty dollars an acre, and nearly all sold between eight and ten dollars an acre.[13] When the state land commissioners heard of this outrage against the school fund, they canceled the proceedings—and were criticized roundly by the newspapers of the lumbering area. The *Oshkosh Northwestern* of September 20, 1883, said the pool was no novelty and that the same thing had occurred every year for the last thirty years. The *Chippewa Times* raged:

The action of the school land commissioners in setting aside the late land sale is a very remarkable proceeding, to say the least. There was no evidence to prove any collusion among purchasers though it was attempted by the commissioners. . . . But suppose they had proven collusion in its wildest possible character in this case. What ground would it then be for setting the sale aside? In the first place, there could be no fraud against the state because the state was protected by the fixed minimum value. . . . It was determined beforehand that the state would take three dollars per acre and just as much more as buyers chose fit to bid. It was not pretended on the part of the state that it was trying to get just what the lands were worth and no more, else it would have had the land appraised and sold according to those appraisals, as any man of sense knows they should have been, instead of all being offered in one class.

The editor then argued that the buyers, at their own expense, had tramped over a large expanse of land, a great part of which was almost

[13] *Chippewa Herald* (Chippewa, Wis.), September 21, 1883.

entirely worthless, and had spent a vast sum in determining what was worth buying.

Is it to be wondered at then that parties who had gone to the expense of looking up lands should desire to stand out of each other's way as much as possible? And could an understanding of this character be regarded in the light of collusion to defraud?[14]

Legal action was taken by the lumbermen and the case was carried to the Supreme Court, which ruled that if the commission revoked the sale, the land had to be offered at private sale since it had been offered once and not sold and since the law provided that offered land had to be sold at the minimum price. The fact is that railroad and timber interests had gained virtual control of the state government. When Horace Greeley went to Madison on a speaking tour in 1869, he said he had never seen "such a pack of drunken rogues and ruffians" as were engaged there in making the laws for the state. In some instances, because lumbermen controlled the county governments, their large and ill-gotten holdings of pinelands were taxed at a very low rate.

Although there was no provision for private entry after 1863, this formula was not necessary for securing vast holdings. The Pre-emption Act had not been repealed with the passage of the Homestead Act, and these two measures became twin agencies for the fraudulent transfer of quantities of timber from the government to lumber interests. By an act of June 2, 1862, pre-emption was extended to all unsurveyed lands. The Homestead Act of 1863 was confined to surveyed areas only, however. The right of pre-emption dated from the actual time of settlement and the settler could occupy his claim indefinitely, without filing, so long as it was not jumped. On the other hand, the homestead right dated from filing rather than from settling. It was a much safer procedure for a man to pre-empt valuable unsurveyed land than to wait until it was surveyed and then homestead. Often a homesteader who had not filed had his claim pre-empted from under him.[15]

The lumber barons used the pre-emption law in various ways; for example, by taking advantage of a clause that extended thirty-three months credit after a man had filed his intention. This was long enough for a logging camp to be established and for cutting all the valuable timber before the payment was due. The loggers would then abandon the tract

14 *Chippewa Times*, quoted in *Eau Claire Free Press* (Eau Claire, Wis.), November 29, 1883.
15 Roy M. Robbins, *Our Landed Heritage* (Lincoln: University of Nebraska Press, 1962), pp. 238, 245.

without paying even the minimum price. The hotel registers of Chicago and Milwaukee were requisitioned to secure the names of dummy pre-emptors. Minors, repeaters under aliases, and purely fictitious pre-emptors turned the trick, which was good for a quantity of land. If land officers were men of integrity, there was a greater show of compliance with the law. A drygoods box, "doctored" so that a man could swear he had a good board house with a shingle roof, a door, and glass windows, might be placed on a claim.

The report of the Commissioner of the General Land Office for 1888 estimated that 99 per cent of the pre-emption entries in the Wausau, Wisconsin, district in that year were fraudulent and that 90 per cent of those in the Eau Claire district were made merely for the purpose of cut-ting valuable timber. Many fraudulent entries in Wisconsin and elsewhere also were made under the Homestead Act. A. R. Greene wrote: "I have seen a mill-owner appear at a land office with seven or eight of his em-ployees and assist them in making homestead filings, giving them the money for the fees."[16]

The story was the same in Minnesota, Michigan, California, Florida, and Alabama—wherever there were enough trees to warrant speculation in timberland or to carry on logging operations. An investigating commis-sion found great numbers of kennel-like structures in the redwood sections of California, totally unfit for human habitation, that had passed for dwell-ing places and had enabled an entryman to prove he had his dwelling on his "farm." In areas where—according to General Land Office records—large settlements of agriculturists were engaged in tilling the soil, the com-mission found only primeval silence, mountain peaks, and canyons where farms were said to be. The only evidence of human occupation was in the form of stumps and waste. As we have seen, after the defeat of the govern-ment by the lumber interests in the 1850's, the government tried to collect stumpage and secure payment for land denuded of trees, but this was an utter failure.

Carl Schurz, who became Secretary of the Interior in 1876 found that in the twenty years since January 1, 1856, $199,998.50, had been collected from depredators and that the cost of collecting this amount was $45,624.76, which left a balance of $154,373.74.[17] This was a mere spark in a dark world of depredation since it was little more than the value of five thousand acres of good pineland. Furthermore, the denuding of the land

---

[16] *Report of the Secretary of the Interior, 1885,* I (5 vols.; Washington, D.C.: Govt. Printing Office, 1885), 202–205.

[17] *Report of the Secretary of the Interior, 1877,* p. 20.

went on constantly during those years. Secretary Schurz, who was a reformer and an able administrator, by an order of May 2, 1877, placed the responsibility for the preservation of forest resources in charge of special agents. In 1879, Minnesota and Wisconsin each had four agents, and Alabama, California, Colorado, Florida, Louisiana, Michigan, Mississippi, New Mexico, Oregon, Washington, and Wyoming each had one. It is easy to see that this small force, spread over such an immense area, could barely touch the problem; and during the 1880's the depredations continued.

In Alabama, Florida, Louisiana, and Mississippi, timberland spoliation consisted of "cutting and boxing" pine trees for the gum that was distilled into spirits of turpentine, which often killed the trees or ruined them for lumber. Furthermore, in attempting to prosecute depredators, the government was restricted by so much red tape and so many delays that witnesses disappeared, and finally the statute of limitations became operative. Although a case was continued from one session to another, a timber company went on with its plundering and endeavored to destroy the evidence against it. In some instances a culprit multiplied the enormity of his offense by setting forest fires. If a case dragged out long enough, there was a chance that the officials in the General Land Office might be changed and the case dismissed. About the time the government had collected its evidence against the Montana Improvement Company and was ready for trial, the Department of the Interior had exhausted its funds for securing witnesses and a postponement was necessary; the case never came to trial and the company continued to commit depredations. Some of the companies became so bold that they brought political pressure to bear upon the government to call off its agents when they were ready to prosecute.[18]

There was great difficulty in securing convictions in an area where nearly all were in sympathy with the lawbreakers. Indeed, the fact that public opinion was with the trespasser was the biggest factor in perpetuating frontier frauds. The experience of Sam Harriman, who was appointed by the governor of Wisconsin to protect land given to the state by the United States government; is typical. He found himself beset with difficulties on every hand. The land-office officials, who had been accustomed to compromise with the lumbermen, were uncooperative and Harriman reported:

The interest of the entire community is in opposition to me and my acts in enforcing the Law. . . . I hate to stand in a community like Ishmael with my hand against every man and every man against me but by the

[18] Harold H. Dunham, *Government Handout* (New York: Edwards Brothers, 1941), pp. 272, 273, 325, 326.

help of God and a few seizures I hope to discharge my duty to the satisfaction of principle.[19]

Even the handful of federal agents must have caused some trepidation in the camps of the spoilers, for once more there was a violent reaction in Congress. A bill was introduced in May, 1879, to relieve trespassers from prosecution for timber depredations committed before May of that year if they would pay the regular price for the land. Many members of both houses favored the bill because the policy of the previous administration had led lumbermen to believe that trespassing would be condoned. That the government would prosecute lumbermen as a result of a sudden change of policy was thought unjust. The debate on this bill, which in due time was passed, reveals the difference in attitude between the old settled areas and the frontier on the principle of cutting timber on the public lands. Wisconsin and Michigan now joined Pennsylvania and New England in resisting this "bill to license timber thieves," as it was called. The land in Wisconsin and Michigan, in large measure, was in the hands of private interests and the lumbermen were on the other side of the question. They did not want competition from companies in the mountain states and in the Pacific West who were obtaining their lumber for little more than the cost of cutting it.[20]

As has been noted, with the passage of the Homestead Act the privilege of private entry was withdrawn and government-owned land could be secured legally only for agricultural purposes. People in the mining and other nonagricultural areas could not legitimately cut a stick of wood for a campfire, the residents of a mining town could secure no wood for fuel, and miners could not procure timber for shoring up the mines. To remedy this unreasonable arrangement, Congress on April 18, 1878, passed the Timber Cutting Act, which authorized residents of mineral lands to fell and remove for building, mining, or agricultural uses any timber on mineral lands not subject to entry under the existing laws. The act was meant to accommodate individual users rather than commercial companies; railroads, for example, were not allowed to cut under this law.

As early as 1879, complaints were received by the General Land Office that miners were cutting small timber—timber less than the minimum eight-inch diameter established by the Commissioner of the General Land Office. Small timber was very convenient for shoring mines, but its cutting denuded great areas that should have been left forested. The smelting

[19] Fries, "History of the Lumber Industry in Wisconsin," p. 345.
[20] *Ibid.*, pp. 332–337.

industry used much charcoal at this time, and in 1880 the Commissioner's report complained that in Colorado alone hundreds of charcoal burners consumed twelve hundred cords of wood daily. This practice was in harmony with the Timber Cutting Act, but the act specified that small timber should not be destroyed, and charcoal producers preferred trees of three to six inches in diameter because they were more easily handled and more quickly charred than larger trees. Since standing trees recently killed by fire were best for charring, large areas around Leadville had been fired. For many months forest fires raged in the mountains; fourteen smelters had no fewer than 100,000 cords on hand; and around nearly every smelter, wood was piled by the acre. The Homestead Act as well as the Timber Cutting Act were used for the purpose of securing land, stripping it, and then abandoning it.[21] A similar situation existed in Alabama, where lands were filed upon as homesteads and stripped of their timber for conversion into charcoal.

On June 3, 1878, by passing the Timber and Stone Act, Congress sought to provide a way in which one could buy timberland. According to its terms, a person could buy a maximum of 160 acres of land unfit for agriculture at $2.50 an acre. The buyer had to swear that the tract was unfit for agriculture, that he was buying it for his own use, and that he had made no agreement with anyone to transfer the title. The law applied only to California, Oregon, Nevada, and Washington, but on August 4, 1892, the act was amended to apply to the whole country.[22] The same methods used to circumvent the Homestead Act were applied to the Timber and Stone Act: dozens of dummy entrymen, employees, or other willing tools bought quantities of land which was immediately transferred to the lumbering interests. John Ise is the authority for the statement that ultimately only a fraction of one per cent of the area acquired under the Timber and Stone Act remained in the hands of the original entrymen, who had sworn the land was for their own personal use.

An instance of how this act was perverted may be cited from the redwood country of California. After James D. Walker and Charles H. King of San Francisco had hired a cruiser to scout the timber in Humboldt County, Walker went to Scotland to interest wealthy men in his project of exploiting the county's redwood forests; and in 1882 he organized the California Redwood Company—with himself as president. Walker, who agreed to furnish fifty thousand acres of land at seven dollars an acre, then returned to California, employed cruisers and surveyors, and set to work to

21 *Report of the Secretary of the Interior, 1880,* I, 578.
22 *Public Land* (Spokane, Wash.), October 22, 1901, p. 5.

fulfill the terms of his contract. One of the men he cunningly employed was a brother of the receiver at the land office at Eureka, and the agents employed to secure the land made not the slightest attempt to keep the program a secret: they openly advertised for four hundred "dummies" to make entries under the Timber and Stone Act. Some of the citizens of Eureka refused to be corrupted, but the agents filled their quota by drafting farmers on their way to or from town and by calling the townspeople from their legitimate activities and persuading them to allow their names to be used in the scheme. Foreign sailors and noncitizens at the local boardinghouse fell into line and marched to the courthouse, where they were aided in getting their first naturalization papers, in entering land, and in executing deeds that sold this land to the company—for which they were paid a fee of from five to fifty dollars. The agents of the company had their headquarters at the back of a saloon near the land office, and it was here that the legal papers were executed and the applications for land presented to the register and receiver, twenty-five at a time. The rest of the requirements for securing the titles from the government were taken care of by other confederates.

Everything proceeded as planned until the agents tried to hurry things along and sent an attorney to Washington to facilitate matters. The officials became suspicious and sent an agent to investigate, but he apparently succumbed to temptation. W. T. Smith, who was sent out later, refused a $5,000 bribe and made a full report to Washington of everything he found, estimating that 100,000 acres had been fraudulently entered. One man signed an affidavit that he had furnished the agents with one hundred men for five dollars each, and evidence was submitted which implicated the land office officials. Smith's report was ignored: 22,000 acres, valued at $440,000, were recommended patented; and as a reward for his impeccability, Smith was dismissed from the service. Commissioner Sparks, who about this time came into the General Land Office with a will to operate it honestly and efficiently, stated that he understood Smith had been dismissed because of great influence brought against him on the West Coast and in Washington. Sparks sent another agent who could not be bribed and whose immediate superiors were not political chameleons.

The economic octopus wound its tentacles tighter around its victim, and held on. Some witnesses were taken out of the area secretly and others were intimidated so that they were of no use to the government. The company employed spies to watch every move of the agent and to report the name of every person who talked with him. On one occasion, two people who were about to enter the agent's room were knocked down and dragged away.[23] Despite all this the agent secured indictments; but with remarkable speed, in thirty days a federal court had quashed the charges. The *New York Times* lashed out at the court's action as a shameful disgrace and a scandalous failure to enforce the laws. The General Land Office did not call off its dogs, however, but canceled the entries and instituted suits against the entrymen for the illegally patented land.

The Scottish owners then sidestepped the frontal attack, formed a new company called the Humboldt Redwood Company, and transferred the holdings of the old company to the new organization. In court, the new corporation argued that it was an innocent purchaser and should not be deprived of its property because of the fraud of others. By this time Sparks, the reform Commissioner, had been relieved, and apparently—as in many other cases of fraud—the action was dropped. There were scores of similar frauds throughout the country, but most of the defrauders were not even discovered, much less indicted and convicted.[24]

Trainloads of women schoolteachers were shipped from Minnesota to Oregon in the 1890's, according to official records, for the purpose of entering lands under the Timber and Stone Act, thus rendering a service to a wealthy Minneapolis timberman while spending a summer seeing the West. In defense of the lumbermen, a historian must point out that since there was no legal way to possess more than 160 acres except under the Timber and Stone Act, they took the only available means of securing the acreage needed in their business: they bought privately entered 160-acre claims. When these could not be obtained fast enough or in usable, compact bodies, lumbermen secured the land by the use of dummy entrymen and other fraudulent means.

Through the years the lumber interests were savage and unscrupulous in their attempts to rid themselves of timber agents who investigated their machinations. At Ashland, Wisconsin, intent upon obtaining several million feet of pine timber on an Indian reservation, the lumbermen set a trap for an agent, a man of integrity who refused to be bribed: they imported a woman of easy virtue, pretty and vivacious, to ensnare the man. When the affair had reached the right stage, the woman invited the agent to her room, and unaware of the plot, he accepted the invitation. When the agent was in a morally compromising situation, suddenly a big, angry man kicked the door in and abused the startled officer for paying attention to his wife. The officer's reputation was so badly tarnished that he was

[23] John Ise, *The United States Forest Policy* (New Haven: Yale University Press, 1920), p. 75.

[24] Dunham, *Government Handout*, pp. 264–268.

compelled to leave town as quickly as possible, and there is no record of his having made a report to the Commissioner at Washington.[25] Timber interests, as late as 1908, arranged a special "farewell" dinner for a government agent, hoping to terminate his service with the government by placing Rough-on-Rats poison in his coffee. Fortunately the plot was unsuccessful. The government's procedure with regard to timber and timberlands showed perhaps more distinctly than that of any other the vacillating inconsistency of the land laws of the United States and the failure of the government to execute those laws. On the one hand Congress failed to pass a genuine workable land law to allow the legitimate harvest of the forest trees, and on the other there was no firm determination to enforce existing laws. The inability of a democracy to pursue an undeviating course in the face of a determined minority far away from the seat of government stands out in bold relief in the ruthless frontier exploitation of the forest riches.

[25] Nelligan, *Life of a Lumberman*, pp. 176–177.

XIII

The Day of the Speculator

In the boom period that followed the War of 1812 and ended in the Panic of 1819, the American people were seized by a veritable land craze. Alabama and Mississippi were particularly affected. At the sales at Huntsville, Alabama, in 1818, the land sold beyond all calculations: forty-two townships brought the government five million dollars,[1] or a little over five dollars an acre. Since the minimum price of land was two dollars an acre, the average price was more than two and one-half times the minimum; and some agricultural land sold for thirty to seventy-eight dollars per acre. But frontiersmen, eager to advance their own interest, would not allow the United States to conduct a fair auction at which the land would be sold at its true value. General John Coffee, a land buyer, stated that a group of speculators, bent on obtaining the land for a fraction of its worth, had sent men out on the different roads leading to Huntsville to meet incoming strangers and solicit them to join a company that was being formed to buy as much land as possible, supposedly for the benefit of all. They proposed to "*run down small capitalists* or such as would not join their company." Learning of this scheme, the register, receiver, and surveyor general felt they should protect the interests of the United States and keep the company from securing the land for the minimum price, which was much below the real value. Accordingly, they sought counsel from the attorney general of the territory on the legality of stopping the sale. The attorney general did not believe it could be stopped legally, and therefore the register, to protect the interests of the United States, bid on the land and ran it up to a high figure, making the speculators pay a just price.

Much of the land sold for twenty dollars an acre and up, and land intended for nonagricultural purposes—such as townsites—sold at even higher figures. Half of one quarter-section sold for $150 an acre and the

[1] *The Alabama Republican* (Huntsville, Ala.), July 4, 1818; Everett Dick, *The Dixie Frontier* (New York: Knopf, 1948), Chapter VI.

199

other half for $251 an acre. The Cypress Land Company bought the tract on which Florence, Alabama, now stands, and the next year its lots—containing one-half acre each—were sold at auction. One lot brought $3,500 and another, on the riverbank with ferry rights, sold for $10,100. But the big interests soon made arrangements among themselves to quiet competition and obtain the land at the minimum price.[2] Since at that time there was no law against collusion, the speculators may have been able to pressure the register and the receiver into allowing the auction to proceed although they were satisfied that collusion had stifled competition.

Even after a law had been passed (1833) proscribing collusion at sales, the flush times just prior to the Panic of 1837 brought to a crest the wave of fraud by combines of speculators. On March 3, 1835, a congressional committee appointed to investigate the situation reported that the most atrocious and outrageous frauds had been committed for the last three or four years. No governmental officers had been removed; indeed, those most guilty had been reappointed and had become bold and fearless. Undue confidence had often been placed in a political favorite or friend of the President, the committee reported.

An example of the widespread fraud is the auction held at Chocchuma, Mississippi, in October, 1833. A number of companies of speculators had federated to form a giant association. Some companies were composed of only a few individuals, but one had a membership of from fifty to one hundred. One person could join as many companies as he chose. R. J. Walker of Natchez was the head of the speculators. Each member was to invest not less than $100 nor more than $1,000, but by using fictitious names or joining several companies, individuals with large sums of money could make unlimited investments. Four representatives were selected to bid for the land under conditions that practically eliminated competition, and later a real auction was held to resell the land bought at the minimum price. Settlers who lived on the land and who had made improvements were allowed to buy eighty acres or 160 acres at the minimum price, provided they had that much under cultivation. The settlers were to hand to the company agents the numbers of their land, and it was understood they would not bid on other lands. Each day after the government auction, in a tavern thirty or forty paces from the land office, the company held its private auction of lands bought during the day, and a Mr. Rather, an auctioneer for the government, sometimes served in the same capacity for the speculators at the tavern. Before the federation was formed, a tract

---

[2] Jennie Hughes Morril, "The Settlement of Alabama" (Master's thesis, University of Wisconsin, 1905), pp. 50, 51.

had brought ten dollars an acre, but after the union almost all the land was sold at $1.25 an acre. From one-half to two-thirds of the land was resold at the second auction, but at an advance of 100 to 200 per cent. One witness testified that his profit was "only" $301.50 on each $1,000 invested.

Before the auction began, a member made a speech to the crowd, promising the great benefit the combine would be to the settlers, appealing to them to cooperate, and arguing that the association would bring the settlers pre-emption privileges that had been denied by the government. At the conclusion of the sales, moreover, the settlers gave the leader of the speculators, R. J. Walker, and some of the other speculators a dinner in appreciation of their efforts to secure their land for them at the minimum government price.[3]

A similar combine operated at Columbus, Mississippi, in the same year, and the register of the land office later testified that he understood the company declared a dividend of $465 for each $1,000 invested. The land sales closed on Saturday, and that evening the company conducted its sale at the courthouse door, about fifty or sixty steps from the land office. The congressional committee which investigated the matter concluded that the loss to the government was $65,000 or $70,000.

At the conclusion of a government auction, land that had been offered but for which no bid had been received was open to private entry at $1.25 an acre, and many stayed to enter such land. This offered another opportunity for the speculator. At Chocchuma, due to the press of entries, the register would receive applications only in the evening for entry the following day. After he had worked them he would open the office and announce the conflicting claims. In almost every instance, several men had applied for the same tracts, and in some cases there were six or eight conflicting applications. It was the duty of the register to allow these applicants to offer bids and he had to sell the tract to the highest bidder. Actually, however, the applicants would withdraw a few yards from the door and bid among themselves; the highest bidder was allowed to enter the tract at the government rate and the difference between $1.25 an acre and the "over" bid was divided among the unsuccessful bidders. One man said that R. J. Walker acted as crier for many of these private auctions, and men who had no intention of buying would require real land aspirants to buy them off in this fashion. A great outcry went up from

<hr />

[3] See Depositions of Congressional Committee of Investigation in *American State Papers, Public Lands*, VII (Washington, D.C.: Gales and Seaton, 1860), 452–456, 469, 497, and VIII (Washington, D.C.: Gales and Seaton, 1861), 775, 776, 786.

small-scale purchasers because a small coterie of moneyed men was allowed access to the land office while the doors were closed to the general public. The applications were kept in a cigar box, and by examining them, the clique could see what land was desired and place a conflicting claim on the tracts. The land officers were suspected of working hand in glove with the big interests to squeeze the little man.[4] A study of the records shows that Walker and other men with a large amount of money went from one sale to another throughout the Southwest, using their money again and again to great advantage.

It also was charged that the land officers at Chocchuma in 1833 cooperated with the speculators in bringing the land into the market without giving sufficient notice; hence, the actual settlers did not have time to raise the money to purchase their claims. As a result, the settlers had to borrow at 50 per cent interest from the speculators or lose their land. Furthermore, the land was bought "for a song" by the speculators since, under the circumstances, there was little competition from local people.

It was very difficult to obtain evidence concerning the widespread fraud because most of those who were large purchasers for the combines, when summoned to give testimony, refused to appear before the investigating commissioner. As a result, the evidence is much less complete than if they had been compelled by the Senate to appear and testify. Many speculators were high officials of the state or territory, and others were men of influence and wealth. All united to discourage anyone from testifying and to render the position of witnesses odious. Naturally this influenced many to refuse to testify to the facts. In some instances the commissioners in charge of the investigation were threatened with personal violence in an attempt to deter them from their duties. In the district of the land sales of Chocchuma, the murder of the acting commissioner was attempted.[5]

Speculators also operated north of the Ohio and west of the Mississippi, but the competition at sales was not so keen, perhaps because the land boom was less acute than in the South—there was no great cash-crop expansion as there was for cotton. Nevertheless, settlers who hoped to secure their homes for the minimum price at the land sale looked with dismay at the troop of well-dressed men who came riding through the

[4] Testimony of Joseph Persons, in *American State Papers, Public Lands*, VII, 498; Deposition of John T. Hammond, *ibid.*, p. 472.

[5] Report of the Committee Appointed to Investigate Fraudulent Practices in the Sale of Public Lands, in *American State Papers, Public Lands*, VII, 732.

country shortly before an auction. An Iowa boy remembered that when these men appeared, wearing jewelry and ruffled shirts even during the week, his father and mother withheld information about land which they would have volunteered cheerfully to actual settlers. The activities of the speculators also were discouraged by force.

At an early day, Hancock County, Indiana, was disturbed by a small party of landlookers, and a group of settlers ambushed them in the woods. When the bullets whistled around them, cutting off tree twigs, the speculators fled. When the landlookers began to ride together in bands, the settlers formed an organization, known as the Home Defenders, to work a ruse on their enemies. Selecting several of their number to keep an eye out for speculators, the defenders organized a group of thirty men, some of them dressed in Indian costumes and others in frontier garb. When the spies reported that the dandies had come into the country (many wore stovepipe hats), they alerted the settlers and sent three of them to meet the city men with an offer to act as their guides. The settlers decoyed the dudes down a road where they met two or three men who reported that the Indians were on the warpath. The homespun-clad frontiersmen, in a simulated battle line, then appeared; they were being pushed back but were stopping now and then to fire at an unseen enemy. The fighters declared they had been attacked by an overwhelming force of Indians, who had killed two of their men, and they appealed to the speculators to help them. Suddenly, a large body of "Indians" came rushing over a hill, whooping and yelling. The city men fled in panic, with the "Indians" hotly pursuing them and the bullets whistling around them. The guides tried to rally their guests, but failing in this, cursed them as cowardly villains. The land hunters went back to Cincinnati, but it was said afterwards that many plug hats were found in the woods. The settlers, according to the story, were not bothered any more but obtained their land at the government price without competitive bidding.[6]

Speculators seemed to have an almost intuitive insight for the best land—land that would be the site of a county seat, a great city, or the key to larger or more valuable tracts. For example, as settlement reached the prairies, where timberland had much higher value than grasslands, speculators bought wooded tracts along streams and thereby controlled the meadow on each side of it. These tracts they could sell quickly at a profit to newcomers who needed timber, and then reinvest their money. They would also discover people who had bought small tracts after an auction

[6] William M. Cockrum, *Pioneer History of Indiana* (Oakland City, Ind.: Press of *Oakland City Journal*, 1907), pp. 406–408.

and would buy the adjoining land. If the settler prospered, he would soon want more land and would buy at a good margin over cost; if he failed, the speculator would buy the improved tract of the failure at the government price.

Railroad land grants presented another inviting opportunity to the speculator who took advantage of the overwhelming desire of the immigrating farmers to live near the railroad line where they could have an outlet for their product. Aaron M. Sakolski in his book, *The Great American Land Bubble*, cites the case of young Grenville Dodge (who some years later was the builder of the Union Pacific). Dodge, who went to Illinois as a surveyor in the 1850's, with acute perception saw that the odd sections within the grant of the Illinois Central would be in great demand shortly. Eagerly, he wrote back East to his father who ran a combination bookstore and post office, urging him to gather up what cash he could command and invest. He promised his father the he could double his money in six months if he would buy up some Mexican War land warrants in the East, where at that time they could be bought for about a dollar an acre, and send them out. Said he:

> I'll locate them in places where land is selling at this minute for $2.50 an acre. . . . Now this is no gun game but the truth. Don't tell anybody about it, but go to work. . . . This will pay better than all the post offices and bookstores in the kingdom.[7]

The speculator paid the minimum tax on unimproved land and did not help build roads, churches, or schools, but his land increased in value because of the improvements of the surrounding settlers. Logan Esarey, in his history of Indiana, has said that the speculator, the note-shaver, and the horse thief were the three most despised men on the frontier.

When the prairie was first reached, people did not appreciate its value, and many miles of grassland in western Indiana and Illinois remained almost unpopulated. Eventually, shrewd men from the East—without competition—bought thousands of acres at private entry for $1.25 an acre. In 1835 and 1836 Henry L. Ellsworth, the Commissioner of Patents and one of the first men to buy large tracts of grassland, acted as a private entrepreneur and as the agent for eastern capitalists in securing whole townships in Tippecanoe, Warren, White, Fountain, and Jasper counties in Indiana, and large areas in Illinois, Wisconsin, Michigan, and Iowa. Ellsworth became the largest land baron of the West in the 1840's. In

---

[7] Aaron M. Sakolski, *The Great American Land Bubble* (New York: Harper & Bros., 1932), p. 283.

Benton County, Indiana, he entered 65,000 acres. Because his vast holdings were not broken up, absentee landownership and tenant farming resulted, which in turn caused soil depletion and only minimum improvements. Today, in three prairie counties—Benton, Newton, and White—more than half the farms are operated by tenants.[8]

Absentee ownership was exceedingly distasteful to pioneers because such holdings remained vacant for years and settlers who were surrounded by ansentee-held lands were without near neighbors. This meant poor schools (if any), poor roads, a long way to market, and a general lack of the conveniences that come about through the efforts of a large number of people working together to secure public comforts and advantages.

Some of the numerous pre-emption acts before 1841 recognized floating claims, or "floats," which were issued on various occasions and were obtained with certificates that could be used to buy land anywhere without the necessity of residing on the tract (as was required for a pre-emption). Some of the earliest floats were the New Madrid certificates. In December, 1811, the populous settlement of New Madrid, Missouri, was stricken by a severe earthquake which demolished the buildings and damaged agricultural land, some of which sank beneath the waters of the Mississippi. In 1815, Congress passed an act that permitted the landowners in the affected area to exchange their holdings with the national government in return for certificates that entitled them to locate an equal area on government land wherever they might choose. This well-intentioned benevolent action was the source of three great evils.

Before the earthquake sufferers were fully aware that a relief act had been passed in their behalf and that their holdings, therefore, were not worthless, speculators from St. Louis began to buy up these valuable certificates (or floats) because they could be applied to land anywhere. Of the 516 certificates finally issued, only twenty remained in the hands of the earthquake victims—Moses Austin and his partner, for example, bought all they could at the lowest figure with the intention of locating them on choice townsites or other extremely valuable tracts. The certificates circulated rapidly and passed through the hands of many individuals. In 1820, William Wirt, the Attorney General, gave an opinion that the warrants were not transferable since the law was passed to help the unfortunates who had been rendered indigent by an act of God, not to enrich the speculators. He reasoned that patents for land located had to be issued to those who were owners at the date of the relief act, but

---

[8] Paul Wallace Gates, "Land Policy and Tenancy in the Prairie Counties of Indiana," *Indiana Magazine of History*, XXXV, No. 1 (March, 1939), 2.

for many years the legislature of Missouri, sympathetic to the speculators, petitioned Congress to accommodate the manipulators.[9]

The second evil that arose from the relief measure resulted from the fact that the certificates had no residence requirement. It therefore was possible for a bona fide settler who had lived up to all the regulations laid down by the pre-emption acts, but had not paid for the land, to find himself dispossessed by the holder of a float who had presented it at the land office and "floated" the settler out of his land (secured a title to the land).

Actually, although the New Madrid earthquake had caused much damage to houses, very little privately owned land had been damaged to the point that it was unfit for cultivation, and this made possible a third evil of this act. In not a few instances owners accepted the certificate, sold it for a tidy sum—or entered it on valuable land—and remained on their old land. The old land not seriously damaged was valuable because it was cleared and improved, and the owners stayed on as squatters. They could pre-empt and buy this improved land for $1.25 an acre, and sell their floats.

Floats provided by the various acts that implemented and followed the Pre-emption Act of 1830 had even more serious effects than the New Madrid certificates because they were more numerous. These floats were issued in an attempt to aid two claimants who, before the surveys had been made, had inadvertently settled on the same quarter section of land but were cultivating it separately (on different parts of the tract). The law provided that in such a case each settler should receive eighty acres of the dual claim and a floating claim for another eighty acres. The claimants were to apply at the land office, secure the float, and enter it a few days later, after examining the land to determine that it was unoccupied. In practice, however, a claimant traded his float to a speculator for enough cash to pay for his half of the 160 acres and thus obtained a clear title to an eighty-acre farm. Speculators acquired as many floats as possible and, finding a promising area, would enter the whole district. All of the squatters in such a region had their land and improvements "floated" out from under them.[10]

Various subtleties were practiced to gain floats. In Louisiana, a father and his son and the wife and another son dwelt in the same household but

[9] Sakolski, *The Great American Land Bubble*, pp. 207–210.

[10] Reports of Inspector V. M. Caresche, in *American State Papers, Public Lands*, VIII, 958–964.

pretended to cultivate separate eighty-acre tracts in an attempt to secure two eighty-acre floating claims. In a letter to President Andrew Jackson in 1835, Benjamin F. Linton, the district attorney for western Louisiana, described a fraud that had been perpetrated at the Opelousas land office:

I regret to say, because I religiously believe, that the most shameful frauds, impositions, and perjuries, have been practiced upon the land office at Opelousas, Louisiana. . . . Two persons living on a quarter-section, or who pretend they do, on lands not worth a cent an acre, men who can neither read nor write, men who have never seen a survey made and know nothing about sections or quarter-sections of land, and who in point of fact, live five, ten, and in many instances twenty miles apart, go before a justice of the peace as ignorant as themselves, and swear to all the facts required by law, to make their entry; this, too, in a section of country never surveyed by the authority of the government, nor any competent officer thereof. Would it be believed that any officer of the government would admit an entry, under circumstances like these upon oaths alone of the parties interested in making them, . . . It is not believed that there are thirty honest pre-emption floats in the whole western district of Louisiana; and yet, since the first of January, 1835 up to the 27th of May, there have passed at the land office at Opelousas, at least 350. And who are the owners of these floats principally? To one and not more than three speculators, since the first of January, of this year, up to the 27th of May, day after day, week after week, I might say months after months, a notorious speculator, and who must have been known as such to the officers of the land office at Opelousas, was seen occupying that office to the almost total exclusion of everybody else; no other person appeared to understand how to get pre-emption floats through, and no one did succeed until an event which will be stated below. He could be seen followed to and from the land office by crowds of free negroes, Indians, and Spaniards, and the very lowest dregs of society, in the counties of Opelousas and Rapides, with their affidavits already prepared by himself, and sworn to by them, before some justice of the peace in some remote part of the country. . . . And would it be believed, that the lands where these quarter-sections purported to be located, from the affidavits of the applicants, had never been surveyed by the government, nor any competent officer thereof, nor approved nor returned surveyed? . . . This state of things has gone on from the first of January until about the middle of April or first of May, of the present year, when it was suddenly announced a more rigid rule would thereafter be adopted, which was this: that a sworn deputy surveyor of the United States should in all cases make the survey, in order to ascertain if the parties were on the same quarter-section and to testify before the register that such was the fact. Besides this, they required the applicants to produce very satisfactory evidence from their neighbors that they had cultivated and improved, as stated in their notice. Pre-emption floats, when tested by this rule, were found to be very few indeed. Governments, like corporations, are considered without souls, and according to the code of some people's morality, should be swindled and cheated on every occasion.[11]

Linton suggested that the President withhold patents from all land entries based upon pre-emption floats between June 1, 1834, and July 1, 1835.

No doubt the land officers were not as alert to the government's interests as they should have been; indeed, it seems that they were criminally responsible for much of the fraud and may have shared in the gain. Had the land officers protected the interests of the United States, much of the theft would have been avoided. On the other hand, they had no means of determining the truthfulness of individuals' sworn statements with regard to improvements or the basis for rejecting floating claims on land a hundred miles from the office. In the last analysis, the blame rests more with the system than with the land officers.

Another government transaction which resulted in dishonesty and skul-duggery was the Indian land-settlement policy, which can be illustrated by the Treaty of Dancing Rabbit Creek, on September 27, 1830, and its execution. The government, pressed by the frontiersmen to move the Choctaws from their homes in Alabama and Mississippi, sought to safe-guard the Indians' property rights and ease the shock of the transaction. The Choctaws, by this time fairly well civilized, lived in houses and culti-vated the soil after the fashion of the whites. In honorable recognition of the situation, the treaty reserved cultivated land to the Indians and their children. If the head of an Indian family had as much as fifty acres of land in cultivation and wanted to become a citizen, he was entitled to 640 acres for himself, 320 acres for each child over ten, and a quarter section for each child under ten. After living on it for five years, he would be given a patent. The land not claimed under this provision was to be sold in

[11] Benjamin F. Linton, District Attorney of Western District of Louisiana, to President Andrew Jackson, August 25, 1835, in *American State Papers, Public Lands*, VIII, 443–444.

accordance with the regular government scheme and the proceeds were to be held for the benefit of the tribe in its new home in the West. If two Indians had been cultivating the same surveyed tract or if there were overlapping claims, the two were given "floating" rights.[12]

As in every situation of this kind, squatters had been moving onto the Indian land in anticipation of a special pre-emption act. The provision that reserved cultivated land to the Indian families was resented by these frontiersmen, who thought the only good Indian was a dead one; and the arrangement whereby the Indians could secure floating claims—because of tracts illegally occupied by white trespassers—was considered intolerable. A company of speculators, formed to secure the land held by these civilized Indians, contacted the settlers and urged them not to oppose the confirmation of the lands located for the Indians; in return, the company would bind itself to sell and convey to the settlers 160 acres at $1.25 an acre and the rest of the section at three dollars an acre.

Because many of the Indians had gone West without registering intent to claim personal ownership of a tract, the company said they did not know their rights and sent agents west of the Mississippi to bring them back to claim their land. The Indians were then induced to sell the land to the company at a nominal price. Public indignation, however, was so strong that the group proposed to enlist popular men to make itself appear more respectable. According to one proposal, the original group was to form a subcompany within the larger organization. How this company fared is not revealed by the official records, but the Indians did not escape despoliation.

If an Indian had a bona fide claim and intended to stay, white men would offer to buy the land at a tempting price and would pay the Indian from one-tenth to one-quarter the price agreed upon, contracting to pay the balance at the time the treaty was ratified. Promissory notes were given to the Indians, to be paid when the titles became perfect. The Indian then made out a bona fide deed, with an acknowledgment of receipt of the whole amount, and emigrated to Oklahoma. The purchaser would sell the land to an incoming settler, and he to another, and the land might pass through a half-dozen hands before the date the promissory note was due, while the first purchaser became rich through many such transactions. By the time the Indians' payment was due, the manipulator had fled to Texas or other unknown parts, cheating the Indian and leaving

---

[12] Memorial in Behalf of Sundry Choctaw Indians (by their agent, Andrew Hays), to the House of Representatives, February 1, 1836, in *American State Papers, Public Lands*, VII, 5–13, 27.

the last white purchaser in danger of losing his land and the improvements he had bought and paid for.[13] A declaration signed by eighty-eight citizens of Mississippi and sent to the General Land Office noted that speculators had produced documents purporting to be powers of attorney from Indians to select lands and transfer their rights, and thus had gained control of the choicest lands. The fraud covered entire districts, which were inhabited and cultivated by citizens who had anticipated that the government would continue its policy of granting pre-emption rights to settlers.

In carrying out the provisions of treaties that set aside land for Indian agriculturists, the government sometimes sent locating officers to place the Indians upon the land that had been provided for them. Many of these agents, however, were corrupt, and located land in the name of dummy claimants or unqualified Indians—minors, wives who were not the head of a family, and Indians who impersonated the real owners. Speculators would bring an Indian before the agent, where he swore he was the person who qualified, and then the land-grabber persuaded the impostor to sell the land to him for a pittance. The floating rights granted to children were even more useful, for the speculator could use them to enter the finest land or townsite tracts, which could be cut up into lots and sold at fabulous prices. Many civilized Indians, cheated and expelled from their lands, suffered privation, poverty, and persecution at the hands of other unscrupulous persons. Driven to desperation, famished and homeless, they became thieves and pillagers. They burned houses, robbed the mail, and in other ways became a menace to the white population. As a result, Colonel J. B. Hogan was dispatched to investigate the Indian discontent. His report incriminated many white men of respectable standing in the area.[14]

As has been noted, veterans of the various wars before the Civil War received land warrants, valued at $1.25 an acre, for their service. Since most of them did not care to go West and live on the frontier, they sold their warrants to brokers in the East. Because a vast number of these warrants were thrown on the market within a few months, the sale price declined to as little as fifty cents an acre. These warrants, bought at perhaps one-half the face value (62.5 cents), were applied in some

[13] William S. Colquhoun to Lewis Cass, September 20, 1833, in *American State Papers, Public Lands*, VII, 14.

[14] Affidavits of Sundry Persons Received in the Investigation of the Frauds in the Sale of Public Lands by the Senate Committee on Public Lands, 1835, in *American State Papers, Public Lands*, VII, 735–737, 740, 741, 745; James Edmonds Saunders, *Early Settlers of Alabama* (New Orleans, 1899), p. 285.

instances to land worth from five to fifty dollars per acre, but this increase was not all profit; an agent in the West had to be paid, and the speculator often had to wait several years for an increase in values. (Fortunately, there have been no military land bounties since 1855.) At the opening of the Civil War there were so many volunteers that there was no need of an incentive to secure troops, and by 1862 Congress had passed the Homestead Act.

Another law, which was passed in 1854 and was similar in its effect to the military warrants, was the Sioux Half-Breed Scrip Act. Many of the Sioux Indians who resided in Minnesota were half-breeds who had adopted the ways of the white man but retained their interest in the tribal reservation. When the tribe was moved into the Dakotas, the government gave each half-breed a certificate that entitled him to enter 480 acres of land that was not occupied or surveyed. The certificates were not transferable, but this provision was easily circumvented, and the act became a vehicle for the conveyance of valuable land from the government to private ownership even before it was surveyed.[15]

Land warrants were very unpopular among settlers in the West, but probably there would have been less feeling against military warrants if the veterans had become settlers. Many thought of the land-warrant system as a form of graft by which the wealthy were able to make exorbitant profits. The system, moreover, encouraged speculation and absentee ownership of vast districts. Agents were able to isolate the settlers, to depress or limit the increase in value of their land, and to deprive them of the assets of living in a thickly settled region. In 1853, settlers near the town of South Grove, Illinois, complained—when it became certain that a railroad would be built near or through the town—that speculators had purchased nine-tenths of the remaining government land, entering warrants bought at eighty cents or less and gaining land which would become valuable with the completion of the railroad.

Henry L. Ellsworth, who operated primarily in western Indiana and Illinois, advertised that he would buy land for investors at 62.5 cents an acre by purchasing soldiers' warrants at $100 for a quarter section. He agreed to invest in the land for capitalists in return for one-half the increase of the investment when it was sold. Ellsworth believed he could sell the land within two years for four dollars an acre, and in five years for five dollars an acre, which he pointed out would be a 700 per cent gain. He said he hoped when he sold to get as much cash as the land originally

[15] William Watts Folwell, *A History of Minnesota* (4 vols.; St. Paul: Minnesota Historical Society, 1921), I, 324–325.

cost, which could be refunded or reinvested as they chose; a mortgage would be accepted for the balance.[16]

Speculators, large or small, had insight and were innately opportunistic. Franklin Steele, the day after the official notice that Indian title had been extinguished in the vicinity of the present Twin Cities in Minnesota, located a claim on the east side of the Mississippi River and abreast of the Falls of St. Anthony. Steele had sufficient frontage to command the waterpower to the center of the channel, and by buying out other claimants, he gained control of a valuable site.[17] Speculators laid out counties on each side of the Minnesota River above St. Paul and set up county seats on the river as gateways to land seekers who came by water. Afterward, many of these seats were changed, but they were key positions for speculator schemes in the 1850's. In the late 1850's the competition among speculators for land in Iowa became so keen that the auction price sometimes was bid above the minimum. J. W. Dennison, an agent for the Providence Land Company of Rhode Island, wrote that at the spring auction of 1856 in western Iowa much of the land sold for $1.35 to $3.00 an acre, although the price was held down because the speculators would get together before the auction, compare notes, and settle among themselves which tract each was to have, largely eliminating competition. In this way, by trading tracts with one another before the sale, Dennison said he got every piece he wanted at the minimum price.[18]

At the Council Bluffs land office during 1856, the rush to enter land was unprecedented. The clerks worked night and day, and 200,000 acres were entered during one month. John H. Charles, who acted as agent for an investment company in the late 1850's, said that it was a common plan to enter a quarter section at $1.25 an acre and sell it immediately on one year's credit for $2.50 to $3.00 an acre. So great was land hunger in the East in that boom period that he said one could get four dollars an acre by going there to sell.

As has been noted, the surest and quickest returns came from the sale of timberlands adjacent to prairie, which could be sold in four or five years at a high figure. Knute Stevenson of southern Minnesota surveyed one hundred acres of timberland into three- to five-acre lots and sold them to the prairie newcomers for forty and fifty dollars an acre. When vast acres

[16] Elmore Barce and Robert A. Swan, *History of Benton County, Indiana* (Fowler, Ind.: Benton Review Shop, 1930), pp. 62–63.

[17] Folwell, *History of Minnesota*, I, 228–229.

[18] J. W. Dennison to the Providence Land Company, April 9, 21, 1856, in *Iowa Journal of History and Politics*, XXXI, No. 2 (April, 1933), 292–295.

were held by absentee owners, the settlers tried by various schemes to make the owners pay a larger share of the taxes than their holdings would warrant. One scheme that was successful in Illinois was a type of gerrymandering whereby the residents built their schools with little cost to themselves. They successively attached the sections that belonged to speculators to every district that wished to build a school, and the residents who were caught in the tax net were reimbursed by contributions from the settlers in the benefit area. In this way fine schools were supplied at small cost to the residents, and a rotation plan ensured that the highest possible taxation was levied on absentee owners—who, if they ever visited the area, must have been astonished that there was not a school within miles of their land although they had been taxed to the limit for that purpose for several years.[19]

In Nebraska in 1875 a shrewd Scotsman from Australia demonstrated how a settler could take advantage of an absentee landlord to forward his own interests. He bought an eighty-acre tract from a speculator in the midst of the latter's holdings and built up a herd of cattle. He pastured them on the absentee speculator's land around him and made an abundance of hay from the wild grass which grew so luxuriantly upon the large holdings of his speculator neighbor, who, from far away, paid the taxes. However, as the one who related the incident said, everybody was so greedy for land that few were "able to avail themselves of all the advantages to be obtained by *not* buying speculators' land."

During the second quarter of the nineteenth century the first requests for flood control and the reclamation of overflow lands in the Lower Mississippi Valley were made, and the Swamp Lands Act of 1849 gave Louisiana the swamplands within her border on condition that the state reclaim them. The state was to appropriate the money for digging ditches

[19] Henry Lamson Boïes, *History of DeKalb County, Illinois* (Chicago, 1868), p. 471. The same condition existed in the pinelands of Wisconsin. Paul Gates states that the cry of the homesteaders of the Chippewa Valley counties who had no title to land and paid no taxes was: "Let's go for the speculators." They urged that the assessments of nonresidents be increased 100 per cent, and since county government was in the hands of the homesteaders, they had their way. Not only did they make the nonresidents pay a disproportionate amount of taxes, but they arranged matters to siphon the lush tax receipts into their own pockets. Expensive schoolhouses and courthouses were constructed, and they laid out little-needed roads through the woods. For making these improvements, they gave lucrative contracts to themselves or their friends. This they felt justified in doing as compensation for the isolation that was forced upon them by absentee landholders who were getting rich at their expense. See Paul Gates, *The Wisconsin Pine Lands of Cornell University* (Ithaca: Cornell University Press, 1943), pp. 86, 87, 143, 144.

to drain the water from the swamps and for building dikes to prevent overflows in flood seasons, and the reclaimed land was to be sold to pay for its reclamation. One proposal envisioned a canal to divert excess water from the Mississippi in times of flood. The problem was national, however, because the water which flooded Louisiana came from many states to the north.

Once a state received aid, other states—whether subject to floods or not—also called for aid, and Congress in 1950 passed the Swamp Lands Act, which extended the law of 1849 to cover all of the states, with the provision that the proceeds from the sale of these lands would be used for levees and for ditches to drain the flooded areas. The original idea was to apply the law only to the areas indicated on the surveyors' records as swampy and unfit for cultivation, but the Commissioner of the General Land Office allowed the states to decide which lands within their borders were swamplands. The states appointed commissioners to make the selections, which resulted in a riot of fraud and corruption. The commissioners usually were paid according to the number of acres they secured; hence, the more swampland they discovered, the more they were paid. Incompetent and unscrupulous, they might swear that land was swampy and that they had gone over it in a boat, but neglect to add the interesting fact that the boat was in a wagon and that they had transferred the spring seat of the wagon to the boat and that they were driving the team over good solid ground. Indeed, in 1857 the Surveyor General wrote that he had received lists of selections "situated among and embracing portions of the Ozark Mountains" that had been described in the surveyors' field notes as "too mountainous and hilly for cultivation." In Iowa, federal agents discovered that of 64,360 acres declared too wet for cultivation in five counties, only 7,400 acres were actually swampy.[20] Ignoring the reason why the land was given, some of the states even requested additional land as indemnity for the swampland that had already been taken by settlers who had selected this "swamp" land by choice over other available tracts.

Another absurdity was discovered in Oregon by the General Land Office: a desert claim and a swampland selection lay side by side. The Commissioner did not know which was valid, if either, and strongly suspected that both were speculator-inspired. According to a special agent, Charles Shackelford, the swampland selected by corrupt state

[20] Roscoe L. Lokken, *Iowa Public Land Disposal* (Iowa City: The State Historical Society of Iowa, 1942), pp. 191–193; William W. Robinson, *Land in California* (Berkeley: University of California Press, 1948), p. 193.

land commissioners included hundreds of thousands of acres of dry and arable land on hillsides, valleys, and even on mountain ranges. According to his report, the chief object of the "swamp ring" of government officers, state land commissioners, and other land-grabbers seemed to be to secure possession of all the water frontage and approaches to water and thereby control all of the grasslands in that part of Oregon for sale to the cattlemen. By means of chicanery, false surveys, bribery, and fraudulent returns, they had conspired to show that highlands and elevated sagebrush plains were swampy. In the meantime, settlers came into Lake County, located fertile claims, and began farming, unaware that the land was swampy. When the ranching companies to whom the state officials had sold the land attempted to dispossess the farmers, the latter would not move and fought the unjust ouster proceedings. The fight began in the local land office, went to the Commissioner of the General Land Office, to the Secretary of the Interior, and to the United States district courts. In 1905 the case was submitted to the Supreme Court, but many settlers, worn out with litigation, had made the best possible terms with the cattle company and had abandoned their homes. Others stayed on the lands, determined that they would keep them, but they had to give up finally.[21]

In California, by means of the Swamp Lands Act, Henry Miller, a famous rancher, was able to garner in a hundred-mile continuous strip of "swamp and overflowed land" along the San Joaquin River, a highly irrigated region today. Nevertheless, California was one of the few states which attempted to do something in harmony with the spirit of the Swamp Lands Act. On the lower San Joaquin and the Sacramento rivers, a considerable body of land was drained. An ingenious system of levies, dams, and tidal gates was set up to control egress and ingress of water from or to the lands according to the needs—whether irrigation or drainage was temporarily desired. The rich tule lands on the bottoms were destined to supply much of the fruit and vegetables for San Francisco. This was the rare exception, however, for very little was done by the states to reclaim flooded lands until the United States in more recent times had spent vast sums in building levees to protect the areas given to the states in 1850 on condition of reclamation.

With the advent of the Republican party as a dominant factor in the government of the United States, the policy of free land for settlers was adopted. Strange as it may seem, at the very time that the Homestead Act was passed by Congress (May 20, 1862), that body was considering other acts which were in large measure to undermine this policy of making

[21] F. A. Shaver, *An Illustrated History of Central Oregon* (Spokane, 1905), pp. 829–841.

available the public lands to homemakers. A million acres to the Union Pacific Railroad was only one of a number of such grants. Moreover, thirteen days after the Homestead Act became law, Congress passed the Morrill Land Grant Act. This gave the states a total of thirteen million acres for the endowment of a college of agriculture and mechanical arts in each commonwealth. Thus we see, in the Civil War era, a clash between the homestead and the grant-in-aid policies. Whereas the Homestead Act would give each actual settler a home and encourage the growth of a thickly settled region of homeowners, the Morrill Act would give the states large tracts which they could sell in order to secure money for their colleges. The latter, however, was an ideal system for promoting the twin evils the frontiersmen despised: speculation and absentee ownership.

The Morrill Act provided that each state not in rebellion should receive thirty thousand acres of land for each senator and representative it had in Congress. The strongest support for the bill came from the northeastern states, which would receive the largest grants; the greatest opposition came from the newest states, which would receive only a small amount of land while yielding large quantities of the land within their boundaries to eastern states. The bill provided that the states which had no federal land within their borders should receive scrip entitling them to land within the borders of the public-land states. This scrip was issued at the customary rate of $1.25 an acre.[22] Since there was no government land in the eastern states, their scrip would have to be used in states farther to the west. Moreover, grants of large quantities of land or the equivalent in scrip gave unscrupulous politicians an opportunity to use the scrip for their personal gain; and, unfortunately, much of the land given to the colleges was frittered away by careless administrators. This agricultural college scrip brought with it all of the evils of the previous kinds of scrip and was more serious because so much was dumped on the market at once.

Because the colleges needed money to get started, there was a demand that the scrip be sold and the interest accruing from the sale be used at once, instead of locating tracts of raw land from which there would be no immediate income. Since the scrip had to be used to purchase large areas rather than single pieces of land, there was no demand for it from the thousands of pre-emptors who would have bought it at only a slight reduction. As a result of the lessened demand and because of the pressing needs of the new schools, whose managers dumped the scrip on the market, its price fell as low as forty-two cents an acre, and several states sold theirs

[22] Thomas Donaldson, *The Public Domain* (Washington, D.C.: Govt. Printing Office, 1884), pp. 223, 230, 231.

for fifty to sixty cents. At this rate, speculators could secure twice as much land with scrip as they could with cash. Gleason F. Lewis of Cleveland, who practically monopolized the market, bought for himself—or as an agent for others—five million of the entire thirteen million acres, which included the entire acreage of a number of states.

To combat the tendency toward absentee ownership of large unbroken blocks of land, the frontier area persuaded Congress to pass a law on July 27, 1868, which provided that the number of sections in a township acquired with scrip be restricted to three, or to one-twelfth of a township. As usual, the General Land Office was slow in sending the notices to the land offices. Speculators, however, heard of the change and, taking advantage of the overland telegraph, entered 66,720 acres in solid tracts in California before the directive reached the land offices in that state.[23]

Cornell University, the agricultural college of New York State, managed its land acquisition the best of any of the land-grant colleges. Instead of selling its scrip at a discount, Ezra Cornell, the "father" of the university and an enterprising man, applied it on land to advantage. He secured the services of an unscrupulous clerk, Henry C. Putnam, in the land office in Wisconsin. With a confederate in the land office, Cornell was favored in various ways over other landseekers. For example, when locators who represented other interests came to the land office to enter pinelands, Putnam would inform them that the land was taken, then mark the sections sold but hold them for entry by Cornell's agents. By buying land wisely, guarding it from depredation, and selling stumpage and lands at an advance in price, Cornell University netted $5,000,000 for its endowment.[24]

During the debate over the passage of the Homestead Act in the 1850's, another force was in the making which partly nullified the propitious influence of the Homestead Act. A precedent for this was the treaty with the Delaware Indians in Kansas in 1854 whereby their land was to be sold at auction, under the supervision of the Bureau of Indian Affairs, for the benefit of the tribe. For a generation thereafter, there were two federal land-dispensing agencies in Kansas: the General Land Office and the Bureau of Indian Affairs. The general pattern for land distribution under the latter agency was that if special interests wanted to secure land owned by the Indians, they would persuade the tribe that it was in its best interest to make a treaty by which it would agree to sell its land through the Bureau of Indian Affairs. The price for the land was fixed by the

[23] Gates, *The Wisconsin Pine Lands of Cornell University*, p. 32.
[24] Cornell also bought smaller acreages in Minnesota and Kansas.

treaty; usually it was the customary $1.25 an acre, but in some instances the Indians demanded that it be sold at an appraised price. At times this was twice the minimum government price, or even higher. (The original agreement on that portion of the Cherokee Outlet in Kansas, a strip along the southern boundary, was two dollars an acre, but because of a lack of sales during the Panic of 1873 the price was halved.) Since Indian lands of this nature did not become part of the national domain or public land, and were not subject to homesteading and pre-emption, large tracts could be purchased. This policy loosed a horde of speculators upon Kansas. A man with enough money could buy any quantity of land he desired and hold it for an increase in price and in the meantime keep the country unsettled.

The large amount of land in Kansas that was removed—by the Morrill Act, railroad grants, and Indian distribution—from what would otherwise have been part of the public domain gave the speculators great opportunities. Land received free by these agencies or purchased cheaply from the Indians was retailed at an advance to the actual land users. Paul Gates states that 42 per cent of the area of Kansas was excluded from the public domain and thus became a speculator's paradise rather than—as we are accustomed to believe—a free gift to the tillers of the soil.

In Kansas during the early 1870's there was a unique use of the public lands for the benefit of a group of unscrupulous frontier rogues. Their plan involved the organization of county governments upon sparsely settled or unsettled lands in central and western Kansas. The state legislature had made provision for the organizing of counties, and since there were almost no permanent residents in the buffalo-hunting country of western Kansas, the region presented a fruitful field for the scheme. The law required that an area, to be organized, should have not less than six hundred bona fide inhabitants, but the fact that the territory they wished to organize as Barber County, for instance, had less than one hundred residents deterred them not in the least. They secured the services of a census taker, whose tools in trade were a hotel register and a ready skill at copying names. When his list was made up, he swore that the names represented bona fide voters of the area and sent the form to the Kansas secretary of state, who approved the petition and authorized organization. A county board was then elected by the rogues, and this body immediately issued $25,000 in warrants to C. C. Bemis for the purpose of building a courthouse. Although Bemis neither constructed the building nor returned the money, the board decided to give him another chance and voted $40,000 more for the courthouse. Although this time the few actual residents of the county objected to the proceedings and defeated the bond issue at the election, the commissioners nevertheless issued the bonds and elected one of their members to the state legislature to "cover" the irregular proceedings. The board issued $40,000 or $50,000 in warrants to build bridges across the streams in the county, but not one bridge was constructed. Next, a mythical corporation—the Nebraska, Kansas, and Southwestern Railroad—was organized, and the conspirators contrived a fake bond issue and authorized the issuance of $100,000 in bonds at 10 per cent interest in the name of their paper corporation. Not a mile of road was built, but the board issued—and sold—the bonds, which finally passed into the hands of a member of Parliament in England. Afterward, when the county was settled, the taxpayers resisted payment on the bonds on the basis of fraud and carried the case to the Supreme Court. They lost their case, however, and forty years later were still paying on this fraudulent obligation. The new settlers, when they learned of the thievery at the county seat, formed a vigilance committee and rounded up part of the gang, but the plunderers agreed to restore the money and leave the country, and the settlers released them, but their confidence was misplaced. The swindlers left, but instead of restoring the ill-gotten money, they took the warrant book and county seal, and from a safe distance continued to issue bonds. They never returned any money and they made a clean getaway. A number of other counties in Kansas were similarly plundered, and huge debts were attached to the land just as though it had been mortgaged before it passed from the ownership of the national government. It is a sad fact that not one of the thieves engaged in the faudulent county organizations in Kansas was punished.[25] A number of counties in northwestern Iowa were plundered in the same fashion.

[25] T. A. McNeal, *When Kansas Was Young* (New York: Macmillan, 1922), pp. 20–24, 64.

XIV

Free Grass, the Cattleman's Paradise

FROM THE TIME of the early English settlements in America, the towns had set aside commons for stock-grazing. As the frontier moved westward, the settlers grazed their cattle, horses, and hogs on free government land to the westward, or on the range as it was called. Immediately after the Civil War the ranching area on the western fringe of settlement expanded into an area larger than the cultivated area of the United States and became an important economic factor in the life of the nation. With the building of the transcontinental railroads, the buffalo herds were killed, leaving vast grasslands to be occupied by cattle. The transcontinental railroads, although they spelled the doom of the Indian and the buffalo, made it possible to market the products from this vast ranching area.

Cattle-raising on the Plains had its beginnings along the trails that traversed the West. As early as 1835 the Bent brothers—at Bent's Fort on the Santa Fe Trail—were doing a limited ranching business in connection with their fur-trading activities. By the late 1850's, so-called road ranches along the trails a little farther north traded fresh cattle and oxen with passing travelers. Many of these ranchers were former trappers and, a little later, unsuccessful miners who squatted at favorable spots along the trails and on the Plains at the edge of the highlands.

In Texas, meanwhile, millions of head of cattle were awaiting a market. The railroads slowly being built across the Plains beckoned to the pent-up Texas herds. Enterprising cattlemen from Texas and the North conceived the idea of driving the cattle to a point on the railroad for shipment east. In 1867 a farseeing Illinois cattleman, Joseph G. McCoy, located a marketing point near the western end of the Kansas Pacific Railroad, at Abilene, Kansas, and invited Texans to drive their herds to that point. This was the beginning of the successful operation of the Long Drive, which was made possible by the open Indian or government-owned land that extended

220

northward from the Texas boundary.[1] Once Abilene became a market, however, more cattle were driven from Abilene to the northern Plains than were shipped east.

The government at this time was contracting for beef for its soldiers scattered over the Plains and for herds to furnish food for the Indians on the reservations, since their food supply was dwindling at the hands of the buffalo hunters. Soon after this—when the Plains were cleared of buffalo and Indians—a vast and unoccupied grassland waited to be stocked with cattle. Ranching promised to be a real "beef bonanza" inasmuch as the United States furnished the range free of charge and the ranching facilities were not subject to taxes. Large cattle interests from Scotland, England, and the Continent, as well as eastern cattlemen, took advantage of the opportunity, while the early ranchers continued to live as squatters, enjoying the free grass, occupying the watering places, and making hay where they pleased. At first, the ranchers did not even bother to enter the land on which their ranch buildings stood.[2] As it became apparent that there was a future in the cattle business, newcomers began to seek locations and to apply the principles of pre-emption in a new way. By squatting on land around a watering place, a cowman was able to hold the land for about seven and a half miles on every side. Cattle will not walk more than fifteen miles a day and therefore would not graze farther away than one-half the round trip to water.

The principle of "priority use of the range" was coupled with another principle, known as the "law of the accustomed range." The latter was recognized in enactments by various states that provided punishment of any person who drove stock from their accustomed range. Although this law was directed at cattle theft, it also held that a man established a claim to a particular area by prior grazing and by the habits of his cattle, similar to the claim of the miner who opened a shaft and could claim the ground around it. For example, land where the Lazy W cattle regularly grazed became known as Lazy W range.[3]

A man would ride across the country looking for a range much as the prospector looked for paydirt. The ideal location was a valley that had plenty of grass, hay lands, coulees extending back from a river or stream,

[1] A large drive had been made in 1866 through semisettled country, but with indifferent success. See Joseph G. McCoy, *Historic Sketches of the Cattle Trade of the West* (Kansas City, Mo., 1874), pp. 1–7.

[2] Addison E. Sheldon, *Land Systems and Land Policies in Nebraska* (Lincoln: Nebraska State Historical Society, 1936), p. 178.

[3] Ernest S. Osgood, *The Day of the Cattleman* (Minneapolis: University of Minnesota Press, 1929), p. 182.

and knolls and hillsides. If clumps of small trees were scattered along the valley, all the better. Trees and coulees provided the cattle protection from winter storms, and hills that the wind swept free of snow provided feed when the coulees were filled with deep drifts. Once the cattleman found his ranch site, he went to the nearest newspaper and posted his claim, somewhat as the miner had posted his, or as the early backwoods farmer had blazed his unsurveyed holding. Wyoming and Montana newspapers ran many columns of claim advertisements, of which Professor Ernest Osgood gives this example, from the *Glendive Times* of Glendive, Montana, April 12, 1884:

> I, the undersigned, do hereby notify the public that I claim the valley, branching off the Glendive Creek, four miles east of Allard, and extending to its source on the South side of the Northern Pacific Railroad as a stock range—CHARLES S. JOHNSON.

Since a man was occupying government land that was subject to entry by others, such a claim was extralegal; in time, therefore, he entered a homestead on which to erect the ranch headquarters with its numerous buildings and corrals. The next step in keeping trespassers off a claim was gaining control of all the water adjacent to the range. If the land lay along a stream, a rancher could pre-empt a second quarter, in addition to his home quarter-section, and a third quarter-section as a timber-culture claim. Still later, the Desert Land Act was useful to the cattleman; if he owned the property along the water, he could fence it and control the hinterland.

Because there was no legal way to purchase land outright, cattlemen were obliged to resort to fraud or to an abuse of the system for dispensing land as provided by law (this is discussed in detail elsewhere in this volume). In order to hold land, cattlemen in a region would also unite and refuse to cooperate with a newcomer. Various operations depended upon cooperation: the use of common corrals; protection against Indians, thieves, and predatory animals; and group participation in the round-up in early summer and the beef drive in the autumn. Here, then, was the old scheme in new garb—"hating out" a newcomer if he presumed to intrude upon the regulations made by the community organization. The new organization, in some respects comparable to the claim club, was called a cattlemen's association, and it denied privileges to those it wished to exclude.[4]

[4] Bruce Nelson, *Land of the Dakotahs* (Minneapolis: University of Minnesota Press, 1946), p. 209.

Cattlemen also secured grazing land by leasing or buying land from the railroads and by leasing tracts on Indian reservations. During this early period, cattlemen in California, Arizona, and New Mexico took advantage of fictitious or exaggerated private claims or old grants from the Spanish or Mexican governments. For many years, cattlemen possessed or used hundreds of thousands of acres of grazing land under pretended grants, many of which eventually were disallowed.

In addition to these sources of land, tens of thousands of acres of public land were "covered" by being surrounded or intermingled with holdings of cattlemen in such a manner as to make them unavailable to farmers. So secure were these ranchers in their holdings and use of the land that they bought and sold this government property as part of their ranches. In 1883, for example, when Coad Brothers sold their ranch holdings in western Nebraska to the English, Scottish, and eastern interests which eventually formed the Bay State Livestock Company, of the ten tracts listed in the contract, Coad Brothers held a clear title to only 527 acres. Another tract of 320 acres was listed as "the title to which is in process of being obtained from the Government." Compared to this insignificant acreage, the inventory listed vast holdings of government land under their control which they were selling as an integral part of their ranching operations:

What is known as the 'Main Pasture' being about eight miles in width and thirty-five miles in length and which is enclosed, to which Coad Brothers have no title except a possessory title or right thereto.

What is known as the 'Mitchell Pasture' which is five miles in width and eight miles in length and which is enclosed and to which Coad Brothers have no title except a possessory one . . . .

In addition to the foregoing the Coad Brothers have a large open and unenclosed ranche with almost limitless boundaries and located on and south of Pumpkin Creek . . . .[5]

According to an estimate made by a son of John F. Coad at a later time, the total acreage of the ranch as sold under this contract was 220,000 acres (of which they had a legal right to sell only 527 acres). This sale, which brought Coad Brothers over $900,000, suggests that in many sales of American ranches to foreign interests in the 1880's, the selling price was based largely on their holdings of government land.[6] Since only 22,000

[5] Coad Brothers: Contract with the Nebraska Land and Cattle Company, Limited, March 30, 1883, MS, Nebraska State Historical Society Library.

[6] A. B. Wood, "The Coad Brothers, Panhandle Cattle Kings," *Nebraska History*, XIX, No. 1 (January–March, 1938), 38.

head of cattle were inventoried, it is obvious that the value of the business was in government land they controlled.

A great hardship on the prairie and Plains country was caused by the absence of trees. As the traveler went west from the Missouri River, into Kansas or Nebraska, or across the Red River in the Dakotas, the number of trees decreased, and beyond the 100th meridian there were scarcely any. Women, especially, missed their former home to the east. By themselves for long periods, they frequently dreamed of the old home: orchards, vineyards, and rippling brooks. In August, when the blistering southwest wind turned the vast prairie into a sea of brown on all horizons, the prairie dweller longed for the trees of Iowa or Wisconsin. In Nebraska, especially, tree planting was encouraged, and a state law granted taxpayers a $100 exemption for five years on their property evaluation for each acre planted to trees. Arbor Day was instituted in Nebraska, which was known as the Tree Planters State, and the intense desire for trees throughout the "sod-house frontier" found a response in Congress. On March 3, 1873, the Timber Culture Act was passed, providing for what was commonly known as the tree claim. The act allowed a person to file on a quarter section of land devoid of trees; then, if he planted forty acres to trees and kept them in good condition for ten years, he could have a patent to the land; there was no residence requirement. In 1878 the measure was amended, reducing the requirement for trees to ten acres and prescribing 2,700 trees per acre at the time of planting and 675 per acre in good condition at the time of patent. As it turned out, the act was a made-to-order land conveyance for cattlemen and speculators.

At best, even if a man went through the motions of fulfilling the requirements of the law, it was primarily a means of adding a quarter section to his holdings. In this way the typical pioneer was able to secure 480 acres by means of the Homestead, Pre-emption, and Timber Culture acts. A common procedure by those who made an attempt to fulfill the requirements of the Timber Culture Act was to plow a furrow, stick cottonwood cuttings erect in the bottom of the furrow, and cover them with the next round of the plow, allowing the switches to stand erect; then they skipped a few furrows and repeated the process. The more conscientious made an effort to keep down the weeds between the rows. Astonishing as it may be, if the earth was marshy or wet, the cottonwood sticks formed roots and grew. In a few places enough effort was put forth to actually plant trees, and a lively demand was created for seedlings. At Chadron, Nebraska, in the fall of 1886 and the spring of 1887, Ben Arnold and Don Pope sold more than a million young cottonwood saplings to land claimants.[7] Nurseries advertised that they would furnish the trees and set them in compliance with the provisions of the law—a boon to nonresidents who did not need to leave the old home. By and large, however, the attempt to make trees grow in the semiarid region was a mockery of nature. A man who went to see an agent about a loan was asked whether he had complied with the law, and he said he had. He had plowed five acres the first year, in keeping with land-office regulations; the second year he raised a crop on the land; and the third year he planted it with tree seeds. On being questioned further, he admitted that he had broadcast the seeds with an oat crop and that he had not seen the land since the oats were harvested and did not know whether the tree seeds had sprouted, but he had planted the land according to the requirements of the law. The claimant could have secured plenty of witnesses among his neighbors to swear that he had fulfilled the requirements since all in the neighborhood were in the same category.[8]

In the semiarid regions, where trees did not grow, it was particularly impossible to fulfill the requirements of the law. The *Nebraska Farmer* of August 22, 1899, asserted that "any man who enters land in good faith and for five years really attempts to grow timber on it will more than earn his land." The editor added that "the Interior Department seems to be run upon the plan that as many barriers as possible should be put in the way of the frontiersman." The newspaperman, in blaming the Department of the Interior, overlooked the fact that a Nebraska congressman, in the interest of promoting a forested Nebraska, had worked hard to get the law passed. As a rule, timber-culture claimants did not intend to raise trees but merely wanted to add a quarter section to their holdings or sell it at an advance. Many of the first settlers' tree claims were sold to the next comers who purchased rather than take homesteads or pre-emptions. A land-office inspector, A. R. Greene, reported in 1884:

I have seen small patches of land (possibly five acres) where the prairie sod had been 'listed' in furrows six or eight feet apart each way, and occasionally a sickly cottonwood sprout, two or three feet in height, of the thickness of a man's thumb, standing thereon. In other cases the land had evidently been honestly plowed at some time, but through neglect

[7] Lewis F. Crawford (ed.), *Rekindling Camp Fires* (Bismarck, N.D.: Capital Book Co., 1926), pp. 278–279.
[8] A. M. Thompson, "Tree Culture on the Western Plains," U.S. Department of Agriculture *Forestry Bulletin*, No. 5 (Washington, D.C.: Govt. Printing Office, 1891), pp. 45–50.

226 THE LURE OF THE LAND

had grown to grass, and the trees (?) were holding up their tiny cattle-browsed, fire-burnt branches in a mute protest against the farcical absurdity of the 'timber culture act.'[9]

The Timber Culture Act lent itself to the rancher more readily than the Homestead Act because residence and improvements were not required; it was necessary only for the cowman to have his cowboys allow their names to be used and for them to perjure themselves at the appropriate moment. There was no building of cabins, even fragile shacks, and no anxiety that someone might be watching to see that the entryman spent a night on his claim now and then. Many tree claims were entered, relinquished after three years, and re-entered by another employee. For example, the southeast section of township 5 north, range 25 west, of the 6th principal meridian at McCook, Nebraska, was entered on March 24, 1879, and between that time and May 25, 1887, it was entered six times and relinquished five times. In Nebraska, Colorado, and Kansas, in the three years prior to 1887, there were 73,908 filings, but only 25,558 claims were perfected. In his report for 1887 the Commissioner of the General Land Office said it was unthinkable that such a large proportion of claimants would abandon claims made in good faith. He pointed out that relinquishments of this magnitude were otherwise unknown and the circumstantial evidence showed that the bulk of them were made for the sole purpose of trafficking in the public domain, not for securing homes.[10] There is, of course, no way of knowing what percentage of these relinquishments was made to hold grazing land; it is certain, however, that great blocks of untaxed rangeland were used for years and that no money was invested in the land that produced the feed for the ranchers' livestock.

In 1888 the land officer at Sidney, Nebraska, stated that there had never been a final proof for a timber-culture claim in that district. The routine, he said, was enter, hold, relinquish, change claims; enter, hold, relinquish, and so on; indefinitely holding and keeping quantities of the public domain from the newcomers until the claims became valuable. The register at Wichita, Kansas, said that in nine cases out of ten the act was used for speculative purposes and that, finally, after several relinquish-

[9] Inspector A. R. Greene to the Commissioner of the General Land Office, November 3, 1884, in *Annual Report of the Commissioner of the General Land Office, 1885* (Washington, D.C.: Govt. Printing Office, 1885), p. 57.

[10] *Annual Report of the Secretary of the Interior, 1887*, I (Washington, D.C.: Govt. Printing Office, 1887), 138, 139, 141.

ments, when the government parted with the land it was by the homestead or pre-emption method.[11]

Almost every section of a ranch had a timber-culture claim in 1885, and the other three quarter-sections often were held by fraudulent use of other land-law provisions, or by sheer force. According to the Commissioner's report for that year it was estimated that 100 per cent of the pre-emptions and 95 per cent of the timber-culture claims were fraudulent. In the eyes of the land officers, the latter act was more harmful than either the Homestead or the Pre-emption act because it permitted the manipulations that kept large areas tied up, and it played into the hands of the big interests. Thousands of settlers were prevented from exercising their legal right to acquire homes. On the other hand, it was a godsend to the rancher, who could not legally secure the land he needed.

Cattlemen, however, were not the only ones who misused the Timber Culture Act. The purpose of the law, of course, was to encourage the growing of trees, and the statute stated that land, to be admissible for taking under the act, had to be "devoid of timber." But by means of the ever useful, ever pliable frontier oath, valuable coal lands—and incredible as it may seem, even timberlands—were separated from the government by the use of this act. The law required the entryman at the time of proof to show 6,750 living and thriving trees as a result of his planting and cultivation. Commissioner Sparks, in his report for 1885, noted that he had found a predecessor's ruling that a partially forested tract, on which not more than 6,750 trees were growing at the time of entry, could be entered as a timber-culture claim, allowing a man to plant a few more trees and fulfill the requirements of the Timber Culture Act—a complete reversal of the intent of the law.

In his report for 1875, the Commissioner of the General Land Office, S. D. Burdett, stated that the homestead law was unsuited to the area west of the 100th meridian because agriculture—as it was known east of that area—could exist only in a few watered valleys where, by the most strenuous labor, water could be diverted for irrigation. Titles to the public lands could not be acquired honestly under the existing laws because it was impossible to cultivate the land as required. Burdett therefore recommended selling or leasing grassland in large quantities for ranching purposes.

Congress, however, ignored Burdett's request to help the cattlemen and, obsessed with the idea of cultivation, passed the Desert Land Act of March 3, 1877, which was intended as an irrigation measure. The act

---

[11] *Annual Report of the Commissioner of the General Land Office, 1888* (Washington, D.C.: Govt. Printing Office, 1888), pp. 51–75.

provided that in the Dakota Territory westward and in the states and territories west of Nebraska and Kansas a land seeker could buy 640 acres of desert land at the old price of $1.25 an acre, on condition that he would irrigate a portion of it. The terms were twenty-five cents per acre down and the balance in three years.

The Desert Land Act was as fine an example of political blundering as can be found anywhere. In the first place, applicants were charged $1.25 an acre for desert land although there was still much land in the rain belt that was available under the Homestead Act merely for the fees. The law also called for an enlarged area for irrigation when only a small area was feasible. Worst of all, most of the land was entirely unsuited for irrigation. Sensing the ridiculous nature of the requirement, settlers made light of the whole thing, evaded the legal requirements, and used the law to their best interests. With a plow or a lister they turned a few furrows between a stream and the uplands—an impossible make-believe irrigation system— in order to secure an addition to their range that could be secured only through trickery.[12] Mounting a barrel on a sled or wagon and accompanied by witnesses, they drove around, dipping out a little water now and then and pouring it into the pseudo-irrigation ditches. This enabled the frontiersman, at the time of final payment, to swear before the land officers that he had "brought water" to the claim. By and large, although the lawmakers in Washington had not intended this outcome, the act was a boon to cattlemen, who used it as they saw fit in their operations. By means of the Desert Land, Homestead, Pre-emption, and Timber Culture acts, a man could accumulate 1,120 acres of land.

Another outstanding weakness of the Desert Land Act was that it did not require surveys, and therefore the government did not know whether it was issuing a patent for 480 or 800 acres or even the type of land in the claim. The act did not require a definite shape for an entry or stipulate the character and extent of the efforts required in reclaiming the section. Although an entryman had to outline his boundaries, the frontier oath was elastic;[13] and a claimant merely had to describe, with as much clearness and precision as possible, the locality of the tract with reference to known and conspicuous landmarks or established lines of survey, so as to admit of its being thereafter readily identified when lines of survey came to be extended.[14]

[12] *Irrigation Age* (Chicago, Ill.), June 1, 1892, p. 65.

[13] Harold Dunham, *Government Handout* (New York: Edwards Brothers, 1941), pp. 30–34.

[14] Thomas C. Donaldson, *The Public Domain* (Washington, D.C.: Govt. Printing Office, 1884), p. 1105.

Descriptions, even if honestly made, often were hard to follow, which made it difficult for anyone to locate a claim. Even officials who were used to inspecting tracts found it almost impossible to detect frauds. Descriptions such as the following were recorded: "At a point 200 feet northeast from rocky point in a certain small creek 55 miles up [another creek] . . . ." Consequently, a person who was looking for a claim might ask a sheepherder about land along a certain creek and be told that it had already been taken in an unsurveyed claim. The prospective settler could not determine the truth of the matter without going to great expense, and sought land elsewhere. Even the land office could not have given him the information he wanted. Thus, large areas were "covered" for many years and used by cattlemen as their own. The Choteau Company of Montana, for example, held many unsurveyed desert claims for twenty years, tax free, for only an initial payment of twenty-five cents an acre.[15]

Speculators selected arable lands—although they swore that they were arid—and held the land for three years, hoping to sell it to a newcomer before it was time to make the final payment. If they could sell their rights in the land for only $2.50 an acre, at the end of three years they could make ten times their original investment. If a cattleman did not wish to pay the purchase price outright, he could hold the land indefinitely through manipulation and the payment of twenty-five cents an acre every three years. When his first three years expired, he could relinquish the claim and have one of his cowboys enter it in his own name, and so on. Of course, land held in this way was not taxed.

The original act of 1877 did not provide for assignment, but an amendatory act of 1891 had a phrase which read: "No person or association of persons shall hold by assignment or otherwise prior to issue of patent more than 320 acres." This was interpreted in such a way as to bring in two new principles which permitted a tremendous amount of fraud: assignment of claims and holding by companies. Assignment was similar to homestead commuting. The theory was that if anyone, while pursuing his irrigation program, ran out of money, rather than abandon the project he could assign it to another. No doubt, "association" was used because the few who actually tried discovered that irrigation projects usually were too big for an individual to handle. The act also reduced the acreage that might be taken by one person under the Desert Land Act to 320 acres, but cattlemen and speculators who wanted to segregate large blocks of the public domain and hold them for their advantage had a picnic.

[15] *Report of the Public Lands Commission, 1905*, S. Doc. 189, 58th Cong., 3d Sess., Appendix p. 86.

According to land-office interpretation, an individual or a company could hold a claim. Accordingly, two men could form a company, ostensibly for the purpose of irrigating their tract, and each could select a claim and take another claim in the name of the company. The same individuals could then form *another* company, under an entirely different name, and repeat the process. New companies were formed ad infinitum, and in each case a half section was alienated from the government. As long as a man did not prove up, he did not forfeit his rights. By forming new companies there was no end to the number of claims he could take, providing he assigned them to new companies.[16] Another dodge used by the cattlemen was to have their cowboys make a desert claim at the employer's expense; but cowboys were nomads, and therefore to protect the cattleman's interest, they had each cowboy execute a blank assignment for the claim he was covering. If the nominal claimant wandered off, a cowman could put another man's name on the document; in a pinch, he might use his own name until he could recruit another entryman. If the cowboy stayed on, in time he would offer proof, receive a patent, and deed the land to his employer.

Sometimes bona fide homesteaders were used by men who furnished them with the money to make desert claims. A husband would claim a 160-acre homestead for himself and a 160-acre desert claim for a cattleman (320 acres was the maximum an individual could hold), and his wife would take a 320-acre desert claim for the rancher. The homesteader and his wife would pay the government for the land, perjure themselves in making the necessary proofs, and turn the title over to the rancher, but that was not the end of the story. The cattleman now held three quarters of the section and the homesteader and his wife one quarter. The rancher naturally wanted his range in one block and, finding it entirely undesirable to have a homesteader in the midst of his pasture, took steps to eliminate the farmer. The latter was entirely at a disadvantage. If he did not come to terms with his big neighbor he found his water shut off (a rancher claimed prior right to water supply) and probably also found himself fenced in on all sides with no right-of-way to his homestead without fighting for it. Eventually he succumbed to the inevitable and either commuted with money furnished by the rancher or made final proof and deeded away his homestead. After a settler had at least theoretically fulfilled his residence and other requirements, he was required to appear at the land office, where he stated this under oath. His two witnesses also were sworn and stated that he had fulfilled the requirements. Face to face with the land

16 *Ibid.*, p. 83.

officers, they were then examined to determine whether the claimant had lived up to the terms. Because land on which a claimant had settled was frequently many miles from the land office, this procedure involved considerable inconvenience and even hardship—in addition to perjury. By law, he must have seen the land before he filed on it; he then had to travel perhaps a hundred miles to the land office of his district to make out the necessary papers and repeat the trip when he proved up.

An act of March 3, 1877, sought to accommodate the settler, and in so doing provided another source of abuse. The new law provided that claimants and their witnesses could appear before the judges and clerks of the various counties, who would administer the oath, and the testimony would then be sent to the land office. The affidavits made by the clerk of the court ordinarily were perfectly legal but there was no opportunity for the land officers to question the claimant and his witnesses, and the judges and clerks of the county courts were not interested in examining the citizen to ascertain the truth of the statements. Indeed, to have looked into these matters too closely would not have been good politics, and the circumstances permitted some highly unethical procedures.

In the Dakota Territory, where the rates for legal procedures were fixed by law, only ten cents per one hundred words was allowed for taking the testimony of witnesses, but the probate judge at Bismarck charged $23.00 for his work on the dubious grounds that he was also the claimant's lawyer and hence was entitled to a lawyer's fee as well. Similar abuses and unethical practices were rife throughout the West. For a fee, agents carried the legal papers from the county office to the land office, and the traffic was heavy.

In the 1880's the land office at Garden City, Kansas, noted that there were fifty or more land agents or attorneys in the town who prepared papers for hundreds of claimants and presented them at one time. In addition, there were numerous land agents in all of the little towns in the valley of the Arkansas River who sent packages of documents to the land agents at Garden City. Said the register:

> I look upon this state of affairs as a real abuse of the privileges designed by law, for a majority of the patrons swept through by these agents never see the land they make entry upon, fail to realize their obligation to the government, and scheme, by following the form to avoid the spirit and intent of the law. We have not time to correct these things; we cannot have time to attend to that patron who is in real need of our assistance.[17]

[17] *Annual Report of the Commissioner of the General Land Office, 1885*, pp. 58, 59, 77, 78, 79.

In any case, it was less embarrassing than facing the land officers with a guilty conscience and trying to prove something that was not true.

The homestead law was used by ranchmen throughout the grazing area, as has been indicated, because it offered a cheaper way of securing land than did the pre-emption law. A cattleman took a number of his cowboys to the land office and had them enter every quarter section along a stream that had a never failing supply of water; and if he did not have enough cowboys, he could have them repeat the process under different names. If the land officers were strict, however, he would build little shacks on the tracts where the cowboys would sleep now and then, but usually houses on wheels or skids were moved from one claim to another to make a show of compliance with the regulations. Ownership of a narrow fringe of one-half mile along the waterfront enabled a cattleman to control an area six or seven miles deep.[18] George A. Benkelman of Denver, who owned twenty miles of waterfront in eastern Colorado, controlled several thousand acres. The Commissioner's report for 1888 noted, after an investigation in the McCook district of Nebraska, that forty pre-emptions and commuted homesteads had been entered in the names of fictitious persons for the benefit of a cattle company.

The successful contests on these speculative entries were rare enough to be newsworthy. The *Keith County News* of Ogalalla, Nebraska, of March 15, 1889, reported the contest of a pre-emption claim which gave promise of considerable value since it was only two miles from the town near the stockyards. J. F. Bishop from Lincoln entered the quarter section as a pre-emption in April, 1884, and went through the formality of proving up on it in October, 1884; but in 1885, before patent had been completed at the General Land Office, Tom Blackburn filed a contest. Testimony in the case showed that Bishop owned 240 acres of land near Lincoln and had resided upon it with his wife and children for several years. About two weeks before he made entry upon his pre-emption he sold his old farm to a minor son for $7,500, taking in payment his unsecured note. In April he built a house, twelve by fourteen feet, on the pre-emption, broke about five acres, and planted some vegetables. Although he had a good supply of furniture at his old home, he took to the claim only some blankets and cooking utensils; and he made a bunk, table, and other furniture of rough boards for use in the claim shack. He left two minor boys to farm the old home place, and although he owned four horses, some cows, and ample farm machinery, he took none of these along but left them on the old home place. His wife and three children came and spent some time with him

[18] Walter Prescott Webb, *The Great Plains* (Boston: Ginn & Co., 1931), p. 241.

during the summer, although his wife was absent a number of times and in September went back to the old home and never returned. He proved up, sold the land immediately, and returned to the old home. After about four years of litigation, the assistant commissioner of the General Land Office ruled that the old home had been his residence prior to, during the time he made the entry and final proof, and afterward—since he continued to live there afterward. According to the decision, the defendant at no time performed acts of settlement that would tend to show in good faith that he intended to make the claim his home. He made the entry as a speculator and did not have a residence on the claim as was contemplated by the law. The assistant commissioner ruled that the sale of the home to an unmarried lad of seventeen was fraudulent and for the purpose of evading the law, which disqualified a person who quit or abandoned his residence on his own land to reside on public land in the same territory or state; therefore, the pre-emption claim was turned over to the contestant.

If a rancher had money and wanted quick title to the land, he could have his men, either real or mythical cowhands, commute and pay $1.25 an acre, but a law of May 27, 1878, provided a convenient way to avoid this payment and simply steal the land. Before 1878 a man's required residence time on a homestead began when he made application at the land office, but application could not be made until the land had been surveyed and the plats had been deposited in the land office. Although a man may have lived up to the spirit of the Homestead Act for four years before the land was surveyed, he could not count any of these years as residence time in fulfillment of the requirement. Now the law of 1880 allowed a homesteader to date his residence from the time he settled instead of from the date of application—the old pre-emption principle.

Instead of repealing the Pre-emption Act, as the commissioners of the General Land Office had repeatedly recommended, Congress perpetuated its evils in the homestead laws, which immediately gave the defrauders a field day. Cattlemen, speculators, lumbermen, coal interests, and others who desired to control large blocks of the public domain employed men to make entries by alleging residence long before the date of entry or even before the land was surveyed. Careful surveys would have prevented much of this fraud, but by swearing they had completed more than their residence requirement, men could secure land patents in a matter of a few days instead of five years.

This fraud was popular in Las Animas County, Colorado, where Mexicans were numerous. A schemer would make a pre-emption claim in the name of a Mexican and allege that settlement had begun more than five years before, which sounded reasonable since they were natives of the land district. The same law permitted an entryman to commute a pre-emption to a homestead. Pre-emptions on surveyed land which had been filed before 1878 could be changed to homesteads, or homesteads on unsurveyed land could be proved up by schemers in the time required to advertise these maneuvers. The register at Las Animas stated that many bona fide claims had been made by these Mexican-Americans but that many more were unquestionably fraudulent.[19]

A law of May 14, 1880, allowed anyone who settled on the public domain, on surveyed or unsurveyed land, with the intention of claiming the tract as a homestead, ninety days in which to file a claim. Benevolent in design, it proved to be the basis for many contests and unfair practices. For example, even though a man had settled on a tract first, another individual could swear that he had settled on it before the bona fide settler. If two men discovered an excellent piece of land at the same time, one might go to the land office and file on it, but the other man, learning his competitor had gone to file, could settle on the land and claim that his right preceded the other's. These contests were a boon to the land lawyers but a curse to the settlers.[20]

Cattlemen used Civil War veterans or their widows in their attempts to procure homesteads quickly. Because the law allowed a veteran to apply his Civil War service in lieu of residence in proving up on the land, many ranchers secured a veteran's warrant and obtained his land in a very short time. Furthermore, a veteran could have an agent make the application for him at the land office. After passage of the Kinkaid Act, the cattle kings combed the country, rounded up all the ex-soldiers they could find, and paid each veteran or dependent fifty dollars and all expenses to file a Kinkaid homestead of 640 acres in the Sand Hills ranching country. Many of these applicants did not know that they were breaking the law by their homesteading activity. In 1906, when the government, under the administration of Theodore Roosevelt, cracked down on the cattlemen, many of these homesteaders appeared as witnesses at the trial in Omaha. The cattlemen were charged with subornation and with aiding fraud by perjury in the entry of land. Testimony showed that veterans or their widows had been gathered and shipped to the Sand Hills by the railroad carload; then,

[19] Register and Recorder of Las Animas Land Office to the Commissioner of the General Land Office, November 15, 1884, in *Annual Report of the Commissioner of the General Land Office, 1885* (Washington, D.C.: Govt. Printing Office, 1885), p. 58.

[20] *Public Land* (Spokane, Wash.), September 17, 1901, p. 5.

before United States commissioners, they had signed papers that had already been filled out for them and had filed on land already selected— even the witnesses were provided. Although they swore that they were taking the land for their own use and had no intention of selling it, they had nimbly dodged this by leasing the sections to cattlemen for ninety-nine years. The trial lasted for twenty days and the United States attorneys piled up evidence that the homesteaders had been lured from their homes by the cattlemen and offered a free train ride to Nebraska, where they followed directions to perjure themselves. So many widows appeared one day as witnesses that the *Omaha World Herald* headlined its account as "ladies' day" at the trial.[21] As a result of this vigorous prosecution, some of the leading cattlemen were imprisoned and fined.

Through the neglect of Congress and the lack of aggressive and efficient administration, the land system, especially during the 1880's, served the land-grabbing interests very well. Unfortunately, members of Congress often had personal interests or had sold out—politically or otherwise—to combines that were grabbing or illegally using the public lands. Land agents, unscrupulous attorneys, and large-scale operators took advantage of every opportunity to create erroneous opinions about the requirements of the law. They induced persons to make illegal and unauthorized entries and to hold the land for them until its value rose. They advised foreign immigrants or people in eastern states that they could swear to the character of land they had never seen, that they could enter land without going to the district in which the lands were located, and that they violated no law in allowing friends to use their names to enter homestead or timber-culture claims. As soon as honest efforts were made to enforce the laws, they sought by every means to prejudice the settlers against the special agents sent out by the General Land Office and to create an impression that the agents were unscrupulous spies who were prying into the private business of the entrymen and seeking to rob them of their land. They were absolutely unscrupulous in dealing with the government or even with their clients, for lawyers often sacrificed their clients' interests in order to make a few dollars. It was a common practice for them to dismiss a legitimate contest without the client's knowledge and immediately institute another contest, upon the same grounds, for another client who would pay a larger fee. The Commissioner's report of 1887 stated that "in some localities the sentiment of the whole community was corrupted by their erroneous advice and dishonest practices and men were led to commit the gravest crimes against

---

[21] Sheldon, *Land Systems and Land Policies*, pp. 198–202.

the laws without knowing or appreciating the consequence of their acts."[22]

During the Cleveland administration, an earnest attempt was made to administer the land in an efficient, honest manner, and Cleveland was forthright in his endeavor to give the country honest government. L. Q. C. Lamar, the Secretary of the Interior, carried out the administration's program and supported the new Commissioner of the General Land Office, William Andrew Jackson Sparks. Sparks, an Illinois man, instituted the most remarkable and vigorous improvement of the office that the country had ever seen. He was a man of high ideals and irreproachable honesty, with a combative and stubborn insistence on clean government and the enforcement of the laws. Sparks, first of all, asked Congress to reform the surveying system. He recommended the repeal of the deposit system, the use of permanent markings (of iron and stone rather than mounds), a penalty for false survey returns, punishment for the removal of markings, and he asked for an appropriation of money to use in inspecting surveys before they were accepted. In executing the land laws, he held up issuance of patents in classes where frauds had been found, and he ordered that new patents be granted only after a thorough investigation. It had been customary, when the General Land Office became glutted with business and entrymen had to wait a year or two for their patents, for land attorneys in Washington to go to the General Land Office with the papers of their clients and secure their patents for them, out of turn. These claims were known as special cases. Sparks abolished the practice. He also abolished the practice of permitting settlers to mortgage their land before they received the patent. If claimants did not pay, of course, the mortgagers received the land. Sparks saw this as a miscarriage of the plan to settle the land with homeowners. Indeed, in many areas on the Plains a mortgage was a sale, for a man never expected to pay off the mortgage. Sparks ruled that a settler did not have title until he had received his patent, and therefore could not mortgage his claim.

Sparks' attempt to administer the land laws according to their spirit and the letter of the law outraged many in the West, as is indicated by the statement of a Nebraska representative: "It is my honest belief that if General Sparks should visit Nebraska the people would mob him before he got out of the State." The *Wyoming Daily Sun* in February, 1887, spoke for the cattlemen and pictured Sparks as assuming the attributes of the Deity because he did not propose to allow the cattlemen to alienate large areas from the government by fraud. It said, derisively: "Thou shalt have no

---

[22] *Annual Report of the Commissioner of Public Lands, 1887* (Washington, D.C.: Govt. Printing Office, 1887), p. 520.

other gods than William Andrew Jackson Sparks and none other shalt thou worship. Thou shalt not raise cattle upon the land, neither sheep nor any living thing but the corn the same as in the state of Illinois."

As soon as Sparks' effort to enforce the laws was felt, land lawyers and agents, who thrived largely on circumventing the law, began a smear campaign. They sought by every means to prejudice the settlers against the General Land Office and its efforts to enforce the laws, and were assisted by members of Congress from the frontier. In February, 1886, Senator Manderson of Nebraska complained that Sparks' withholding of patents until their validity could be investigated had "caused a wonderful amount of suffering this winter."[23] The suffering lay in that the homesteaders who had sworn they were filing on land to make homes for themselves were not allowed to mortgage the land and leave the country, or to turn it over to a speculator or cattleman who had been waiting for it. Sparks' action, however, came at the peak of the boom period in the 1880's, during the great rush into the West, and probably affected more people than any other land office departmental ruling.

The railroads were building westward in the 1880's. New towns were mushrooming and tens of thousands of people were spreading over the Plains. The word had gone out that a penniless person could file on land, put up a soddy or tar-paper shack and live in it a few summers, make proof, and secure a patent for a homestead, and at the same time secure a tree claim. Or, if a man had a little money, he could secure a pre-emption in addition to the homestead and tree claim, and could hold his 480-acre tract until a buyer paid him a good price—or mortgage it for $500 to $1,000 and go back East. However, when patents were issued only on valid grounds, many bubbles burst, and the West turned on Sparks, who said he could not believe that settlers who had taken land for a home were suffering for their inability to mortgage it. If a man had taken up land to mortgage or sell it, he had made a fraudulent entry and had no honest grievance. Said Sparks:

It is inconceivable that whole communities of farmers are anxious to mortgage their actual farms. Ordinarily, where people live upon land as homes, they want to keep them from the grasp of the money brokers and usurers as long as they can.

A particular case which your correspondent presents is the case of a man who, after an apparently doubtful "settlement" for six months and the most meager "improvements," wants to sell or mortgage his asserted

23 Sheldon, *Land Systems and Land Policies*, p. 122.

"home" in the public lands in Nebraska for the most he can get and return to his actual home in some eastern state. This is a very common case. I do not believe that the population of a state is increased by a settlement that is abandoned as soon as its temporary purpose is accomplished, nor that the wealth of the state is augmented by an influx of money that is immediately carried out of the state in this manner.

Another case is where a man made an entry, sold the claim for $800 and the purchaser finds his title is not good. The real hardship in this case is that an honest settler, who wants to get a home upon the public lands, is compelled to remain homeless or buy off a fictitious claim. This kind of hardship I am endeavoring to prevent.[24]

Sparks found that the complaints to his office were not from homemakers, who in fact cared so little for patents that thousands lay in the land offices uncalled for. The clamor, he said—and his investigation bore out—was made by the procurers of false entries who wanted patents issued before the falsity of their claims could be ascertained by the government.

The vigorous steps of the new Commissioner produced results almost immediately. Sparks took office in 1885, and by 1888 attempts to acquire land by fraud had decreased markedly; nevertheless, politics was against the fearless Commissioner. The western states in which the public lands lay were Republican, and since President Cleveland represented the East by residence and thinking, Republicans made it appear that it was the policy of the Democrats to hinder the development of the West. Sparks and his defenders vainly sought to show that the abuses he was attacking had been pointed out by his Republican predecessors and that he was merely trying to correct the situation, that by halting land-grabbing frauds by the big interests he was preserving the public domain for homemakers. But the western clamor was effective; after only a one-year trial, the Secretary of the Interior revoked the order that suspended the issuance of patents until after an investigation had been made. After three years of fighting, Sparks resigned, worn out and discouraged by the seemingly impossible task of securing the cooperation of Congress and his superiors in the great work of executing the laws and preserving the land for homemakers.

Two factors worked in favor of the defrauders after the Civil War: (1) the statute of limitations, which freed miscreants from prosecution after five years and gave them permanent immunity from the penalties they deserved, and (2) the inconsistency of the Supreme Court in upholding the land laws. In the Throckmorton case, the Court passed over some cases of

[24] *Ibid.*, p. 123.

fraud on the grounds that the administration of the land laws had always permitted fraud and that a decision against the claimants would open up innumerable cases and mean the beginning of a whole train of evils. In a later case, although the Throckmorton decision was cited as a precedent, the Court reversed itself.

In the meantime, the land officers continued to have their difficulties with the cattlemen, but in justice to the graziers it must be said that the land laws made no provision for the business of grazing. The system of parceling out land by quarter sections as homestead, pre-emption, and tree claims allowed only 480 acres to be secured legally, although later this was increased to 960 acres. In many parts of the West beyond the 100th meridian, ten to twenty acres were necessary to keep a cow the year round, with the result that ranchers would have been compelled to go out of business or into small-scale operations.

In the late 1870's, suggestions were made that the government lease land to the cattlemen. Although the Union Pacific Railroad was anxious to do this, it was impractical inasmuch as the railroad owned only alternate sections, and anyone who desired a block of territory for a range needed both government and railroad land. Carl Schurz recommended that the government trade its alternate sections on one side of the track for the railroad land on the other side, which would allow the railroads to lease their land in blocks for grazing. The Secretary of the Interior later suggested leasing all government land west of the 100th meridian in blocks of fifty to five hundred square miles to responsible cattlemen for a term of years that would justify the cattlemen in fencing them.[25] Congress, however, refused to make any provisions for leasing lest the public raise the cry of monopoly.

In 1879, the public lands commission, in search of a legitimate means for cattlemen to secure land for their use, proposed a homestead of four square miles on grazing lands. This "enlarged homestead" idea did not gain the support of Congress, however, and for another quarter century the ranchers were obliged to resort to fraud in order to secure enough grazing land to carry on their business. The Kinkaid Act, sponsored by Moses P. Kinkaid of Nebraska in 1902, provided for a homestead of 640 acres; this was experimental and applied to Nebraska only. Since, in western Nebraska—where the land open to entry lay—it took from ten to twenty acres per head, as mentioned previously, this was still insufficient to feed a hundred head of cattle—the number necessary to support a family. Nevertheless there was a tremendous increase in the number of entries; within two years the number of applications increased nearly tenfold. The Commissioner of the General

25 Dunham, *Government Handout*, p. 40.

Land Office and other land officers approved the way the new experiment worked out to the advantage of the homemaker. In 1909, when many of these claims were being proved up, the Commissioner reported that the great majority of these claims had been made in good faith; only about 25 per cent were found deficient and suspect of fraud. After a short trip through western Nebraska, the Commissioner said he was agreeably surprised at the success of the project. Settlers had combined tilling of the valleys with the grazing of tablelands, and thanks to some years of more than average precipitation, comfortable farmsteads were in evidence where it would have been impossible with the old 160-acre homestead. This, of course, was advantageous primarily to the small rancher, but as the years passed, many of these Kinkaiders, as they were called, "dried out" and their tracts gravitated into the hands of the big ranchers, thus legitimately giving them secondhand the added range which they sought.[26] The provisions of the Kinkaid Act were extended to the remaining portion of the public lands in the form of the grazing Homestead Act of December 29, 1916, but it was a case of too little and too late, for by this time the remaining land was such that 640 acres was not nearly enough to form even a small ranch.

A better way to help the big rancher legally acquire the land needed was proposed to Congress by Major John Wesley Powell in 1880. He accurately prophesied that the area west of the 100th meridian would have enough rainfall for crops and prosperity for a series of years, but that this period would be followed by a cycle of dry years when disaster would smite thousands. To meet the problems of the changed climatic conditions beyond the 100th meridian, he advocated congressional legislation to supersede the Homestead Act, which was unsuitable in the semiarid region: (1) Any nine men could settle along an irrigable stream—each man to have a private eighty-acre plot for small farming, gardening, and haying. These men would form their own irrigation district, enabling them to manage an irrigation project that would be too big for any one man. (2) The nine men would each be given four sections of grazing land as near to the irrigated land as topography would allow. The grassland would be formed into an unfenced grazing district to be used as a communal pasture much as the cattlemen were using the government land as a range. The rectangular system of surveys would give way to whatever shape would be necessary to allow each man his share of land and water. With this plan, water rights would always be attached to the land. Unfortunately, the idea was far too

[26] Sheldon, *Land Systems and Land Policies*, pp. 159–167; *Annual Report of the Commissioner of the General Land Office, 1909*, p. 20.

advanced for its day. The cattle kings fought the recommendation—strangely enough—on the ground that it would create a monopoly, when at that time they were holding thousands of acres. This plan was to be carried out in a very limited way with the resettlement program during the New Deal in the 1930's.[27]

[27] Nelson, *Land of the Dakotahs*, p. 141; Wallace Stegner, *Beyond the Hundredth Meridian* (Boston: Houghton Mifflin, 1954), pp. 215–219, 225; Webb, *The Great Plains*, pp. 353–355.

XV

The Range Wars

FOUR FAIRLY DISTINCT RANGE WARS over the use of government land were fought between the Civil War and World War I : the fight between the trail drivers who drove large herds of cattle from Texas to the northern Plains, and the faint line of farmers who were pushing out onto the prairies; strife between the ranchers who had established prior rights, and the homesteaders who located on their grazing grounds; a struggle between the big rancher who had gained control of the waterholes and range, and the little rancher who was just getting started and wanted a share of free grazing privileges (since homesteaders usually had some cattle, there was often a gray area between the homesteaders and the little rancher, especially after the advent of the enlarged homestead, making the differentiation between the second and third of these wars hazy in some instances); and a bloody conflict between the ranchers who held their range by prior use, and the sheepmen who attempted to drive across the area grazed by the cattle or sought to graze on government land. Since these conflicts overlap in point of time they will be treated topically rather than chronologically.

The first of these wars was the war of the trails. The Civil War had caused a shortage of cattle in the East while in Texas the herds had multiplied beyond comparison. As a result, enterprising men drove great herds of Texas cattle hundreds of miles north to shipping points on the railroad in a movement known as the Long Drive. Often the cattle were driven 1,000 or 1,500 miles across the public domain to favorable locations where ranches were being established. Naturally the farmers who were beginning to occupy the prairie country objected to the trail drivers pushing a herd of wild cattle through their part of the country. Not only was there danger of stampeding across cultivated fields, but the problem was aggravated by the fact that Texas cattle usually were afflicted with a disease known as Texas fever. Although the cause of the disease was unknown at the time,

242

it is now known that it was carried by ticks, but the Texas cattle had built up a measure of immunity over the years that prevented them from dying, although they did not thrive. When the northern herds came in contact with Texas cattle, however, or even walked across land over which the latter had recently been driven, they contracted the disease and died by the dozen. Understandably, farmers and other cattlemen did not want their animals wiped out by this plague.

As early as 1867, when the settlers in the eastern part of Dickinson County, Kansas, learned that great herds of Texas cattle were expected at their county seat, Abilene, they organized a company to stampede the herds and keep them away from the county. Scores of these herds, each numbering several thousand, were to be held on the railroad and government lands while awaiting buyers or shipment, but Joseph G. McCoy, the founder of the Abilene cattle market, was able to persuade the settlers that a prosperous trade would open a brisk market and that they would be able to sell their produce readily at a good price. This, he argued, would offset any inconvenience the cattle trade might cause.[1] Thus the first Kansas skirmish was won by the cattlemen, but other victories were not to be won so easily.

In the same year, 1867, the Kansas legislature passed the Texas Cattle Prohibitory Law, which reflected the rising tide of sentiment by forbidding cattle drives across the eastern portion of the state. The law was not enforced, but it was the first of a series of similar acts that were intended to push the trails and the markets westward before agrarian settlement. One by one, Abilene, Newton, Ellsworth, and Wichita, each a little farther west, were killed as cattle markets, until finally an act of 1885 sounded the death knell of Dodge City, the most westerly and most famous of the Kansas cow towns.

To make matters worse for trail drivers, settlers and small ranchers had pushed out from the mountains in Colorado some distance and attempted to keep the Texas trail drivers out of their area. Charles Goodnight, driving through Colorado from his ranch in the Texas panhandle, was threatened in Colorado about 1870, but by courage and a show of Winchester rifles he forced his way through. The Coloradans then formed the Colorado Cattlemen's Association and pledged themselves to prevent Texans from using the public domain between the Arkansas River and the South Platte unless the cattle had been in Colorado for a year. This legal provision was a defense measure against Texas fever. Cattle wintered

[1] Joseph G. McCoy, *Historic Sketches of the Cattle Trade of the West* (Kansas City, Mo., 1874), pp. 63–65.

in the northern climate were freed of the ticks and did not infect the settlers' native cattle. Goodnight then laid out a trail from his ranch to the north that ran east of the mountain settlements. By the late 1870's and early 1880's, however, the trails had moved farther west and Goodnight's ranch was astride them—the shoe was on the other foot.[2] It was north Texan against south Texan, and Kansan against both.

In 1884, at the first national stockmen's convention, the Texans tried to pass a resolution requesting the United States government for a three and a half mile wide national cattle trail from the Texas boundary to the Canadian border, a distance of 690 miles. They proposed to ask the government not only for 1,324,000 acres of land but also for the surveys, fencing, artesian wells, and bridges. Because northern stockmen maintained that their ranges were crowded and because they did not want them to be a dumping ground for surplus Texas cattle, there was a lack of unity among the cattlemen and the plan came to naught at the hands of Congress.

In the summer of 1885, Mart Culver, a citizen of Dodge City, drove his herd through the neutral (Cherokee) strip in present-day western Oklahoma and attempted to move it into Kansas, but was met at the border by mounted riflemen who prevented entry into the state. Culver turned his herd westward, but soon he obtained permission from the federal government to drive his cattle northward from the Cherokee Strip along the western boundary of Kansas in Colorado without touching Kansas. He established a new market at a point on the railroad near the Arkansas River just west of the Kansas boundary. The cattle trail, which he marked with piles of buffalo bones, ran along the main street of the town, which Culver called Trail City. By August, 1885, the town had developed into a booming city from which, during its short life, thousands of cattle were shipped. Thus, after a fashion, a cattle trail was laid out, but it was not national or permanent. By 1890 the agricultural boom of the 1880's, by settling the Plains, had almost cut off the trails; then, too, the northern ranges were becoming overstocked, all of which sharply reduced the flow of cattle from Texas.

In the meantime, the second serious conflict over government land developed into a running fight between the cattlemen who had old established ranches with possessory rights and the "nesters," or agriculturists, who were encroaching upon them. In the early 1880's, the profits in

[2] Mari Sandoz, *The Cattlemen* (New York: Hastings House, 1958), pp. 272–276. Goodnight's range was Texas range rather than government land, and therefore has no further place in this delineation.

ranching on the northern Plains was so great—often 50 to 100 per cent per annum—that they naturally attempted by every possible means to keep their prior rights which had given them the use of their grazing areas for so many years that they were accustomed to consider it their own. They opposed the proliferation of railroads since they did not need these arteries—they could easily drive their marketable commodity a hundred miles to shipping points—and at the same time they knew that these iron spear thrusts into their grazing grounds would bring settlers, which meant the extinction of the range. This conflict between ranchers and homesteaders, which lasted until about 1910, began in the 1870's when the "sod-busters" began to push into the ranchers' pastures with mild forms of intimidation. Indian scares sometimes were conjured up causing the temporary depopulation of a whole area and even scaring many settlers away permanently; or prospective settlers were told that it never rained, that the land was unproductive, and that a homesteader's family would starve. Jules Sandoz, a settler near the Running Water River in western Nebraska, was accosted by a cowboy who addressed him:

"You aimin' to raise corn here? Why, man, you're crazy. Look at the heat, drying up the prairies so it'll burn like powder by the first of August. Don't be a —— fool! . . ."

Old Jules came back with: "If the country is so —— bad, why you staying?"

"Wall I aint stayin' to stir dirt as hard as dobe bricks, nor to encourage poor little sunflowers to commit suicide by tryin' to grow on it. I been through this country with cows from Texas for six years, hand runnin' and I aint seen more than a drop of rain in July yet."[3]

If a homesteader was not easily scared and attempted to settle on a fertile spot on a cattleman's range, a group of cowboys would ride up and threaten him with death; any but the most resolute would turn back to a less-favored spot nearer other grangers.

Although the ranchers ordinarily had the advantage of the advancing homesteaders—and it is customary to think that their position made them invincible—as a matter of fact they often felt vulnerable. This was especially true among the little ranchers, and the coming of a colony was of great concern. Grant Shumway tells us that when John Maycock greeted the first grangers who arrived in the Snake Creek area north of the North Platte River, he immediately rode like the wind up and down the valley spreading the word that a whole colony of nesters was settling on the river

[3] Mari Sandoz, *Old Jules* (Boston: Little, Brown, 1935), p. 67.

below Scottsbluff and that they had brought along a post office. The latter was an error, but the coming settlers certainly created a near panic among the cattlemen. The experience of Edward Abel of Cherry County, Nebraska, is typical of force used on an individual. In July, 1895, Abel appealed to Governor Holcomb for protection against the ranchers. Two families had filed on adjoining land. Eight days later, fifteen cattlemen appeared and tried for half a day to force Abel and the two nearby families to vacate their claims and leave the country. The families nevertheless refused; the cattlemen then threatened their lives and from a distance fired at least twenty shots in their general direction, some of which struck within six feet of them. The terrorists returned early the next morning and fired two shots through the wagon in which the homesteaders were sleeping. According to Abel the cattlemen had been operating in this manner for years, intimidating settlers and forcing them to abandon the range.[4] Despite threats and violence, however, small groups of nervy men moved in to stay.

Before 1880 the big cattlemen had started to fence their water supply, and in 1880 they began to fence vast areas of rangeland and to patrol their fences with armed riders. In 1882, the Arkansas Valley Land Company held thirty townships within fences on the north side of the Arkansas River in Bent County, Colorado. In California, Henry Miller and Charles Lux, who had started as poor men only a few years earlier, enclosed 600,000 acres. By 1883, the Brighton Ranch Company in the Loup Valley of Nebraska had enclosed 125,000 acres and had even fenced off the mail route (the mail carrier complained that in order to reach the post office he had to open and close such gates as the land company chose to erect). This vast Brighton area was far more than was necessary for their six thousand cattle; they were simply fencing out the farmers rather than fencing in the stock. Brighton claimed that the land they had shut off was marginal and unproductive, fit only for cattle raising, but an inspector found very good crops in South Loup Valley, and the ranch had raised an excellent crop of millet. A settler, Eber Barber, cut two tons of hay on government land within the Brighton big pasture and attempted to haul it away, but the ranchmen drove him off and used the hay to feed their own cattle.[5]

As early as 1883, in the case of Alexander H. Swan of Wyoming, the courts decided that his fencing of public land was illegal and that the

[4] *Lincoln State Journal* (Lincoln, Nebr.), July 11, 1895.

[5] Louis Pelzer, *The Cattlemen's Frontier* (Glendale, Calif.: Arthur H. Clark Co., 1936), pp. 177, 179.

wire had to come down. The Secretary of the Interior, H. M. Teller, attacked the evil in three ways: he brought suits to compel the removal of fences from the public domain; he authorized the settlers to cut the fences; and he requested a law of Congress to prohibit the fencing of public lands.

Where the farmers were numerically strong, they were delighted to co-operate with the Secretary, and one night in 1885, some settlers cut fifteen miles of barbed wire around the big pasture used by the Brighton company in Custer County, Nebraska. In the fall of 1884 a few settlers had located homesteads in this huge pasture on government land and had served notice that Brighton should remove its wire fence within thirty days. At the expiration of the time, however, the company had paid no attention to the notice and the homesteaders tore down the wire and took the fenceposts for use as rafters in the sod houses they were building. The ranch foreman had the settlers arrested and taken to the county seat for trial; then he and a number of cowboys rode from home to home, tearing down the settlers' houses and recovering the posts. They would hitch a team to a ridge pole and in a few seconds each soddy was a shapeless mass of earth, brush, and hay mixed with bedding, utensils, furniture, and personal effects. The rollicking cowboys then extricated their posts from the debris, put them in their wagon and drove off. While the cowboys were about their work of destruction, a boy rode to the county seat for help, and a posse of men who were friendly to the homesteaders was im-mediately formed. The foreman and his party, however, having been warned by a cowboy who had been in town, fled to the hills and escaped the wrath of the posse.[6]

For a time, by making full use of their employees, ranchers had con-trolled the county governments, and decisions had gone against the farmers; but later, with the influx of homeseekers, the grangers out-numbered the graziers and had things their own way. In areas where the greater part of the country was better adapted to ranching than to farm-ing, there were long-drawn-out struggles that lasted for forty-five years— from 1875 to 1920—but the farmers often were scared out, starved out, or they sold out to the ranchers, whose domains absorbed the homesteads on their borders.

On February 25, 1885, the act forbidding fencing of public land was passed, but the government had difficulty in enforcing the law. It was possible to compel a livestock man to take down his fence if it was on

[6] S. D. Butcher, *Pioneer History of Custer County* (Broken Bow, Nebr.: Merchants Pub-lishing Co., 1910), pp. 185, 186.

government land, but it was difficult if the fence was on the rancher's land, even though it enclosed thousands of acres of government land. One maneuver, known as checkerboarding, was to buy or lease the railroad's odd sections along one side of the track. (In many places this was ten miles wide.) If the rancher wanted to enclose a tract twenty miles long the width of the grant, he fenced the railroad sections on the perimeter of the thirty-by-twenty-mile tract. This was done by placing a fence four or five inches from the section line, using care never to fence a government section. Where the railroad section cornered with a government section, a gap of a few inches was left in order to avoid placing any part of the enclosure on government land. The cattle, of course, could not pass through the little gap, and hence this perimeter fence enclosed almost as much government land as that controlled legitimately. This presented a legal conundrum that could be solved only by Congress or the courts, and nothing was done for another decade. The Swan Land and Cattle Company of western Nebraska and eastern Wyoming purchased 450,000 acres from the Union Pacific and fenced this land and the alternate government-owned sections in this checkerboard fashion. Along the Northern Pacific in North Dakota and Montana, a strip twenty miles wide on one side of the track could be secured. If a rancher wanted more land he could buy on both sides.

Two remedies were proposed to cure this cunning evasion of the law: a bill that would establish a public highway four rods wide around each section, and a bill that would permit the government to lease its land to owners of adjacent land. The latter bill would help ranchers secure adequate grazing land and at the same time would bring some income to the government and set up a defensible economic balance between the farmer and the rancher. But neither of these two proposals was acted upon. Fence removal from other than railroad grants made some progress but much government land was still illegally enclosed. In 1887 the Commissioner stated that 465 illegal enclosures, with an area of seven million acres, had been reported, but in only 165 cases were the special agents able to report complete removal or removals in progress. The removals restored 3,395,000 acres to public use. In 1895, when a case of checkerboard fencing in Colorado came before the United States Circuit Court of Appeals, the fencing of alternate sections was declared an illegal enclosure.

Fencing, as it turned out, was harmful to the cattle business; it prevented uniform grazing and increased winter losses. Cattle would drift mile after mile before a blizzard and had a good chance of survival as long as they kept moving, but once they came to the cruel barbed barrier they huddled together and were lost unless the storm abated shortly.[7] Indeed, the winter of 1886–1887 weakened the cattle barons in their struggle against the government, the homesteaders, small-scale stockmen, and the sheep men.

Up to that time, it was not customary for ranchers to make hay for winter feeding, and sheds for winter protection were unheard of, but the summer of 1886 had been dry and stock was lean and in poor condition to face the winter. In early November there was such a heavy snowfall that in many places the cattle could not get down to the cured wild grasses below; the few ranchers who had hay fed it to the cattle, and those who did not prayed for a chinook. A warm wind came early in January, melting the snow and leaving the high ground exposed. Ranchers took hope, thinking they might yet escape ruin, but the latter part of January brought the worst blizzard that had ever been experienced up to that time. The hungry cattle drifted before the merciless storm, and thousands huddled among aspens or cottonwoods in the coulees or against barbed wire barriers, slowly dying of starvation and exposure. Charles M. Russell, later to become famous as a cowboy artist, and Jesse Phelps were caring for a herd of five thousand in the Judith Basin in Montana, when their employer in Helena anxiously inquired about his cattle. Phelps did not have the heart to write the whole truth, but Charles Russell painted the now-famous watercolor depicting a gaunt, starving cow waiting for the wolves to make a meal of her. He entitled the picture "Waiting for a Chinook." Phelps sent the picture, without comment, in a letter. The subtitle, "Last of 5,000," which was added later, told the story of the whole northern Plains better than words. Ranchmen of finer instincts suffered untold agony as they realized their cattle were slowly starving. A few of these famished creatures moved about gaining a little sustenance from the sagebrush and cottonwood twigs.

The spring thaw revealed the full extent of the disaster—in sheltered places thousands of rotting carcasses and only a few gaunt, bony, skeleton-like survivors that had to be "tailed up." Even these, the remnant of the great herds of the previous autumn, suffered frozen ears, tails, feet, and legs, and were so weak they were scarcely able to drag around. Many ranchers found the whole range system revolting. Granville Stuart, a big Montana cattleman, later wrote: "A business that had been fascinating to me before, suddenly became distasteful. I wanted no more of it. I never

[7] Ernest S. Osgood, *The Day of the Cattleman* (Minneapolis: University of Minnesota Press, 1929), p. 193.

wanted to own again an animal that I could not feed and shelter."[8] The hard winters finished the open range system. Nature had delivered a devastating attack—this time on the side of the homesteaders.

After the blizzards subsided, homesteaders searched out the carcasses and skinned them for the hides. In the winter of 1871–1872, however, in Rice County, Kansas, the ranchers believed that the homesteaders were not "biding their time" but were killing some of the cattle that might have survived if let alone. The ranchers served notice that the first man found skinning an animal would be killed on the spot; the settlers responded with an ultimatum that if any settlers were killed, the prairie would be fired. Each side had the other at a disadvantage, and the matter rested, but it was only a step from skinning dead cattle or killing dying ones to rustling.

The settlers in Sherman County, Kansas, in their fight against the ranchers, organized the Homesteaders' Protective Association, a secret organization with many oaths, passwords, and the like. The final and most solemn oath was:

> I do solemnly swear not to tell anything that may in any way lead owners of cattle which are running at large contrary to law and destroying settlers crops to discover who had killed or crippled or in any way injured these same cattle, . . . If I do, then I shall expect this society to use me thus.[9]

At this point, a straw man with a rope around his neck was lowered from a rafter and dangled before the astonished candidate.

In March, 1867, the manager of the Anglo-American Cattle Company wrote that the loss of cattle on Hat Creek in western Nebraska had been frightful. The homesteaders, he said, had not confined their slaughter to meat for their own use but had killed wantonly. In a stretch of only a mile and a half, over thirty cattle had been found dead, and every one of them had been killed by rifle or pistol fire.[10] It is not surprising that in the course of killing ranchers' cattle, the homesteaders should supply themselves with ranchers' meat. In fact, a standing joke in the ranch country was that the only time a rancher learned how his own beef tasted was when he ate with a neighbor.

In 1877 in Custer County, Nebraska, I. P. Olive, a wealthy rancher

---

[8] Granville Stuart, *Forty Years on the Frontier* (2 vols.; Cleveland: Arthur H. Clark Co., 1925), II, 237; Osgood, *The Day of the Cattleman*, pp. 219–221.

[9] E. E. Blackman, "Sherman County and the H.U.A.," *Transactions* of the Kansas State Historical Society, 1903–1904, VIII (Topeka: Kansas State Historical Society, 1904), 51.

[10] Osgood, *The Day of the Cattleman*, p. 242.

who had recently come from Texas, suffered heavy losses from those whom the cattlemen regarded as rustlers, and Olive decided to rid the Loup District of these thieves. A man whom the cowmen later hanged implicated a homesteader, Ami Ketchum, as one of those who was overfond of the ranchman's beef. Print Olive's brother, Bob, had just come from Texas with a record of having killed some men, and on complaint of Print, the sheriff deputized Bob Olive to arrest Ketchum. The latter lived with a man named Luther Mitchell in a sod house astride the line between their homesteads; this was also a center of activity for the homesteaders of the community. The homesteaders, having heard of the sheriff's plans, hooked the team to the wagon ready to take Mrs. Mitchell to a safe place— Ketchum was single—but suddenly a troop of horsemen, four abreast, dashed up and demanded Ketchum's surrender. A sharp fight ensued in which Mitchell's arm was broken and Bob Olive was mortally wounded. The posse having been repulsed, the homesteaders started for their former home in Merrick County, Nebraska. After they had gone, the cattlemen returned and burned the roof off the homesteader's soddy—the only part which was combustible. In Merrick County, Mitchell and Ketchum decided to give themselves up and were placed on a train under custody, and the sheriff started back to Custer County with the prisoners. When the train reached Plum Creek, Print Olive and a crowd of his cowboys met the sheriff and his prisoners and accompanied them north toward Custer County. After an all-night ride, they came to the Custer County line and the sheriff turned his prisoners over to Print Olive and his gang, who took the prisoners to Devil's Gap, a wild canyon halfway between Wood River and the Loup River. Two lariats were thrown over a tree limb, the nooses were adjusted, and the two men, manacled together, were hanged. Then a can of kerosene was dashed over their clothing and the bodies were set afire.

Whatever sympathy the cattlemen may have had now vanished as the press of the state cried, "Man Burners!" and Judge William H. Gaslin, a fearless official, caused the arrest of the gang. At the trial, Olive and his foreman were sentenced to the penitentiary for life, but before they had served a year the state supreme court granted a new trial on the technicality that the legislature had neglected to assign Custer County to the western judicial district and therefore the trial was an erroneous procedure. When a second trial was called, no one appeared against the accused and the "man burners" went free.[11]

[11] W. L. Gaston and A. R. Humphrey, *History of Custer County, Nebraska* (Lincoln: Western Publishing & Engraving Co., 1919), pp. 160–166.

Some of the fiercest attacks on homesteaders took place in the first decade of the twentieth century. In 1905, not far from St. Francis, Kansas, John Barry and his four sons filed claims on the range of the Dewey Cattle Company. The cattle company, observing the threat to their range by settlers coming in, erected fences which enclosed 51,040 acres, or about eight square miles. The Barry family then foresaw their homesteads completely encompassed by the barbed wall of the cattle company; and cowboys threatened to kill the whole family if its members disturbed the newly strung wires. The Barrys saw that they had to fight or they would be run out, and they resolved to stand their ground. One night, as Barry and his sons were returning from town, they found it necessary to cut the fence in order to get home, but just as they rode through the opening a gang of cowboys swooped down upon them and opened fire. The father was hit but managed to keep his seat in the saddle, and the family was soon beyond range of the cowboys' guns. About twenty cowboys, however, followed the grangers to their home and took them by surprise, killing two at the outset. Defending themselves, the settlers killed three of the cowboys, and the attackers, incensed by the unexpected resistance, set fire to the house. When the three men within sought to escape, they were shot to death.[12]

A lawyer of Mullen, Nebraska, O. F. Hamilton, apparently possessed by righteous zeal to help the little man in his struggles against the big cattlemen, had kept tab on illegally and fraudulently held public land. He was threatened more than a dozen times and warned that he would be killed if he did not desist. As a witness, he testified in a federal court for the United States on the illegal activities of the cattlemen. After his house and outbuildings were burned, he appealed to the United States for protection with no success. At the trial of the cattle barons at Omaha in 1906, at which Hamilton was a witness, he was so dogged by thugs that the government guarded him with secret service men. After he returned home, he received threatening letters warning him to get out of the country, and his law office was ripped apart by an explosion. In April, 1908, Hamilton disappeared; later, his body was found, and eventually his alleged murderer was tried but was acquitted.[13]

At this time the matter of illegal fencing came up again. The federal law of February 25, 1885, forbade the construction and maintenance of fences

[12] Henry S. Brown, "Punishing the Land Looters," *Outlook*, LXXXV (February 23, 1907), 437.

[13] *State Journal*, October 4, 1905; *ibid.*, April 21, May 2, June 18, June 19, June 21, 1910.

upon public lands under penalty of $1,000 and one year in prison. During the Sparks regime, as we have seen, attempts to enforce this law had met with partial success, but in response to the uproar in the West, the reform was dissipated and illegal fencing continued into the first decade of the twentieth century. It was thought by some who did not know their man that Roosevelt, having been a rancher himself, would overlook the illegal practices of the cattlemen, which seemed to them to be necessary in order to preserve their existence; but, for Roosevelt, to see an infringement of the law which was abridging the rights of the common man was for him to enforce the law. Secretary of the Interior E. A. Hitchcock singled out Bartlett Richards and Comstock, two of the biggest cattlemen in Nebraska, for prosecution. Indictments were returned against these men and others in 1903, but by means of continuance the cases dragged on interminably. In their affidavit seeking a continuance, Richards and Comstock had sworn that the land in question was unsurveyed and that if it were surveyed no government land would be found enclosed by their firm. The government then sent a large force of special agents and surveyors into the Sand Hills to run out the original survey lines and re-mark the corners obliterated by the cattlemen. When their work was complete, they had a map showing the location of fences which enclosed 212,000 acres of the public domain. In the face of this, at the trial in the United States district court in Omaha in November, 1905, the defendants pleaded guilty and were fined $300 and sentenced to six hours in custody, which the United States marshal interpreted to be of no significance except that they could not leave town for six hours. That official accordingly appointed the prisoners' attorney to take custody of the prisoners for six hours. It was the old story of the frontier court making a farce of enforcement of the laws of the United States when the interests of a large segment of the public ran counter to the law. Roosevelt was indignant when he saw that the court was in entire sympathy with the flouters of the law. He dismissed the district attorney and the United States marshal and declared that he would have cut off the head of the judge if he were subject to dismissal.[14] His vigorous manner brought an end to the fencing of the public domain.

The third range war, closely akin to and oftentimes merging with that of the cattleman-homesteader conflict, was the battle between the big

[14] Addison E. Sheldon, *Land Systems and Land Policies in Nebraska* (Lincoln: Nebraska State Historical Society, 1936), pp. 196–197, 200–203; *Omaha World Herald*, December 13–25, 1905. The *Omaha World Herald* stated that about a million acres of fenced land was involved in the court proceedings of that session.

cattleman and the little cowman. The small-scale rancher was usually a homesteader who had just started a herd and was "on the make" as a cattleman. This beginner was accused of rustling and every means was used to crowd him out. In 1901, Charles Tirman charged that Miller and Leith had procured twenty-nine Negroes to file homesteads on government land in such a way as to completely surround his ranch and prevent his cattle from going to and from his watering place. Because homesteading with the intent to turn the land over to a company was a fraudulent proceeding, Tirman was granted an injunction against Miller and Leith for shutting him off from his entrance. The press hailed this as the forerunner of legal redress for the small rancher who had been suffering for years at the hands of the big firms.

One of the first attempts by the little man to compete with the big outfits was the formation of cattle pools. In southwestern Kansas in 1882, for example, the Smoky Hill Pool was formed in Lane County with a membership of seventeen; and in 1883 they branded fifteen hundred calves. Each member had his own herd and the cattle ran together on the government range, but the organization hired the cowhands and prorated the expenses. In 1883 the cost per head for a month was only 12.5 cents. The Forrester Pool in Lane County, Kansas, had six partners and ran four thousand cattle. It must be admitted that these pools were an economic halfway station between the homesteader and the big rancher; they were as much anti-homesteader as they were anti-big-cattle rancher, and there was a tendency for them either to die out or combine into regional or state cattlemen's associations.

More often than not the little cattleman was a former cowhand who had learned the tricks of the trade from his boss and was ready to set up business on his own. It was customary for such an enterprising individual—after having his brand registered—to brand mavericks and buy a few cattle to form the nucleus of his herd. Whatever his beginning or the source and composition of his herd, it often was difficult for the big cattleman to distinguish between a little cattleman and a thief. In fact, any man who filed upon government land on the big man's range was looked upon as a rustler, and unfortunately, there was much rustling. Even today it is impossible for the historian to distinguish between the legitimate small-scale cattleman and the rustler. An occasional loss of cattle was tolerable but the loss of grazing land was a more serious blow to the rancher, and since filing on government land was legitimate, the only way the big cattleman could get at this small competitor was by freezing him out or by charging him with stealing stock. For example, two settlers with small herds homesteaded on a level spot not far from some coulees which ran back into the hills, with the intention of securing an outlet to the grazing land in the hills beyond, but the manager of the ranch which had formerly used the whole area located his cowboys on claims just back of them and put up a legitimate fence along the front of the bluffs, completely shutting the little cattlemen out of their grazing ground. In Huerfano County, Colorado, big companies grazed their cattle outside their fenced pastures until the grass was short and then drove them into the enclosure, leaving the little man's cattle to starve on the overgrazed area outside. Finally the later comer gave up and left.[15] The passage of the Kinkaid Act of 1904 loosed upon the ranchers' pastures in Nebraska a flood of homesteaders who, because of the enlarged homesteads, posed a double threat to the big cattlemen: (1) they took four times as much range as the ordinary homesteader; (2) they were potential small ranchers. Of course the cattlemen made use of the act also.

In Wyoming, after years of sniping by the big cattlemen, a last battle known as the Johnson County War took place in the northern part of the state in 1892. Since it was common knowledge that small cattlemen were branding mavericks—calves which were not following branded mothers— the Wyoming State Live Stock Commission, an organization controlled by the big ranchers but with the power of the state government behind it, decided to put an end to this gray area between raising one's own cattle and rustling—mavericking. The commission made a list of small cattlemen who they thought were guilty of rustling and/or mavericking, and determined to stamp out the practice. An order known as the "maverick law" was sent to the commission's inspectors at the market centers (Chicago, Omaha, and Kansas City) ordering them to confiscate all Wyoming cattle bearing the outlawed brands. During the first ten months under this maverick law, 16,306 head of cattle that carried the brands of small cattlemen were confiscated, although the owners had not been convicted of rustling and most of them were not even accused of it. Indeed, the maverick law was in large measure contrary to the training the big men had given their cowboys, for it had been customary to pay a cowboy $2.50 to $5.00 for each maverick he branded for his boss. The branding custom, which the big cattlemen had considered legitimate for themselves, had become a crime if practiced by their small competitors.[16]

[15] Pelzer, *The Cattlemen's Frontier*, p. 176.

[16] A. S. Mercer, *The Banditti of the Plains* (Norman: University of Oklahoma Press, 1954), p. 14.

The opposition organized its own association, but the small cattlemen, one by one, were shot from ambush. A man and woman suspected of rustling were hanged in a lonely canyon, although a charge of stealing had never been made.

The big operators, having had their way for years with impunity, decided to organize an expedition and clear the country of what they termed rustlers. One morning in the spring of 1892 a special train from Denver, shrouded in secrecy, arrived in Casper carrying saddle horses, wagons, provisions, ammunition, and other equipment for an expeditionary force, and between fifty and sixty men, of whom about one-third were hired Texas gunmen armed to the teeth. They cut the telegraph line and headed north. On the morning of April 9 they surprised two supposed rustlers at the K C ranch and after a day's siege killed them. They then rode on, followed by wagonloads of provisions and ammunition, including a quantity of giant powder, fuses, and poison. It had been the intention of the invaders to keep their expedition secret and, driving all before them, to advance on Buffalo and clean out that nest of little cattlemen and their sympathizers; but the siege at the K C ranch had given them away, and riders had carried the message of the progress of the gunmen to Buffalo. Meantime the gunmen rode rapidly on, hoping to surprise the "doomed city of the Plains," as they called Buffalo, and to kill the sheriff and others on their list. Upon learning that their intent was known, they turned in at the T A ranch and, awakening to their danger, prepared for a siege. Word of the invasion and the killing of the two men at the K C ranch was carried throughout the area and into Buffalo, and the small ranchers and citizens of Buffalo swarmed like the minutemen of Lexington and Concord; the hunters now became the hunted. No doubt the whole party of gunmen would have been killed if one of the besieged had not slipped through the surrounding lines with a message for help. By the morning of April 11, three hundred or four hundred men surrounded the invaders. Since the ranch house was made of logs, it appeared that it could be defended indefinitely if the defendants were properly supplied, but unfortunately for them their four supply wagons had been captured by the besiegers. The little cattlemen now determined to make use of the captured supplies. They lashed two of the wagons together and fastened a breastworks of logs to the back of them to form a movable fort which they called a "go-devil." They were just ready to push it down the hill and from its protection throw the captured dynamite into the fortifications when the besieged were rescued by United States troops. The messenger had gotten through to the governor, who was sympathetic with the big cattlemen, and at his frantic request three companies of United States cavalry were dispatched to arrest the besiegers, but when the commander learned the true state of affairs, he arrested the gunmen.[17]

Legal technicalities prevented bringing the gunmen to justice, but public opinion was inflamed to the point that the herds of those responsible for the invasion were practically annihilated.

In some places, however, force of circumstances decreed a marked degree of cooperation between the big and the little cattlemen. John Bratt, who controlled a spacious range in western Nebraska, recalled in his reminiscences that when his range became overstocked, to relieve congestion he placed the excess cattle out on the shares with small cattlemen on the periphery of his big pasture, giving them half of the increase—the small cattlemen to make good the original number except those which died a natural death. Often, too, the big outfits allowed the little men to share in the roundups, with each small rancher sending one cowboy to represent his small ranch. These were known as "Reps."

The fourth range war was between sheepmen and cattlemen. The first sheep to be brought to the New World—like the first cattle—came from Spain. The silky-fleeced merinos of Castile multiplied in Mexico and with settlement moved north into Texas, New Mexico, Arizona, and California. They were the base stock for the millions of animals that were herded on the Plains, in the mountains, and on the West Coast.

When California was occupied by the miners in the Gold Rush, its demand for livestock made stock driving to California profitable, and this turn of affairs ushered in the first great sheep drives across the public domain. From Taos, New Mexico, on June 24, 1852, "Uncle" Dick Wooton, a former mountainman (who later turned road builder and keeper of the Raton Pass tollroad), started to California with a herd of nine thousand sheep, twenty-two Spanish herders, and eight American guards. Eight goats were taken as herd leaders, a string of pack mules to carry supplies, and a dog to urge on the stragglers. Wooton and his herd arrived safely in California before the big snows fell in the Sierras, and he sold over 8,900 sheep and grossed $50,000. Although authorities regarded the feat as unparalleled for herd survival in a cross-country drive, the next year Kit Carson drove thirteen thousand sheep to California in two

---

[17] Robert B. David, *Malcolm Campbell, Sheriff* (Casper, Wyo.: Wyomingana, Inc., 1932), Chapters V–XIV; Frank M. Canton, *Frontier Trails* (Boston: Houghton Mifflin, 1930), Chapter IV; Mercer, *Banditti*, Chapters IV–VIII.

divisions. He traveled north to Fort Laramie and thence by the Overland Trail to the coast.[18]

Because Colorado was on the main artery of travel and close to the source of breeding stock in the Southwest, sheep raising developed in that state rather early; by 1880 there were 1,091,443 sheep in Colorado. In the meantime, California and Oregon became the source of breeding stock for Montana and Idaho, and thousands of sheep were driven from the Pacific Coast into the northern mountain states. Cattle ranching, however, was established earlier than sheep raising on the northern Plains and in the intermountain region, so that cattlemen thought the ranges belonged to them by prior use, and they objected to sharing the ranges with the sheepmen. The former usually had not the slightest title to the land they used but they did not propose to be "sheeped out" of their grazing land, and as the first comers, they determined to defend themselves—in the bloodiest war in the history of the public lands.

Sheep, in the natural course of things, would have supplanted cattle. They could live on a range where cattle could not thrive. They could crop shorter grass than cattle, eat salt sage which cattle would not touch, feed on browse, and graze on steep hillsides. It might appear, then, that sheep and cattle would be a good combination, with the sheep using the poorer grazing land and the cattle the better. Unfortunately for the peace of mind of the cattlemen, the sheep preferred first-rate pasture and competed with cattle for the superior grass until it was eaten bare; then they would live on the less desirable feeding grounds while the cattle starved out. In the end, if the range was overstocked, the sheep survived over the cattle, and hence they could take over a range, crowding cattle completely out. If a number of cattlemen had decided to quit the cattle business and had gone into sheep raising, the conflict might have been resolved with less difficulty, but most cattlemen "believed" in their cattle as the sheepmen "believed" in their flocks. This was even more true of the cowboys, who could imagine nothing worse than being reduced to the lot of the despised sheepherders. Since there was little range that was not claimed by some cattleman, the first sheep were brought by newcomers onto an occupied range, but the sheepman had the same legal rights to the land as the cattleman.

By 1881 the number of sheep in Wyoming exceeded the number of cattle. They were not distributed evenly over the territory, however, for

[18] Edward N. Wentworth, *America's Sheep Trails* (Ames, Iowa: State College Press, 1948), pp. 168–169. On his return to New Mexico by the southern route, Carson met 100,000 sheep on the way to California.

the sheep counties were in the west and the cattle country was in the north. A general increase in the number of sheep in proportion to cattle also obtained in the semiarid regions of the West. The war between the two groups seems to have begun in the 1870's, the last incident was in 1920, and the most intense flare-up occurred between 1890 and 1909.

The dubious allegation the cattlemen made against sheep was that cattle could not go where sheep had gone. A flock of three thousand sheep, they asserted, would march across the country, leaving it bare by eating the grass down to the roots; what they did not eat, it was claimed, twelve thousand sharp little hoofs tramped into the ground. Their hoofs, moreover, compacted the earth so solidly that it was claimed the grass would not grow after the flock had passed. A cowman who had to share his range with flockowners would say: "I've been sheeped."[19] It was also charged that sheep polluted the watering places and left an intolerable odor that cattle could not endure.

This long list of charges against the sheep, for the most part, were rationalizations for the determination not to share an already overstocked range with a new economic force that threatened to make the graziers' situation even more difficult. A writer noted in 1902 that damage to the rangeland existed primarily in the minds of men who owned cattle only and saw their range in danger, and not in the mind of the man who ran both sheep and cattle. Many ranchers, he said, profitably raised both animals on the same range, each in its separate area, placing the sheep on the rougher, higher lands unsuited to cattle.[20]

The sheepmen were at a tremendous disadvantage in their contest with the cattlemen. It took a number of cowboys to look after the cattle on a range, and each was mounted and armed with a six-shooter. A flock of two thousand sheep, on the other hand, was handled by one man and a pair of dogs. The sheepherder, usually a mild man, tended to travel on foot and seldom carried a weapon; his charges, moreover, were meek, docile, gregarious animals, upon whom great damage could be inflicted without fear of personal harm or retaliation.

The hostilities followed a typical pattern. Cattlemen would meet among themselves and arbitrarily set aside certain ranges for the exclusive use of

---

[19] Alfred J. Mokler, *History of Natrona County, Wyoming, 1888–1922* (Chicago: R. R. Donnelley & Sons, 1923), p. 363.

[20] E. P. Snow, Secretary of the Wyoming State Board of Sheep Commissioners, to the Editor, *Outlook*, LXXIII (April 4, 1903), 839; Will C. Barnes, "The Forest Service and the Stockmen in 1917," *American Sheep Breeder and Wool Grower*, XXXVIII (February, 1918), 88.

cattle; then they warned the sheepmen to get off or stay off their range. They often drew a "dead line" beyond which—by dictum of the cattlemen—sheep would not be tolerated. For example, a rancher near Laramie, Wyoming, near the source of Horse Creek, found a notice posted on a board bearing a grim warning to sheepmen to keep off that range. According to the *Cheyenne Leader*, it was signed, "Salt Peter." The next step was poisoning the grass beyond the dead line, or an attack by the cattlemen upon the sheep and their herders. The least violent of these actions was spreading a strip of saltpeter or blue vitriol where sheep were expected to graze; these chemicals were not harmful to cattle but were deadly to sheep.

As early as 1875, Idaho passed a law forbidding anyone to drive a herd of sheep, cattle, or horses within two miles of an occupied ranch, which presented a constitutional question. What right did a territory have to legislate upon the use of federal property by persons the federal government permitted upon its property? But the doubtful constitutionality of the Idaho law did not deter the states and territories, and in 1883 the cattlemen—with the aid of the homesteaders—pushed through the legislature of that territory the Priority Rights Law forbidding the ranging of sheep where cattle had been grazed.[21] Sheepmen, of course, who knew that the Two Mile Law and the Priority Rights Law were unconstitutional, would move into the cattle territory and attempt to exercise their legitimate right to share in the generosity of the United States. This precipitated attacks upon herders and sheep by the "gunny-sackers," as they were called. As early as 1884 the cattlemen drove the sheepmen out of the Big Bend Country of Washington and killed some of their sheep and dogs.

A typical attack occurred in 1904 upon a sheepman and his flock near Christmas Lake in the heart of the Great Oregon Desert. One night, as the herder was bedding down his sheep, five masked men emerged from ambush and held the herder at gunpoint while they placed a sack over his head, pulled it down to his knees and wrapped a rope around the sacked herder. Then—with rifles, pistols, knives, and clubs—they destroyed the sheep. The slaughter began about dusk and continued through the night. About eight hundred sheep in the herd of three thousand stampeded, but most of them were disposed of by coyotes.[22]

A sheepman in cattle country was in the hands of his enemies. In Montana, when masked men attacked and clubbed to death all but twelve sheep in a herd of 2,500, the sheriff—an old cattleman named

---

[21] Wentworth, *America's Sheep Trails*, p. 527.

[22] F. A. Shaver, *An Illustrated History of Central Oregon* (Spokane, 1905), pp. 646–647.

O. C. Cato—was appealed to for help. When the sheepherder complained that he did not think the sheriff was trying to catch the criminals, the sheriff asked the man to be patient and to give him time—he had a scheme by which he was going to catch every one of them. He had gone to the scene of the killing, had looked things over, had brought the clubs to his office, and was going to arrest the first man who came to claim his club.

But clubbing sheep to death was hard work, and the cowboys thought up easier and more efficient forms of slaughter—such as fitting dynamite charges with percussion caps and throwing them among flocks feeding close together in corrals. In 1887 at Tie Siding, Wyoming, 2,600 were burned in the corral of Charles Herbert. The combustibles fired the oily wool, and because the animals could not scatter, they burned to death or suffocated when they crowded together. Another method of slaughter was to take advantage of the natural flocking instinct of sheep which caused them to follow leaders blindly. If a flock was on a suitable highland, the attackers would drive the animals over a cliff. Once the great mass was in motion, the leaders could not turn back but were pushed over the edge and the others in turn followed, jumping blindly to destruction on the bottom of the chasm. This was known as "rimrocking." Stampeding was another means of destruction.

In 1884 near San Francisco Peaks, north of Flagstaff, Arizona, ten bands of sheep that were camped in close proximity in a natural park were set upon by a hundred galloping horses, many of which dragged huge cowbells on long rawhide lines attached to their tails. Then cowboys rode out of the timber shouting and shooting. The sheepherders turned the horses away with volleys of rifle fire, but this only started them milling around through the defenseless flocks. Twenty-five thousand sheep trampled each other, causing death to many and mixing the herds so thoroughly that it took several weeks to unscramble the disordered mass.[23] A variation of this tactic was to stampede cattle through a flock. In 1884, on the Colorado River in Arizona, cowboys overcame a group of sheepherders, tied them to trees, and drove their sheep into quicksand, where they mired. Sheepmen, unfortunately, were unable to obtain legal satisfaction for these attacks.

In 1904 in Lake County, Oregon, men who were thought to know anything about the activities of the gunny-sackers were threatened and warned to keep still. Warnings were tied to their doorknobs, threatening letters were mailed from widely scattered post offices, and a merchant

[23] William MacLeod Raine and Will C. Barnes, *Cattle* (New York: Grosset & Dunlap, 1930), p. 253; Wentworth, *America's Sheep Trails*, p. 525.

who was thought to know too much was found shot to death. In 1902, Charles Michelson, writing in *Munsey Magazine*, stated that a score of sheepmen had been killed within the past ten years along the borders of Colorado, one hundred had been wounded, and 600,000 sheep had been slaughtered—all in range warfare. For the whole West, Michelson estimated sheepmen's damages at the hands of the gunny-sackers at $5,000,000 for the decade. E. P. Snow, of the Wyoming State Board of Sheep Commissioners, was more conservative, but he estimated that between 1893 and 1903 in the western United States about fifty sheepmen had been killed and 25,000 sheep destroyed. Sheepmen sometimes poisoned the ranchers' waterholes in retaliation, but in general they were at the mercy of the cattlemen.

The war in Wyoming reached its climax in 1909 when a flock of five thousand sheep that had been driven across a cattle range was followed and attacked by twenty men in sheep-grazing country on No Water Creek in the Ten Sleep country. Two sheepmen were burned alive in their wagon when they refused to come out, and the third herder was shot. Because the telephone wires had been cut, it was not until the next day that the sheriff received word of the tragedy. The cattlemen, oversure of themselves because of their long immunity from prosecution, talked too much and the facts became known. The National Wool Growers' Association took up the matter and backed the prosecution, but threats and social pressure were brought to bear against anyone who talked freely. While the grand jury was deliberating, however, one of the witnesses committed suicide and left letters that implicated a number of prominent citizens. Numerous arrests were made and the state militia was called out to guard the prisoners. At the trial, two men turned state's evidence on the promise that they would not be prosecuted. Penitentiary sentences, which served to cool the ardor of the cattlemen, also showed that the sheepmen, small-scale cattle raisers, and farmers were now in the majority. This ended the attacks on sheepmen in Wyoming.[24]

The establishment of the United States Forest Service in 1905 did much to regulate grazing and to give each interest its proper share of the range. Sporadic outbreaks of hostility, however, occurred in various sections of the United States as late as 1920. In that year, a herd on its way to the national forest near Craig, Colorado, was attacked at a camp near Blue Mountain. A herder and an owner were killed and twelve hundred sheep were rimrocked in this last battle of the range wars.

[24] Tacetta B. Walker, *Stories of Early Days in Wyoming* (Casper, Wyo.: Prairie Publishing Co., 1936), pp. 104–106; Mokler, *History of Natrona County*, pp. 365–366.

XVI

Town Building on the Public Lands

FROM THE BEGINNING of the public lands system, certain locations on government land stood out as particularly desirable for nonagricultural uses. It was obvious to the discerning that towns would be located at strategic points and that a break in transportation was certain to promote town growth. For example, the falls of the Ohio made it necessary to unload and reload flatboats or, in time of low water, to wait for a rise in order to navigate the falls; and taverns, inns, stores, blacksmith shops, and places of amusement soon were built nearby to accommodate the public. The resultant city which grew up at that point was Louisville, Kentucky. Another prospective townsite was near a ford on a road that crossed a wide stream, and where in floodtime people were compelled to camp until the water subsided. And it was likely a town would develop at a point where a road crossed a stream that was too deep to ford and where there was a sloping bank to accommodate a ferry landing, as at Council Bluffs.

A good harbor on a lake, as at Milwaukee or Kenosha, Wisconsin, was certain to stimulate urban growth. Similarly, a town could be expected to rise at the confluence of two rivers, as at Kansas City, where the Kansas River meets the Missouri, and at Sioux City, where the Big Sioux River flows into the Missouri.

The discovery of mineral deposits was certain to tempt promoters to build a town nearby. The first settlement on the site of Lincoln, Nebraska, came about through the belief that the salt deposits in the vicinity would be developed into a basic industry. In this case, however, urban growth was delayed until two other factors came into being: designation of the town as the county seat and later as the state capital. A millsite, as at Black River Falls in Wisconsin, or a site near a spring of sufficient volume to furnish water for a frontier town, as at Huntsville, Alabama, also were sought for urban development. The new canals, with their series of locks, offered urban prospects, as did junctions between two or more main arteries of rail transportation.

The number of towns in the United States that bear the prefix "Fort" attests to the potential of favorably situated strongholds as urban centers. Indeed, prior to 1800 there was a consistent pattern of community movement from the East and the building of protective forts; then streets were laid out, along with small in-lots for the residences and larger garden out-lots; then fields for farming and a large common grazing area. As in New England and Europe, the people lived about the fort, ready to duck in for protection, and went out into the country to farm. A congressional act of 1812 took note of this custom in providing that all town lots, out-lots, and field lots not claimed by individuals should be reserved for the support of schools in each village.[1]

Until 1844 an individual town builder or town company—like an individual upon the cutting edge of the frontier—would squat upon a piece of land that gave promise as a townsite, lay out a town, and sell the lots. In some cases a town of considerable size was erected even before the Indian title had been extinguished and often before the land had been surveyed or bought from the government. The Townsite Act of May 23, 1844, however, provided for the entry of 320 acres on condition that it be cut up into lots and disposed of under the rules and regulations established by the territory or state in which the land lay. This was in effect an extension of the Pre-emption Act of 1841, which allowed twice the amount an individual could buy at the minimum price of $1.25 an acre. If the project was not the work of a town company or an individual promoter, but was simply the desire of a group to form a town, it was quite customary for the laws of the territory to permit the authorities of the town or the county authority to pre-empt the land in behalf of the citizens of the town. Long before the passage of the Townsite Act, however, men of foresight were seizing upon the good locations, known as points of "natural opportunity," and building towns.

Townsite speculators were an important element of the first westward wave of squatter occupants, and competition rose to a high pitch during each boom period. So fervid was speculation in 1818 that the *Richmond Enquirer* warned:

> There is an astonishing rage at the present day for the establishment of new towns. Does a man possess a tract of land convenient to river transportation; if he is a man of enterprise he starts the plan of a town; lays

[1] *American State Papers, Public Lands*, VI (Washington, D.C.: Govt. Printing Office, 1860), 188.

off his land into lots and expects to make his fortune by selling out. What pains to puff his situation; to dress off with every advantage of health, navigation and fertility which the most plastic imagination can supply.[2]

In the instances where free and fair competition prevailed at public sales, the price of land was high for prospective townsites—as in northern Alabama. In 1818 the land on which Huntsville was later built was sold at auction for $251 an acre. The Indian Creek Navigation Company laid out the town of Triana, Alabama, and at the first sale took in $90,000. These quick returns were realized while the titles still rested with the United States; the land had been auctioned on the installment plan, and the subsequent transactions had been made before the final payment to the government.

During the next tremendous boom, in the 1830's, town building became a mania over the entire frontier, but of the hundreds of towns laid out in that period the vast majority came to naught. The outstanding boomtown was Chicago, which in 1832 was a village of 550 inhabitants around a frontier fort, but by 1836 Chicago was the fastest growing town in America. During that year, when Harriet Martineau, a British traveler, visited the town, she said:

I never saw a busier place. At the time of our arrival the streets were crowded with land speculators, hurrying from one sale to another. A negro, dressed up in scarlet, bearing a scarlet flag and riding a white horse, with housings of scarlet announced the times of sale. At every street corner, where he stopped, the crowd flocked around him; and it seemed as if some prevalent mania infected the whole people. A young lawyer of my acquaintance there had made five hundred dollars per day the five preceding days by merely making out titles to land.[3]

When the canal land grant within the Chicago city limits was sold at auction, lots brought from $9,000 to $21,400, but the Panic of 1837 pricked that bubble and the price of lots dropped so precipitately that scarcely any of these credit sales was consummated. After the crash, land that earlier sold for $1,000 would not bring $100.[4]

[2] Nina Leftwich, *Two Hundred Years at Muscle Shoals* (Tuscumbia, Ala.: Press of Multigraphic Advertising Co., 1935), pp. 37, 38.

[3] Harriet Martineau, *Society in America* (3 vols.; New York, 1837), II, 259, 260.

[4] Aaron M. Sakolski, *The Great American Land Bubble* (New York: Harper & Bros., 1932), p. 429.

The story was similar on the west bank of the Mississippi, where speculators and settlers used government land directly for their activities. At the
close of the Black Hawk War in September, 1832, the Sac and Fox chiefs
ceded the United States a strip of territory fifty miles wide just west of the
Mississippi. The lands in this Black Hawk Purchase were to remain in
Indian control until June 1, 1833, when they were to pass into the
government's hands, but they were not to be opened to settlement until
they had been surveyed and purchased. Land-hungry men in Illinois,
however, paid little attention to legal details. In October, 1832, twelve or
fifteen individuals crossed the river, landed at the head of Big Island on
the site of present-day Burlington, and laid out claims for future settlement
—driving stakes, blazing trees, or by other means marking off claims. In
February they brought their stock across the river and began to clear the
land in preparation for cultivation, but troops from Fort Armstrong (at
Rock Island) expelled them and burned their cabins and fences.

After returning to the east side of the river with their property, the
settlers held a council and agreed to hold their claims. They built a flat-
boat and crossed the river from time to time to keep their claims alive and
to give evidence of cultivation. They formed a claim organization and
planned to keep their foothold until such time as they could legally occupy
the area. After June 1, 1833, the soldiers withdrew and the settlers moved in
unmolested although the land had not been surveyed and certainly had
not been sold, as no land office was opened in Iowa until 1838. Two men
laid out the town of Burlington in the fall of 1833, and by July 1, 1836, the
best lots were selling for $500.[5]

In the meantime, the Iowa delegate in Congress had secured the passage
of an act by which the United States government became the town proprietor of Mineral Point, Wisconsin, and of several Iowa towns, including
Dubuque and Burlington. (Iowa and Wisconsin were part of Michigan
Territory at this time.) The law provided that the United States should
survey these townsites and that the Secretary of the Treasury should sell
the lots at auction, with the proceeds to be used for public improvements in
the towns. No claimant was to be allowed more than a half-acre in in-lots or
more than two acres in out-lots, with preference going to bona fide settlers.
A commissioner appointed by the President was to represent the United
States government in each town and see that there was fair play and that
actual settlers received first chance at the sales.

Over ten thousand people were living in Iowa when the surveyors began

---

[5] Augustine M. Antrobus, *History of Des Moines County* [Iowa] (2 vols.; Chicago: S. J.
Clarke Publishing Co., 1915), I, 49–51, 144.

to run the township and section lines in the Black Hawk Purchase, and probably fifteen thousand when the land was first offered for sale in the autumn of 1838, but all of the lots in Burlington and all the land for miles around had already been claimed. Hundreds of houses had been erected in the town and in the surrounding area; the town already had a mayor and alderman, and had been the capital of the territory for more than a year. Most of the first claimants had sold out to advantage and other men had bought and sold lots for years, and had even given deeds, but not a single lot in town or an acre of farmland was legally owned by an individual.[6]

At the time of the land sale at Dubuque it was discovered that seven or eight men, including the President's commissioner, had made an arrangement by which they could pre-empt large tracts within the town limits, which was contrary to the provision of the law, which gave first chance to actual settlers. A number of citizens, therefore, held meetings and made plans to force the sale of the lots according to the law. They threatened to tear down the land office if the lots were not sold in regular order. As a result of this popular demonstration, the sale was suspended. Apparently, however, the land officers were in collusion with the speculators, for when the sale was resumed, a handful of speculators got most of the land that was intended for the citizens, despite all attempts to prevent this outcome.

Many leading statesmen made a competence by town speculation. Daniel Webster was one of these; he raised money in New England and sent it to his agent in Dubuque, G. W. Jones. The latter made the locations and they shared the profits; and according to John G. Parish, at the end of about one year the senator's share was $50,000. Madison, Wisconsin, was also an important scene of their investments.[7] Stephen A. Douglas had large investments and figured prominently in the building up of Superior, Wisconsin. By the 1850's another generation of town organizers was ready to infect the West with the town-building disease, which was to become a veritable epidemic. In Missouri and Iowa, promoters fairly drooled in anticipation of tasty morsels along the west side of the Missouri River— even long before the Kansas-Nebraska Act became law. Missourians had platted a series of towns along the Kansas shore; and before Indian title had been extinguished, Iowans were projecting cities across the river in present-day Nebraska. Colonel Barnabas Bates recalled that so many town promoters came to Nebraska in the 1850's feeling that they had been

[6] Charles A. White, "The Early Homes and Homemakers of Iowa," *Annals of Iowa*, 3d series, IV (Iowa City: October, 1899), 186–188.

[7] John C. Parish, *The Life of George W. Jones* (Iowa City, Ia.: State Historical Society of Iowa, 1912), pp. 21, 96–98, 152.

ordained to found some mighty city that it began to look as if the whole Missouri bottom would be laid off in townsites. While serving as a member of the territorial council, Bates facetiously vowed that the agricultural interests would be protected, and he forthwith introduced a bill in the legislature that "reserved every tenth section for farming purposes." It was jokingly said that a steamboat captain was a fool to haul passengers when he could have made a fortune freighting town stakes for Kansas and Nebraska.

In Dakota, the "chain-store" idea of town-founding blossomed. The territorial governor of Minnesota, Samuel Medary, learning through his political connections that the area west of present-day Minnesota was soon to be cut off and formed into a new territory, organized the Dakota Land Company, with himself as president. The company's avowed purpose was to seize every valuable townsite on the James, Vermilion, Wanari, and Missouri rivers in that region and start a series of new towns. Feeling sure the capital of the new territory would be located at the falls of the Big Sioux, the company sent an expedition racing to claim the site in June, 1857—only to find that the Western Townsite Company of Dubuque, Iowa, had already laid claim to the land about the falls and had named the townsite Sioux Falls. The latecomers had to be content with an adjacent half section of land, upon which the principal part of the city lies today.[8] Several counties were organized and at least six towns were founded at the time. Four years later, in July, 1861, the government got around to open a surveyor's office and started surveying, preparatory to selling the land.

Ordinarily, a group of perhaps half a dozen financiers would get together and lay claim to a half section of land, as allowed by the Town Site Act and then, in order to enlarge the site and have more lots to sell, would squat on adjacent land and stake it out in lots with streets and alleys. Next, the group secured the services of an artist to work up an attractive plat, had it lithographed, and distributed hundreds of copies of these beautiful works of art in the East. These pictures showed broad, shaded streets, churches, opera houses, elegant residences, magnificient wharfs, and puffing steamers. John J. Ingalls, who later represented Kansas for eighteen years in the United States Senate, was lured to Kansas by one of these master-pieces, which he later called "a chromatic triumph of lithographed mendacity." The "engraved romance" which lured him from his Massa-chusetts home depicted Sumner, Kansas, as a commercial city of large

[8] George Kingsbury, *History of Dakota Territory* (2 vols.; Chicago: S. J. Clarke Publishing Co., 1915), I, 100; Everett Dick, *The Sod-House Frontier* (New York: D. Appleton-Century, 1937), pp. 42–43.

proportions. Upon his arrival, however, Ingalls found none of the four churches represented, no schools, and shacks instead of residences. As for the college that had been so beautifully pictured, no one in Sumner had even heard the idea advanced. Instead of a magnificent busy wharf where five steamboats called simultaneously, there was a rickety dock and scarcely enough business to warrant an occasional stop by a steamboat.[9]

The most spectacular land fraud in the fifty or more Missouri River towns that were laid out in northern Nebraska occurred in Cedar County. A town named Curlew was laid out and ten thousand lots were sold, but not one house was ever built there.

Reverend Henry T. Davis, in the beginning of his ministry in Nebraska, made an appointment for a preaching service at a town called Fairview, which was clearly printed upon his map. He rode on and on over the undulating prairie, thinking it was surely time he was reaching the town. Finally he saw a settler's shack on the side of the road, and after asking for directions to Fairview, was told he had ridden through town a couple of miles back. "How's that?" exclaimed the astonished divine; "I haven't seen a house for miles until I saw yours." "Oh, there are no houses in Fairview," replied the settler; "it was laid out only a few months ago." The squatter then told the circuit rider to ride back and look in the grass for the white stakes. Davis did so and, from a settler some distance off the road, learned that arrangements had been made to hold his meeting in a pioneer's shanty in the general area.[10]

Town builders who genuinely wished to develop a city used every conceivable means to boom and puff the new city, and one of the most important means was the newspaper. This subsidized mouthpiece, often rightly named the "Bugle," "Herald," or "Advertiser," lived up to its name, tooting, crying, and advertising the town long before it had subscribers, advertisers, or any real support other than optimism and the subsidy of the town company, which sent issues of the paper all over the country "back east" as an agency for recruiting new residents.

Town promoters also built, or pursuaded an enterprising proprietor to build, a hotel. Lots were given away on the condition that houses of certain specifications would be erected. Churches and lodges also received building lots, and many lots were set aside for anyone who would at once build a house worth a certain sum. A Kansas town company, advertising in the *Tribune* of Liberty, Missouri, in 1855, announced that fully half the lots

[9] John J. Ingalls to his Father, October 5, 1858, in *Collections* of the Kansas State Historical Society, XIV (Topeka: Kansas State Historical Society, 1918), 100.

[10] Dick, *Sod-House Frontier*, Chapter III.

would be given away to sober, industrious homemakers who would in a short time erect houses. The proprietors, of course, expected to reap a rich harvest from the sale of the other half.

Sometimes business establishments were enticed to a town by the gift of an entire block. The fact that the land on which these towns were located belonged to the Indians or the federal government did not seem to bother the town boomers. However, the proprietors of Delaware, Kansas, advertised that buyers

> will be required to pay one-third and the balance to be paid when a complete title is made (when the townsite has been bought from the U.S. Government). That portion of the purchase money paid will be deposited in the bank of the state of Missouri at Lexington until said title is perfected and if never perfected will be refunded to the purchaser.[11]

Various towns, having fortunate combinations of location, resources, transportation, and the like, grew rapidly. The *Omaha City Times* traced the growth of Omaha:

> 1853 June—Town claim made by the Company and kept by them by paying tribute to the Indians whose title had not been extinguished.
> 1854 June—No settlements; but a single log house, "old St. Nicholas" of round logs, 16 feet square, built by the company as an improvement to hold the claim.
> 1855 June—Number of inhabitants from 250 to 300. Best lots sold at $100. . . .
> 1856 October—Number of inhabitants sixteen hundred. Best lots sold for $2,500.
> 1857 April—Number of inhabitants two thousand. Best lots sold for $3,500.
> June—Number of inhabitants three thousand. Best lots sold for $4,000.

The editor of the *Omaha Arrow*, on October 13, 1854, wrote:

> Omaha City commencing as it has done upon unsurveyed territory, with even the Indian land title unextinguished already claims a degree of respect recognized second to none on the soil of Nebraska, and bids fair . . . to take the lead of all Nebraska cities.

All of these developments, at Omaha and other places in Nebraska, took

[11] *Liberty Tribune* (Liberty, Mo.), April 6, 1855.

place before the first land sales, which occurred in July and August, 1858.[12]

Leavenworth, one of the earliest towns in Kansas, was laid out on Indian lands in 1854 and grew by leaps and bounds, with the buying and selling of lots taking place at a furious rate and at high prices. In February, 1857, however, the lots were sold at a mock auction and at the low prices at which they had been appraised due to the intervention of the local claim club.

The rushes at the openings of Indian lands were accompanied by town-building speculation. This was especially prominent in connection with the land rushes in present-day Oklahoma. In the winter of 1879–1880, David Payne founded two claim organizations—Payne's Oklahoma Colony and the Oklahoma Town Company. These organizations were intended to function as a sort of extraterritorial claim club which operated from Kansas soil. The town company sent scouts into Oklahoma to lay out towns at promising spots, and each member had his town lot reserved according to this plan. The number of members of the organization is not definitely known but by 1884 it is said that receipts for membership dues numbered well over fourteen thousand.[13] The two principal towns of the several projected in the territory were to be Guthrie and Oklahoma City, and since these townsites were on the railroad and were centrally located, many of the town boomers (as these people, who incessantly agitated the opening of Oklahoma to settlement, were called) arranged to move in by train when the territory was opened. The old boomers, or leaguers, planned to be there first and make their selections according to their explorations and squatter association plans of many years' standing. The Santa Fe Railroad had even designated locations for depots at these points and all was ready to move in and occupy the plotted area. A few days before the opening, a meeting was held at Arkansas City and a town was prefabricated and readied for the opening date. Newspapers reported that over a thousand businessmen were preparing to go in, and a newspaper, a bank, grocery stores, a hotel, and other institutions were ready to operate immediately upon arrival on opening day. A printing press, bank equipment, prefabricated business houses, tents, and stocks of goods were loaded on flat cars on railroad sidings, ready to be moved to Guthrie and Oklahoma

[12] A number of pre-emption claims had been entered, however, after the surveyors' plats had been deposited at the land office in June, 1856; Addison E. Sheldon, *Land Systems and Land Policies in Nebraska* (Lincoln: Nebraska State Historical Society, 1936), p. 35.

[13] Carl Coke Rister, *Land Hunger* (Norman: University of Oklahoma Press, 1942), pp. 51–66, 70, 77, 78, 93, 210–213.

City as soon as the passenger trains had gone ahead with the settlers. Since Guthrie was close to the Kansas line, from which the majority of immigrants came, it developed faster than Oklahoma City. On the morning of April 22, 1889, there was one building on the site of Guthrie—the Santa Fe depot—and a few shacks.

At the northern border of Oklahoma were fifteen passenger trains, all of them crammed with settlers. In order that all might have a fair chance (most of the settlers went in by horse conveyance), the train engineers had orders not to run faster than fifteen miles an hour. Meantime, before the signal had sounded for the race to begin, during the whole forenoon people began to drift into Guthrie from mysterious sources. By ten o'clock, two hours before the legal time for the rush to start from the boundary, tents began to rise, and by the time the bugle sounded for the run to start, the townsite was covered with tents. (Those who went into Oklahoma before the legal hour are known as Sooners.) Correspondents were allowed a place on the first train, which left at noon, and when it stopped at Guthrie, correspondent Hamilton Wicks of *Cosmopolitan* crowded out of the train window, baggage in hand, and sped across the townsite. Since this was the leading train, the passengers had anticipated no competition, but when these legitimate first arrivals found the townsite covered with tents and the ground studded with stakes, their curses were loud and explosive. Wicks described his experience:

> The race was not over when you reached the particular lot you were content to select for your possession. The contest still was who should drive their stakes first, who would erect their little tents soonest, and then who would quickest build a little wooden shanty.
>
> The situation was so peculiar that it is difficult to convey correct impressions of the situation. It reminded me of playing blind-man's buff. One did not know how far to go before stopping; it was hard to tell when it was best to stop, and it was a puzzle whether to turn to the right hand or the left. Everyone appeared dazed and all for the most part acted like a flock of stray sheep. Where the boldest led many others followed. I found myself, without exactly knowing how, about midway between the government building and depot. It occurred to me that a street would probably run past the depot. I accosted a man who looked like a deputy, with a piece of white cord in his hands, and asked him if this was to be a street along here.
>
> "Yes," he replied, "We are laying off four corner lots right here for a lumber yard."

"Is this the corner where I stand?" I inquired.

"Yes," he responded, approaching me.

"Then I claim this corner lot!" I said with decision, as I jammed my location stick in the ground and hammered it securely home with my heel. "I propose to have one lot at all hazards on this townsite, and you will have to limit yourself to three, in this location at least."

An angry altercation ensued, but I stoutly maintained my position and my rights. I proceeded at once to unstrap a small folding cot I brought with me, and by standing it on its end made a tolerable center-pole for a tent. I then threw a couple of my blankets over the cot, and staked them securely into the ground on either side. Thus I had a claim that was unjumpable because of substantial improvements, and I felt safe and breathed more freely, . . .[14]

Every fifteen minutes, when another train arrived, the rush of hundreds of new lot seekers pushed the town limits out farther, until the staked area extended beyond an eminence out of sight of the depot, at least two miles away. Later, the bounds were pushed out even farther, until the staked area was big enough to accommodate 100,000 inhabitants. Major Pickles, who had been sent to Guthrie by the Department of the Interior, reported that although he had arrived before noon on the day of the opening, the ground "was literally covered with men who were selecting, measuring, and staking out lots." Some of these men, no doubt because of their number, were very bold in their admission that they were Sooners—that they had jumped the legal deadline.

W. W. Howard, a *Harper's Weekly* correspondent, arrived at Guthrie on the first train from the north and stopped beside a man who had already pitched his tent.

"Where did you come from, that you have already pitched your tent?" the inquisitive newspaper man asked.

"Oh, I was here," said he.

"How was that?"

"Why, I was a deputy United States marshal."

"Did you resign?"

"No; I'm a deputy still."

"But it is not legal for a deputy United States marshal or anyone in the employ of the government, to take up a town lot in this manner."

"That may all be, stranger; but I've got two lots here, just the same; and

14 Hamilton S. Wicks, "The Opening of Oklahoma," *Cosmopolitan*, VII, No. 5 (September, 1889), 470.

about fifty other deputies have got lots the same way. In fact, the deputy marshals laid out the town."[15]

As the day wore on and the observations of the first trainload of arrivals concerning the occupancy of the site before the opening spread among the later claimants, indignation rose to a dangerous level against those who had entered the territory before the legal opening.

The honest land seekers were particularly incensed because people whose work legitimately called them into the territory had taken advantage of the situation to grab land before the legal opening. Indeed, it was charged that two United States marshals, Jones and Needles, had appointed about 450 friends and "land sharks" as deputies and that these pseudo lawmen had taken the choice lots in Guthrie and Oklahoma City. It was even claimed that the marshals, who were there to enforce law, drove off a party of Sooners concealed in the bushes on the townsite of Guthrie and took for themselves the identical lots the Sooners were attempting to hold.[16]

Smoldering indignation on the part of latecomers was blown into a blaze. A meeting was held that very evening in protest of the violations of the rules of the opening (announced by runners who had been sent through the town). A committee, composed of one man from each state, was appointed to protect the honest settlers against the frauds perpetrated by the officers and others, and the group determined to put a squatter on the lot of every man who had taken a claim before noon of April 22. They selected one hundred choice claims that they planned to jump simultaneously, under the protection of two hundred armed men. If the Sooners gave possession peaceably" well and good; if not, they were to be ejected and their possessions thrown off the lot after them.[17] Bloodshed was threatened for a time, but finally the protestors dropped the matter in the mistaken belief that the government would set everything right.

In the meantime, however, confusion reigned in the tent town, which in one day had grown from a grassy prairie to a human anthill of eight to ten thousand settlers. Town lots were staked out, with their lines running in every direction; there were no streets or alleys and no semblance of a planned city. The original attempt of the Sooners was to hold three or four lots, but as more and more settlers arrived and jumped their claims, they were able to hold only one or two. The situation grew tense, and every man had to stay on his claim; if he went to the river for a drink, someone was

[15] W. W. Howard, "The Rush to Oklahoma," *Harper's Weekly*, LXXXV (May 18, 1889), 391.

[16] *Caldwell Journal* (Caldwell, Kan.), April 25, 1889.

[17] *Arkansas Traveler* (Arkansas City, Kan.), April 25, 1889.

apt to occupy his claim. Some men at the corner of Pennsylvania and Washington streets—according to the plat laid out by the Sooner founders —began to argue and then to fight; then they whipped out their revolvers and started firing. A large crowd quickly gathered, and when they went back to their claims they found that they had been jumped by members of the gang who had started the mock pistol fight as a ruse.[18]

On the evening of April 22, some of the settlers tried to plow a furrow around the lots they claimed, which provoked much objection and reaching for guns. In a mighty tug-of-war among the factions on April 23, the form of the townsite was altered a dozen times. The major points at issue were where the streets were to run and who would lose his claim when a definite survey was made. An eyewitness remarked that a town had never been in such a muddle. Even the lots on which the land-office tent stood, which had been reserved from entry by proclamation, was jumped, but soldiers drove the squatters off. The Sooners, of course, wanted their plats recognized and insisted that the streets according to their "survey" be cleared of later comers. On the other hand, the legitimate settlers could scarcely tolerate the Sooners' having any claims at all.

Despite the uncertainties of the situation, frontier optimism triumphed and a city rose rapidly. Even on the evening of the first day of the run, the first hotel, the Guthrie House, consisting of fifty tents (five used for dining and the rest for lodging) was in operation. The same day, the first issue of the daily *Oklahoma Herald* was published. On the next day, April 23, the Bank of Oklahoma, with capital of $50,000, opened for business, and a postal clerk was running a post office. The newspaper later declared that the freight business at Guthrie had exceeded the business at Wichita and at Kansas City for two weeks after the opening and that acres of freight and thousands of pieces of baggage were piled up. Within three days after the rush, fifty lawyers had established themselves near the land office at Guthrie, and it is not particularly surprising that they were reported to be doing a flourishing business. Within ten days after the opening, about fifty buildings had been erected and mounted on runners in such a way that they could be moved after the final survey established their proper locations. On May 21 the *Oklahoma Optic* announced that a waterworks had been put in, an electric power franchise had been granted, and streetcars would be running in time for the Fourth of July celebration.[19]

Congress had thrown Oklahoma open to settlement so hastily that for over a year it neglected to provide for a government, either territorial or

[18] *New York Times*, April 25, 1889.
[19] *Oklahoma Optic* (Guthrie, Okla.), May 21, 1889; *Omaha Herald*, April 23, 1889; *Arkansas Traveler*, April 23, 1889.

local, in the newly opened area, but the frontier genius for self-government soon filled the vacuum. Tents had scarcely been pitched in Guthrie and claims recognized before a call was issued for an assembly that would organize a town government and elect its officers. Considerable political skirmishing followed, but finally the number of candidates for mayor was reduced to two. The manner of voting was unique. The two candidates took their places in an open field, adherents of each man—several thousand strong in each case—formed a column of four abreast behind him, and the columns marched past two tally committees which counted the "votes" by fours. All went well until the men in one column, seeing that the column of the opposing candidate was longer, sought to compensate for this inconvenience and, after being counted, circled back and formed ranks once more at the rear of the losing candidate's column for a repeat. When this trick was discovered, some emphatic language was used, but fortunately no gunplay, and all was settled peaceably.

As soon as city government was organized and order was brought out of chaos, the first problem was opening or laying out the streets; and this was effected in keeping with the spirit of the frontier. A heavy pole as long as the width of the street-to-be was cut and placed crosswise on the proposed street. A team was hooked to this gauge and it was pulled across the town, opening up the street. Men, whose claims obtruded the right-of-way were compelled to vacate such portions. A committee then divided the land that was left among the claimants and settled other claim disputes. Within a few weeks Guthrie was operating like a long-established community. Unlike Oklahoma City, in spite of many disputes, there was very little gunplay. Some have chosen to credit all this to an innate ability of American citizens to govern themselves in the absence of established authority, but United States marshals and troops were always on hand and materially aided in this matter.

Although the law provided that 320 acres was the maximum acreage that could be claimed for a town, Guthrie had so many claimants that the people overflowed the original plat and formed four towns of that size adjacent to one another. For over a year, until Congress provided a means to secure title and to set up a legal government, the citizens settled their own problems and lived on government land. By the act that was passed for them in 1890, the adjustment of disputes was placed in the hands of a board of trustees appointed by the Secretary of the Interior, and towns of 1,280 acres were legalized.[20]

[20] Roy Gettinger, *The Formation of the State of Oklahoma* (Berkeley: University of California Press, 1917), pp. 156, 157, 159, 161.

Space forbids a discussion of other towns except to say that Oklahoma City started out slower than Guthrie and had less than one-fifth as many people on the first day. Sooners—marshals and railroad construction workers—laid out the town. William L. Couch, successor to David Payne and the long-time leader of the Boomers, secured employment on a construction gang that was building the Santa Fe Railway conveniently near the site of Oklahoma City, where he had selected land. He and the common-law wife of David Payne, Mrs. Haines, who was employed as a cook for the construction company, went into the area well within the city limits of present-day Oklahoma City and staked out their claims.[21] The legitimate settlers, however, were not as docile as those in Guthrie and a pitched battle with rifles and revolvers seemed imminent, but a reinforced body of deputies prevented bloodshed. In the bitter feud that arose between the two rival groups, Indian names were used. The Sooners, under the leadership of Couch, were known as Seminoles, and the legitimate settlers went under the name Kickapoos. The Seminoles won out at first and elected Couch first mayor of Oklahoma City; but as time went on, daring and determined men pressed their challenge to the ownership of the land claimed prior to the legal hour or by people who were in the territory before the rush began. Eventually, Couch was killed while defending his claim and a court decision took Mrs. Haines's claim away from her. Much of the land which the Boomers had sought and actually claimed by means of the efforts of their extraterritorial claim club (formed in Kansas) and which they entered illegally, lay in what became a rich oil-producing area.[22] Riches seemingly within their grasp slipped away.

The townsite of Edmond also was occupied by Sooners long before the legal opening. The Sooners claimed the choice lots, but parties of colonists from Missouri and Illinois drove them off and took possession as the legal firstcomers.

In 1893 at the opening of the Cherokee Strip—the last and greatest "run" of all—the government divided the area into seven counties and designated them by letters "K" to "Q," presumably to allow the settlers to select the names themselves. Four acres were reserved in each county for a county seat. Towns were platted and blocks and lots designated on the official plat of survey. The rules laid down by the General Land Office

---

[21] David L. Payne and Mrs. Rachel Haines, a widow, had formed an attachment for one another and lived together but had postponed their marriage until Oklahoma was opened in order that each might secure 160 acres rather than only the single claim to which they would have been entitled as a married couple.

[22] Rister, *Land Hunger*, pp. 211–213.

allowed a claimant to homestead a quarter section or a town lot, but not both. To prevent early illegal entry, registration certificates secured within five days before the opening were required the same as for homesteading rural tracts. Despite these provisions, the rule was circumvented by sending members of a ring into the strip as Sooners to hold the most valuable lots while other members stayed behind and secured the certificates. When the latter arrived at the town, after the legal opening, the Sooners relinquished their claims in favor of their confederates. When the spoils were divided, each got a half-lot, but since these were the best lots a handsome gain was realized.

According to a *New York Times* correspondent, a group of fourteen women Boomers, who had been among the most successful town organizers in the past, reached the boundary of the strip several days before the run and worked out a scheme to displace one of the county seats for their advantage. Government regulations in connection with the opening allowed any four persons taking adjoining 160-acre tracts to start a town. Fifty people were required to organize a town company, and all land within the townsite had to be paid for at the rate of ten dollars an acre, rather than at the rural rates of $1.00 to $1.50 an acre. Since a county seat had the advantage in building rapidly into a city with valuable lots, the ladies planned to displace one of the government-designated county seats with one of their own founding. They intended to squat in numbers along the railroad line and by trading with neighbors to secure the required 640 acres to form a townsite; then the others would join them, lay out the town on the selected tract, and control all of the lots instead of one per person. These women, led by Miss Effie Williamson, were immediately joined by two hundred men, and the correspondent remarked that it looked as if they would start the race with a membership of one thousand. Their plan was to have a public drawing to determine which of their number should have the choice lots and then sell the rest for the profit of the company.[23] A town with such backing could be expected to wrest the county seat from one with less initial support.

Another factor which changed the location of some of the towns was the activity of some of the Indians. According to the treaty by which the Indians had given up their land, certain Indians were allowed to take claims before the regular opening. Accordingly, someone in the Department of the Interior who knew where the towns were to be located—possibly confederates in the scheme—allowed this information to reach the Indians, and seventy of them selected land that was intended for towns.

[23] *New York Times*, September 7, 1893.

This connivance necessitated the relocation of towns without regard to the appropriateness of the new sites as to water, soil, and other factors.

With the opening of the twentieth century, the day of the town builder was about over; thereafter, either a railroad that preceded an opening or normal economic procedures dictated the new town locations.

XVII

"Run for Your Land"

In the 1880's, as people realized that the public domain was melting away like a late spring snow, there was a frenzied rush for the land that remained. In earlier times, people had often ignored the laws when they were contrary to their desires and immediate interests, but in the final rush for the soil, agitators and determined promoters worked systematically to crash the gates of unopened territory. The Indian reservations began to appear as more juicy morsels than ever before to the land-hungry borderers. In 1870, when the Osage diminished reserve lands were sold to settlers, there was a feeling that other reservations also would be opened if the subject was agitated.

The first big body of land to become the subject of agitation in this era was the area known as Oklahoma. This was not the region that comprises Oklahoma today but only a small part of it—the central core in which Oklahoma City is now located and which is the area called Oklahoma in this chapter. In the Jacksonian era, various tribes from east of the Mississippi River had been given the land in the eastern portion of present-day Oklahoma, which for about three-quarters of a century was known as Indian Territory. When the Cherokee tribe was located in the northeast corner of present-day Oklahoma, they insisted on a corridor through which they could travel, unmolested by wild tribes, to the buffalo-hunting grounds in the West. This area—about sixty miles wide, extending from the Kansas boundary to Oklahoma, and from the 96th meridian on the east to the 100th meridian on the west—was called the Cherokee Outlet, or Cherokee Strip. Oklahoma was a rich area extending from its south boundary to the Canadian River, consisting of more than two million acres. During the Civil War, the Five Civilized Tribes, who held the lion's share of the central and eastern part of the state—as of today—had the misfortune to choose the wrong side and supported the Confederacy. As a result, the federal government compelled the Seminoles and Creeks to cede the smaller area, known at that time as Oklahoma, to the government to be devoted to the benefit of loyal Indians and freedmen (former slaves of the Indians). In the turmoil of the carpetbag period the ceded land was not disposed of as planned, and the Creeks and Seminoles claimed an interest in it. The opening of these two Indian domains—Oklahoma in 1889 and the Cherokee Strip in 1893—were the two most spectacular and famous land rushes in American history. Town building in connection with these runs has been discussed; we now turn our attention to the distribution of the land itself. As happened with the Platte Purchase in Missouri in the 1830's and the opening of Kansas in the 1850's, a flood of white migration was dammed up on the border of the Indian Territory, and the frontiersmen started a campaign to open the area to white occupation. Groups of men gathered in Kansas preparatory to staking out claims on the Indian lands to the south. Those who waged this ten-year crusade for the opening of Oklahoma to settlement, as we have seen, were called Boomers.

In the spring of 1879, several thousand covered wagons were said to be moving toward the southern border of Kansas. Newspapers reported that expeditions were springing up like mushrooms, and several expeditions actually crossed the line. One reporter stated that over fifty thousand acres had been staked out. C. C. Carpenter of Independence, Kansas, a colorful border figure, who wore a fancy velvet vest and a beaver hat from under which descended long curls, led one of the most formidable of these invasions, which was partly funded by a $500 contribution from the merchants of Independence. Kansas newspapers reported a general gathering on the border.

An administration of a strong stamp was at the helm in 1879—or stronger than that in the 1850's, when settlers squatted on the Delawares' lands with impunity. Carl Schurz, the Secretary of the Interior, called on President Hayes to warn the intruders out of the Indian Territory, and the President held a meeting of his Cabinet that voted for prompt and vigorous action. Hayes warned against the intrusion, pointing out that the land (Oklahoma) taken from the Indians after the Civil War was not open to homestead entry. He told the would-be squatters that they would be expelled by force, but Carpenter scornfully declaimed that his group would appeal to the God of Battles and the United States Congress to protect them in their constitutional rights if the President interfered. As for the military men, Carpenter didn't care a "fig" for General "Bull Run" Pope, saying that if Pope did not cut a better figure on the frontier than he had at Bull Run he would again be forced to retreat—this time before the homeseekers' army. The vigorous action of President Hayes nevertheless broke up the Invaders' plans, and Inspector John McNeal of the United States Indian Service informed the blustery Carpenter that he had better leave the country or he might be forced to wear handcuffs to complete his outlandish costume.[1] Carpenter, who went back to Kansas City and disappeared from sight, was pictured by the *Kansas City Times* as a Moses who instead of leading the people into the Promised Land had hidden in the bulrushes.

Dave Payne, a Kansan who had come from Indiana, had served in the Indian wars on the Plains, had risen to the rank of Brevet Major of Volunteers, and had been a member of the Kansas legislature, now became Carpenter's successor as the Boomer leader. During the winter of 1879–1880 he founded a sort of extraterritorial claim club known as Payne's Oklahoma Colony for the purpose of ensuring its members first right to a particular tract in the Indian country when it was opened to settlement. Payne soon issued a proclamation that Oklahoma was subject to entry and that his association planned to occupy it with a colony of five to ten thousand settlers. He claimed to have arranged for a daily paper and for schools, and said that three days after they arrived on the site of their city the schools would be in full operation. Threats of removal by federal troops, however, caused the invasion party to melt to almost nothing, for a cordon of soldiers was stretched along the boundary where the invasion was expected.

Not to be thwarted, Payne and twenty-one adventurers—using scouts and great secrecy—eluded the troops on the night of April 26, 1880, and by May 2 were camped on the site of Oklahoma City. Payne then announced that Oklahoma not only was open to settlement but that it had been settled, and that he would have a thousand people there in thirty days. Soon, however, they were captured by federal troops and escorted to Kansas, where they were released. At Wichita, the men received a hero's welcome. Payne later boasted that the soldiers had handled his men very carefully: that they had been treated more like guests than prisoners and that they had not been turned over to a court for trial.

One month later Payne's group slipped away to the spot they had correctly prophesied would be the capital of Oklahoma and found that their gardens, planted a month before, were growing nicely. Soon, however, they were again discovered by troops, and the first offenders among them were very politely escorted to the Kansas line; but the old repeaters were taken to Fort Smith, Arkansas, for trial at the United States district court,

[1] Carl Coke Rister, *Land Hunger* (Norman: University of Oklahoma Press, 1942), pp. 36–38, 46–49. I am indebted to this volume for much of the material on Oklahoma.

where the federal judge released them for appearance at the November term of court. Payne went to St. Louis, where he was given a great reception, and he was lionized in Wichita. Two bands, a troop of cavalry, and a great crowd met him at the Wichita depot and conducted him to a hall, where he was welcomed with speeches. Had his expedition been a success, thousands would have rushed into the Indian Territory before autumn. The Boomers received powerful support from the newspapers along the frontier and from the commercial interests of St. Louis and closer towns.

While waiting for his trial, Payne organized another invasion and went into camp not far from where Troop H of the 10th Cavalry was bivouacked. The Boomers expressed their determination to cross the line at all hazards, but the commander of the troops warned that his men had orders to shoot. On a Sunday, when religious services were held in camp, women and children came and the crowd sang lustily "Hold the Fort" and "Oklahoma Still," with the soldiers joining the Boomers in singing the "Star-Spangled Banner." The Boomers' chaplain, preaching from a text in Exodus, likened President Hayes to Pharaoh, Oklahoma to the Land of Canaan, the Boomers to the Israelites, the military commander of the Boomers to Moses, and the chaplain himself to Aaron. Later, two spies who were sent into the "Promised Land" found that many wagonloads of emigrants had entered the territory, but because they had no channel of supplies their settlement withered. Finally, faced with the impossible, the expeditionary force again melted away.[2]

Shortly after this, Payne's trial took place at Fort Smith on charges that he had violated United States laws of 1834 and 1856 which forbade whites on Indian Territory. In his defense, Payne argued that Oklahoma was not Indian Territory but part of the public domain, that it had been ceded by the Indians to the government after the Civil War, and that the government had recognized it as public domain in granting the Atlantic and Pacific railroads alternate sections along the right-of-way. The Boomers, then, had staked off the nongranted even sections. Federal Judge Isaac Parker, in rendering his decision, cited the laws that held that reservation lands and lands reserved by treaty or by proclamation of the President were not subject to pre-emption unless this right was provided for by special law. He ruled that Oklahoma was still Indian Territory and fined Payne $1,000. The government could not collect the fine, however, because Payne had no property and the law made no provision for seizing wagons and other chattels. Since there was no jail sentence, Payne was

2 Rister, *Land Hunger*, pp. 81–88.

released; whereupon he organized more expeditions and kept the border in a state of excitement. The *Oklahoma War Chief*, an organ of the Boomers that was published in southern Kansas, expressed the frontier doctrine by proclaiming that the history of every territory showed that the people had gone in first and occupied the land, and that the land offices had followed soon after.[3]

Payne invaded Oklahoma again and again, only to be brought out by the soldiers, who now treated the Boomers less like refractory comrades and more like prisoners. In June, 1884, while the soldiers cordoned off his camp near Arkansas City, Payne slipped away and surveyed a townsite, which he named Rock Falls, five miles below Hunnewell, Kansas, on un-disputed Indian land in the Cherokee Strip, which again indicated his in-difference to the Indians' rights. More than fifteen hundred people came to the settlement and thousands of claims were laid out for members of Payne's society. They erected a building for the *Oklahoma War Chief* and actually printed an issue or two. When it seemed that the plan was going to succeed, word reached the settlers that the soldiers were coming, and wagon after wagon was loaded and headed for the Kansas line; by evening hardly 250 people were left. When the soldiers arrived, they loaded the press and other valuables in wagons, hauled them back to Kansas and fired the town, leaving the place deserted. A few months later, Payne died.

Payne was succeeded by W. L. Couch, who led an expedition of three hundred men into the forbidden land. When the Boomers were appre-hended but refused to submit to arrest, the military commander sent for more troops; then he camped between the Boomers and the Kansas line, turned back all their supplies, and starved the settlers out. Finally they were marched back to Kansas by federal troops.

The army officers were incensed that they had to patrol such a vast area, submit to insult, and risk bloodshed. They felt that a firm policy should be followed and a stiff penalty provided for a repetition of the offense. The Boomers, on the other hand, complained that the government had dis-criminated against agrarians (Boomers) but had favored the cattlemen and the railroads. Ranchers had been allowed to lease vast tracts in the Chero-kee outlet, they complained, but the government prevented a poor man from homesteading a quarter section. In one case, they asserted, a Boomer was allowed to stay in Indian country simply because he had a few head of cattle.

The situation was complicated by several powerful interests that worked at cross purposes. The Indians, of course, wanted to keep their reservations

[3] *Oklahoma War Chief* (Arkansas City, Kan.), May 3, 1884.

intact and had collected a large fund to fight for their cause; they were sure that Payne had been only a front for their worst enemies—the railroads and the commercial interests. On the other hand, the frontiersmen, wanting the land opened to settlement, maintained that an "Indian ring," a group of "sharpers" who profited from the funds paid to the tribes by the government, and "New England sentimentalists" who believed in honoring the terms of Indian treaties, were blocking progress. Cattlemen, because they had a highly satisfactory grazing arrangement and did not wish to see it spoiled, also backed the Indians.

The railroads, standing to profit by settlement, backed the Boomers and kept a lobby in Washington to urge the opening of the Indian lands. Settlements would mean profitable traffic on their lines and would bring much trade to the merchants of St. Louis, Kansas City, and Wichita, for the rail lines ran directly between these cities and the Indian country. A railroad lobbyist at one time took all of the Kansas state officers by special train into the middle of the unopened Indian country and wined and dined them in an effort to influence the Kansas government to support the opening of the territory. Some Kansans, however, were cool toward opening Oklahoma since this would drain off tens of thousands of people from the state.

For a decade, army troops and United States marshals were constantly busy removing settlers until the tremendous pressure for opening Oklahoma bore fruit. In January and February, 1889, Congress passed laws granting a little over $4,000,000 to the Creeks and Seminoles for withdrawal of their claims to Oklahoma, and a bill to open the area was signed by President Cleveland on March 2, 1889. These laws stipulated that any homesteader who intruded before the official opening would forfeit his right to enter land, and President Benjamin Harrison, in a proclamation, set the opening of Oklahoma at noon on April 22, 1889, as previously mentioned. A large force of marshals and deputies was hired by the government to aid the soldiers in repelling and/or expelling intruders, but infiltrators would make a dugout in a secluded spot in an attempt to escape the notice of the soldiers.[4]

A party of Texans, led by Ed McIntosh, had meanwhile determined to defy authority and go into Oklahoma and stay there. They crossed the Canadian River below Purcell, Oklahoma, a few days before the opening, and when the deputies went after them they barricaded themselves and battled the United States troops. When these Sooners from Texas surrendered, they were taken to Purcell and jailed, but the party was only a

[4] Colonel Homer W. Wheeler, *Buffalo Days* (Indianapolis: Bobbs-Merrill, 1925), p. 298.

vanguard of a larger party which planned to follow this probing move-ment. The *New York Times* reported that on the morning of April 17 an Old Soldiers' Colony left Wichita, Kansas, for the Kansas boundary with about seven hundred wagons in the column. As they were ready to start, cheer after cheer arose.[5]

When the long-looked-for day drew near, it was estimated that 100,000 people stood on the borders in the neighboring states, waiting anxiously for the word to go, although only twelve thousand quarter-sections were available. Troops were stationed along these state lines to keep anyone from going into the land before the opening signal. Military officers gave the word that on the morning of April 19 at 8:00 o'clock the waiting throng would be allowed to start the march across the intervening Indian-held territory to the border of Oklahoma. On the Texas side the soldiers left for the Oklahoma line the evening of the eighteenth, and hundreds of the hopeful followed them, traveling all night. The movement across the intervening country to the line was made in a leisurely way. As the long columns of covered wagons moved across the space to the starting positions, it was obvious that the travelers had staked everything on this big gamble. Many had brought cattle and chickens; one reporter observed prebuilt claim shacks on some of the wagons. Because heavy rains had made the roads difficult and Salt Creek was too high to ford, boats were built and the Santa Fe Railroad installed decking on a bridge to permit the land seekers to drive their wagons across.[6] Starting points were designated along the Oklahoma line and the crowds gathered at these places. Much good-natured bantering took place and the contest of speed soon became known as "Harrison's Hoss Race."[7] As the hour of twelve approached, the multi-tude formed along the boundary. Blue-coated cavalrymen stood by to restrain overly anxious Boomers. When the bugle blared, the mass of humanity stiffened, bulged and broke, and they were off. It was "every man for himself and the devil take the hindermost." The shouts and curses of the vehicle drivers, the scream of terrified women, and the noise of pounding hoofs mingled in wild confusion as the contestants fanned out, seeking the coveted lands. Early arrivals in a short time occupied select tracts and latecomers dashed on seeking unoccupied plots or entered into angry quarrels over select claims. Others who eschewed quarrels wandered here and there only to find lucky runners had preceded them. Inevitably,

[5] *New York Times*, April 20, 1889, p. 1.
[6] *Omaha Bee*, April 20, 1889, p. 1; April 21, 1889, p. 1.
[7] Hamilton S. Wicks, "The Opening of Oklahoma," *Cosmopolitan*, VII, No. 5 (September, 1889), 470 ff.

there was much overlapping of claims, and claimants had to guard their quarter sections against all comers. According to the government's "ground rules" for the "Harrison Hoss Race," a man could step over the line after the bugle blew, drive a stake, and sit near the stake and claim a quarter section; but there was nothing to keep ninety-nine others from doing the same thing within the limits of the same claim. Even more exasperating was the problem of Sooners—those who went into the area sooner than the proclamation allowed. Many Sooners slipped into the area by night, one or two days before the legal opening. Even as men galloped across the country, the Sooners, who had concealed themselves in bushes or slough grass, seemed to rise out of the ground and lay claim to the land just as a horseman was about to stake it out. One man said he stopped seven times to claim land and each time a man arose out of nowhere and said he had already claimed it.

Several smaller areas were opened in the years that followed the opening of Oklahoma, one of which was the Sisseton Sioux and Wahpeton Reservation in northeastern South Dakota in April, 1892, in which a cloak of piety was used to hide the scheme that pressured the Indians into parting with their lands. The Watertown Board of Trade called a meeting of all the counties interested in opening the reservation to settlement and a committee was elected to meet with the Indians. The committee provided a bountiful feast, which was served in a beautiful grove at the Big Coulee, and the negotiations were opened by prayer and a request for heaven's blessing upon the treatymaking. Soon, a delegation was on its way to Washington to assure Congress that the Indians were ready to part with their heritage, and Congress responded with plans to parcel out the land by the usual land rush.[8]

Another distressing feature of this race, however, was confusion over the surest method of securing the land. The General Land Office prescribed two alternate methods for acquiring title after the opening signal: rush to the tract, take possession of the land, and make improvements on it; or stand in line at the land office, file on the land, and pay the two-dollar filing fee. The first homesteader by either method secured the land, it was stated, and if a filing and a settlement were simultaneous, the settler was given the preference. As the inspector of surveys and land offices pointed out, not more than thirty filings an hour could be made at the land office, but within one and a half hours every quarter section would be squatted upon by a settler. Hence according to the law of chance it would be best to run for the land. This double-jointed manner of securing land was a made-

[8] *Public Opinion* (Watertown, S.D.), April 15, 1892.

to-order troublemaker and certain to add to the income of the land lawyer. How could it be determined who had prior right to a claim!

We have noticed before how the cattlemen used Civil War veterans to act as their dummy entrymen. The *Grant County Review* of Milbank, South Dakota, now uncovered a land agent's racket in connection with this opening. A law provided that Civil War veterans might grant a power of attorney to an agent who could represent the soldier and file on a claim for him at the land office, which would take precedence over settlement. The agents in and about Watertown had sent circulars among the Grand Army of the Republic posts announcing that for fifty dollars they would enter claims for veterans. The game was so inviting that some agents sent letters to old Civil War comrades in the East, offering a commission of five dollars for each declaratory statement (the first step in making a claim) they could rustle up from other veterans. One of the agents no doubt spoke for all of the others when he said: "There will not be one-tenth of these old soldiers ever prove up on his claim and that is where we will make our money." If veterans asked a land officer the best way to obtain a claim, they were usually advised to have a land agent file for them, which probably revealed collaboration. The Milbank paper charged that the whole thing was a swindle and predicted that since soldiers' filings took precedence over squatters' rights, the agents would get a place in line and make proxy filings by the thousands, each one of them eliminating a settler from a claim which he had staked in the run. Thus, thousands of settlers would soon learn that a soldier's claim had been filed on the homestead upon which they were living. These settlers, prognosticated the editor, would live under sentence of losing their homes while yet hoping that the soldier might not come to settle upon the land. The agent would then inform the settler that he had lost his land to the veteran but that he was the agent for the veteran and for $250 to $500 he would relinquish his claim to the actual settler; the agent would split with the veteran, who never had any intention of coming to the West but merely allowed the agent to use his name to collect a modest sum. The paper further reported that agents had even offered to advance veterans the filing fee if they did not have the money and promised better service than a man could secure for himself since the agent would make it a point to be near the head of the line. One agent, the editor reported, had boasted that he expected to file a thousand claims the first day.

The newspaper's fulminations seem to have brought results, for an order was issued by the government that only one veteran's certificate could be filed by an individual in a waiting line. Even so, because soldiers' entries took precedence, such entries even at the end of the line eliminated settlers or registrants who were not veterans.[9]

Because a show of improvement was as important as prior occupancy, the most common proof of improvement in this treeless country was to start digging a well or a cellar. Of course, a man could carry a spade on horseback while making a run for land. A young man and his sister at the starting line, mounted on horses and waiting to make the run, were excited and anxious, for they knew where they wanted to locate. "Now, Betty," the brother said, "be sure to follow me and keep up with me if you can, for I have the spade to commence our improvements and I am going to ride on a dead run." But in the wild rush following the bark of the signal guns, the brother and sister were separated. When the young man reached the location he found that his sister had outrun him and, having no implement, was burrowing in the ground with her hands like a badger.[10]

The last great race for land was in the Cherokee Strip in 1893, about four and one-half years after the opening of Oklahoma. This tract of land, with an area of 6,500,000 acres, was about sixty miles wide and 168 miles long and lay just south of the southern boundary of Kansas. Owned by the Cherokee Indians, it had been leased by them to ranchers for grazing purposes until 1887 when the cattlemen's illegal fences were torn down. Squatters then sought to settle the area.[11] The government obligingly purchased the strip from the Indians and by a law of Congress passed on March 3, 1893, provided for its opening to settlement at such time and on conditions laid down by Presidential proclamation. The President set the date of the opening at noon on September 16, 1893. The proclamation temporarily set aside a strip of land one hundred feet in width around and immediately within the outer boundaries of the entire tract of country to be opened to settlement. This temporary reservation was used for a place of assembly for those waiting to make the run on the appointed day. Although the law provided that the land should be distributed as homesteads, in addition to the regular requirements the settler had to pay a specified price beyond the regular land-office fees. The land was graded into three classes on the basis of the amount of rainfall in the region where it was located, and this determined its appraised worth: land east of 97° 30′ cost $2.50 an acre; land west of 98° 30′ cost $1.00 an acre; and the land between cost

[9] *Grant County Review* (Milbank, S.D.), April 7, 15, 1892.

[10] Willard A. Burnap, *What Happened During One Man's Life Time* (Fergus Falls, Minn.: privately printed, 1923), pp. 120–121.

[11] *Annual Report of the Secretary of the Interior*, 1887 (Washington, D.C.: Govt. Printing Office, 1887), p. 23.

$1.50 an acre. Four per cent interest was charged from the time of filing until payment was made. A man was ineligible to homestead if he was the owner of 160 acres in fee simple or had at any time taken a homestead.[12] Soldiers who were sent to patrol the outlet and to find and expel Sooners burned the tall grass that would serve as hiding places. Despite these efforts, many Sooners provisioned themselves and went into hiding in caves as early as September 1.

In another effort to dispense justice and to guarantee fair play, officials in Washington, as we have seen, devised a plan to turn the tables on Sooners by requiring each person to have a certificate in order to enter land. These certificates were to be issued not earlier than five days before the run and were meant to eliminate those who might go in early. Accordingly, within the reserved corridor on the main routes of travel into the strip, land-office representatives set up booths to register the land seekers—five on the northern line and four on the southern border. Here, officials took an applicant's sworn statement that he was qualified and issued him a certificate that qualified him to enter land. Five days before the opening, the officials were ready for business. With thousands waiting to make the run it was anticipated that applicants would crowd in to be sure that they were not left out at the end of the registration period. A correspondent at Orlando, Oklahoma, reported that all was quiet until about 6:15 P.M. of the day before the registration, when some eager ones started to form lines. By 9:00 P.M., four thousand persons had formed in four lines, and they held their places all night, dancing, singing, and howling. When the booth opened at 7:30 the next morning, the places toward the front were bought and sold. Some of the positions brought up to $5.00, and after they had been registered, some of the men even sold their certificates.[13] The broiling sun, the furnace-like wind, and great clouds of dust caused much suffering. One witness testified:

I saw hundreds of men in line waiting to be registered who were over sixty years of age. They stood there for three days, and at the end many of them were lying in the dust gasping for water, and too weak to move. Other and stronger men only laughed at their misery. It was the survival of the fittest, and nothing but selfishness abounded on all sides.[14]

At Hennessey, Oklahoma, an ingenious man arranged a scheme whereby people did not have to wait in line for hours. The waiting lines were

---

12 *United States Statutes at Large*, XXVIII, 1229.
13 *Oklahoma State Capital* (Guthrie), September 16, October 13, 1893.
14 *The Clipper* (Hennessey, Okla.), September 22, 1893.

organized into divisions, each man was given a ticket that denoted his position in the division, the data were recorded in a book, and the roll was called every two hours. A man who was absent at two consecutive roll calls lost his place. Later, each man received a card and was not called until his division was formed and ready to go to the window; this was done in the evening and the individuals did not have to wait throughout the preceding twenty-four hours.

The operation came very close to getting out of hand. The representatives of the Department of the Interior, seeing that they did not have enough clerks to register the immense crowds in five days, hired extras from the applicants, and new booths were erected at points where the crowds were the greatest. As a result of this wise move, by the hour of opening every applicant had received a certificate and was ready for the race. One hundred and fifteen thousand certificates were issued.

The army was diligent in rounding up Sooners and ejecting them, but it was impossible to keep the latter from crossing the lines at night and hiding out. A Sooner who had dug a small trench and covered himself with leaves was nevertheless discovered and arrested. The soldiers had grown weary of ejecting these cheaters, and in one instance, at least, they decided to make the swindlers pay for their chicanery. A soldier, upon discovering a hidden Sooner, allowed himself to be bribed by a ten dollar bill to permit the land hunter to stay in the forbidden area. The blue jacket would then tell a comrade, who would "discover" the trickster, take a bribe from him, and so on, until the Sooner's money was exhausted; then the last soldier to flush him out, receiving nothing, would in the most military manner march the culprit to his commanding officer and receive his commendation for fidelity to duty, which was not as desirable as a ten dollar bill but was better than nothing.

At noon on opening day, after the soldiers along the lines had given the signal by firing their guns, according to plans, the Boomers, running in pairs, were to rush until they found themselves in the clear, then diverge from each other about a half-mile so that they would not lay claim to the same quarter section, and set up a flag with the name of the claimant and the number of his certificate as a sign that the land was taken. The next step was to note the time of day, since the legal time of entry was the time of setting up the flag, and each partner was prepared to bear witness to the time the flags were erected. After setting the flag, the partners were to go to the corner mounds and stake off their land.

The plan was all right on paper, but in the confusion the partners sometimes became separated. Then, too, there might be several other people, just over a hill or out of sight, staking out the same claims. Another draw-back was the fact that the federal government had set aside four sections in each township for public schools. The Boomers, however, could not stop to search for a cornerstone and determine whether they were on school land or on land that was subject to private entry. By the time they had set their flags and discovered that their claim was on school land, the adjacent tracts would have been claimed.[15]

The Department of the Interior's regulations stipulated that there could be no chartered trains, that the regular fares had to be charged, that only certificate-holders were allowed on the trains, that the trains travel no faster than fifteen miles an hour, that they stop every five miles, and that no one be allowed to board the trains within the strip.[16] On the day of the opening it was 100° F. in the shade and there was a searing wind from the Texas panhandle wilting everything. Long before noon the land-hungry had lined up, and out in front, one hundred or two hundred yards apart, were the soldiers, resting on their rifles and watching the crowd.

Near Liberal, Kansas, a few hundred feet from the line, a Rock Island train engine coughed gently, its tender and the tops of its ten cattle cars alive with men. Inside, where the cattle ordinarily were carried, were jammed hundreds of standing men. The time of the start was to be an-nounced by the firing of a cannon at the east end of the strip, and relays of soldiers, firing rifles, were to carry the signal to the west end. At quarter of twelve, the line stiffened and, like a huge animal straining at the leash, waited impatiently. Somebody accidently discharged a revolver and a man galloped across the line. "Come back!" roared the crowd, but the man could not hear or did not want to hear. "Halt!" a soldier commanded. When the rider did not heed the order, a Springfield blazed and the man went down with a bullet in his head. At Orlando, Oklahoma, on the southern side of the strip, nonpaying Boomers hung all over the waiting engines and cars and refused to get off. "Shoot us if you will but we won't get off;" and they could not be dislodged. Six big trains followed the first one to the points where the Boomers wished to stop. A reporter for the *Oklahoma State Capital* wrote: "One of the grandest sights that it is given to men to witness is that of a mighty mass of men rushing for 160 acres of land."

When the signal sounded, a great roar went up; the whole line swayed, pushed, cursed, and then broke into fragments. Dust rose in dense clouds

[15] Seth K. Humphrey, *Following the Prairie Frontier* (Minneapolis: University of Minne-sota Press, 1931), pp. 233, 234, 236.

[16] *Oklahoma State Capital*, September 16, 1893.

and men knocked each other down, and then rushed heedlessly on. Women were hurled to the ground and trampled underfoot. Mrs. Charles Barnes of El Dorado, Kansas, was knocked from her horse and trampled to death by other riders. Three men were killed when they rode their horses over bluffs.[17]

The winner of the race for a quarter section usually was the man who rode a wiry western pony, sure-footed and tough. Few men, however, had anticipated the hardships of a waterless country; they did not take enough water even for themselves, let alone for their horses. Those who ran near a railroad helped themselves at the railroads' tanks. Men who had been in the waterless hinterland told of horses dying and of men in desperate circumstances for want of water. One man told Seth Humphrey, who made the run on a bicycle, that he got his horses to town only by giving them spoonfuls of whisky along the way. Those on bicycles were able to travel faster than those on foot, and did not need water by the bucketful as did the horsemen, but the short, sharp grass sometimes punctured the tires.

During the afternoon, two men in the lead, to discourage competition, set fire to the prairie, and many Sooners were unintentionally smoked out in this way. Some who had made the run legitimately and were staking out land had a gun poked in their face and were commanded to move on by a man who did not have a certificate—or any means of conveyance from the line. Feelings ran high against such land seekers, and sometimes the Strippers combined and visited sudden death upon the Sooners where their activities were too obvious.[18] Some settlers came upon a ravine where a man had been hanged from a tree; pinned on his shirt was a placard with a simple but eloquent explanation: "Too Soon."

A futile attempt had been made to disarm the land seekers in the law-abiding state of Kansas in order to lessen shooting and bloodshed in the strip. The first night after the rush began, and while Seth Humphrey was sleeping on a claim, he was awakened a little past midnight by distant hoof beats, shouting, and shooting. A gang of gunmen was riding about, shouting the number of a section, township, and range, and warning: "Get off and keep off!" This was followed by gunfire after each call. A gang on horseback was clearing a number of quarter sections of claimants by the well-known method of "shootin' past the ears." A few well-placed shots whistling through the air served to send many easterners back to their native state to tell tales of the rough ways of the wild and woolly West. As one witness observed, the race might go to the swift but the land went to

---

[17] *The Clipper*, September 22, 1893.

[18] *New York Times*, September 17, 1893.

the tough; or, as another expressed it, the farms went to the gun-toters rather than to the farmers.[19]

The Department of the Interior had set up four land offices in the strip —at Perry, Enid, Alva, and Woodward—and a few minutes after noon on the day of the opening these opened to receive entries. Shortly, claimants who had staked out their claims began to form lines at these offices. In a short time, five thousand were in line at each place; many weeks elapsed before the lines broke, but the General Land Office was able to announce that before the three months had passed—the time allowed between staking out the claim and entry—the business was done and no one was prevented from getting his entry in on time.[20]

The frenzy for land, which was becoming scarcer every day, brought about such abuses in connection with the rushes of the early 1890's that volleys of criticism were fired at the army and the Department of the Interior immediately after the Cherokee Strip opening. It was charged that innocent people had been burned to death when the soldiers fired the high grass to destroy the hiding places of Sooners, that the army shot and killed a man who had started too soon, that bribes had been accepted for unfair advantages, and that partisanship had been shown in administering the race. Moreover, the rush method allowed the unscrupulous, lawless, and desperado class to take the land at the expense of more-or-less honest, peaceable, law-abiding citizens. At last, rugged individualism had to give way to cooperation. As miners who had attempted to hold a whole gulch had been compelled to disgorge and give later comers a chance, public opinion also compelled a revision of the land-distribution procedure, which resulted in the land lottery, or raffle.

The first experiment with the lottery system was made in connection with the opening of the Kiowa, Comanche, and Apache reservations in present-day Oklahoma. During the sixteen registration days provided for those who wished to file, 167,000 applicants registered for the thirteen thousand available claims. The registrations were shuffled, drawn, and numbered, and one's number represented one's turn to file. The first few men whose names were drawn were fortunate indeed, for they had the privilege of filing upon choice quarter sections, estimated to be worth $25,000 each, adjoining Lawton, Anadarko, or Hobart, Oklahoma. The object of the plan was to eliminate the abuses occasioned by the rush and disputes over claims; but James R. Wood's claim adjoining Lawton was

---

[19] Humphrey, *Prairie Frontier*, pp. 236, 257.

[20] *Annual Report of the Commissioner of the General Land Office, 1894* (Washington, D.C.: Govt. Printing Office, 1894), pp. 100–102.

jumped by two hundred squatters. There seemed to be no way of avoiding contests occasioned by the frontier custom of squatting.[21]

From time to time, however, other Indian reservations were opened for settlement by the land-drawing system with little or no difficulty, as was the Rosebud Reservation in South Dakota in the summer of 1904. Registration took place at four towns simultaneously—at Yankton, Chamberlain, Bonesteel, and Fairfax—and thirty-two clerks sent out by the Department of the Interior handled the registering. Clerks at Yankton registered applicants at three booths—fifteen hundred men who formed lines two or three blocks long. A Negro shipped in a quantity of chairs which he rented to the weary waiters. At first, some of the applicants slept in the street in order to retain their places near the head of the line, but an ingenious individual had cards with consecutive numbers printed which read: "Rosebud Land Registration. This holds your place in line. Authorized by the mayor." The man vainly tried to sell each card for twenty-five cents, but the crowds finally agreed to pay five cents per card. The card device may well have been inspired by the merchants and vendors, for it provided time for the land seekers to part with their cash.

The registration towns had the appearance of a carnival, with sideshows, shooting galleries, and other concessions. At Bonesteel, the city officials gave concessions to gamblers for $100 a day, and the *Yankton Press and Dakotan* charged that crooked gamblers and pickpockets were having a field day. Many men in line represented whole communities, such as an Illinois man who said his neighbors had paid two-thirds of his fare on condition that he look the situation over and, after having registered and viewed the land with the thought of their coming, bring them a report. Many aliens desired to register. Since a sworn declaration of their intention to become a citizen was a prerequisite for registration, the courthouse officials were busy making out first papers in the naturalization process.[22]

A typical land lottery in the closing years of the public-lands distribution was that of the Fort Niobrara Military Reservation in Nebraska, which was opened for settlement in October, 1913. For a period of thirteen days, land seekers were allowed to register at one of three points in Nebraska— Valentine, Broken Bow, or North Platte—and the drawing was to take place the third day after the registration was concluded. Registration was free, although each registrant was required to have his signature notarized, for which the notaries charged twenty-five cents. The ninety-one notaries in Custer County were notified to be present at the opening of registration and

21 *Public Land* (Spokane, Wash.), August 20, 1901.
22 *Yankton Press and Dakotan* (Yankton, S.D.), June 10–25, 1904.

were organized into eight-hour shifts for work on a twenty-four-hour basis.

Registration began at midnight on Sunday, but early Sunday morning at Broken Bow, a woman planted herself in a chair in front of the registration booth and held her place the livelong day. She was a leading Lincoln suffragette, and while she waited she gave the swelling crowd a spirited lecture on women's suffrage. At intervals, someone would start a popular song or a hymn in which everyone joined, but as the deadline drew near, the excitement became intense. As midnight approached, the government official in charge gave the last-minute instructions. As the hour struck, the sheriff shouted: "Let her go!" The big rush was on. There was no reason for this crowding to be first, however, since the last registrant had as good a chance for land as the first. Every train into these cities bulged with humanity. Some trains, jammed from engine pilot to the last coach, carried a thousand people. Regular trains ran extra sections and special trains ran from Lincoln. The rush continued for two weeks. The city of Broken Bow provided a large information tent thirty feet in circumference, with a telephone, a counter with timetables, and many other things of help to strangers.

The land seekers were a heterogeneous lot, and many were entirely unsuited to face the realities of homesteading in a semiarid country. A widow from Des Moines, with her little daughter, had spent all of her money except twenty dollars; she had been doing housework for a livelihood and hoped to draw a home. A waitress from St. Louis hoped to get her invalid mother away from the city and into the healthful atmosphere of the high Plains. A Civil War veteran from Missouri announced: "I'll make a good homesteader . . . Uncle Sam won't have nothin' to complain of in me." A big Iowan registered at Broken Bow and then went to North Platte to be on hand when his name came up at the drawing; he was so certain of his success that he had a prewritten telegram to send to his wife as soon as his name was drawn.[23]

Judge James W. Whitten, who on behalf of the United States had supervised the drawings for more than a decade, was in charge of the Fort Niobrara operation. As announced in the newspaper prior to the event, the drawing was to be in the North Platte opera house and a band would render special music during the procedure. The stage was to have an enclosure, twelve by eighteen feet, made of woven-wire fencing four feet high, forming a visible bin into which envelopes, each containing a registrant's name, were to be placed and then stirred thoroughly with a pitchfork. After tens of thousands of envelopes had been deposited and the mass

[23] *Custer County Chief* (Broken Bow, Nebr.), October 17, 24, 1913.

thoroughly shuffled, two little girls were to enter the cage before the expectant crowd, select two thousand envelopes, and hand them to the officials, who would read the names aloud and announce the numbers that determined the order of choice. When two thousand names had been read, the drawing would be over and the rest of the 76,689 would be eliminated. The fortunate ones, most of whom would not be present at the drawing, were to be notified by mail of the day and hour to be on hand for filing; in the meantime they could look over the land and be ready to make entry, beginning on November 17, at the North Platte land office.[24]

At the mammoth drawing at the second Rosebud Reservation opening in South Dakota in 1908, town companies and businessmen offered $10,000 for claim number 1. As usual, Judge Whitten conducted the drawing, in a huge tent at Dallas. As the little girls took their places to select the names from the shuffled pile, the great crowd became tense and alert, waiting breathlessly as the official took the first envelope, slit it open, and read the name. Most of the winners had gone home, to be notified by the list of names published in the newspapers, but the winner of the first choice on this occasion, an Oklahoma farmer, was present. He was greeted with tremendous applause and many demands for a speech, but he was a timid soul unused to speaking, and the best he could do was to rise with a sheepish smile, feel through his pockets, and pull out a rabbit's foot which he waved triumphantly.[25]

After the drawing, the locators now had their inning. Day after day they did a wholesale business. They loaded the winners, popularly known as "lucky numbers," on hayracks padded with hay and drove them many miles into the reservation, charging them $15.00 to $25.00. Selecting a choice quarter section was not difficult for those whose names had been drawn very early, but those whose names were drawn last found it difficult to find a place and had to take what was left. The entering of the lands did not necessitate long waiting lines since the land office staggered the candidates' times for filing over a period of several days.

All in all, the lottery method of distribution was satisfactory—except that only a small amount of land was available, which necessitated the disappointment of many people. It is probable, however, that land just as good as much that was drawn could have been secured at private entry at the numerous land offices over the country which still were dispensing free land at this time.

24 *North Platte Tribune* (North Platte, Nebr.), October 7, 14, 24, 28, 1913.
25 Edith Eudora Kohl, *Land of the Burnt Thigh* (New York: Funk & Wagnalls, 1938), pp. 161–162.

XVIII

Beyond the 100th Meridian

As LATE AS THE 1870's the maps of the United States showed a vaguely defined region called the Great American Desert. Zebulon Pike, the first American explorer to traverse the area between the Missouri River and the Rocky Mountains, and the originator of the desert idea, reported that the territory that lay between the meridian through present-day Kansas City and the Rocky Mountains, and north as far as the 48th parallel, was without question a desert and "might in time become as celebrated as the African deserts." He referred to the sterility of the soil, the lack of rainfall, the absence of trees, the lack of fuel, the scarcity of water, and the sparseness of the vegetation. One is inclined to believe, however, that Pike's judgment was in part conditioned by the contrasts with the area he had explored just previously: the wooded, well-watered Mississippi River basin from St. Louis to north-central Minnesota. But Pike also thought that the desert might be a blessing because it would restrict the westward movement and lead to a more compact population, and thus ensure the continuation of the Union. (This was a reflection of the thinking of some that the rapid extension of settlement would result in the breaking away of the self-sufficient westerners from the rest of the nation.) Pike judged, however, that a limited grazing business might be conducted on the marginal grassland to the west of civilization.

The historian of the Long expedition of 1819–1820 moved the eastern boundary of the desert farther west, to the 98th meridian, but he was even more emphatic about the utter worthlessness of the Great Plains. He pronounced the area between the 98th meridian and the Rocky Mountains a "dreary plain, wholly unfit for cultivation, and of course uninhabitable by a people dependent upon agriculture for their subsistence." He thought it should "forever remain the unmolested haunt of the native hunter, the bison, and the jackal."[1]

[1] Wallace Stegner, *Beyond the Hundredth Meridian* (Boston: Houghton Mifflin, 1954), pp. 215–216.

The Great American Desert had never been bounded definitely, and by 1850 it was commonly believed that it began at the Missouri River. In spite of adverse reports, when the Kansas-Nebraska Act was passed, settlers swarmed across the river before the Civil War and occupied the immediate trans-Missouri area. Moreover, when travelers along the overland trails saw that crops could be grown, they stopped and established road ranches, leading later comers to believe that crops could be grown almost anywhere. These early settlers, however, had failed to note the gradual decrease in annual rainfall as settlement moved westward. Anxious to secure immigrants and build up the country, the inhabitants puffed the country and began to think of the entire Kansas and Nebraska area as highly productive.

People in the East failed to discern that the productive lands were fairly close to the Missouri River, and they began to think of the Great Plains as the garden spot the reports had pictured. Professional promoters, such as Governor William Gilpin of Colorado, said there was no American desert—that the area all the way across the Plains was productive. Gilpin represented the land west of the 100th meridian as a pastoral Land of Canaan. According to his exuberant recital, most of the Great Plains was arable, the climate was the finest to be found anywhere, and although there was little timber, a beneficent nature had provided a plant (sagebrush) with an abundant root system that the settler could dig and have ample firewood. Gilpin was merely the mouthpiece for the area's boomers, politicians, the railroads (eager for settlers), and the speculative town builders.

Major J. W. Powell, in his famous *Report on the Lands of the Arid Region of the United States*, in 1878, drew the line of an average of twenty inches of rainfall a year as the western limit of successful agriculture, as it was known in the rainfall belt. He approximated this line at the 100th meridian and this is the definition used in this chapter. The 100th meridian is used to indicate a line separating the area of sufficient rainfall for farming without special techniques—such as dry farming and irrigation—from that where such techniques are required.

Settlement gradually pushed westward, unmindful or innocent of the fact that beyond the 100th meridian the average rainfall was not over twenty inches a year—inadequate for farming as carried on east of the Missouri—and that the wet year-dry year sequence was utterly unpredictable. In the late 1860's a cycle of wet years began that, with only one short drought, lasted until the late 1880's. People who came from the humid area accepted this occasional wet cycle as normal, and continued to farm much as they had in Iowa or Illinois. When a dry year overtook them, they considered it unusual, and with frontier optimism staked their faith on a bumper crop next year. Another idea—propounded when some dry years suggested that perhaps there was an arid region after all—was that settlement would in some way lead to greater rainfall. Ferdinand Hayden, the director of the United States Geographical and Geological Survey in 1867, predicted that settlement would reduce the number of prairie fires and this would increase the amount of timber. He stated that the planting of trees had increased the amount of rainfall in the eastern section of Nebraska. He forecast that this change would continue across the dry belt to the very foot of the mountains. Samuel Aughey, professor of natural science at the University of Nebraska, summarized the idea with an immensely popular and wishful slogan: "Rain follows the plow."[2]

Charles D. Wilber, a town builder, joined Professor Aughey in proclaiming that the western advance of settlement was extending the humid area into the Great Plains. In an address to the Nebraska State Horticultural Society in 1878 he declared:

The amount of rainfall per year is steadily increasing west of the Missouri River. The average for nine years past at Omaha is twenty-nine inches. With the year ending June 1877, it was thirty-eight inches in southeast Nebraska—an amount equal to the average of Northern Illinois. From similar statistics we are able to show that the rainfall is steadily increasing westward, following the pioneer farmer and his plow, which is the primal cause of all these changes.

With a logic that cannot rest we are forced to this conclusion, that the agencies of civilization now in action are such as will secure a complete victory over the wilderness and waste places of western territory. The plow will go forward; "God speed the plow." The rich carpet of grass will continue to advance. The rains will assume the regularity of times and seasons. By this wonderful provision, which is only man's mastery over nature, the clouds are dispensing copious rains upon millions of acres of surface that were for centuries parched and desolate.[3]

A popular work, *Our Western Empire*, by Linus P. Brocket spread the idea far and wide that the existence of an arid area in the trans-Missouri region was pure fiction:

[2] Henry Nash Smith, *Virgin Land* (Cambridge: Harvard University Press, 1950), pp. 180–182.
[3] C. D. Wilber, "The Relation of Geology to Horticulture," *Annual Reports of the Nebraska State Horticultural Society, 1878 & 1879* (Lincoln: Journal Co., 1879), p. 92.

Nearly the whole region lying between the Mississippi river and the Rocky Mountains was regarded fifty years ago as a desert land, incapable of any considerable cultivation, and given over to the buffalo, the panther and the prairie wolf; yet in no part of the vast domain of the United States, and certainly in no other country under the sun, is there a body of land of equal extent in which there are so few acres unfit for cultivation, or so many which, with irrigation or without it, will yield such bountiful crops.[4]

The promoters were quick to capitalize upon the erroneous beliefs and statements. LeRoy Hafen quotes a Burlington Railroad pamphlet of the late 1880's:

The rain belt has moved westward to within less than eighty miles of Denver. . . . So much rain now falls in the eastern portions of Colorado that it is no longer fit for a winter range for cattle. . . . What has brought about this great change cannot be accurately determined.[5]

A few years later—1892—another Burlington advertising folder attempted to explain why this land, which until recent years was part of the Great American Desert and regarded as having insufficient rainfall for raising crops, had seemingly become a garden spot of the nation.

As a matter of fact, rain has fallen in its proper season, and in greater or less quantities, ever since the first settlement of the country, and with the gradual cultivation of the soil the rainfall has been considerably increased, until now it is amply sufficient for all purposes. This remarkable fact accords with the experience of the early settlers throughout almost the entire West, for while the unbroken sod is almost impervious to water, the rain running off into the creeks and rivers, the cultivated ground readily absorbs the heaven given moisture and treasures it up, and what it loses in evaporation it gets back in those local rains which but a few years ago, were almost unknown.[6]

During this time, Kansas, Nebraska, and Colorado were enjoying a land boom. The register of the land office at Garden City, Kansas, wrote:

[4] Linus Pierpont Brocket, *Our Western Empire* (Philadelphia: Bradley, Garretson & Co., 1881), p. 131.
[5] LeRoy Hafen, *Colorado and Its People* (4 vols.; New York: Lewis Historical Publishing Co., 1948), II, 434.
[6] More recent research has proved that soil covered with vegetation holds the water much more effectively than does cultivated soil; see "Burlington Route, Cheap Lands West of the Missouri River," a pamphlet (Chicago: Burlington Railroad, 1892).

The rush for land in this section of Kansas is unprecedented. Every train brings in a crowd of land-seekers. For more than an hour before the office opens a mass of humanity throngs the doorway, and it is a remarkable sight to see the press and excitement.[7]

Fifty thousand acres were taken daily, and thriving towns sprang up from the Plains around isolated windmills and water tanks along the railroad lines. Counties were laid out and the location of their governmental seats was disputed and fought over with a vengeance by the lusty, growing population. Then, a normal series of dry years, in the climatic character of the Plains, began in 1887 and lasted into the middle 1890's.

Many of the homesteaders were fairly well-to-do farmers from the rain-belt region who had come West to use their homestead rights to get rich in the new Garden of Eden, but they moved away from the searing, blazing sun and the furnace-like southwest wind, back across the Red River into Minnesota and across the Missouri River into Iowa or Missouri. Half the population of western Kansas moved out, defeated, between 1888 and 1892, and vast portions of the Plains to the north were almost entirely depopulated, from Nebraska to the Canadian line. Twenty towns in western Kansas were said to have been entirely abandoned. Wichita, "Peerless Princess of the Plains," although just east of the 100th meridian, lost thirteen thousand inhabitants, and her real estate business suffered almost total collapse. Long lines of covered wagons now moved from Kansas into Missouri, bearing such signs as "In God we trusted, in Kansas we busted."[8] The dry cycle that began in 1887 lasted nearly ten years, and those who could afford to leave packed up and went "back to the wife's folks," as the saying had it.

Here and there a settler too poor to get away or one too stubborn to admit defeat stayed on, adapted his tillage system to the prevailing conditions, and succeeded. To accomplish this, an entirely new system of farming had to be developed, which would drastically affect the occupation and distribution of the remaining public lands. In 1890 the Bureau of the Census declared that the frontier line had ceased to exist, and on the strength of this declaration the great American historian, Frederick Jackson Turner, in 1893 wrote *finis* for the frontier. Nevertheless, with the development of the new system called dry farming, or dry-land farming, in the 1890's and early 1900's, once more the Department of the Interior

[7] *Annual Report of the Commissioner of the General Land Office, 1885* (Washington, D.C.: Govt. Printing Office, 1885), p. 79.

[8] Fred A. Shannon, *The Farmers' Last Frontier* (New York: Farrar & Rinehart, 1945), pp. 307–308.

began its land-office business with a flourish. Indeed, more land was distributed under the Homestead Act in the twentieth century than in the nineteenth. In the thirty-year period between 1868 and 1897, seventy million acres were homesteaded, but during the twenty years between 1898 and 1917, 100 million acres were given away by homesteading—a 43 per cent increase over the nineteenth-century period.[9]

Recognition of the arid conditions beyond the 97th to the 100th meridian, the discovery of new techniques for tilling dry soils, and the adaptation of the land laws to fit dry farming and grazing conditions account for the tremendous land-office activity after the frontier was thought to be at an end. Although the principles of dry farming were advanced by various people, the outstanding advocate and promoter of the system was a homesteader in South Dakota, H. W. Campbell, who, after suffering the reverses of the dry years, by observation, study, and experimentation worked out his scheme of farming. Campbell had migrated from Vermont in 1879 and had taken a homestead in Brown County, South Dakota, fifteen or twenty miles northeast of Aberdeen, just west of the 98th meridian. The first few years were exceptionally wet, and Campbell raised good crops. In the midst of this cycle, however, a wheat crop failure had occurred in 1883, and Campbell had begun to study soil production scientifically. One by one, he discovered the principles that were to make crop-growing much more certain on the Great Plains. One of these principles, packing the soil, Campbell discovered by accident. He tells of the experience:

In the fall of '85 a neighbor had driven four mules, four or five times across one of our plowed fields, very much against our judgment. We then believed plowed land should go into the winter loose to admit the air freely, but we later found this a very erroneous idea. This field was harrowed in the spring and drilled into wheat. Favorable spring weather with ample rain brought fine prospects for a good crop, but hot dry July weather not only blasted the prospects for this field, but another interesting condition developed. A green strip of rank, healthy wheat with long well filled heads appeared across the field where the small feet of the mules had penetrated deeply and made the plowed soil or seed bed firm to the bottom. Here was another clear demonstration of a new and important principle to be carefully considered.[10]

[9] Louise E. Peffer, *The Closing of the Public Domain* (Palo Alto: Stanford University Press, 1951), p. 134.

[10] Hardy W. Campbell, "Dry Farming in the Western Plains Region," MS in the Nebraska State Historical Society Library, pp. 1–14.

Campbell immediately used his New England ingenuity to invent the subsurface packer, which was designed to do what the neighbor's mules had done. The packer used a series of wheels, like those in a disc harrow, except that each wheel worked independently of the others, making it possible for the machine to pack uneven as well as level spots. The wheels had a sharp, wedge-shaped felly, which not only pulverized the clods and left a fine granulated seedbed but packed the ground. The *Nebraska Farmer* called the machine a "rainmaker" because it preserved the moisture.[11]

The system known as dry farming, worked out by Campbell and others, consisted of:

1. Plowing deep.
2. Compacting the soil.
3. Maintaining a soil mulch by cultivating after every rain.
4. Growing a crop on a field every second year, and on the off year cultivating the field, preserving a dust mulch, and keeping down vegetation, in this way conserving the rainfall of two years for one crop. This is known as summer fallowing.
5. Thin seeding. Available moisture is used to grow one-half the crop that would be expected on humid farming soil.
6. Raising the types of plants that thrive in semiarid climates.
7. Developing strains of ordinary humid farming crops which are drought-resistant.[12]

By 1905, the dry farming idea had been accepted, but the system entailed two requirements for homesteading in the rain belt: more land and more capital. East of the prairie region the farm unit was forty acres, tended by one man, one small plow, and a horse or mule; but on the prairie, where it was unnecessary to clear the land, the unit increased to eighty acres, and a little later to 160 acres. It was therefore on the tall grasslands that mechanized agriculture began. Beyond the 100th meridian, where summer fallowing was practiced, the system required two quarter-sections—320 acres—one to raise a crop each alternate year (but both quarters were cultivated every year).

It was evident that the amount of land in a homestead should be

11 *Ibid.; Nebraska Farmer* (Lincoln), March 24, 1898.

12 *Dry Farming Congress Bulletin*, III, No. 4 (Spokane, Wash.: February 15, 1910), 300; B. C. Buffum, *Arid Agriculture* (No place given: privately published, 1909), pp. 42–76; *Annual Report of the U.S. Department of Agriculture* (Washington, D.C.: Govt. Printing Office, 1908), p. 66.

doubled, and Congress by an act of February 19, 1909, increased the amount that could be homesteaded to ⋅320 acres. This applied only in twelve western states, however, and was intended to satisfy settlers of the semiarid lands.[13] The second need of the homesteaders of the Plains was for more capital than was needed by the earlier homemaker, who crossed the Missouri River with little more than grit and a willingness to work. A number of horses and more machinery were required to succeed in subduing nature in the semiarid region. In fact, the need for greater horsepower in the dry farming system caused it to be dubbed "horse-leg irrigation." Enthusiasm for the new system grew inordinately. One popular writer interpreted the practical statements of James Wilson, the Secretary of Agriculture during the administration of Theodore Roosevelt, to mean that the whole arid region could be made fruitful by dry farming; and that since America had agricultural explorers in every corner of the world finding crops which had become acclimated to dry conditions, in time America would have plants thriving upon all of our so-called desert lands. John L. Cowan, writing in *Century Magazine* in July, 1906, expressed his enthusiasm:

> Western Kansas and Nebraska and eastern Colorado are known all over America as forming the most desolate and God-forsaken regions on the continent . . . It now seems as if the history of the prairie lands a thousand miles further east are about to be paralleled. Forty years ago it was commonly believed that the prairies of Iowa, Missouri, and Illinois were irreclaimable wastes where nothing but poverty and starvation awaited the settler. Just as these lands yielded in time to the plow and harvester, so will the inexhaustible soil of the Great Plains richly reward the toil of those who adapt farming methods to natural conditions . . . Last autumn the little settlement of Limon, situated on the dry plains of Lincoln County, Colorado, leaped into wide-spread prominence on account of the surprising exhibit of agricultural products made at the second annual harvest festival of the Eastern Colorado Fair Association. The surrounding country is far from the possibility of irrigation and its agricultural future depends absolutely upon the success of dry farming methods. The exhibits of garden vegetables, cereals, and forage crops were equal to any made at any county fair in the country, and were amply sufficient to silence the critics who have long claimed that Eastern Colorado never can become a prosperous farming country. A twenty-pound squash, a thirty-five pound head of cabbage and an

[13] Walter Prescott Webb, *The Great Plains* (Boston: Ginn & Co., 1931), pp. 387–394, 423.

eight pound sugar beet were among the prizewinners; as also were specimens of potatoes that yielded 200 bushels to the acre, of winter wheat that yielded thirty-five bushels to the acre, of corn that yielded forty bushels to the acre.[14]

But the frontiersman needed little encouragement; for land hunger was never satisfied on the middle border, and hopes became so extravagant that the second highest number of acres in the history of homesteading was entered in the fiscal year 1909–1910. Enthusiasm ran so high that the Department of Agriculture felt obliged to caution people against the hallucination that dry farming was a sure road to fortune.

Just when the public was convinced that the arid lands were all productive, the reaction set in. By 1912, it was observed that even dry farming worked better during a cycle of wet years. With a new series of drier seasons dry farmers faced ruin and there was another demand for relief. Congress again came to the rescue and lowered the residence requirement for proving up on a homestead to three years instead of five. This act seemed to grow out of the belief that the character of the remaining land was such that the average family could not hold out for five years. Since it was thought the point of starvation would be reached before the culmination of the required residence, it was a realistic as well as a humanitarian measure to shorten the period to three years. A further endeavor to relieve human suffering allowed the homesteader to absent himself five months out of the year, presumably so he could earn enough money to keep body and soul together while basking in the joy of living on his free homestead.[15]

Booming agencies continued to advertise agricultural production under the new dry-farming system. At St. Paul, the gateway to the Northwest, the Great Northern Railroad displayed an almost unbelievable exhibit of the grains and fruits grown on the lands available along the company's lines. Their superb quality and yields per acre were almost beyond credibility, but of course nothing was said about the number of crop failures the producers had endured while waiting for the good year when the sample products were raised.

A year or two of above-average rainfall, accentuated by the more lenient homesteading law, started a new rush—the scramble for land in Montana, Wyoming, Colorado, and on other remnants of the public domain. The peak came in 1913, when, according to Benjamin Hibbard, nearly twice as many entries were filed as in any previous year in the

[14] John L. Cowan, "Dry Farming—the Hope of the West," *Century Magazine*, LXXII (July, 1906), 444, 446.

[15] Webb, *The Great Plains*, p. 423.

homestead era. Miles and miles of prairie were broken by farmers, most of whom were men of moderate means from farther east who had brought enough machinery and capital to tide them over a few lean years. Once again, little towns sprouted, and hamlets blossomed into cities. Where only a little time before, the cattleman had reigned supreme, surrounded by his cowboys, every half section had a tar-paper shack or a house. Miles of barbed wire enclosed homesteads, and thousands of cattle and sheep were pushed off the ranges they had grazed for years. Much bitterness was engendered in the cattlemen, who were certain the newcomers could not make a home for themselves but were nevertheless ruining their ranges.

Irrigation, another important feature of settlement beyond the 100th meridian, was first carried on in the United States by the Indians of New Mexico, who were watering the soil when the Spanish conquered their lands. The Spanish, however, learned from the Indians and made the desert around the missions blossom. The first Anglo-Saxon irrigation was by the Mormons who on the very day the "Pioneers" entered Salt Lake Valley began to run ditches and turn the waters of the Jordan River onto the thirsty land. This system made the Mormons prosperous. Usually, however, irrigation began as an adjunct of mining. Because miners needed water for their operations, they formed water companies to lead the precious fluid from streams into their cradles and sluice boxes. This led to use of the diverted streams to raise produce.

The unheard-of prices that miners had to pay for foodstuffs and the uncertainties of gold digging caused some of them to decide that they had missed their calling. Concluding that there were more riches in raising potatoes, onions, and other provisions, they began farming operations. On May 23, 1860, a Denver newspaper quoted potatoes at sixteen dollars a bushel, and during the first six years of Montana's history, flour sold between $20.00 and $25.00 for one hundred pounds. Bayard Taylor reported that in 1867 a strip of agricultural land a mile or more in width along Clear Creek in Colorado was producing the finest of crops. It was from such beginnings, therefore, that irrigation farming pushed out onto the Plains from the mountains, with no idea that the government would take part in irrigation as such, although government land was used.

The first irrigation ditches usually were dug by farmers—often by one man who simply dug ditches which led the water from the stream onto the land through the fall of the mountain stream. These early ditches were virtually laterals, in irrigation parlance. Later, several men would unite in a partnership or community effort to bring water in canals from a stream some distance from the source and distribute it by means of laterals.

The Larimer and Weld Canal in Colorado, built in 1864 by a single owner to water eight hundred acres, is a good example of this evolution. In the 1890's it was enlarged to water forty thousand acres, and several hundred men joined the association to build large lead ditches to supply big districts. The Fort Lyon Canal was constructed in 1884; a corporation project, it was 105 miles long and capable of irrigating 120,000 acres serving the famous Rocky Ford melon area. The Greeley, Colorado, settlement apparently was one of the first out-and-out pioneering irrigation projects by settlers who came for the explicit purpose of farming arid land; it was laid out by a colony on government land for the avowed purpose of irrigating the region.

By 1873 irrigation was so important that the first irrigation congress in the United States was held at Denver; moreover, the Congress struck a new note by voting to ask the United States to give the states one-half of the nonmineral land of the public domain within their borders to support a program of watering the semiarid lands. In response to this request, President Grant, in his message to Congress in December, 1873, recommended the encouragement of an irrigation canal to run from the Rocky Mountains to the Missouri River. The President observed that:

> An irrigating canal would make a belt as wide as the supply of water could be made to spread across this entire country, and would secure a cordon of settlements connecting the present population of the mountain and mining regions with that of the older states.[16]

Such a project, of course, was too large to be considered seriously at that time; however, another project had set a precedent for federal aid in irrigation projects. In the early 1860's the United States had granted $150,000 for an irrigation canal in Arizona.[17]

Irrigation was just the reverse of dry farming in its implications in regard to the size of farms. Maximum returns were realized upon land well tilled and watered; indeed, settlers could become self-supporting on ten or twenty irrigated acres. Forty acres was a great plenty and usually eighty acres was too much, and a big mistake in the early times was to secure too much land and too extravagant water rights. It was actually easier to be "land poor" with eighty acres of irrigated land than with a section of dry land.

[16] Jerome C. Smiley, *Semi-Centennial History of the State of Colorado*, I (2 vols.; Chicago and New York: Lewis Publishing Co., 1913), 574–575.

[17] Charles D. Poston, "Irrigation," *Annual Report of the U.S. Department of Agriculture* (1867), p. 193.

The Desert Land Act was another product of the awakening interest in irrigation. Congress, in response to pressure from irrigation enthusiasts, passed this act on March 3, 1877.[18] Among several other ill-conceived features, the Desert Land Act permitted claims for the largest acreage that had been allowed since direct land sales had ceased—for the purpose of irrigation. An entire section was allowed, although one-eighth of a section would have been more than ample for irrigation, and this feature made the law an inviting vehicle by which ranchers could secure needed public lands they were not allowed to obtain otherwise.

Nevertheless, in some instances an effort was made to carry out the spirit of the law and actually water the parched agricultural land. In fact, irrigation had its first real boom as a result of this act.

As we noted earlier, the Desert Land Act allowed a desert claim to be made on unsurveyed land, and although the entryman was required to describe his boundaries under oath, western oaths were unreliable, and the government never knew whether it was issuing a patent for five hundred acres or for eight hundred acres. The law, furthermore, did not specify the shape of an entry or stipulate the character and extent of reclamation, and this was to become a source of perplexity even to the irrigator who in good faith sought to carry out the law's provisions. In his report for 1877 the surveyor general of Arizona explained some of the oddities in the operation of the law.

Fearing that possible abuses of the privileges permitted by the law would lead to such strict application of its provisions as to compel the reclamation of the entire tract embraced in the application, and which, in a large majority of cases, would be an impossibility honest settlers and residents have almost ceased to regard the law as valuable to them. In order to comply with its provisions, some applicants have taken their land in zigzag shape, thereby confining it to the lands on or near a level with the streams. In one instance, I am assured that a claim is so taken as to embrace forty-four corners! The law requires claims on unsurveyed lands to be described as nearly as possible without a survey. No connection is required to be made with the public surveys, but evidently the public surveys must eventually be connected with the lines of such claims, . . . Think of a deputy surveyor closing on one claim with forty-four corners![19]

[18] This is discussed more fully in Chapter XIV, "Free Grass, the Cattleman's Paradise."
[19] Report of the Surveyor General of Arizona, in *Annual Report of the Commissioner of the General Land Office, 1877*, pp. 322–323.

Since this was the first land law that recognized the critical importance of water in arid regions, its application brought to the fore the principles of water usage and water rights. The only law with which Anglo-Saxon Americans were acquainted was the custom of riparian rights which was in vogue in England, under which a man with riparian rights owned one or both banks of a nonnavigable stream and therefore had access to it. He also had the right of full use of the water which flowed past his land, provided he did not diminish the flow appreciably, since all riparian owners were entitled to the same rights. This was a satisfactory custom in England, where the streams were used for mills to furnish water power, and all of the water then flowed back into the stream; but if this principle of equal rights had been recognized in the West, it would have made irrigation impossible even among riparian owners. When the riparian owners nearest the source of a stream took out enough water to irrigate their land, the stream was diminished to that extent, so that men farther down the stream may have had riparian rights to a dry creek bed. Legal recognition of riparian rights, therefore, would have forbidden the use of water for irrigation because it is impossible to replace water which has been taken from a stream and has been soaked up by the land. Nevertheless, some firstcomers felt that their prior claims gave them the right to a monopoly of the waters of a stream. In Lassen County, California, for example, Isaac Roop located a water right by posting this notice:

> I, the undersigned, claim the privilege to take all of the water out of Smith Creek at the junction of the two forks where this stake stands. I shall build the dam some six feet high, and carry the water along the south hill to emigrant road. August 1854.[20]

This was an example of what was later known as the doctrine of appropriation—the firstcomer established the right to take all of the water with no guarantee of returning it to the stream. Eventually, a middle ground had to be found to make irrigation feasible along the streams in arid regions.

The famous suit of the Miller and Lux cattlemen against Carr and Haggin, irrigators, occurred in 1881 in Kern County, California. The cattlemen contended that they were the owners of riparian lands along the lower reaches of the Kern River and that the natural channel was through their ranch; hence, they were entitled to have its waters flow over, through, or upon their lands in undiminished quantity—riparian rights. The defendants claimed the right to divert the water for irrigation pur-

[20] *Illustrated History of Plumas, Lassen, and Sierra Counties* (San Francisco: Ferris and Smith, 1882), p. 341.

poses by prior appropriation. The suit, then, was a contest between riparian rights and the right of appropriation. After the case went through the district court and the state supreme court, the riparianists won the decision, which meant that nobody could take water out of a stream and spread it over his land inasmuch as he could not restore it to its natural channel in an undiminished volume. As a result of the decision in the Haggin case, as it is called, irrigators throughout California set up a howl of indignation, and a series of conventions was held to draft bills for submission to the legislature for the voiding of the riparian rule. Finally, the laws were amended in such a way as to effect a compromise. Those who held riparian rights were to have one-third of the water during the high-water season each year—during March, April, May, June, July, and August—and those who held appropriation rights were to have the remainder. Also, the two parties were to join in building levees and reservoirs. Thus the Haggin case set a precedent in California, which became known as the Western Doctrine of Riparian Rights, or the California Doctrine.[21]

One the other hand, eight states in the Rockies and in the basin west of the Rockies abrogated the common law in favor of a modification, substituting for the English riparian-rights idea the arid-region doctrine of appropriation, or the Colorado system—so called because Colorado was the first state to substitute the new doctrine for the old.

If land was actually sought for irrigation under the Desert Land Act, water was more important than the land, and this fact determined the course for claiming land. Since claims could be made on unsurveyed land— and the act envisioned that an individual farmer would take water directly from a stream—the inevitable result was that claims were made in long strips adjacent to a stream in order to use the water at its lowest level. It was early seen that the man who could hold stream frontages held the key to the irrigation of the benchlands immediately behind. Since the benchlands could be irrigated only if their owners bought the vested interests of the landowners along the stream, there was a rush for these riparian lands.

In the late 1880's the expansion of irrigation was so rapid that the director of the Geological Survey expressed concern lest this process cripple irrigation in the future. In order to use water to its fullest extent, it would be necessary to buy out early comers' interests along the streams, at a cost of several hundred million dollars; otherwise, it would be impossible to utilize natural resources to the full. It then became apparent that cattlemen

---

[21] Wallace M. Morgan, *History of Kern County, California* (Los Angeles: Historic Record Co., 1914), pp. 102–110.

were not alone in securing large districts along the streams by means of the Desert Act; speculating companies, whose members often lived in the East and even in foreign countries, were soon off to a good start to tie up the land along small streams and with it the water to irrigate the benchlands. Men envisioned wealth in water rights, canals, and other appurtenances of irrigation. Commissioner Sparks, having received reports that the lands along the streams were falling into the hands of those who had not secured them according to law, took vigorous action. In his report of 1888 he stated that a vast area of 350,000 acres, upon which no attempt had ever been made to irrigate and much of which bordered upon streams, had been restored to the public domain through the cancellation of entries in the preceding fiscal year.

Even the farmers who conscientiously attacked the problems of bringing water to their land found the matter a big undertaking. Again, although a number of entrymen united and pooled their efforts, they did not have enough capital to dig big ditches. This eventually led to the formation of irrigation districts which sold bonds and did business as companies. Such projects, however, even though managed by efficient men, usually lost much of the original capital, to say nothing of operating losses. Investors were misled by the fact that it usually cost more to dig a canal and its accompanying works than the estimate indicated, but a more important factor was the mistake of thinking that all of the land that would ultimately be "under the ditch" in the project would be taken immediately and that all of the owners would furnish a market for water. Rainfall farmers—who previously had received free land from the government and water gratis from God—grumbled at the idea of paying $1.25 an acre for arid land, but they rebelled at paying ten dollars an acre for water to put on that land. It is true, of course, that they did worse by settling on the arid Plains and starving out, but in the meantime the canal companies went bankrupt because only a portion of the lands they served was occupied although their expenses covered the entire operation and benefit areas.[22]

An enterprise in one of the territories lost its promoters more than $2,000,000 and another project sold under judgment for about one-tenth of its cost.

The Desert Land Act, although entirely unsatisfactory, as we have noted, did promote irrigation and caused a land boom in the late 1880's by promoting the idea that the desert could be made productive. This, no doubt, was as much a reaction to the dry years which had blasted farm

[22] *Irrigation Review* (Denver, Colo.), September, 1897, pp. 21–22.

hopes and to the hard winters that had jolted the cattle industry as to the act itself. Before this time, in Wyoming, about one company a year—with capital of less than $100,000—was formed, but in 1882 eleven companies were incorporated, and nine in 1883, including one that was capitalized at $300,000 and another at $1,000,000. In Arizona in 1887, there were about four hundred miles of canals that cost more than $1,000,000.[23]

The country was becoming more and more aware that the irrigation of its vast, arid empire was too big an undertaking for individuals and even for companies. The surveyor general of Nevada, in his report to the Commissioner of the General Land Office in 1888, pointed out that simply encouraging the digging of ditches along streams for watering the soil was not enough. In the mountains that year, he stated, snow had been plentiful, and in late spring, while the snow was melting, the streams were swollen with the runoff. Plenty of water was available for a few weeks, but then the streams dried up, leaving irrigation ditches absolutely bone dry. He urged the government to build big dams and impound the melted snow water to be distributed throughout the whole summer when the growing crops needed it.

Major John W. Powell, the great pioneer in the advocacy of better use of the public lands, had long recommended that the government's lands should be classified and distributed in the best interests of all the people and that the water resources should be made to serve the people of the nation. His ideas had been set forth in his *Report on the Lands of the Arid Region of the United States* of April 1, 1878. A decade later, the seed sown by Powell was beginning to bear fruit. Senators Stewart of Nevada and Teller of Colorado found a following when they proposed a restudy of the land system. Their proposal resulted in the passage of an act of October 2, 1888, that authorized the investigation of the arid region, the segregation of the irrigable lands, and the selection of reservoir sites for the storage of irrigation water. All lands that might be selected for irrigation reservoirs, ditches, or canals and all lands susceptible of irrigation were reserved from sale as property of the United States. The act provided, however, that the President could at his discretion open any or all of the reserved lands for settlement under the homestead law.

This arrangement was very sensible and universally accepted; but it should have been forseen that the minute it became known an area was shortly to be set aside for an irrigation project, speculators—big and little—would crowd in and squat on the land, which was sure to become

---

[23] John T. Ganoe, "The Desert Land Act in Operation, 1877–1891," *Agricultural History*, XI (Baltimore: Waverly Press, April, 1937), 147.

valuable. An early indication of speculative reaction came in August, 1889, in a memorial from the Idaho constitutional convention, which was arranging the affairs of that territory preparatory to statehood. The memorial stated that the government's plans were threatened by speculators who had men follow the government surveyors to make filings at advantageous points along projected canals and reservoirs. It had also been learned, the memorial said, that a corporation was seeking to acquire Bear Lake together with large areas of land on its shoreline with the intention of making the lake a great storage basin. The same corporation, moreover, also was seeking to control the waters of Bear River and its tributary gulches for 150 miles in Idaho with a view to monopolizing the water and selling it to users in Utah—to the loss of Idaho. The memorial asked that Bear Lake be retained as a public reservation and that the land around it be withdrawn from entry.[24]

Accordingly, the acting Commissioner issued a retroactive order to all land offices that closed the public lands as of the date of the passage of the bill. The action was legally sound, and if there was any room for criticism, it was that he should have done it before the speculators and settlers had begun to follow the surveyors, but instantly the country was astir. "They can't do that; they have no right to invalidate claims and deny the hardy pioneer his just rights to free land," were the anguished cries which arose. Speculators and settlers throughout the West raised such an outcry that their congressmen, whose ears were ever attuned to the wails of their constituents, heard it in Washington, and congressmen who had voted for the act now found that they had outdone themselves in doing the right thing. Inasmuch as they were dependent upon votes for re-election, they could not ignore the powerful water and land companies in the states. It was plain that the surveys would take several years to complete and that it was not politically expedient to make the land-hungry speculators wait. Major Powell and his surveyors were made the goats of the land withdrawals, and a law of August 30, 1890, repealed the provision of 1888 that had called for the withdrawal of land in the arid region, except that located reservoir sites were reserved from the date of their location.

Once more, when it seemed that the wise and equitable thing was to be done in connection with the nation's resources, political pressure crushed the unselfish plans for the development of America's assets. It was a triumph of local interests over the welfare of the whole people—a victory for those who monopolize that which should be apportioned equitably— and it meant the continued ascendancy of those who, for reasons of per-

[24] *Annual Report of the Commissioner of the General Land Office, 1890*, pp. 72–73.

sonal advantage, feared government supervision and preferred the un-controlled settling of land that had prevailed from the beginning of the distribution of the public domain. Another decade of exploitation and monopoly was to pass before the public's suspicion of the national government would be allayed to the point that its land regulations would, hesitatingly, be accepted.

Idaho's Bear Lake controversy with Utah over diversion and use of water that should be shared by Idaho did not imply that there were no speculators in Idaho ready to take advantage of the opportunity of speculation, nor that Utah had no complaints against Idaho. Because of several conflicts of interest between the two new states, the Secretary of the Interior in 1890 wrote that he thought the solution of their problems was for the irrigated lands in each state to be subject to superior title and further control by the United States. A similar conflict arose between Wyoming and Nebraska because Wyoming had extended her citizens' doctrine of appropriation with regard to water rights to herself, as a state right, which if carried to its logical conclusion, would have meant a dry North Platte River entering Nebraska.[25] But the time was not ripe for the solution of such problems as interstate water rights: advanced thinkers scarcely dared ask for more than government aid in irrigation.

Under the leadership of William E. Smythe, a series of irrigation congresses was held across the country, beginning in 1891. At the very first state irrigation congress held in Nebraska, a resolution was passed asking that the national government grant a subsidy to each state, in the form of land, for irrigating their arid lands. This proposal was patterned after the Swamp Lands Act of 1850. Congress responded to public sentiment by passing the Carey Act on August 18, 1894, which ceded up to one million acres to each state in which arid areas were located. The states, in turn, were to reclaim the land by irrigation and cause it to be settled. Cultivation of twenty acres of each 160-acre tract was required and a ten-year limit was set for meeting the terms of the act. The law did not specify whether the states should construct the reservoirs, ditches, and irrigation system, or that they should contract with private agencies for this work, but in most cases the latter procedure was followed. The statute was ill designed, however, for ten years was entirely too short a period for a state to select the lands, build the dams and ditches, reclaim the land, and have it settled and in cultivation. Five states accepted the offer but only one—Wyoming—completed a canal by 1899. The feature that made the bill superior to the Swamp Lands Act was that it granted land conditionally

[25] *Omaha Weekly Bee* (Omaha, Nebr.), February 25, 1891.

and the United States government held title until the land was irrigated and in production. This provision prevented fraudulent land-grabbing of vast areas.

The fact that many irrigation companies were proving to be money-losers rather than lucrative investments tended to dampen the ardor of individuals who had money to invest, and the states did not wish to venture too much at this time; however, the states began to make regulations which would bring order out of chaos. Idaho passed a law forbidding irrigation companies to require the purchase of a water right as a condition of their furnishing water to owners of land along their canals, thus breaking the hold of the water monopolists who had gained control of the land along streams via the Desert Land Act. Texas, although not a public-lands state, set an example in 1897 that was bound to have an effect on national land policy. It passed a law that reserved all unappropriated water to the state and provided for the use of eminent domain in connection with securing rights-of-way for running canals and ditches. The United States followed this precedent in 1901 by granting rights-of-way over public lands and Indian reservations for this purpose. Nevertheless, state-sponsored monopolists, interested only in their money-making projects and making no attempt to cooperate with neighboring interests, began to create a chaotic situation and threatened to distort the entire irrigation program. Colorado was taking water from the Arkansas River that Kansas needed and had been using. A group of New Mexico monopolists used the government of that territory for their own interests by projecting canals across irrigation ditches that had been used by villagers for many years—and they even defied the federal government.

In 1888 an international dam was projected across the Rio Grande just above El Paso, but while the bill for the project was pending in Congress, entrepreneurs secured a charter from the legislature of New Mexico to build a dam at Elephant Butte, 125 miles up the river, thereby circumventing the El Paso project. Although Mexico had claimed the waters of the Rio Grande by prior use, the United States had reached a compromise with her Spanish neighbor, but New Mexico—in an ill-mannered show of states rights—refused to recognize the compromise, contending that she owned the river and would dam it where she pleased. Meanwhile the New Mexico water interests had taken so much water from the Rio Grande ditches in Mexico that had been used for generations that they ran dry and the United States fought New Mexico three times through the Supreme Court in order to secure a decision enabling her to honor her agreement. Finally, the pledge of the United States to Mexico to share the water of the Rio Grande was redeemed and several years later a dam was built—not where originally planned but at Elephant Butte—by the United States government.[26] It had become abundantly evident to thinking men that the authority of the central government was necessary to supervise the complex problem of watering the arid regions.

The series of irrigation congresses also had influenced public opinion. Elwood Mead, chief irrigation and drainage investigator, United States Department of Agriculture, in his report in 1899, stated that

the National Government alone can make the best and broadest study of the various economic questions related to the development of agriculture on arid lands. The nation alone can deal with conflicting rights in interstate and international streams and with the construction of great reservoirs at their headwaters, with a view to benefitting the several states lying along their course. The National Government is already active along all these lines, and the field for the expansion of its efforts is wide and inviting.[27]

As a matter of fact, the projects undertaken earlier by private capital were simple diversion ditches compared to what was demanded at the turn of the century: expensive storage works, high diversion dams and, in places, tunnels and long, expensive canals or aqueducts along the sides of hills. The time had come when private interests, having tried the easy undertakings and failed, were ready to allow the government to take over the difficult projects. To Francis G. Newlands, at that time the representative from Nevada, goes the credit for getting the United States to undertake reclamation. Before 1901 it had been customary for members of Congress to introduce bills providing for reclamation projects only in their own states or districts, but usually they were unsuccessful because the East was against them and the West was not able to unite for mutual support of the local projects. Newlands, who was later a senator, introduced several bills on reclamation, which, when discussed as a whole, were known as the "Newlands bill." Later proposals by him indicate an evolution in his thinking that had advanced to the position that the United States government should use the money it received from the sale of public lands in government projects to reclaim the arid land.[28] This

[26] Stegner, *Beyond the Hundredth Meridian*, pp. 310–312; Anson Mills, *My Story* (Washington, D.C.: Privately printed, 1918), pp. 266, 273, 278.

[27] Elwood Mead, "The Rise of Irrigation," *Agricultural Yearbook, 1898* (Washington, D.C.: U.S. Department of Agriculture, 1899), p. 609.

[28] William E. Smythe, *The Conquest of Arid America* (New York: Harper & Bros., 1905), p. 275.

method for financing the program removed the East's objection to the appropriation of money from the Treasury for such an unorthodox purpose; then Newlands, in the spring of 1901, called a conference of seventeen senators and representatives from the arid states and thus formed a bloc for his plan. Even so, the bill was not passed until 1902, but Theodore Roosevelt had intervened beneficially in the meantime.

Immediately after President McKinley's assassination and upon Roosevelt's installation as President, F. H. Newell of the Geological Survey, and Gifford Pinchot, the Chief Forester of the United States, called upon Roosevelt and laid before him the need for the government to take over the irrigation of the West. To Roosevelt, to see a need was to act, and he asked the men to provide him with more information on the subject. As a result, in his first message to Congress, Roosevelt recommended that the nation take over the work of building dams to hold back the flood waters and to use them for irrigation. Thus, Newlands started the idea, but the irrepressible Roosevelt seized upon it and pushed it through Congress to become the reclamation law of the nation. He was so fully committed to the idea that when an amendment was added to Newland's bill which would have played into the hands of the land-grabbers, Roosevelt said he would not sign it in that form, and the original items were restored.

The Newlands bill—or Reclamation Act—was a monumental accomplishment in the land policy of the United States. It set aside the money received from the sale of public lands in sixteen states in a reclamation fund, administered by the Secretary of the Interior, for the purpose of examining arid areas, surveying projects, and building dams and other works for irrigation. It directed the Secretary to withdraw from entry all land that it was contemplated to irrigate and the land that was needed for irrigation works. (If in the progress of the work it was seen that all of the land withdrawn was not needed, it was to be restored for entry.) Land irrigated under the act was to be open to entry under the homestead law in tracts of not less than forty acres nor larger than a quarter section. The exact size of the tract was to be determined by the Secretary, who was instructed to limit the size to that reasonably required for the support of one family, and the cost of bringing water to the land was to be paid in not more than ten annual installments.[29] The Reclamation Act looked forward to local management and control of the distribution of the water, although the real title to the projects was to remain in the United States

[29] Charles R. Price, *Irrigated Lands of the United States* (Los Angeles: Pan Pacific Press, 1909), pp. 14–16.

government. A tremendously important feature of the act was that it gave the Secretary of the Interior a large and ever increasing sum that could be used over and over. Congress had set up a revolving system which was to operate for years to come, free from the hazards and necessity of securing a periodic lease on life by securing an appropriation from Congress.

A departure from regular homestead usage was the requirement of both residence and the cultivation of at least one-half of the irrigable area. Also, residence had to be maintained even though water was not secured as soon as had been anticipated, and homesteads could not be commuted. Despite every precaution the law attempted to provide, there was a big rush for arid land, and although the Secretary was authorized to withdraw from entry all land he assumed would be within the project, he could not withdraw it until the surveys for the work had been completed. Speculators noted areas which they thought would probably be the scene of a project and rushed to grab land, within the benefit area, by means of the Timber and Stone Act and the Desert Land Act.[30]

The government's plan was to give a man a homestead of not more than 160 acres and to charge him for the irrigation works in annual installments. The government would maintain the ditches, reservoirs, and other works, and would sell the water to the users. Then, in 1916, the federal government provided for irrigation districts that would act as agencies of the water users in entering a contract with the government. The irrigation districts were formed under the states' laws as a political subdivision of the state, with defined geographical boundaries, and were empowered to issue bonds and to secure revenue from taxes levied upon the land. A certain percentage of the landowners of the area in a proposed district had to approve of their formation, and the districts were to be governed by a board of directors or commissioners.

Between 1900 and 1910 it was common to look upon irrigation as a panacea for all of the farmer's troubles, and promoters made the new program look rosy indeed. William Smythe, the outstanding irrigation Boomer of the day, resigned his position as farm editor of the *Omaha Weekly Bee* and started his own paper to publicize irrigation; in 1907 he wrote a book that promoted irrigation, *The Conquest of Arid America*. Smythe's enthusiasm is indicated by typical chapter titles: "The Blessing of Aridity," "The Miracle of Irrigation," and "The Better Half of the United States." Smythe and other enthusiasts related stories of "typical" products: huge potatoes, enormous heads of cabbage, gigantic cornstalks, and mammoth pumpkins. They also spoke of the virtues of the desert soil,

[30] Peffer, *The Closing of the Public Domain*, p. 45.

the continuous sunshine, the absence of weeds, the pleasure of watering one's own land, the freedom from anxiety about rainfall, and the complete assurance of a crop each year.[31]

Although the unhappy farmer on a sun-baked homestead in dried-out Kansas or South Dakota may have gathered the impression from this propaganda that the irrigation farmer's life was a continual round of pleasure, the problems of an irrigation farmer were legion. He had first of all to clear his homestead of sagebrush, often done by dragging a railroad iron across the area and snapping off the sage even with the surface. Next, he had to level his field and dig the ditches which were to lead the life-giving water from the main ditches out upon his parched soil. He also had to do the work which accompanied homesteading in the rain belt: make fences, build a house and a stable, and the like. On the average, less than half of his claim was irrigated and cultivated during the first year of settlement, but he had to pay his obligation on the whole tract. Because it took five years to get all of the farm under irrigation, it was argued that the irrigation farmer needed help to get started; moreover, settlers were allowed to move onto land before it was irrigated, even several years before water was available. In their endeavor to hold their homesteads, many irrigation farmers spent all of their capital and starved, until they had nothing with which to make their improvements, purchase equipment, or prepare their land for crops.

To remedy this situation, the government in 1914 passed the Reclamation Extension Act, which extended the period of payments from ten to twenty years. Even with this relief, however, many were unable to make a success of the venture. The difficulty in subduing the soil was greater than the rosy pictures had indicated and the costs exceeded the irrigation farmer's expectation; he still had a hard time making a living while also paying for the water system for his farm. It was now seen that only the most capable could succeed and that there should be a screening of candidates so that only those who were likely to succeed were allowed to enter reclamation land. Unfortunately, however, there was no legal basis for screening or selecting settlers, and the officials were obliged to accept filings from "on paper" eligible applicants whether they were likely to be successful or not.

By 1912, irrigation projects had readied the land faster than it was being occupied by competent settlers, which led to government attempts to promote settlement. The need to settle irrigated land more quickly than

[31] A. E. Parkins and J. R. Whitaker (eds.), *Our National Resources* (New York: John Wiley & Sons, 1939), p. 123.

dry land was acute because a completed project represented a large invest-ment of capital by the government on which there were heavy interest charges.[32] In an attempt to settle reclaimed areas with qualified occu-pants, an act was passed in 1924 which required the land officers to exam-ine prospective settlers and determine that they would be likely to succeed before they were allowed to enter land. A board of three members was set up to investigate a candidate's industry, farming experience (at least two years), and character, and he was required to have a minimum capital of $2,000.

The difficult state of affairs, however, was aggravated by the general agricultural depression in the 1920's, and there was another call for aid. In response, a bill was introduced in Congress in January, 1928, that even-tually authorized the Secretary of the Interior to advance up to $3,000 to any one farm for improvements, such as preparation of the land for irriga-tion, the development of a supply of water for domestic or stock use, or the erection of permanent buildings. In case of default, all rights to the property were to revert to the government and all payments and improve-ments were to be considered rent for the use of the land.[33] Thus, govern-ment policy had made a complete circle in the course of a century and a half. From the policy of expelling squatters on the public lands, the government now lent settlers money to induce them to settle upon its land.

There was an evolution in the reclamation idea as well. At first, even under the Newlands or Reclamation Act many projects considered feasible were rejected by the Reclamation Service because they were deemed within the reach of profitable private investment[34] and therefore outside the province of United States business, but some of these projects were now taken over by the government after years of unsuccessful efforts to enlist private capital in their construction. Indeed, almost all of the earlier projects were those that had been abandoned because the attempts to finance them as private projects were unsuccessful, or the projects were so difficult that they could not attract private capital. The first dam com-pleted under the Reclamation Act was Roosevelt Dam, which was part of the Salt River project that supplied Maricopa and Gila counties in Arizona. A private development in this area had been undertaken, under

[32] *Agricultural Yearbook, 1912* (Washington, 1913), pp. 483–484.

[33] Dorothy Lampen, *Economic and Social Aspects of Federal Reclamation* (Baltimore: The Johns Hopkins Press, 1930), p. 115.

[34] *Fourteenth Annual Report of the Reclamation Service* (Washington, D.C.: Govt. Printing Office, 1915), pp. 1–2.

the terms of the Desert Land Act. The government soon found it impossible to bring water to public lands without also serving the larger areas that had passed into private hands under the Desert Land Act or the Carey Act. From 1902 to 1922, only 1,675,000 acres were irrigated under the Reclamation Act, and a little less than a third of this was government land.[35]

Wyoming had undertaken numerous projects under the Carey Act, many of which had been found to be unworkable because of the limited resources which the act provided. Naturally that state was interested in salvaging the Carey projects. In response to the desire of his constituents, Senator Francis E. Warren of that state was able, in 1911, to secure passage of the Warren Act, which authorized the Secretary of the Interior to contract for the storage and flow of excess water for irrigation systems that operated under the Carey Act. The Secretary thus was enabled to make contracts with individuals, corporations, associations, and irrigation districts that distributed water for irrigation. First rights to water were to go to new entrymen on the public lands under this reclamation plan, but users under older irrigation schemes could hook onto the new government projects for service inasmuch as the original irrigation works were inadequate. Companies with which the government contracted for water were to deliver the water to users at a reasonable rate, and the maximum amount of water the company could furnish to an individual was that sufficient to irrigate 160 acres. Money received from the sale of water was to be held in the reclamation fund for future projects. Thus, thanks to the Warren Act, land that had been transferred to private hands under the unworkable schemes—such as the Desert Land Act and the Carey Act— in effect became, by the Warren Act, part of the national irrigation program.[36]

In recent years the money for undertaking large projects has not come from the reclamation fund; instead, Congress has simply appropriated money for them. A modification of the Carey Act in 1921 authorized the Secretary of the Interior to restore to the public domain the segregated lands that had been given to the states for irrigation, unless reclamation construction had been started three years after segregation. Thus, much of the land which had passed into the hands of private individuals who had intended to use it for speculative purposes was restored to the public domain, and some of it was later included in projects under the federal

[35] Peffer, *The Closing of the Public Domain*, p. 198; George Wharton James, *Reclaiming the Arid West* (New York: Dodd, Mead and Company, 1917), p. 65.

[36] Roy E. Huffman, *Irrigation Development* (New York: Ronald Press, 1953), p. 28.

reclamation program. Little by little over the years the reclamation pattern took form under national supervision, and although the whole might suggest a crazy quilt, it resulted in a unified program for the irrigable lands Uncle Sam had for half a century tried to sell, give away, or entice men to take by lending them money.

XIX

Saving the Remnants of Our
National Resources—Conservation

UNTIL THE LAST DECADE of the nineteenth century it was commonly thought that the chief duty of the Commissioner of the General Land Office was to parcel out the public domain as fast as possible. Now and then, of course, a lone voice proclaimed the need of conserving the nation's resources, but this advice was largely unheeded because Americans lived under the misguided idea that the assets of nature were unlimited in the richest nation on earth.

The first attempt to save some of nature's bounty for all the people was made in 1832, when Congress established a reservation of four sections in the Ouachita Mountains of Arkansas. These sections contained a group of hot springs, and it was thought proper that the ownership of these curative waters should be retained by the public for the good of the people rather than pass into private hands for commercial exploitation. Another reserve was made—for the preservation of wildlife and natural curiosities—in the Yosemite Valley in California in 1864. Congress ceded this area, including the giant sequoias, to California on condition that it be maintained as a reserve by the state—the Yosemite Grant. The words of the act as signed by Abraham Lincoln well state the purpose of the national park of later day: "The premises shall be held for public use, resort, and recreation . . . inalienable for all time." In 1890, after the development of the national park concept, Congress responded to the pleas of John Muir and other public-spirited naturalists by setting aside the Yosemite National Park, a large area of mountains and forest land completely surrounding the Yosemite Grant. The anomaly of a national park enclosing a state park, together with a degree of friction in administration, caused Congress in 1906

to accept the recession of Yosemite Grant and unite it with the area surrounding it, thus forming the present Yosemite National Park.[1]

In the meantime the national park idea had been born—as an out-
growth of the Washburn-Langford-Doane expedition of 1870. Having
spent several weeks exploring the region of present-day Yellowstone Park
to verify the tales of old-time trappers about the wonders of that country,
and impressed by what they had found, the explorers camped one night
near the Firehole and Gibbon rivers. While sitting before the campfire, a
member of the expedition suggested that the men enter quarter sections at
the most outstanding points of interest, and others suggested scenic spots
which would become great profit-makers to their owners in the future, but
Cornelius Hedges said he did not favor any of these arrangements. Hedges
opposed private ownership of these great natural assets and asserted that
the entire region should be set apart as a national park that the people of
the nation could freely enjoy for all time to come. The suggestion met a
hearty response, and as the days passed, the men became more and more
enthusiastic about the park idea and resolved to work toward this end.
Their plan was successful, for in 1872 Congress established Yellowstone
Park—the first national park in the world—to preserve its natural curiosities for the people to enjoy.[2] Over fifty nations have followed the precedent.
By the time of Woodrow Wilson's administration, fifteen additional
national parks had been established in the United States.

Since there was no organization to care for the new parks, the army
administered them through a cooperative arrangement, although the
Department of the Interior was in general charge. Later, since the army
had no foresters and much of the area of the parks was wooded, it was
thought best to turn the parks over to the Department of Agriculture. In
1916, however, after all the smoke from the congressional discussion had
cleared away, the National Park Service was set up as a Bureau of the
Department of the Interior.

Forests were the first natural economic resources to receive consideration in the field of conservation. Scientists and other men of learning, who
observed with alarm the rapid disappearance of the forests of the nation,
urged that steps be taken to stop the prodigal exploitation of the forests.
These men argued for a wise use and protection of this great asset of the
country to the end that future generations of Americans would have

[1] Henry Clepper and Arthur B. Meyer (eds.), *American Forestry: Six Decades of Growth*
(Washington, D.C.: Society of American Foresters, 1960), p. 151.

[2] Richard G. Lillard, *The Great Forest* (New York: Knopf, 1947), pp. 261–262.

lumber needed for legitimate uses. They also pointed out that stands of trees with their consequent fall of foliage formed an absorbent blanket upon the hillsides which prevented the rapid runoff of rainfall, thus preventing flooding in the river valleys below. The absorption of moisture on the slopes, they argued, would diminish erosion and thus prevent the denuding of the hillsides of soil. It was also pointed out that the shade of the coniferous forests would cause the deep mountain snows to melt slowly instead of pouring out quick runoff floodwaters upon the lower valleys. In 1877, Carl Schurz, as Secretary of the Interior, had urged the withdrawal of land for national forests but Congress had failed to act.

In 1891, Congress got around to a general revision of the land laws. Conflicting bills had been passed by the two houses and were sent to a conference committee where the differences between the two bills were to be ironed out by members from the two houses. It happened that the conference committee was dominated by midwestern conservationists. The Secretary of the Interior, who was present, suggested that they add a new section, which they did—although this was against the rules, which did not allow any new clause to be added by a conference committee. This bill was rushed through during the closing hours of the session without being printed and with little chance for debate. By this chance circumstance, a sleeper in the legislation opened the door for a revolutionary change in the whole forest policy of the United States. The section that had been slipped in at the conference authorized the President of the United States to set aside:

> any part of the public lands wholly or in part covered with timber or undergrowth, whether of commercial value or not, as public reservations and the President shall by public proclamation, declare the establishment of such reservations and the limits thereof.[3]

This amendment proved so important that the land law of 1891 became known as the Forest Reserve Act of 1891. In 1817, Congress had authorized the President to withdraw certain lands for public purposes, but the withdrawals had been small; now, however, the gate was wide open to the Chief Executive. Benjamin Harrison promptly created the first reserve, the Yellowstone Timberland Reserve in Wyoming, and before his term was over, thirteen million acres had been set aside.

Unfortunately, there was no administrative agency to protect the forests, and Congress could not be induced to provide one; it seemed that the forest reserves would exist only on paper. It was proposed that the army be

---

[3] *Ibid.*, p. 264; Gifford Pinchot, "Progress of Forestry in the United States," *Agricultural Yearbook, 1899* (Washington, D.C.: Department of Agriculture, 1899), p. 294.

employed to protect and administer the forests, but the Secretary of War rejected this plan. Then, when Grover Cleveland became President, he asked the National Academy of Sciences to devise a plan for the forest reserves. The academy appointed a forestry commission, financed by government funds, which traveled through the West to study the problem. Even before the commission made its report, the chairman wrote a letter that recommended the withdrawal of another 21 million acres. Gifford Pinchot, the commission's forester, advised that before this was done, the purpose for which the forests were being withdrawn should be stated and provisions for administering them should be formulated. On Washington's Birthday, 1897, Cleveland, in deference to the day, just ten days before going out of office, issued a proclamation that set aside thirteen new reserves in seven states, more than doubling the number of forest reserves.

The reaction of the West was immediate and belligerent, and newspapers in Colorado and westward generally burned the President to a crisp in their editorials. The congressmen from the timber states were especially vitriolic in their criticism. John L. Wilson of Washington, referring to the National Academy of Sciences, asked scathingly:

"Why should we be everlastingly and eternally harassed and annoyed and bedeviled by these scientific gentlemen from Harvard College?"

Wilson, like most of the West, did not want "scholars" to interfere with the exploitation of natural resources that masqueraded as "development of the West." Representative Curtis H. Castle of California blasted the President: "There was never exhibited by any government a more brutal object lesson of might making right than in this treatment of peaceable citizens of California." And Charles S. Hartman of Montana called the proclamation "a parting shot of the worst enemy the American people have ever had."[4]

Graziers' interests as well as those of the timber barons and mining companies were represented in Congress by these vocal outbursts. The people on the frontier, who had always helped themselves to the nation's resources, saw this action of an eastern gold-standard man as an unbearable encroachment upon the rights of the West. Their rights of entry upon the withdrawn land were cancelled, and apparently their timber rights also would be abrogated, and they would be harassed by "senseless regulations from Washington bureaucrats." All of this left the West in a fighting mood. In short, the West saw the setting aside of forest reserves not as the forester saw it—as a means of saving the forests and protecting them for the

[4] John Ise, *The United States Forest Policy* (New Haven: Yale University Press, 1920), pp. 135–137.

permanent use of the whole people for generations to come—but as a portent that tremendous areas were to be locked up and permanently frozen.

Timber barons were not the only ones concerned; ranchers who grazed their cattle on the large open areas on the new reserves feared the new move. Representative Mondell of Wyoming, a typical champion of the stock raiser's cause in Congress, attacked the idea that forests were conservers of water, asserting on the floor of the House that it was his opinion that one acre of well-cultivated land was worth ten acres of woodland in conserving water.

The anticonservationists now tried to nullify the forest reserve program by means of a "rider." Six days after Cleveland's order on Washington's Birthday, an amendment was attached to an appropriation bill that provided for the restoration of the withdrawn lands to the public domain. Telling arguments used in the Senate were that the President had not consulted the senators and that the proclamation adversely affected the entire West. This amendment set off a lengthy discussion, which ended in a compromise. Congress placated the West by suspending Cleveland's February 22, 1897, proclamation in all of the states except California until March 1, 1898. This allowed nine additional months for speculators to go onto the land and establish claims and for the mining companies to cut large supplies of wood—a final fling at looting the nation's forests. When western congressmen attempted to extend the suspension beyond March 1, however, public sentiment rallied behind the forest program and the efforts for another suspension failed. Gifford Pinchot, in speaking of Cleveland's contribution to the preservation of the forests, said: "Cleveland deserves immense credit, for his courageous action led directly to the beginning of Government Forestry in the woods."

The truth of the matter and the cause of the difficulty was that Cleveland had failed to "communicate," as it would be stated in more recent usage: the West should have been educated concerning the reason for forest reserves and the advantages of preserving them. Westerners saw the move as one in which this land was to be taken away from them and locked up permanently; this misconception played into the hands of the big interests who opposed the principle for selfish reasons.[5] There was much talk that settlers had been robbed of the opportunity of taking a home on the good "agricultural" lands of the forests, and that settlers who had taken such homes were left stranded. The latter would have no neighbors, or schools

---

[5] Louise E. Peffer, *The Closing of the Public Domain* (Palo Alto: Stanford University Press, 1951), p. 26.

and churches; worst of all, it was contended, the value of their land would not rise, as it could be counted upon to do with settlement.

This concern about settlers, which always made good propaganda for the land-grabbers, became the basis for the Forest Lieu Land Act of June 4, 1897 (not to be confused with railroad lieu lands statutes of an earlier time). This law provided that any landholder with an unperfected title from the government or a patent within the limits of a forest reserve could exchange his land for public land of his choice outside the reserves. Although the law seemed fair and in keeping with the public interest, George Chamberlain—for eight years the governor of Oregon—declared that the Lieu Land Law originated "not by the fireside of the poor settler, but in the office of a great railroad company of the Middle West." In the hands of the big interests, the law was a heads-I-win—tails-you-lose proposition, since the claimant would not relinquish land unless he could gain by the transaction. Worthless land within the forest reserves was traded for valuable timber or mineral land without. Some of the relinquished land was originally poor, but in other cases it had been denuded of timber, and this cutover land was exchanged for virgin timber of the best quality. The railroads, particularly, profited by the law by obtaining some of the very best timberland on the public domain. In January, 1904, the Commissioner of the General Land Office estimated that there were 3,500,000 acres of railroad lands in the existing reserves and an equal amount in the projected reserves.

Interestingly enough, after the passage of the Lieu Land Law, the forest reserve policy increased tremendously in popularity in certain parts of the West. In 1901 the Commissioner of the General Land Office had on hand a list of petitions and recommendations from different places in the West asking that some fifty million acres be set aside as new reserves. A sizable part of the area requested consisted of lands in the possession of railroads and other private owners who desired to trade their inferior tracts for good lands by the lieu provision. At one time three congressmen were indicted and charged with attempting to secure the establishment of forest reserves upon their landholdings, as a part of a scheme to defraud the government.

In California, after 1900, a small group led by F. A. Hyde learned, apparently from employees of the Land Office, of the tracts that were to be withdrawn for reserves. For a pittance they obtained title, from pliable state officials, to worthless state school lands within the proposed reservations in California and Oregon. The men were in the midst of exchanging these worthless school lands for valuable timberlands when a new surveyor general took office in California and noticed that the lieu lands were almost entirely controlled by Hyde. By the time the fraud was discovered, nearly forty thousand acres had been patented. E. A. Hitchcock, the Secretary of the Interior, immediately stopped issuing patents and had Hyde and the other men arrested. After more than a year of litigation, Hyde and another man were convicted. Fortunately, in 1905, after some three million acres of valuable land had been separated from the government, the Lieu Land Law was repealed.

Earlier, in 1902, Hitchcock found evidence of widespread fraud and dishonesty in other areas, and when an honest Secretary of the Interior was backed by an honest and fearless President—Theodore Roosevelt—things began to happen. Hitchcock had learned somehow that the General Land Office was a party to a mammoth land steal, and he asked Binger Herman, the Commissioner, for a report he had received from J. S. Holsinger, a special agent working out of Phoenix, Arizona. When Herman brought the report, Hitchcock noted that it had been in the Commissioner's hands for nearly six weeks and that prominent and wealthy men seemed to be a party to frauds against the government, which involved hundreds of thousands of dollars. The Secretary called in the Commissioner a few days later and asked him pointedly: "Can you give me any explanation as to why you have never called my attention to this important matter?" According to Henry Brown, Herman "hemmed, and hawed, and stammered, but he did not give a satisfactory explanation," and Hitchcock reacted immediately: "Well, Mr. Herman, by the direction of the President, I must ask you for your resignation." The Commissioner, who refused to believe his ears, blustered and demanded the reason for this decision, but Hitchcock merely tapped a finger on Holsinger's report.

This action brought forth immediate pressure upon the Secretary because Herman was a powerful figure in the Republican party, in the West, had held several offices in the state of Oregon, had been a member of Congress for six terms, and had been the Commissioner of Public Lands for six years. His dismissal brought strong repercussions, but Roosevelt heartily backed his Secretary and the decision stood. Unfortunately, however, Herman was allowed thirty days to evacuate his office, and in that time, it was charged, he destroyed thirty-four letterpress books that contained thousands of documents relating to the frauds for which he was dismissed. Herman went to Oregon, where a representative had recently died, and sought vindication against the "autocratic powers in Washington" by running for Congress. His opponent asked for a statement from Hitchcock, who refused to make one; this was, of course, taken for weakness in the case, and Herman was elected. A statement by Hitchcock could have resulted in many guilty persons' escaping justice; agents were in Oregon at that very time gathering data for the indictment of Herman on criminal proceedings.[6]

In the end, three of the four men who represented Oregon in the Senate and the House of Representatives were indicted for fraud. Senator Mitchell, who rose in the Senate on January 17, 1905, and denied the charges against him, gained the sympathy of his colleagues but was convicted and sentenced to jail, as was Representative J. N. Williamson. Because of legal technicalities or statutes of limitations, the others escaped justice. After several years in court, the case against Binger Herman was dismissed.

The extent to which corruption had infected the body politic is indicated by proof that many members of Congress had accepted bribes. Also, the testimony indicated that it was part of the plan for the Attorney General to allay suspicion and, if necessary, to bring suit in such a way that failure of the cases would be certain.[7] Nevertheless, fearless in the face of personal and political pressure, Hitchcock—backed by the thoroughly honest Roosevelt—secured results. The *Nation*, in recounting events of 1906, stated that 490 persons had been indicted for land frauds; of these, eighty-nine were convicted and 401 were still under indictment.[8]

Theodore Roosevelt gave Hitchcock all the credit for pushing the prosecution of those who had defrauded the government in securing land and suggested that efforts against fraud be combined with the study of the public lands to create a clearer understanding of the need for reform of the land laws. The study to which the President referred had been made by a commission appointed in 1903, which had recommended classification of the remaining public lands, repeal of the Timber and Stone Act, reduction of the size of a desert claim to 160 acres, abolition of the policy of commutation of homesteads, and a flexible plan for administering grazing on the public lands. These principles ushered in the era of conservation.

Another rare individual in public service now appeared upon the scene, one who combined genius, a unique training for his task, and a drive to serve the best interests of all the people of the United States—Gifford Pinchot. Born of a wealthy family and a graduate of Yale, Pinchot studied forestry in Germany and France and was the first man to practice scientific forestry in the United States, in the Biltmore Forest of the Vanderbilts in North Carolina. Becoming chief of the Division of Forestry in the

[6] Henry S. Brown, "Punishing the Land Looters," *Outlook*, LXXX (February 23, 1907), 427–437.

[7] Ise, *United States Forest Policy*, pp. 187–189.

[8] *The Nation*, LXXX (December 20, 1906), 526.

Department of Agriculture in 1898, he also became the first United States Forester, and soon gained the confidence of President Roosevelt, who gathered a group of forward-looking young men akin to himself in progressive ideas. Roosevelt wrote:

> Gifford Pinchot is the man to whom the Nation owes most for what has been accomplished as regards the preservation of the natural resources of our country. He led, and indeed during its most vital period embodied, the fight for the preservation through use of our forests.[9]

Pinchot, who soon was looking beyond the immediate problems of forestry, believed that

> The earth . . . belongs of right to all its people and not to a minority, insignificant in numbers but tremendous in wealth and power. The public must come first.
> The rightful use and purpose of our natural resources is to make all the people strong and well, able and wise, well taught, well clothed, well housed, full of knowledge and initiative, with equal opportunity for all and special privileges for none.[10]

Pinchot's concept applied not only to the forest resources but to water, grass, soil, minerals, and the problems to which they gave rise, such as erosion, irrigation, water power, navigation of inland waterways, coal, and iron. He saw that all of these were becoming critically important but that each was being dealt with as though it stood alone. Said he:

> I was riding my old horse Jim in Rock Creek Park one day—I think it was in February 1907—when suddenly the idea that put the stone on the end of the club occurred to me. The idea was that all these natural resources which we had been dealing with as though they were in water tight compartments actually constituted one united problem. That problem was the use of the earth for the permanent good of man. We had been dealing with our continent piecemeal, and of course, we were losing an immense amount of steam and effectiveness by acting as single scouts scattering our efforts like using birdshot to kill a bear—not attacking the problem in a united battalion.
> The idea was so new that it did not even have a name. Or course it had to have a name. Our little inside group discussed it a great deal.

[9] Theodore Roosevelt, *Autobiography* (New York: Macmillan, 1913), p. 409.
[10] Gifford Pinchot, *Breaking New Ground* (New York: Harcourt, Brace and World, 1947), pp. 509–510.

Finally Overton Price suggested that we call it "Conservation" and the president said "O.K." so we called it the conservation movement.[11]

When Pinchot became United States Forester, the national forests were under the direction of the Secretary of the Interior and the foresters were in the Department of Agriculture. In 1905, Congress moved the forest reserves from the General Land Office in the Department of the Interior to the Department of Agriculture and at last the foresters were with the forests. With the change, the name Forest Reserve, was dropped to indicate that the forests were not to be locked up for nonuse but were to be of service; the new name was Forest Service of the Department of Agriculture. On July 1, 1905, the Forest Service placed in the hands of its field men a small pocket manual, *The Use of the National Forest Reserves*, which was promptly dubbed, the *Use Book*. The preface of this 100-page book, which contained regulations concerning the forests, declared: "The timber, water, mineral, and other resources of the forest reserves are for the use of the people. They may be obtained under reasonable conditions without delay. Legitimate improvements and private enterprises will be encouraged."[12]

Probably the greatest single immediate benefit which the nation and the community derived from the Forest Service was the protection from forest fires. The *Use Book* of 1908 noted that during the past three years the total area burned over had steadily diminished so that during the previous year it was less than one per cent of the total area of the national forests.[13]

Under the previous arrangement, the organization in charge of the forests had been anything but efficient. The employees were at the mercy of public opinion in the areas where they worked, and followed frontier usage with regard to government land. In the rare case when an officer tried to carry out government policy by protecting the forest, he was helpless even if he caught a trespasser in the very act of violating the law. It was often necessary for him to go twenty miles or more to secure a judicial process since he could not arrest anyone on his own. His supervisors, of course, were political appointees—as Pinchot remarked, "Too many Congressmen had jobs for their deadhead friends." Binger Herman, of whom we have heard, appointed several relatives to positions—three brothers-in-law, a brother, a son-in-law, and a nephew. Pinchot, in his notes, evaluated the three brothers-in-law thus: one was "an old man absolutely worthless in his

11 Gifford Pinchot, "How Conservation Began in the United States," *Agricultural History*, XI (October, 1937), 262–263.

12 Pinchot, *Breaking New Ground*, pp. 264, 265.

13 *The Use Book, Regulations and Instructions for the Use of the National Forests* (Washington, D.C.: Govt. Printing Office, 1908), pp. 152, 153.

position"; another was "ignorant—general report makes him incompetent, and in league with the sheepmen who are running their flocks legally or illegally on the Forest Reserves"; and a third was "an ideally unfit man, utterly useless in every way." Pinchot did not comment on the son-in-law, who was on duty in Roseburg, Oregon, Herman's hometown, "where there were neither forests nor public lands."[14] "Uncle Joe" Cannon, who opposed changing the supervision of the forests from the Department of the Interior to the Department of Agriculture, and who was very suspicious of "college professors, students, wise men and so on and so on who go throughout the length and breadth of the country, who investigate,"[15] appointed a supervisor who "made the Forest Reserve a sort of private benevolence, recommending the appointment of many consumptives who had gone to Santa Fe for their health." Uncle Joe's appointee in Oregon was a man with one lung and one leg. Many of these appointees, moreover, were eastern men who knew nothing of forests but had to superintend forestry work with several supervisors under their jurisdiction.

Major F. A. Fenn, the forest superintendent of Idaho, stated that the forest service had become "a political catch-all into which was cast whatever discarded baggage the dominant party could not deposit elsewhere. The Forest Reserve was purely political." One of the supervisors on the Bitteroot Reserve under Fenn's predecessor

> conducted a saloon and although it was notorious that he never was on his Reserve but once during the time he held office, his service reports showed that he regularly "patrolled out and looked over the Reserve." As a fact he walked out with scrupulous regularity from the interior of his saloon to the front porch thereof and from that observation point "looked over" his Reserve, which was in plain view from there.[16]

The other supervisor was no better. Pinchot, in recalling the matter, said:

> The reports of the other supervisor, which were "models in form and elegant chirography, showed the supervisor most zealous in patrolling his territory 'with saddlehorse and pack horse,' for which he was allowed $1.00 a day each when in actual use. What he actually used them for was delivering beef for a butcher," for which he was paid $2.50 per day.

Dereliction of duty was bad enough, but a betrayal of the public trust by positive acts contrary to orders was even more reprehensible. Pinchot tells

[14] Pinchot, *Breaking New Ground*, pp. 162–163.
[15] Ise, *United States Forest Policy*, p. 156.
[16] Pinchot, *Breaking New Ground*, p. 166.

us that "many a worthless Supervisor ordered his ranger to hold trespassers to strict account, and then notified the trespassers that he had told the ranger the exact opposite." In the Battlement Mesa Forest Reserve the supervisor told squatters to drive rangers off with guns if they tried to interfere with their illegal use of government land. Another supervisor's excuse for not pushing a trespass case was that he believed "some mill crews would vote right when it came time for election." Trespass cases were frequently cancelled for political reasons.

The rangers could scarcely have been expected to be more efficient than their superiors. Ranger Anderson of Kooskia, later of Stites, Idaho, was a veterinary surgeon who, although he drew pay of sixty dollars a month, had never left his place of business or set foot on the reserve. Ranger Beaudette, a jeweler and watch repairman in Kooskia, performed the same nonservice for the government. Ranger Malcolm Glendening, a son of the supervisor, collected his sixty dollars a month but did not let his service interfere with his duties as an accountant at a salary of $125 a month in Concord, Idaho. Out of twenty-five men on the Idaho reserves when Major Fenn took charge, only three were good enough to continue in the service. Pinchot remarked: "Being mostly city men, the political forest officers stayed in town and out of the woods all they could. Take it by and large, the Interior Department's field force on the Forest Reserves was enough to make angels weep."[17]

Some noteworthy examples of conscientious attempts to serve the interests of the United States government and protect the forests from plunder can be cited, however. Since time immemorial, people had been accustomed to exploiting the natural resources about them, using what they pleased and often wasting nearly as much. But when the forest reserves were set up, this was trespassing and the rangers were instructed to stop the practice. Their task was well nigh an impossible one, and all but the most intrepid and faithful to duty quailed before the customary exploiters of the government forests. Many incendiary fires were set, igniting slashings and destroying thousands of acres of standing trees, but it was difficult to prove this incendiarism.

William R. (Bill) Kreutzer, the first ranger assigned to the forest service in Colorado, even without the benefit of police power, like a marshal without a gun, protected the forests of the Centennial State. Tiehacks had been accustomed to cutting railroad ties on government land, and two of them defied Bill and positively refused to cooperate when he explained that under the new order they were trespassers and would have to cease their

[17] *Ibid.*, pp. 164–167.

cutting. Learning of their intransigence, Bill went alone to their camp and after a little maneuvering disarmed the cutters and talked them into a co-operative state of mind.

On another occasion timber operators, used to "stretching the chain," would not desist when warned that they were cutting across the line on government-owned land. Rather than precipitate a head-on collision, Bill approached the problem obliquely. While the gang members ate dinner some distance from their cuttings, the intrepid ranger carried off their tools and hid them several miles away, refusing to tell them where they were until the trespassers promised to stay on their own holdings.[18]

Pinchot completely overhauled the forest supervisory organization as soon as it came under his jurisdiction, and within two or three years he had a reasonably efficient service. Moreover, those who lost their jobs were those who had been hostile to the idea of national forests.

Although by 1900 many of the big ranchers had become reconciled to the idea of forest reserves as a means of keeping the use of their accustomed grazing lands in the forests, others who were not suffering from competition were opposed to the whole idea. As firstcomers, they had established vested rights in the public domain on which they did not propose to allow any restrictions. Their attitude was: let those city dudes sent out here by a crowd of eastern bureaucrats try to enforce their newfangled regulations, and they will go back to Washington a whole sight quicker than they came. They sent delegations to Washington to influence members of Congress and voiced their protests in scores of frontier newspapers that served as town criers for the grazing interests. The cattlemen often overgrazed the forests, and as soon as an attempt was made to reduce the number of animals grazed on this acreage, the sheepmen occupied the vacated forests.

Indeed, the sheepmen were even more hostile to the new arrangement than the big cattlemen. The forest superintendent, referring to the Sierra Forest Reserve, wrote that early in 1901 three sheepherders took their sheep into the reserve and that in May, 1903, there were seventeen bands comprising about forty thousand sheep grazing in the reserve illegally.[19] It is probable that their intense opposition stemmed from the fact that sheep, for a time, had been banned from the forests because it was thought they would feed on the young growth and thus injure the forests. At any rate, sheepmen and cattlemen were pitted against each other. This situation was

---

[18] Len Shumaker, "The First Forest Ranger," in Nolie Mumey (ed.), *Westerners' Brand Book for 1951* (Denver: The Westerners, 1952), pp. 95–99.

[19] *Annual Report of the Secretary of the Interior, 1903* (Washington, D.C.: Govt. Printing Office, 1903), pp. 26.

changed with the reorganization of the service by Pinchot and the passage of an act of February 6, 1906, giving power to forest officers to arrest violators.

In 1907, as an agricultural appropriations bill was making its precarious way through the Senate, Senator Fulton of Oregon secured adoption of an amendment that rescinded the power of the President to set aside additional national forests in the six northwestern states. If President Roosevelt signed the bill, some sixteen million acres of potentially valuable timberland and other resources would be left to the land-grabbers, in whose interest the amendment had been drawn up. The President was in a dilemma, for he could scarcely veto the important appropriation bill, and yet the rider was not in the public interest. But again Pinchot was equal to the occasion. For four years the Forest Service had been gathering data on the land that should be set aside as forests, and was prepared to act. The wily Forester suggested to Roosevelt that he withdraw the remaining areas which should be reserved for forests, designate the forests, and then afterward sign the amended appropriation bill. When Roosevelt accepted this plan, Pinchot's staff worked around the clock for two days to finish the job of drawing up the proclamation. The bill was passed February 25, but the President had until March 4 to sign it, and the proclamation setting aside the new parks was issued in the interim, very effectively locking the barn. Then the President signed the bill. When the friends of special interests in the Senate found that their victory was a hollow triumph, great was their wrath. As Roosevelt said: "The opponents of the Forest Service turned handsprings in their wrath; and dire were their threats against the executive."[20]

The opponents of the President's conservation policies, then led by the governor of Colorado, called a convention to organize against him, which met on June 19, 1907. According to the *Review of Reviews*, which characterized the meeting as "The Land Grabbers' Last Stand," the entire affair was a "packed" assembly inspired by Presidential opponents, and the program committee did not provide for a single utterance in favor of Roosevelt's policy. The convention, furthermore, was run by Colorado, which had 386 of the 664 delegates; Wyoming had 145, and the other states had 133. Roosevelt sent a letter explaining that his purpose was to protect homemakers and that the real benefactors of the opening of the timber and coal lands would be the big companies. The convention heard much talk of despotism, bureaucracy, and oppression, and the Denver press, serving as an amplifier, filled the country with strident anticonservation propaganda, giving the impression that the country from the Rocky

[20] Roosevelt, *Autobiography*, p. 440.

Mountains westward was seething with indignation against Pinchot and conservation. As the howling of two coyotes sounds like a whole pack to the tenderfoot, so the press made it appear that the whole West was in revolt against the administration. The packing of the meeting created a backlash, however, and a well-organized minority—including Pinchot and Secretary of the Interior James Garfield—was present and happy to add its discordant notes to the symphony. In the end, despite all the arrangements and precautions of the anticonservationists, resolutions were passed that endorsed the "active and successful efforts of the administration in the enforcement of the land laws of the country."[21]

Roosevelt now resolved to bring the conflict home to the opposition and called a nonpartisan White House conference of all the states for the purpose of promoting conservation. In addition to the governors of the states and territories, the President invited the leaders of industry, the Cabinet members, William Jennings Bryan—the leader of the opposition party— and many other representative Americans. The meeting was held in May, 1908, and carried the voice of conservation to the people and resounded in the ears of Congress. Less than a year later, the President invited Canadian and Mexican representatives and domestic leaders of industry and labor, livestockmen, irrigationists, scientists, and tycoons such as James J. Hill and Andrew Carnegie to the North American Conservation Conference in February, 1909. This conference developed many slogans, such as "The greatest good to the greatest number—and that for the longest time," and a policy that took in not only the forests but coal and other valuable mineral lands, and water power as well as irrigation.

Roosevelt and Pinchot not only enforced the laws vigorously but often went beyond the requirements of the law when this was necessary to protect the public interest; they did not hang back and wait for Congress to give specific directions but took the initiative if conditions demanded action. Pinchot even resorted to a bit of chicanery when Congress did not move fast enough in a conservation case that demanded immediate action. In the first decade of the twentieth century, damsites were sought by power companies, and because many excellent sites were on the public domain there was danger that they would be secured by these interests. Unfortunately, the Bureau of Reclamation had no authority to withdraw lands to reserve them for future dam construction; hence between 1905 and 1907, in order to keep the sites from falling into the hands of the power monopolists, Pinchot inspired the Secretary of the Interior to withdraw 2,565 water-

[21] "The Way of the Land Transgressor," *Review of Reviews*, XXXV (September, 1907), 379–380.

power sites on the pretext that they were to be used as ranger stations (in the Department of Agriculture). In 1909, Roosevelt warned that the large corporations were acting with self-seeking foresight and vigor to control the water power of the nation, and he threatened to veto any water-power bill that did not provide a time limit—a lease with stipulations that the power site be returned to the government at a definite time—and the right of the government to collect reasonable charges for the use of the site.

The Timber and Stone Act and the Timber Cutting Act, as we have seen, were passed in 1878 to accommodate settlers and mining interests who could not legally secure wood for their immediate needs. The Timber and Stone Act sought to safeguard any wholesale transfer of large tracts by limiting the maximum sale to 160 acres at a minimum price of $2.50 an acre. Well intentioned, it turned out to be the ideal vehicle for monopolistic acquisition by lumber interests who used dummy entrymen to alienate vast areas from the government by fraudulent means. According to John Ise, between 1878 and 1913, by means of the Timber and Stone Act, twelve million acres of timberland were sold to private interests for $30,000,000, although they were worth much more. By 1920, not over a fraction of one per cent of the timber secured under the act was held by the men and women who made the entries. Land under this act had been disposed of at the minimum rate as though there were no alternative, but on November 30, 1908, the Department of the Interior ruled that in the future, timberland would be sold at appraised values.[22] Coal lands, for example, fell under an act of 1873, which made these lands subject to ordinary preemption or to private entry, with a maximum of 160 acres open to an individual or 320 acres to a company. The sale price varied between ten and twenty dollars an acre depending upon the distance from the railroad.

According to President Roosevelt:

The present coal law, limiting the individual to 160 acres, puts a premium on fraud by making it impossible to develop certain types of coal fields and yet comply with the law. It is a scandal to maintain laws which sound well, but which make fraud the key without which great natural resources must remain closed.[23]

Accordingly, on June 29, 1906, the President directed the Secretary of the Interior to withdraw from entry all valuable coal lands. These lands, therefore, were examined and classified, and between 1906 and 1909 coal land was sold for from $75 to $100 an acre. Another precedent was established

[22] Peffer, *The Closing of the Public Domain*, pp. 104–105.
[23] *The Nation*, LXXXIII (December 20, 1906), 526.

in 1906, when a special act of Congress granted the Edison Electric Company of California a permit to construct a power plant in the San Bernardino Reserve with the provision that the company pay an annual rental.

In 1911, Congress passed the Weeks Act, which enabled the Department of Agriculture to buy land for forest reserves in the White and Appalachian mountains—even the East was benefited by conservation. The government had again made a complete circle in its land policy—from an effort to sell, then to give away, and now to buy land from private owners for permanent ownership and development. This precedent led the government into buying back much of the very land it had sold or given away in earlier years.

Although conservationists had not overlooked water power as a resource that required conservation and control by the government, it did not become a major issue until 1915, when the need for electricity and its potential as a money-maker for big business were recognized. In February of that year the Senate asked the Forest Service to make a study of the water-power situation, and the report—submitted in 1916—revealed that a large percentage of developed water power was monopolized by a few companies. The Ferris bill put the issue squarely before the country in 1916: it proposed to lease water-power sites to individuals or other interests for as long as fifty years while reserving title to the site and the right of the government to acquire the improved properties for the price of the investment. The bill was violently assailed by the power interests, who persuaded their friends in Congress to introduce the Shields bill the same year.

Gifford Pinchot, although now retired from public office but president of the National Conservation Association, wrote letters to various publications and pointed out that the Shields bill, which proposed to give power interests the right to use water power on navigable streams, would mean the surrender of one of the public's resources which should remain the property of all the people. He pointed out that the bill authorized private corporations to seize any land, private or public, that they chose to acquire for power use. Although the bill allegedly made the land and installations available to the people after fifty years, Pinchot said, the government would have to pay a sum far above the original value because of unearned increments, and also would have to pay for the installations merely to recover the land.[24] James Middleton in *World's Work* pointed out that the California Public Utilities Commission, in attempting to set reasonable rates, had called upon the Northern Power Company for a statement of its

[24] Gifford Pinchot to *Wallace's Farmer* (Des Moines, Iowa), December 1, 1916, p. 7561.

assets, and the company had included a $9,000,000 item as the value of its water-power site, which had cost the corporation practically nothing.[25] The power companies, if permitted to operate in this fashion, would profit from natural resources that belonged to and should benefit the people.

By 1915 the National Conservation Congress had made a complete about-face and had fallen under the control of the anticonservation forces. At a conservation convention at Portland in September, 1915, the congress declared that riverbanks belonged to the states in which the river flowed and therefore that power development belonged to the state in which it was located. The states rights forces and the pseudo National Conservationists collided head on with true conservationists: eastern conservationists affirmed that the national government had the right to control water power and the West claimed that this right resided in the states. In harmony with this western concept, the state of Utah attempted to exercise the right of eminent domain and to seize United States government property in Bear Valley in behalf of its creature, the Utah Power and Light Company. In the case of *Utah Power and Light Company* v. *the United States*, the company contended that state law and local custom recognized its vested rights and that the Forest Service had exceeded its authority in issuing regulations concerning power sites. The case went to the Supreme Court, which handed down a decision on March 19, 1917, giving complete victory to the federal government. The decision stated that only the Congress of the United States could determine the manner in which lands of the United States might be acquired; therefore the exercise of eminent domain by a state upon federal property or in violation of the government's rights could be justified only by congressional approval. The decision also upheld the right of the national government to charge rental for the use of government land. Thus the attack by the states rights proponents ended in complete victory for the nation.[26]

On June 10, 1920, after a twelve-year struggle between the National Conservationists and the states rights interests on the one hand, and the government on the other, Congress passed the Federal Power Act—a compromise measure. The federal government was given the right to issue licenses for the acquisition and use of power sites on government land and navigable streams, but the states were given the authority to regulate the service licensees. This law was a landmark in power development, for it removed the uncertainties which had existed previously; as a result, in the

[25] James Middleton, "The New West," *World's Work*, XXXI (April, 1916), 679.
[26] *Utah Power and Light Company* v. *the United States*, *United States Reports*, Vol. 243 (New York: Banks Law Publishing Co., 1917), 389–411.

eight months immediately following passage of the act, applications were made for plants that would produce nearly six times as much horsepower as had been developed in the preceding twenty-year period.[27] The law also set up an agency to control the power programs on all government land and navigable streams—the Federal Power Commission, which consisted at that time of the Secretary of War, the Secretary of the Interior, and the Secretary of Agriculture. The commission was given authority to issue licenses for fifty-year periods, and the state in which a site was located was given the right to regulate rates and service; but a power company was not allowed to count the value of a site as an investment in computing rates.[28] When the national forests were transferred to the Department of Agriculture in 1905, some urged that the national parks should also be administered by that department since most of the national parks have vast areas of forest lands. The Forest Service favored that arrangement, but on August 25, 1916, Congress created the National Park Service in the Department of the Interior to supervise the national parks.

The rush of applications for power sites posed a new danger. In the *Saturday Evening Post* of September 20, 1920, Emerson Hough sounded the warning that power interests were projecting dams and other water-impounding works in Yellowstone, Grand Canyon, and Yosemite parks. He cited the building of a dam on Jackson Lake near the Yellowstone boundary and stated that plans were being made to turn the water of various park rivers into the Snake River for use in irrigation projects. This, he warned, would submerge valuable natural curiosities and ruin the scenic value of the park. Fortunately, these projects were not allowed by the Department of the Interior.

With the second decade of the twentieth century came the building of gigantic dams by the federal government. The first such project after the passage of the Federal Power Act of 1920 was in Boulder Canyon and later was known as Hoover Dam. Private power interests fiercely fought this government construction job. It was argued that the great size of the dam would render it unsafe, that the land it irrigated would compete unfairly with other land in agricultural economy, that the reservoir would soon silt up, and that its water would be too salty for irrigation. Moreover, the Arizona congressmen were against the project because its water was to be used in other states. But the dam was built despite these objections and set

[27] Roy M. Robbins, *Our Landed Heritage* (Lincoln: University of Nebraska Press, 1962), pp. 393–394, 397.

[28] O. C. Merrill, "A Hundred Million Horse Power Waiting to Be Used," *The Independent*, CIII (August 14, 1920), 195.

the precedent for a series of similar construction works in the Far West, Northwest, on the Missouri River, and elsewhere.

It has been seen that as early as 1878, John W. Powell had advocated community grazing areas and community use of land, but Congress, not fully aware of the semiarid condition of the West and occupied with the 160-acre homestead-farm concept, paid little attention to the idea. By the time of Theodore Roosevelt's administration, however, the idea that grazing land should be leased and the cattlemen allowed to fence it had taken hold. Roosevelt himself felt that this would be desirable. Because of their history of lawless acts against the homesteaders and sheepmen, the ranchers were thought to be opposed to the control of the range, but actually by the first decade of the twentieth century many of the big ranchers were not; they had simply tried to hold the range by the only method then available. Indeed, in 1900 the National Livestock Association endorsed the idea of a system of grazing leases for the public domain, and at their conventions in 1907 and 1908 the cattlemen voted for government-controlled grazing.

When Pinchot took charge of the Forest Service and allowed the cattlemen to graze the forests, the ranchmen were not unhappy, but it was another story when Pinchot felt it only fair that the cattlemen should pay for the grazing privileges. Easterners had to pay for their pastures; why, then, should the West object to so fair a proposition? He was sure, however, that he could not get such a bill through Congress. The eyes of such representatives of the cattle interests as Senator Frank W. Mondell of Wyoming were open to seek out any legislation that would, in their judgment, be inimical to the ranching business. Pinchot was certain that a frontal assault would be soundly defeated and he resolved to make a flank attack. Backed by Roosevelt and armed by the precedent that the Department of Agriculture had charged a company for use of forest reserve land for a fish saltery, oil, and fertilizer plant in Alaska, Pinchot secured an opinion from the Attorney General that it was legal to charge for grazing in the national forests. This action, in the summer of 1906, met bitter opposition from those ranchers who had been accustomed to use the forests without charge, but the Department of Agriculture collected.[29] At first, silviculturists had thought that sheep-grazing injured the forests; it was argued that these voracious animals would kill the little seedlings and otherwise injure the woodlands. But in time it was conceded that sheep- and cattle-grazing could be conducted on the same ground and at the same time without harm to the forest or the animals. As one forest ranger put it: "The stock

[29] Pinchot, *Breaking New Ground*, pp. 271–272; Roosevelt, *Autobiography*, p. 439.

seemed to agree with each other much better than did their owners." Each animal preferred different forage, and sheep could utilize ranges that could not accommodate cattle.

For example, sheep can subsist on less water than cattle and can use arid ranges. According to the *American Sheep Breeder*, experiments showed that in mountains where succulent plants and heavy dews were available sheep needed water only every third day; and in one experiment, in the Uinta National Forest in southern Utah, a herd of sheep was kept one hundred days, from June 10 to September 20, with no water except from dew and showers.[30] Again, although it had been thought that in order to restore an abundant coverage of grass it would be necessary to allow the forests to lie unpastured for a series of years, it was discovered that by proper management the pastures could be restored to maximum capacity while in use. Moreover, it was soon discovered that much of the damage to the range had been caused by ranchers' rushing their stock into the mountains early in the spring in order to beat other ranchers to the best grazing areas. This early grazing before the grass was ready killed the grass. To make matters worse, latecomers crowded in and overstocked the grasslands.

Under the direction of the Forest Service, rules were made indicating when stock could go onto the range, how many head could be grazed, and when the herds should be taken off in the fall. It was found that good management in these respects increased the efficiency of the range by about 30 per cent over what it had been under competitive individualism. Moreover, in a short time the cooperation of the graziers made possible the opening of new ranges for the excess stock not allowed on the pastures at first. The range was extended by cleaning out seeps and springs and by piping the water to troughs on ranges that previously had been dry and un-usable, by making trails into formerly inaccessible canyons, and by fencing areas in which special categories of animals could be run, for example, segregation of riding horses, beef steers, and "young she-stuff."

The Bureau of Plant Industry, which was set up in 1907 to study ways to improve the range and to make and to implement plans, was responsible in a large measure for range improvement. Albert Potter stated that the number of head of stock the ranges would support increased over 50 per cent between 1905 and 1917. This increase made it possible to allow new ranchers and small flockowners a fair share of the range without reducing the number of stock allowed by the grazing permits of the senior permitees.[31]

---

[30] Will C. Barnes, "Adaptation of National Forests to the Grazing of Sheep," *American Sheep Breeder and Wool Grower*, XXXVI (February, 1916), 73.

[31] Albert F. Potter, "How the Forest Service Has Helped the Stockmen," *American Forestry*, XXIV (March, 1918), 165 ff.

Instead of ruining the range business, the forest reserve policy helped it. Will C. Barnes, writing in the *American Sheep Breeder*, said that grazing permits were at a premium. When a man who had a grazing permit sold his business, the buyer was given grazing-permit preference in the forests, and so valuable was this preference that the custom arose of paying a bonus for it. The Secretary of Agriculture forbade this, however, under the penalty of revocation.

As for the nonforest lands of the national domain, which remained under the supervision of the Department of the Interior, millions of acres were not inviting enough to be homesteaded—not even with the help of the enlarged Grazing Homestead Act—but although twenty or more acres might be necessary to support a cow, the range was of some use. And during the years the forest ranges were being upgraded and made more profitable, the nonforest lands were being grazed by big ranchers with less and less restraint.

In 1928, when Hoover became President, he advocated states rights by stating that the

Federal Government is incapable of the adequate administration of matters which require so large a matter of local understanding. . . . Western states have long since passed from their swaddling clothes and are today more competent to manage much of these affairs than the Federal Government.

At a conference of western governors at Salt Lake City, he proposed selling the arid and semiarid lands suitable for grazing and also said he would appoint a commission to study his recommendation of turning the lands over to the states. The commission, which reported in 1932, recommended that the land be given to the states and that the states be urged to sell it at auction, but the recommendation applied only to arid grazing lands and not to forest reserves, oil lands, Indian reservations, and national parks. The governors of the affected states applauded the move, but the members of Congress from the affected areas were cool toward the recommendation. It was presumed that big stockmen would buy large units of the offered land, to the detriment of homesteaders and small stockmen—and even crowd them out. Senator Borah scorned the gift of land "on which a jack rabbit could scarcely live," and other senators, knowing the government would cede only the surface rights and keep the mineral rights, referred to the dubious gift as "skim milk." The recommendation did not prevail and the Secretary of the Interior of the incoming administration summed up the attitude of the conservationists toward the cession idea:

I feel certain that the selfish and shortsighted influences which have done so much to plunder our public domain and bring upon our heads the problems that now vex us would find it simpler to have their way with State Governments than with the National Government.[32]

While administrators recommended and Congress argued, the range—which was overgrazed, even in 1904—had continued to deteriorate, and more noticeably now that grazing management in the national forests had succeeded so well. The steady deterioration of plant life had brought about a decrease in water-storage capacity, leading to floods and erosion—a problem of great proportions. It was now known that the mountainous and arid land in the national domain had a direct effect upon the waters of the valleys, and an increase in the coverage of plant life on the overgrazed, un-cultivated areas would not only hold moisture and prevent erosion, but would decrease the silting of the reservoirs.

In 1928 the Secretary of the Interior obtained authority from Congress to undertake an experiment for the purpose of improving grazing. Some of the poorest grazing land in southeastern Montana, the Mizpah-Pumpkin Creek area, was selected. The land had been abused and was all but un-usable. The department then separated 108,000 acres, part United States land and part privately owned, but of minimum use to the owners; the land was given a rest, then leased to a private association at twenty dollars a section. The association put up fences, improved the waterholes, built corrals for handling stock, made it a service grazing institution, and charged cattlemen $1.25 a head for grazing. As a result of regulated graz-ing, after three years there was twice as much grass in the area as before, even though the land's capacity had been increased to five thousand head of cattle from three thousand head. Furthermore, it was said that the calves weighed twelve pounds more than at the same age on the previously un-regulated range.[33]

Franklin D. Roosevelt, an ardent conservationist, then came to the Presidency and supported his Secretary of the Interior, Harold Ickes, in a program of classification of the public lands and grazing conservation. Ickes' revolutionary program, patterned upon that of the Forest Service which had been developed over the years and upon the Montana experi-ment which had been set up under Hoover's administration, was based on the idea that the remaining grazing lands of the public domain should be placed upon the same basis as the national forests—that they become a

[32] Marquis James and Harold Ickes, "The National Domain and the New Deal," *Saturday Evening Post*, CCVI (December 23, 1933), 11.
[33] *Ibid.*

permanent grazing land. Representative Edward Taylor of Colorado, formerly an active states rights advocate who had belabored Washington bureaus and charged them with meddling, now turned conservationist and guided through the House the bill that bears his name, the Taylor Grazing Act, which became law on June 28, 1934.

The Taylor Grazing Act directed the Department of the Interior to set aside eighty million acres of the public domain as a permanent grazing preserve. After sounding out local reactions, the Secretary entered into agreements with other government departments, state land officials, and graziers and encouraged the formation of a grazing district in each community. Grazing permits for periods as long as ten years were authorized and the receipts from grazing were divided three ways: half went to the counties in which the grazing district lay, a fourth went to the Department of the Interior for range maintenance and improvement, and a fourth went to the general Treasury. Fees were made high enough so that they precluded charges of favoritism, inequity (roughly corresponding to the cost of other grazing), or of subsidizing livestockmen. They were based upon a sliding scale, with the earning capacity of a range—as measured by the market values of livestock—being the final criterion. In keeping with other New Deal acts, the users of a range had a voice in formulating the policy of the new grazing districts. Graziers elected an advisory committee, composed of one member for every 100 to 150 stockmen, who proposed equitable apportionment of the range in each district.[34]

This last feature evoked more criticism than any other aspect of the program. Arthur Newton Pack, the editor of *Nature Magazine*, felt that this was a scheme that had been worked out in behalf of the cattle barons who had used the land as their own for many years, without regard to law.

> Those who know this act know . . . that its fundamental principle lies in turning over the public range lands to the tender mercies of "Advisory Committees" of stockmen who have exploited those lands to their own advantage.
>
> If Mr. Ickes and those who think as he does, really believe . . . the Taylor Grazing Act is a blow at "special privilege," then Heaven help democracy. If through the enactment of this bill, this sort of philosophy should be applied to our National Forests turning them over to "advisory committees" of lumbermen, in the name of conservation, we had best begin praying for our children and our children's children.[35]

[34] *American Forests*, XII (March, 1935), 129.
[35] *Nature Magazine*, XXXI (January, 1938), 46.

With the coming of the New Deal in 1933, a genuine conservationist took the driver's seat. When he accepted the Democratic nomination at Chicago in 1932, Franklin Roosevelt stated:

> Let us use common and business sense. . . . We know that . . . means of relief, both for the unemployed, and for agriculture, will come from a wide plan for the converting of many million acres of marginal and unused land into timber land through reforestation. . . . In doing so employment can be given to a million men.[36]

Just seventeen days after his inauguration Roosevelt started the Civilian Conservation Corps, and on April 17, the first CCC camp was established, in the George Washington National Forest near Luray, Virginia. By August, 1940, the corps had planted nearly two billion trees, had spent over 5,500,000 man-days fighting fires, had built 5,250,000 erosion-control dams, and had improved 3,500,000 acres of forests.[37]

The New Deal recognized the fact that many people had settled upon marginal or subproductive land that could not support a family on a fair standard of living. To cite an example, the new government agencies recognized that in 1909, when the government passed the enlarged homestead act, thus inviting Tom Scott to leave his home in Illinois and settle on a half section in Montana with the intention of dry farming, it had made a mistake.

Scott had intended to return to Illinois in the fall, after the first crop, and marry his neighborhood sweetheart, but he did not raise his first good crop until five years later. Nevertheless, the couple married, lived in a tar-paper shack, and fought the Montana drought together. Their hopes soared when a good rain finally helped them out of debt, but a series of dry years followed during which their children would not have had enough to eat if it had not been for their mother's garden and flock of turkeys. By 1936, the Scott family was on relief, having lost everything in the drought years. Then, by good fortune, Scott became one of the first to participate in the New Deal's submarginal land plan and resettlement program. Scott's land and approximately a million acres of other homesteads that had suffered a similar experience were acquired by the government for a grazing district. The Scotts were moved to a small, irrigated valley where, with the money from the sale of their half section (about five dollars an acre), they could

[36] F. A. Silcox, "Our Adventure in Conservation—the CCC," *Atlantic Monthly*, CLX, No. 6 (December, 1937), 718.

[37] L. H. Robbins, "Training Youth the CCC Way," in *New York Times Magazine*, August 11, 1940, p. 8.

buy a tract and Scott could run his cattle upon the land of the grazing district at a reasonable cost.[38] Thus a modification of the recommendations of J. W. Powell a half century before was carried out in a limited area.

Drought and hardships in a semiarid country had broken down the rugged individualism of many frontiersmen and made this cooperative program welcome. By the end of the Depression, it seemed that the battle for conservation had been won and that a frazzled remnant of the original magnificent heritage of the American people had been saved for the enjoyment of posterity. Nevertheless the spirit of individualism with its threat of exploitation appears from time to time supported by the argument that state or individual control is more effective than federal control in developing the natural resources. Although the national government with its bureaus and political intricacies is not perfect, it has been freer from corrupt rings than have local and state governments; and history indicates that the national government should guide in the use and enjoyment of the remaining remnant of our national resources.

But to all intents and purposes, the passage of the Taylor Grazing Act of June 28, 1934, sounded the death knell of the public domain, as it was originally known, in the forty-eight states (leaving the territory of Alaska with special considerations); and President Franklin D. Roosevelt by Executive orders of November 26, 1934, and February 5, 1935, withdrew the remaining land from private entry. To cap it off, the General Land Office, which had dispensed land continuously since its formation in 1812, was merged with the Grazing Service to form the Bureau of Land Management on July 16, 1946.[39]

[38] Rexford G. Tugwell, "Our New National Domain," *Scribner's Magazine*, XCIX (March, 1936), 166.
[39] Peffer, *The Closing of the Public Domain*, pp. 224, 313–318.

XX

A House Divided Against Itself

LONG BEFORE ABRAHAM LINCOLN'S famous statement, on the eve of the Civil War, that the United States was a house divided against itself, the nation had been divided, with East and West forming the two sections. By the time the public domain was established following the Revolutionary War the eastern seaboard had become more conservative in its thinking and sought to control the frontier. The western edge of settlement where land was available was always more radical in its outlook than the older, longer-settled portion. The seemingly inexhaustible supply of land, with its boundless natural resources, which lay at the western edge of settlement awaiting exploitation by the enterprising, had a tremendous molding influence upon the American character and sense of nationality. The settler living in that environment of plenty thought of these resources as one would think of air or the wilderness streams.

Fortunately, the two sections were fluid and were able to accommodate each other, avoiding the conflict that threatened to rend the country asunder during the Civil War. As the squatter line moved on, the new settlers gradually became old settlers and their attitude and thinking became more eastern, and yet they retained a measure of the western outlook. This fluidity preserved the equilibrium between the two sections and prevented the breakup of the Union which had been feared by far-seeing men in the early days of the republic. The Midwest or land which had so recently been frontier was an ameliorating influence between East and frontier, and indeed held the balance of power in Congress, which slowly responded to the desires of the frontier.

The eastern viewpoint toward the frontier is voiced in a speech in the Senate in 1838. In 1807 the East had passed the Intrusion Law which forbade squatting on the public domain, and for years that section had been trying to keep the door closed against unauthorized occupancy of the land; but the West with the aid of its Midwest friends, who not so long

350

ago were pioneers, forced the door ajar with a series of limited pre-emption laws. When another pre-emption bill came up in 1838, John C. Calhoun in the Senate expressed the viewpoint of the East on the extreme frontier as he reported that

> if he was correctly informed, the Iowa country had been already seized by a lawless body of armed men, who had parcelled out the whole region, and had entered into written stipulations to stand by and protect each other—and who were actually exercising the rights of ownership and sovereignty over it—permitting none to settle without their leave—exacting more for the license to settle, than the Government does for the land itself.[1]

This statement picturing the activity of frontier speculation on the edge of settlement was fairly accurate. That the frontiersman was lawless, or at least paid no attention to the laws of the United States, was admitted by Senator Linn in a speech in favor of the Pre-emption Bill of 1841. He said he would like to see the man who would avow that it was possible to "remove by force those who are usually termed 'Squatters' from the public domain." And later in the same speech he

> repeated his position that it was utterly useless to pass laws to restrain the American people from going forward to settle on the public lands. Congress might pass such edicts as often as they pleased, but they never could carry out one of them.[2]

During the same debate Senator Oliver H. Smith of Indiana gave a defense of the squatter:

> More than twenty years of my life have been spent on the frontier. I have seen my state in her infancy, with the fairest and largest portion of her territory in the possession of the Indians. I have seen her pass through the different gradations of improvement until she has arrived at her present high grade in comparison with her sisters. I have seen the first rude hut, the first log cabin, erected by the first occupant of the wilds of what is now the most beautiful and highly improved

---

[1] Richard Cralle, *Speeches of John C. Calhoun* (New York: D. Appleton and Company, 1883), p. 135. Although Calhoun's speech illustrated the attitude of the East, Calhoun—himself the son of a colonial pre-emptionor—was sympathetic with the actual settler and would have been glad to see him have a tract for a home, but he did not want to see speculators profit at the expense of the real farmers who would have to buy them out.

[2] Blair and Rivers (eds.), *The Congressional Globe*, 26th Congress, 2d Sess., Appendix (January 6, 1841), p. 34.

portions of my state. I have seen, heard, and conversed with the early settler, and let me assure (the) senators he is the last man that would willingly do injustice to his country, and the very first, in times of peril, to bare his manly bosom and nerve his strong arm in her defense; and although he may be as rough and rude as his own log tenement, his heart beats with patriotic emotions for his country; he is a warm friend, a kind neighbor, ever hospitable to strangers, and, still better, an honest man; his poverty and his enterprise, with the hope of bettering his condition and providing for his family, stimulate him to leave his old friends, the home and graves of those who are dear to him, plunge into the wilderness, and undergo the perils and deprivations incident to the settlement of a new country.[3]

And he was right, as the westerners saw themselves. As the frontier moved westward, those left behind became more conservative in their viewpoint until finally the whole country had become eastern enough in its outlook to adopt and accept conservation with the setting up of national forests and grazing districts.

From decade to decade, for generations, until the 1930's there was always free land on the "cutting edge" of the frontier. Legally this was not true until the Donation Law became effective in the middle of the nineteenth century, but in practice, to the man who would live on the edge of the middle border, land was free. He could squat on land offering "natural opportunities," monopolize it by claim-club procedure until it became valuable, sell his "rights," and repeat this process until by a series of petty speculations—using his time and nerve rather than money— he accumulated enough money to secure title to a tract.

Major John Gilpin, recently returned from the Mexican War, in a Fourth of July address to a group of immigrants ready to leave the Missouri River for California in 1849, referred to this process of securing free land in military terms:

> Up to the year 1840, the progress whereby twenty-six States and four Territories have been established and peopled has amounted to a solid strip, rescued from the wilderness, 24 miles in depth, added annually along the *western* face of the Union, from Canada to the Gulf of Mexico.
>
> This occupation of wild territory, accumulating . . . like the annual rings of our forest trees is . . . at this moment sweeping onward to the Pacific with accelerated activity and force, like a deluge of men. . . . Fronting the Union is a vast *army of pioneers* . . . recruited by single

[3] *Ibid.*, January 14, 1841, pp. 69–70.

individuals, by families: and in some instances by whole communities. . . .

Each *man* . . . is in force a platoon. He makes a farm on the outer edge of the settlements, which he occupies for a year. He then sells to the leading files pressing up to him from behind. He again advances 24 miles, renews his farm, is again overtaken and again sells. As *individuals* fall out from the front ranks, or fix themselves permanently, others rush from behind, pass to the front, and assail the wilderness in turn.[4]

Free or cheap land was the bait which lured millions of the propertyless westward in the hope of bettering their economic condition. Professor Roy M. Robbins quotes a Belgian investigator who in 1846 minimized the democratic political organization in America as an inducement for emigration and insisted:

Land which is cheap of an almost unlimited extent, fertile enough to make capital unnecessary for its exploitation is a powerful attraction for the agricultural populations of Europe. During the nineteenth century this attraction has been more powerful than any institution made by men.[5]

The Reverend A. King, an immigration agent of the Burlington Railroad, wrote in an English newspaper that Nebraska had

a magnificent climate, and social and educational advantages more rapidly and abundantly provided than has ever before been known in the history of the world, *millions of acres of land of the richest and most fruitful character, may be had, at prices so low that it seems almost incredible, and like a mockery to call it purchase.*

The price, in fee, does not average the amount of a year's rent of ordinary farms in this country. . . . Nay in many parts, *fine farms may be had for nothing* by any families from any part of the world, who choose to come and live on them; and "homesteads" are sacred, so that no misfortune, bringing a man into debt, can result in the pauperizing or "eviction" of his family.[6]

---

[4] William Gilpin, *The Mission of the North American People* (Philadelphia, 1873), pp. 117–118.

[5] Roy M. Robbins, *Our Landed Heritage* (Lincoln: University of Nebraska Press, 1962), pp. 148–149.

[6] *Sterling Observer and Midland County's Advertiser* (Sterling, England), February 22, 1872, p. 259, from "Scrapbook of English Clippings, Burlington Papers," Newberry Library, Chicago.

Newspaper articles such as this excited people to fever pitch and brought droves of Europeans who had only their passage money.

At home the European thought of land as a plot of ground to which a family was rooted for generations, where children were born, reared, and spent their lifetime. Transplanted Europeans in America, however, moved by the thousands into open prairies and lonely forests, exploited the virgin areas, built towns, and moved on, perennially repeating the cycle. Whether Americans were foreign-born or native-born, this conquest and exploitation of the wilderness imparted distinctive traits of character and strongly influenced the formation of the American system of individual enterprise and the molding of American economic and political institutions.[7] Europeans observed in amazement the gypsy-like character and movements of Americans, who darted about like quicksilver, seeking valuable "natural opportunities." At times the seeking was headlong and inexorable. Relentlessly, the gold-seeking forty-niners jumped the trans-Missouri region and reached the Pacific, but some turned back upon the Missouri.

The remoteness of the land from the seat of the national government made it very difficult to formulate an ideal land policy and even more difficult to enforce a policy once it was formulated and adopted. As Great Britain found it difficult to fashion colonial policies and enforce them in America, Congress found it equally cumbersome to oversee the distribution of lands in the faraway wilderness; nor, in a democracy, could Congress speak with one voice and with the authoritative directness of a monarchy. Frequently, the East spoke conservatively but often passively for the good of the whole nation while the West clamored for the immediate interests of the exploiter and the individualist. Democratic institutions, furthermore, weakened the enforcement of government policy. Violators were allowed to try their own cases and make a farce of justice by being assessed five cents in damages for a flagrant violation that involved hundreds of thousands of dollars, or by being sentenced to a few hours in the custody of a sheriff in lieu of a jail sentence.

An incident in Turner County, South Dakota, typifies the frontier spirit that pervaded even the judiciary. Two settlers who had taken several loads of wood from government land were apprehended, but the judge before whom their case was tried decided that no damage had been done; he ruled it was simply a case of moving timber from one piece of government land to another. After the men were discharged the judge

[7] John Ise, *The United States Forest Policy* (New Haven: Yale University Press, 1920), p. 11.

shook hands with the culprits and said: "Boys, I'm sorry you are walking home. I wish you had your teams so you could go home by way of the gulches and get another good load."[8]

With the administration of George Washington, land sales were placed in the hands of the Treasury Department since land was a source of income to an impoverished government. The Secretary of the Treasury set up land offices in the area of the lands to be sold, with a register and a receiver of public moneys in charge of each; and in 1812 within the Treasury Department the General Land Office was established with a Commissioner in charge. With the establishment of the Department of the Interior in 1849, land business was transferred to it. In 1905 the national forests were placed under the supervision of the Department of Agriculture, but other lands, including national parks and the Bureau of Land Management, are under the supervision of the Department of the Interior.

The scheme adopted in 1785, by which the government surveyed the land in rectangular patterns before settlement was permitted, was a revolutionary improvement over the old haphazard custom in the South of allowing private individuals to go onto the land, select the choice areas, mark them in whatever shape they might choose, and record them as claims at the county seat. Unfortunately, however, the value of the new system was considerably vitiated by the heedless rush of settlement ahead of the land surveys. This allowed overlapping claims and consequent personal conflict, bloodshed, neighborhood feuds, and inequitable procedures that too often gave the advantage to the lawless, unscrupulous, and strongest.

Although most of the surveying was done honestly, nineteenth-century democratic processes permitted the employment of those with indifferent qualifications and now and then an unscrupulous individual whose work was done in a careless manner; and sometimes fraud was practiced over large areas. Such practices, which could have been prevented by rigid inspection before the surveyor received his compensation, were apt to provoke boundary disputes and make land titles insecure. Furthermore, laudable as the rectangular system was for fertile level land, it was unsuitable for semiarid or arid country and mountainous terrain, which called for classification and a different type of measurement.

On two major occasions, moreover, Congress departed from the principle of the rectangular survey system. The Oregon donation acts of the 1850's allowed settlers to select their claims in any shape they desired,

---

[8] W. H. Stoddard, *Turner County Pioneer History* (Sioux Falls, S.D.: Press of Brown and Saenger, 1931), p. 259.

which permitted them to claim the valleys and cut the country into odd shapes. This resulted in confusion and inequity to later comers, and impeded the growth of many areas. The Desert Land Act of 1877 also allowed settlers to select odd-shaped claims that for many years "covered" thousands of acres under obscure descriptions without surveys, depriving other settlers of their rights to the public domain.

Under the Articles of Confederation in 1787, land was sold in huge tracts to companies at a few cents an acre, but gradually the land laws were shaped to sell acreages in smaller quantities on easier terms to accommodate the homeowner. From 640 acres in 1796, the minimum was decreased to 320 acres in 1800, eighty acres in 1820, and forty acres after May 1, 1832. Congress, convinced that the public lands should be a financial asset to the nation, provided for auctions but set a minimum price for the land with the thought that much of the land would be sold at a figure above the minimum. The minimum price set in 1796 was two dollars an acre with a decrease to $1.25 in 1820.

The land law of 1800 provided for the sale of land on a four-year installment plan. When the buyers failed to make their payments, failure of the government to enforce the terms of the purchase agreement brought a deterioration of public morals by weakening the will to pay one's honest debts. Even after relief measures had been passed in favor of the delinquents and easy terms were offered for settlement, settlers continued to live as squatters upon the land for which they had not completed payment. By and large, the squatting habit of the borderers, learned in colonial days, was at the heart of the ineffective enforcement of the land laws. According to the federal laws, land was to remain vacant until it was purchased by a settler, but in practice, the valuable tracts were occupied long before they were sold. And often—even before tracts were surveyed—towns had been built on them. From time to time the government made halfhearted efforts to enforce the laws against intrusion, but too often the officials who attempted to carry out the laws lost the support of the government because of pressure from members of Congress or because a vacillating administration usually bowed to the cry of the frontiersmen.

The auctioning of land to the highest bidder amounted to little more than a sale at the minimum price shortly after 1800. The sales were accompanied by all sorts of chicanery and skulduggery in order to sidestep an honest auction; then, in time, claim clubs were formed to guarantee that their members could buy land at the minimum price. Auctions were largely a farce; the auctioneer received his fee for officiating at a sale where little was sold above the minimum although much valuable land was offered.[9] Of far greater harm than the loss of revenue to the government was the fact that much of this land was resold at a sizable increase. Squatting and the squatter associations (claim clubs) permitted speculation at the expense of the actual farmers and homemakers who came later.

Eventually, the passage of the Pre-emption Act in 1841 made squatting legal and guaranteed that the squatter-settler should have his claim, if used for a home, at the minimum price, which by that time had been lowered to $1.25 an acre. The act merely legalized the irregular proceedings that had been carried on for years. Senator Oliver H. Smith said in 1841: "I consider the pre-emption law merely declaratory of the custom or common law of the settlers."[10] As one writer said, the settlers handed the law up to Congress.[11] The pre-emption law, however, was as readily evaded as the stipulations and conditions of the auction. A lack of supervision and inspection by the government made it possible for an alleged homemaker to secure land with no intention of fulfilling the legal requirements that it would become the home of the claimant and that he would make certain minimum improvements.

By acts in 1785 and 1807, the government attempted to reserve the mineral deposits on the public lands for all the people by keeping title in government hands. In 1821 the government set up a system to collect a percentage of the metal mined in the lead mines in Missouri and in the tristate lead-mining area of Illinois, Wisconsin, and Iowa. The miners paid for a time, then refused to pay further, and the government did not press the point. In the 1840's the government gave up and offered the land at auction when it was secured at the appraised double minimum price ($2.50 an acre) by claim-club procedure. The lands of the Mexican

---

[9] The limited amount of land sold above the minimum price is accounted for by the fact that special pre-emption laws covered only limited areas; squatters with their claim-club arrangements sometimes were not numerous enough to buy more than the choice lands at the sale, allowing some to be sold at a free auction; and big speculators were not always able by collusion to arrange matters to get all of the land they wished at the minimum. The average prices per acre at which land sold in the third decade of the nineteenth century were:

1820—$1.40	1823—$1.30	1826—$1.33	1829—$1.26
1821—$1.50	1824—$1.27	1827—$1.42	1830—$1.26
1822—$1.28	1825—$1.35	1828—$1.26	

Congressional Globe, 26th Congress, 2d Sess., Appendix, January 4, 1841, p. 19.

[10] *Ibid.*

[11] Roscoe Lokken, *Iowa Public Land Disposal* (Iowa City: The State Historical Society of Iowa, 1942), p. 26.

Cession fell like ripe fruit into the public domain after 1848. Knowledge of the peace treaty's guarantees of title to those who had received grants of land under Spanish or Mexican sovereignty came as a shock to land-greedy Americans, whose habit for decades had been to swarm over the frontier area. They did not, however, allow the knowledge to deter them from occupying vast stretches of unpeopled, although privately owned, California country. As they had done for a hundred years on government land, they now squatted wherever they pleased, built towns, and exploited the country. Even land which had been held for a generation was not free from squatters' occupation, and the claim clubs were resurrected to retain their seizures. In some instances the Spanish grants were fraudulent or over-extended in size, and the Americans saw the holders of the grants as speculators who were robbing them of their rights as American citizens, but the squatters fell on the just and the unjust alike. The resultant squatter versus antisquatter activities kept the state in a turmoil for years and resulted in a vast amount of injustice.

A horde of gold-hungry prospectors spread over the mining area digging wherever their desire dictated, turning the very earth upside down whether on public or private property. Frontier lead-mining custom with only slight changes was transplanted to the gold fields. The miners formed their mining associations, laid out districts, and decided the size of claims, very much as the claim clubs had done earlier.

The congressional action which opened the way for perhaps more fraud than any other was the Swamp Lands Act of 1850. The intention was to reclaim the flooded or marshy lowlands in various states by giving them the land within their borders that was listed on government records as "swamp and unfit for cultivation."

The states were to drain these rich bottoms, sell them, and use the money to pay for the engineering procedures incidental to the reclama-tion; unfortunately, however, the states were allowed to select the drowned lands. Unscrupulous politicians selected desirable lands and managed to secure the tracts for themselves, leaving the swamps unre-claimed and the state governments very little richer. Mountainous sec-tions of the Ozarks and tracts in areas later designated arid in the Oregon country were taken at this time. Genuine swampland was not reclaimed until many years later, by the United States government.

In the rapid advance of settlement the land buyers purchased only the most desirable land, leaving much good land unpurchased along the way. The states, in which this passed-over land lay, appealed to the government to reduce the price since it evidently was not worth the minimum price or it would have been purchased. In response to this demand, Congress passed the Graduation Act of 1854, which lowered the price of land that had been offered and remained unsold for as long as ten years to one dollar an acre; if it had been on the market for thirty years or more, it was priced at 12.5 cents an acre, with proportionate rates for the years in between. Thousands upon thousands of acres of good land thus passed into the hands of buyers at minimal prices as a result of this act.

Over the years there had been calls from the West for the government to make a free gift of land to the settler who would make his home on it. In harmony with the general reluctance of the East to make land terms easier, this had been consistently rejected by that section. The first break came with a series of donation acts giving land to persons who would settle in Oregon, Florida, and New Mexico. But the campaign for a general homestead act was defeated by a coalition of the East and the South during the 1850's. The South opposed it since such an act would encourage the formation of new antislavery states and thereby diminish her relative voting power in Congress. With the outbreak of the Civil War and the withdrawal of southern delegations in Congress, it was possible for the West to secure passage of the Homestead Act, which became effective January 1, 1863. It now seemed that the day of the speculator was over. Unfortunately, three troublesome types of land distribution came to the fore about the same time, which to considerable extent negated the plan to distribute the remaining land to homemakers in family tracts: (1) internal improvement lands, (2) lands given for the establishment of colleges of agriculture and mechanical arts, and (3) direct sales of Indian land to commercial companies that precluded homestead entries. Under all of these provisions large amounts of land were acquired by the big interests to be sold immediately at an advance or to be held until rising property values warranted profitable sales. Great quantities of land were excluded from homesteading, and the homestead law did not make available nearly as much land as has been popularly thought. So huge was the amount of land given to the railroads that as late as 1909 twice as much had been received by them as had been taken under the Homestead Act.[12]

Although the settlers complained loudly about the great land giveaway to the railroads—and it goes without saying that the latter abused their

[12] Gifford Pinchot, *Breaking New Ground* (New York: Harcourt, 1947), p. 82.

privileges—the railroad land-grants had several virtues. They permitted rail extensions into regions which otherwise would have been uninhabited for years to come. Not only did the railroads make great expanses accessible but they promoted settlement with their intense propaganda in the East and in Europe. Although land within a railroad grant cost the settlers more, it was worth more because of the railroad, even though it would have been better to have given the land to the people and to have subsidized the railroads with money. Squatters, nevertheless, moved onto the choice railroad land-grants and disputed prior rights with the railroad. Where this did not occur, the vast amount of unsettled and often untaxed railroad land handicapped settlers who wanted neighbors and deprived them of additional tax money with which to build schools and other public improvements.

The Morrill Act, which gave scrip to the states to establish agricultural colleges, encouraged the entry of large blocks of land, which caused scattered settlement and deterred the development of a community.

Speculators, often representing eastern money interests, made use of every land act to buy or control large tracts of land and hold them for a profit, also leaving large areas unsettled and handicapping the homemakers. Speculators were despised by the actual settlers: they felt these people were making a profit without working for it and without enduring the hardships required to turn the country into more than bare unimproved land. Since speculators did not improve their blocks of land, it threw a greater burden upon the scattered settlers than would have been the case if the whole country had been settled evenly. At the same time, in some areas, almost every squatter frontiersman was in a way a speculator; guilt differed in this respect merely by degree and according to one's opportunity and financial backing. The settler who condemned the absentee landholder became a speculator when he formed or joined a claim club and held a quarter section of prairie and another quarter section of woodland. He divided the former into small tracts and sold them at high prices to those who came too late to obtain forest land. Speculation or aggrandizement motivated the man who claimed a wooded quarter section along a stream in the prairie country, saved his own trees by using those on the vacant quarter next to him, and later sold logs to the newcomer, possibly to the one whose quarter had been denuded. Horace Greeley, whose sympathy was with the bona fide settler, hated speculation; after a trip through the West in the 1850's, he remarked that Kansas suffered much from speculation. He said there were speculators in broadcloth and those in rags, neither more pernicious than the other. It was the only business a man could enter with no capital but an easy conscience, he observed.

The homestead bill was passed at the time the frontier was poised ready to advance beyond the rain belt. As settlement pushed westward across the 100th meridian, the country became increasingly inhospitable and it was more and more difficult to wrest a living from the soil. Many homesteaders could not live on the free land of the government long enough to secure title to it. When, at last, in response to the cries for help, the government permitted the mortgaging of homesteads, thousands mortgaged their claims for all they could borrow and left, never intending to return. Vast districts became the property of mortgage companies in the East, leaving much of the land unoccupied. Under the circumstances, it would seem that the government should have screened the applicants and required them to have agricultural experience and a minimum amount of money to tide them over the first rough years of living on the Plains—or perhaps have lent them the money to get a start.

Part of the area beyond the 100th meridian was occupied by ranchers who followed their great herds of Texas cattle to the northern Plains and settled down to stay. The country was a natural grazing area, not suitable for the type of farming conducted in the area east of the Missouri River. Large acreages were required for the support of a family but there were no legal provisions by which the cowman could secure more than a homestead designed for the humid country and the purchase of a pre-emption. Three hundred and twenty acres and after 1873 the possibility of another quarter section under the Timber Culture Act was only a beginning for ranching. A rancher therefore squatted or held by prior occupancy the lands he needed. When the homesteaders began to press in upon his domain, he determined to hold by force what he had been using for years and regarded as his. As a result, the homesteader-cattleman wars erupted, with intimidation, illegal fencing, and various forms of violence. After these means failed, the cattleman resorted to various types of fraud to secure control of the range he was using: dummy entrymen, repeat entries and relinquishments, and control of water sources.

The failure of Congress to make the land laws realistic was not due to a lack of information. In 1878, John Wesley Powell, the government's geological expert, issued his *Report on the Lands of the Arid Region of the United States*, which stated that there were three classes of land in the arid region of the United States: irrigable lands, pasturage lands, and timberlands. Each should be handled differently, he insisted. Powell's greatest innovation pertained to the first two classes, which were of immediate importance, and he drew up two bills for Congress to consider. The bills provided that in order to have enough pasturage for a family unit in regions of sparse grass, the claims should be enlarged from the standard 160 acres to 2,560 acres and arranged so that each family would have sufficient water for cattle and a small acreage that could be irrigated for a garden and for hay land. The second recommended type of claim pertained to land that could be farmed with the help of irrigation, and Powell envisioned a maximum eighty-acre tract for a family unit. For each type he recommended that the rectangular survey system be abandoned and that settlers be allowed to form districts and divide the land so that all might have an adequate share of the available water. Powell's recommendations, however, were unheeded.[13] Later, the government increased the acreage that could be taken for grazing, but the action was taken too late—in 1916.

Those who desired to harvest the forests by legitimate means were stymied by the lack of legal methods for obtaining possession of forest lands. They could obtain land only by skulduggery, or strong-arm methods, or by inducing others to perjure themselves. Farseeing lumbermen, anticipating the day when all of the timberland would be gone, grabbed while the getting was good. This, together with the attempts to secure mineral land, ushered in a land-grabbing era that debauched public men and reached into Congress and the Department of the Interior. During the latter part of the nineteenth century, great areas of forest land fell into the hands of the lumber barons.

On the Great Plains in 1890–1895 a tremendous recession in frontier settlement occurred due to the fact that agrarians had gone beyond the rain belt in the mistaken belief that the area was suitable for farming in the established way. The dry years of the 1890's compelled these hardy, venturesome settlers to "go back to the wife's folks" or to seek new ways of farming in order to utilize their free land.

Two methods were adopted by those who stayed, one of which was irrigation. At first, lateral ditches were run directly from streams out onto the thirsty land. Then, in the 1890's, a number of main ditches were dug and many more projected, but experience proved that watering the land was a job too big for one man, one company, or even one state. The cry went up that Uncle Sam would have to provide water to make his gift of land worth having. The response was the Reclamation Act of 1902, which made possible the impounding and use of the spring runoff from

13 Walter Prescott Webb, *The Great Plains* (Boston: Ginn and Co., 1931), pp. 420–421.

the melting snow in the mountains. Irrigation, as we have noted, necessitated intensive farming of a small acreage.

The second method for cultivating arid land was dry-land farming, which involved cultivating fallow land thoroughly while conserving the scant moisture in order to raise a crop the next year. This method necessitated a larger area because only half of the land was cultivated for crops, each half in alternate years. As a result of the demand for larger farms, the Kinkaid Act of 1904 and the enlarged Homestead Act of 1909 were passed by Congress. In 1913, as a result of these acts, nearly twice as much land was entered—most of it by dry-land farmers—than had been entered in any previous year.[14] Dry farming, however, was entirely successful only as an adjunct to grazing or irrigation farming.

As the United States government approached maturity and most of the country passed beyond the frontier stage, a reaction to frontier exploitation set in and the age of conservation began. It was a last-minute attempt to save the remainder of the national resources for the benefit of all the people rather than let them fall completely into the hands of monopolists. Conservation began, in a limited way, with Cleveland; it reached full definition with Theodore Roosevelt, whose administration advocated shaping policy in a way that would bring the greatest good to the greatest number for the longest time. The remaining worthwhile forest lands were set apart as national forests, and water-power sites were reserved.

With the coming of the New Deal, conservation was reinvigorated. Some of the near-starving settlers were moved off the marginal land they had been allowed to take from the cattlemen and to homestead, in the mistaken idea that dry land could be made to produce crops successfully. The government resettled these farmers on the basis of the plan that Powell had advocated a half century earlier. Although millions of acres in the arid regions produced only sparse foliage, when rightly managed, this land could support limited numbers of cattle. The Taylor Grazing Act, therefore, set such land aside as a permanent grazing area and granted the graziers extensive local autonomy in using the lands.[15]

The frontier with which the distribution of the land of the public domain is so closely intertwined died a lingering death. In 1893 the great

[14] Benjamin Hibbard, *A History of the Public Land Policies* (New York: Macmillan, 1924), pp. 397–398.

[15] Louise Peffer, *The Closing of the Public Domain* (Palo Alto: Stanford University Press, 1951), p. 170; Wallace Stegner, *Beyond the Hundredth Meridian* (Boston: Houghton Mifflin, 1954), pp. 355–356.

apostle and interpreter of the frontier, Dr. Frederick J. Turner, in his revolutionary address on the significance of the frontier accepted the appraisal of the Superintendent of the Census of 1890, who wrote: "Up to and including 1880 the country had a frontier of settlement, but at present the unsettled area has been so broken into by isolated bodies of settlement that there can hardly be said to be a frontier line."[16] Turner and the historical profession after him thereafter spoke of 1890 as marking the close of the frontier. Thousands of settlers, however, oblivious of the historians' declaration, poured into the unoccupied West, entering land, putting up tar-paper shacks or soddies; or they took advantage of Indian land openings. In fact, more land was entered under the Homestead Act after 1890 than before that date. Later historians, with the advantage of greater perspective than was possible in 1890, have interpreted 1890 as the date when it was certain that settlement had passed beyond the rain belt; and hence the frontier had ended because it was felt that land beyond that line was not worth occupying.

Granted that there was a change in the nature of the frontier after 1890, in this volume I have chosen to consider that the frontier closed with the two Executive orders of Franklin D. Roosevelt dated November 26, 1934, and February 5, 1935, which withdrew from entry the remaining land in the "unreserved and unappropriated public domain." Thus ended in the United States, aside from Alaska, "private land settlement which has strongly influenced the shaping of American character, and the establishment of individual enterprise as the dominating feature of American economic life."[17] The General Land Office continued to function until July 16, 1946—one hundred and thirty-four years to a day from the time of its establishment in 1812—when it was merged with the National Grazing Service and given the title of the Bureau of Land Management. Henceforth there would be a public domain, but it was reserved for the use of the people for all time to come.

In retrospect it may be said that the history of the dispersal of the public lands, as viewed from our time, sounds like one long orgy of fraud, skulduggery, and general dishonesty. The records do indicate that most of the land laws were evaded or used to further the interest of the frontiersmen. But what per cent of the land was subject to these practices is difficult to determine. It is axiomatic that in a well-regulated community the

[16] Frederick Jackson Turner, *Significance of the Frontier in American History* (New York: Henry Holt, 1920), p. 1.

[17] Rexford G. Tugwell, "Our New National Domain," *Scribner's Magazine*, XCIX (March, 1936), 168.

violation of a law is newsworthy. The law-abiding man who is regular in every respect never gets his name in the newspaper. Likewise the land seeker—be he homesteader, recipient of a donation claim, entryman on a desert claim, or a timber-culture claimant—who honestly lived up to the law was seldom mentioned in the reports of the Commissioner of the General Land Office, reports of a congressional committee of inquiry, or the report of an inspector in the field. Certainly these and other sources reveal much fraud, but how universal this was cannot be known. The researcher, however, gains the impression that in certain areas and under given conditions a law was carried out in good faith whereas in other places the same law was used in a manner entirely unintended by the national government and contrary to the spirit of the law. For example, in the rain belt, as proof that many, perhaps a vast majority, of the homesteaders acted in good faith is the fact that a quarter century later many farmers were living on their original homesteads. And yet, as indicated previously, in many other places the same law was often fraudently used to secure land for cattlemen, lumbermen, or mining companies.

The course of action of the frontiersman is better understood when we remember the difference in viewpoint toward law on the frontier from what it was in the East. The easterner considered law and governmental regulation as necessary, requiring obedience. On the other hand, the western man saw land as the property of the government—a government of the people of whom he was one, and he regarded the land as "ours." Trespassing, cutting government timber, or breaking the land law in any other manner he considered in no way dishonorable. Cattlemen, who were the soul of honor in their business dealings with one another—whose word was as good as gold and their cattle count in a sale was not even questioned to the point of making a tally—did not hesitate to prevent a homesteader from exercising his legal right or to fence public land contrary to law; and they were equally free to monopolize land to prevent a little stock raiser from using range land to which the latter had as much right as they had.

To their mind it was the thing to do—in fact was the only way open to them—to preserve the range cattle system. The lumber and mining interests were in the same predicament and reacted in a fashion suitable for their needs. Moreover, the rank and file of settlers who used the land laws for their own purposes instead of obeying them in letter and spirit were honest citizens and good neighbors to the great majority who saw things in the same light as they.

The seeming anachronism lies in the fact that the nation was a house divided against itself. The West gradually won the privileges she wanted from a reluctant East. As the frontier neared its close many westerners began to look at the situation from the eastern viewpoint, and when government land was gone the frontier outlook vanished with it; the western outlook became eastern.

Bibliography

1. GOVERNMENT DOCUMENTS AND MANUSCRIPTS
   Agricultural Yearbook. Department of Agriculture, 1898, 1899, 1906, 1908–1910, 1912.
   American State Papers. Vols. I–VIII.
   Annual Report (14th) *of the Reclamation Service,* 1915, General Land Office, Department of the Interior.
   Annual Reports, Department of Agriculture, 1867, 1908.
   Annual Reports of the Nebraska State Horticultural Society, 1878 & 1879. Lincoln, Nebr.: Journal Co., 1879.
   Blair and Rivers (eds.). *The Congressional Globe,* 26th Cong., 2d Sess., January 6, 1841.
   Carter, Clarence Edwin (ed.). *The Territorial Papers of the United States.* Vols. V, VI, VII. Washington, D.C., 1938.
   Correspondence of the Commissioners, 1816, MS, General Land Office, Department of the Interior. National Archives.
   Forest Service Bulletin, Nos. 66, 67. Department of Agriculture.
   Forestry Bulletin, No. 5. Department of Agriculture.
   General Land Office Circular 18. Department of the Interior. Washington, D.C.: General Land Office, 1867.
   Instructions to the Surveyor General of Public Lands of the United States for those Surveying Districts Established In and Since the Year 1850; containing also, a Manual of Instructions to regulate the Field Operations of Deputy Surveyors. Washington, 1855.
   Letters of Deputy Surveyors to the Surveyor General of Kansas and Nebraska Territory and of Iowa and Nebraska. Vols. I–III. Nebraska State Historical Society.
   Letters Received by the Register, Muskoday Land Office, Vol. I, MS, General Land Office, Department of the Interior. National Archives.
   Letters Received from Register and Receiver, Monroe, Mich., 1823–1830, MS, General Land Office, Department of the Interior. National Archives.

Letters Received from Shawneetown, Ill., Vol. 140, General Land Office, MS, Department of the Interior. National Archives.

Letters Received from Vincennes, Ind., Vol. 20, General Land Office, MS, Department of the Interior. National Archives.

Miscellaneous Letters to the Commissioner of the General Land Office, 1830–1833, Vols. 25, 34, 35, MS, General Land Office, Department of the Interior. National Archives.

Nebraska, State of, Board of Educational Lands, "Surveyors' Correspondence," Book I. Statehouse, Lincoln, Nebr.

Pre-emption and Homestead Laws. Lincoln, Nebr.: Journal Co., State Printers, 1874.

Private Law 391, H.R. 3768, 80th Cong., General Land Office Records. National Archives.

Records of Proclamations for the Public Land Sales, Nov. 19, 1807—July 14, 1838, Vol. I, MS, General Land Office, Department of the Interior. National Archives.

Registers' and Receivers' Letters to GLO from Kaskaskia, Ill., 1804–1833, Vol. 13, General Land Office, MS, Department of the Interior. National Archives.

Registers' and Receivers' Letters to GLO from Palmyra, Mo., 1824–1833, General Land Office, MS, Department of the Interior. National Archives.

Report of Commissioners, General Land Office, Department of the Interior, 1858, 1862, 1863, 1865, 1866, 1874, 1875–1885, 1887, 1888, 1890, 1892–1896, 1905.

Report of the Grand Jury, District Court, Detroit, Mich., May 24, 1830, Miscellaneous Letters to the Commissioner of Public Lands, Vol. XXV, MS. National Archives.

Report of Idaho Constitutional Convention, 1889. Caldwell, Idaho, 1912.

Report of Public Lands Commission, S. Doc. 189, 58th Cong., 3d Sess., 1905.

Report of the Secretary, 1877, 1879, 1880, 1885, 1886, 1887–1903, General Land Office, Department of the Interior. National Archives.

Resources of the Semi-arid Region, S. Doc., 58th Cong., 3d Sess., 1905.

Suggestions to Homesteaders and Persons Desiring to Make Homestead Entries, 1906, General Land Office, Department of the Interior.

Surveyors' Correspondence. Book I. Nebraska State Historical Society.

The Use Book, Regulations and Instructions for the Use of the National Forests, 1908, Department of Agriculture.

United States Public Statutes at Large, Vol. 28.

2. MISCELLANEOUS MANUSCRIPTS

Backus, James. "Journal." Ohio Archeological and Historical Society Library.

Barstow Statement. Bancroft Library, University of California, Berkeley

Blount, William. "Correspondence of William Blount, 1777–1797." McClung Collections, Lawson-McGhee Library, Knoxville, Tenn.

Burlington Railroad, Land Department Scrap Book 1, English Agents. Newberry Library, Chicago.

Burlington Railroad, Scrap Book, Clippings, English Newspapers. Newberry Library, Chicago.

Burlington Railroad, Letter Book of the Land Commissioner, 1880–1881. Newberry Library, Chicago.

Burlington and Missouri Railroad, Land Department Scrap Book of English Clippings, 1871–1872. Newberry Library, Chicago.

Burlington and Missouri Railroad, Letter Book of the Land Commissioner, 1874. Newberry Library, Chicago.

"Cahaba." From the *Young American.* In Towns. Alabama Department of Archives and History, Montgomery, Ala.

Campbell, Hardy W. "Dry Farming in the Western Plains Region." Nebraska State Historical Society Library.

"Claim Association Papers, Lee County, Illinois" (1834). Illinois State Historical Society Library.

"Coffee Correspondence." Robert Dyes Collection of Coffee Correspondence, Tennessee Historical Society Library, Nashville.

Coffee, Mary. "Papers." Robert Dyes Collection of Coffee Correspondence, Tennessee Historical Society Library, Nashville.

"Crapo Papers." Michigan Historical Collection, William L. Clements Library, University of Michigan, Ann Arbor.

Dry Farming Congress Bulletin. Spokane, Washington, III, February 15, 1910.

"Ferry Letters." Michigan Historical Collection, William L. Clements Library, University of Michigan, Ann Arbor.

"Land Warrants, Letters Concerning." State Historical Society of Iowa Library, Iowa City.

"Landt Manuscript." Vol. II. Wisconsin State Historical Society Library, Madison.

"Little, Statement." Bancroft Library, University of California, Berkeley.

"Merriwether Papers." Kentucky Historical Society, Frankfort.

Moore, Augustus. "Pioneer Experiences." Bancroft Library, University of California, Berkeley.

Olsen, Charles Oluf. "History of Linn County, Oregon." Mimeographed book, 1941.

Pickett, A. J. "Conversation with John Bibb." Alabama State Department of History Library, Montgomery, Ala.

Ramsey, Rev. A. C. "A Sketch of the Life and Times of Rev. A. C. Ramsey," as written by himself in 1879 at the age of 72. Alabama Department of Archives and History, Montgomery.

Richards, W. A. "Diary Kept by W. A. Richards the Summer of 1873." Wyoming Historical Society Library, Cheyenne.

Snelling, Henry Hunt, "Memoirs of a Life From My note book and Journal, with additions and reflections, 1829–1867." 3 vols. Vol. I. Edward E. Ayer Collection, Newberry Library, Chicago.

Wheaton, Milton A. "Statement." Bancroft Library, University of California, Berkeley.

3. CONTEMPORARY WRITINGS

Beadle, Erastas. *To Nebraska in Fifty-Seven.* New York: N.Y. Publishing Library, 1923.

Borthwick, J. D. *Three Years in California.* Edinburgh and London, 1857.

Brocket, Linus Pierpont. *Our Western Empire.* Philadelphia: Bradley, Garretson & Co., 1881.

Brunson, Alfred. *A Western Pioneer, 1872–79.* New York: Carlton & Lanshan, no date given.

Buffum, E. Gould. *Six Months in the Gold Mines.* Philadelphia, 1850.

Curley, Edwin A. *Nebraska, Its Advantages, Resources and Drawbacks.* London, 1875.

Featherstonhaugh, George William. *Excursion Through the Slave States.* 2 vols., Vol. I. New York, 1844.

Flint, James. *Letters from America, 1818–20.* Edinburgh, 1822.

Fordham, Elias Pyn. *Personal Narrative of Travels.* Edited by Frederick Austin Ogg. Cleveland: Arthur H. Clark, 1906.

Gilpin, William. *The Mission of the North American People.* Philadelphia, 1873.

Hodgson, Adam. *Letters from America Written During a Tour.* 2 vols., Vol. I. London, 1824.

Hutton, William Rich. *Glances at California 1847–1853: Diaries and Letters of William Rich Hutton, Surveyor.* San Marino, California, 1942.

Jackson, Albert T. *The Diary of a Forty-Niner and Guide.* Berkeley: University of California Press, 1947.

Martineau, Harriet. *Society in America.* 3 vols., Vol. II. New York, 1837.

Mercer, A. S. *The Banditti of the Plains.* Norman: University of Oklahoma Press, 1954.

Murray, Charles Augustus. *Travels in North America.* 2 vols., Vol. I. London: R. Bentley, 1839.

Nuttall, Thomas. *Journal of Travels into the Arkansas Territory during the Year 1819.* Philadelphia, 1821.

Peeper, David Rohrer. *The Argonauts of 'Forty-Nine.* South Bend, Ind., 1894.

Pigman, Walter G. *The Journal of Walter Pigman.* Mexico, Mo.: W. G. Staley, 1942.

Shaw, Pringle. *Ramblings in California.* Toronto, 1851.

Taylor, Bayard. *Eldorado.* New York, 1856.

Tillson, Mrs. Christiana H. *A Woman's Story of Pioneer Illinois*. Chicago: R. R. Donnelley & Sons Company, 1919.

4. REMINISCENT WRITINGS

Anderson, Mary Jane Hill. *Autobiography*. Minneapolis, Minnesota: Agnes A. Twichell, 1934.

Burnap, Willard A. *What Happened During One Man's Life Time*. Fergus Falls, Minnesota: Privately printed, 1923.

Burnet, Jacob. *Notes on the Early Settlement of the North-Western Territory*. Cincinnati, 1847.

Canton, Frank M. *Frontier Trails*. Boston: Houghton Mifflin Co., 1930.

Chetlain, Augustus Louis. *Recollections of 70 Years*. Galena, Illinois, 1899.

Cox, Sanford C. *Recollections of the Early Settlement of the Wabash Valley*. Lafayette, Indiana, 1860.

Crawford, Lewis F. (ed.). *Rekindling Camp Fires*. Bismarck, North Dakota: Capital Book Co., 1926.

David, Robert B. *Malcolm Campbell, Sheriff*. Casper, Wyoming: Wyomingana, Inc., 1932.

Downie, William. *Hunting for Gold*. San Francisco, 1893.

Gardiner, Robert Hallowell. *Early Recollections of Robert Hallowell*. Place of publication not given: White and Horne Company, 1936.

Garland, Hamlin. *A Son of the Middle Border*. New York: Macmillan, 1917.

Goulder, William A. *Reminiscences in the Life of a Pioneer*. Reagin, Oregon, 1909.

Graves, J. A. *My Seventy Years in California*. Los Angeles: Times-Mirror Co., 1927.

Grey, William. *A Picture of Pioneer Times in California*. San Francisco, 1881.

Haskins, C. W. *Argonauts of California*. New York: Fords, Howard & Hulbert, 1890.

Hollman, Frederick G. *Autobiography of Frederick G. Hollman*. Platteville, Illinois: R. I. Dugdale, no date given.

Howells, William Cooper. *Recollections of Life in Ohio*. Cincinnati, 1895.

Hughes, Richard B. *Pioneer Years in the Black Hills*. Glendale, California: Arthur H. Clark, 1957.

Kip, Wm. Ingraham. *The Early Days of My Episcopate*. New York, 1872.

Knower, Daniel. *Adventures of a Forty-Niner*. Albany, 1894.

Mills, Anson. *My Story*. Washington, D.C.: Privately printed, 1918.

Roosevelt, Theodore. *Autobiography*. New York: Macmillan, 1913.

Saunders, James Edmonds. *Early Settlement of Alabama*. New Orleans, 1899.

Shaw, D. A. *Eldorado, or California as Seen by a Pioneer, 1850–1900*. Los Angeles: B. R. Baumgardt and Company, 1900.

Stephenson, Isaac. *Recollections of a Long Private Life, 1829–1915*. Chicago: R. R Donnelley and Sons, 1915.

Woods, James. *Recollections of Pioneer Work*. San Francisco, 1878.

5. INTERVIEWS

Ard, Newt. Personal interview with Everett Dick, January 2, 1934.

Norton, Clarence. Personal interview with Everett Dick, December 29, 1933.

6. NEWSPAPERS

Ainsworth Journal, Ainsworth, Nebraska (June 24, 1886).

Alabama Republican, Huntsville, Alabama (August 5, 1817—May 3, 1822).

Arkansas Gazette, Little Rock, Arkansas (May 21, 1822—June 17, 1823).

Arkansas Traveler, Arkansas City, Kansas (April 23, 24, 25, 1889).

Baxter Springs Examiner, Baxter Springs, Kansas (September 14, October 26, 1871; January 28, June 8, 1872.

Bellevue Gazette, Bellevue, Nebraska (October 23, 1856—April 29, 1858).

Caldwell Journal, Caldwell, Kansas (April 18, 25, 1889).

Chamberlain Register, Chamberlain, South Dakota (July 7—August 18, 1904).

Chariton Herald, Chariton, Iowa (April 5, 1904).

Cherokee Sentinel, Baxter Springs, Kansas (March 20, 1869—October 26, 1871).

Chicago Times (May 26, 1894).

Chippewa Herald, Chippewa, Wisconsin (September 21, 1883).

Clipper, The, Hennessey, Oklahoma Territory (August 1—October 30, 1893).

Custer County Chief, Broken Bow, Nebraska (June 24, 1904—October 28, 1904; October 1—November 15, 1913).

Dubuque Herald, Dubuque, Iowa (June 27, 1860).

Eau Claire Freepress, Eau Claire, Wisconsin (August 8, November 29, 1883).

Fort Scott Monitor, Fort Scott, Kansas (January 20, 1869—September 1, 1869).

Frontier, The, O'Neill, Nebraska (June 1—July 30, 1904).

Grant County Review, Milbank, South Dakota (April 1–30, 1892).

Herald Advance, Milbrook, South Dakota (April 1–22, 1892).

Herald and Advertiser, Milbank, South Dakota (April 1, 1892—May 30, 1892).

Herald of Freedom, Lawrence, Kansas (October 21, 1854—August 25, 1855).

Iola Register, Iola, Kansas (April 6, 1878; July 9, 1886—January 28, 1887).

Iowa Territorial Gazette, Burlington, Iowa (December 1, 1838).

Irrigation Age, Chicago, Illinois (June 1, 1892).

Irrigation Review, Denver, Colorado (September, 1897, February, 1898).

Jefferson Enquirer, Jefferson City, Missouri (January 8, 1853—September 30, 1854).

Kansas Weekly Herald, Leavenworth, Kansas (September 15, 1854—September 29, 1855; September 1, 1856—January 10, 1857; July 8, 1857—September 1, 1857).

Kanzas News, Emporia, Kansas (June 6, 1857—October 17, 1857).

Keith County News, Ogallala, Nebraska (1885–1888).

Lake Superior News, Mackinaw, Michigan (July 11, 1846).

Liberty Tribune, Liberty, Missouri (April 15, 1853—April 18, 1856).

Lincoln Evening News, Lincoln, Nebraska (December 3, 1891).

Lincoln State Journal, Lincoln, Nebraska (July 11, 1895; June 7, 1901; October 4, 1905; December 31, 1907; April 21—June 21, 1910).

Missouri Argus, Far West, Missouri (May 1, 1839—July 1, 1839).

Missouri Gazette, St. Louis (November 6, 1818).

Missouri Intelligencer (December 16, 1823—February 15, 1824).

Montgomery Republican, Montgomery, Alabama (January 6, 1821—May 8, 1824).

Nebraska Advertiser, Brownville, Nebraska (June 7, 1856—March 3, 1859).

Nebraska Farmer, Omaha, Nebraska (March 24, 1898).

Nebraska Palladium, Bellevue, Nebraska (July 15, 1854—October 11, 1954).

Nebraska Statesman, Lincoln, Nebraska (July 29, 1871).

Nevada Journal, Nevada, California (March–November, 1853).

New York Times (April 10—May 8, 1889; September 1–30, 1893).

New York Times Magazine (August 11, 1940).

New York Tribune (July 15, 1855; October 15, 1856—January 10, 1857; May 18, July 27, August 14, 1857—September 1, 1857).

North Platte Tribune, North Platte, Nebraska (October 1–31, 1913).

Oklahoma Optic, Guthrie, Oklahoma Territory (May 20–29, 1889).

Oklahoma State Capital, Guthrie, Oklahoma Territory (August 12, 1893—October 21, 1893).

Oklahoma War Chief, Arkansas City, Kansas (January 12, 1883—May 10, 1884).

Omaha Arrow, Omaha, Nebraska (July 28, 1854—December 29, 1854).

Omaha Herald, Omaha, Nebraska (April 23, 1889; December 2, 1906).

Omaha Nebraskan, Omaha, Nebraska (1856).

Omaha Weekly Bee, Omaha, Nebraska (April 15–29, 1889; February 25, December 3, 1891; February, 1897; December 13–25, 1905).

Oshkosh Northwestern, Oshkosh, Wisconsin (September, 1883).

Pacific News, San Francisco, California (September, 1849).

Public Land, Spokane, Washington (August 20, 1901—June 3, 1902).

Public Opinion, Watertown, South Dakota (April 1–22, 1892).

Sacramento Transcript, Sacramento, California (April 18, 1850).

St. Joseph Commercial Cycle, St. Joseph, Missouri (January 5, 1855—May 4, 1855).

St. Joseph Gazette, St. Joseph, Missouri (January 7, 1852—January 29, 1856).

Squatter Sovereign, Atchison, Kansas (February 3, 1855—September 2, 1856).

Sterling Observer and Midland County's Advertiser, Sterling, Midland Co., England (February 22, 1872).

Watertown Public Opinion, Watertown, South Dakota (April 15, 1892).

Yankton Press and Dakotaian (June 1—August 1, 1904).

7. PERIODICALS AND HISTORICAL COLLECTIONS

Anderson, George L. "The Administration of Federal Land Laws in Western Kansas, 1880–1890," *Kansas Historical Quarterly*, XX (November, 1952), 233–251.

———. "The El Paso Claim Club, 1859–1862." *The Colorado Magazine*, XIII (March, 1936), 41–53.

"Around with the American Forestry Association: Ickes Outlines Grazing Policy," *American Forests*, XLI (March, 1935), 129.

Bagley, Clarence. "The Mercer Immigration," *Oregon Historical Society Quarterly*, V (March, 1904), 1–24.

Baker, Ray Stannard. "The Great Southwest: the Tragedy of the Range," *Century Magazine*, LXIV (August, 1902), 535–545.

Barnes, Will C. "Adaptation of National Forests to the Grazing of Sheep," *American Sheep Breeder and Wool Grower*, XXXVI (February, 1916), 73–75.

———. "The Forest Service and the Stockmen in 1917," *American Sheep Breeder and Wool Grower*, XXXVIII (February, 1918), 88–89.

Beal, W. J. "Pioneer Life in Southern Michigan in the Thirties," *Michigan Pioneer and Historical Collections*, XXXII (1903), 236–246.

Bek, William G. "The Followers of Duden," *Missouri Historical Review*, XVII (October, 1922—July, 1923), 28–56.

Bien, Morris. "The Public Lands of the United States," *North American Review*, CXCII (September, 1910), 387–402.

Billington, Ray Allen. "The Origin of the Land Speculator as a Frontier Type," *Agricultural History*, XIX (October, 1945), 204–212.

Blackman, E. E. "Sherman County and the H.U.A.," *Transactions* of the Kansas State Historical Society, 1903–1904, VIII (Topeka, 1904), 50–62.

Bogue, Allan G. "The Iowa Claim Clubs: Symbol and Substance," *Mississippi Valley Historical Review*, XLV (September, 1958), 231–253.

Boyd, G. D. R. "Sketches of History and Incidents Connected with the Settlement of Wapello County from 1843 to 1859, Inclusive," *Annals of Iowa*, VI (January, 1868), 37–44.

Brown, Henry S. "Punishing the Land Looters," *Outlook*, LXXXV (February 23, 1907), 427–439.

Butler, Nathan. "Boundaries and Public Land Surveys of Minnesota," *Minnesota Historical Society Collections*, XII (1908), 649–670.

Chatelain, Verne E. "The Public Land Officer on the Northwestern Frontier," *Minnesota History*, XII (December, 1931), 382–389.

Clarke, Robert E. "Notes from the Copper Region," *Harper's New Monthly Magazine*, VI (March, 1853), 433–448; (April, 1853), 577–588.

Colgrove, Kenneth W. "The Attitude of Congress Toward the Pioneers of the West," *Iowa Journal of History and Politics*, VIII (January, 1910), 3–129.

Cowan, John L. "Dry Farming—the Hope of the West," *Century Magazine*, LXXII (July, 1906), 435–446.

Dunham, Harold H. "New Mexican Land Grants with Special Reference to the Title Papers of the Maxwell Grant," *New Mexico Historical Review*, XXX, (January, 1955), 1–22.

——. "Some Crucial Years of the General Land Office, 1875–1890," *Agricultural History*, XI (April, 1937), 117–141.

Gallaher, Ruth A. "This Iowa," *Iowa Journal of History and Politics*, XXXIX (January, 1941), 3–51.

Ganoe, John T. "The Beginnings of Irrigation in the United States," *Mississippi Valley Historical Review*, XXV (June, 1938), 59–78.

——. "The Desert Land Act in Operation, 1877–1891," *Agricultural History*, XI (April, 1937), 142–157.

——. "The Desert Land Act Since 1891," *Agricultural History*, XI (October, 1937), 266–277.

——. "Origin of a National Reclamation Policy," *Mississippi Valley Historical Review*, XVIII (June, 1931), 34–52.

Gates, Paul Wallace. "The Homestead Law in an Incongruous Land System," *American Historical Review*, XLI (July, 1936), 652–681.

——. "Land Policy and Tenancy in the Prairie Counties of Indiana," *Indiana Magazine of History*, XXXV (March, 1939), 1–26.

Gould, J. "Wanderings in the West in 1839," *Indiana Magazine of History*, XXX (March, 1934), 71–103.

Grahame, Pauline. "The Promised Land," *Palimpsest*, X (May, 1929), 187–198.

Graves, Henry S. "The Public Domain," *The Nation*, CXXXI (1930), 147–149.

Gray, L. C. "The Resettlement Land Program," *American Forests*, XLII (August, 1936), 347–349.

Green, Charles Lowell. "The Administration of the Public Domain," *South Dakota Department of History Collections*, XX (1940), 7–280.

Hafen, LeRoy R. "Mexican Land Grants in Colorado," *Colorado Magazine*, IV (May, 1927), 81–93.

Haney, E. D. "Experiences of a Homesteader in Kansas," *Collections* of the Kansas State Historical Society, XVII (Topeka, 1928), 305–325.

Hanson, Joseph R. "Reminiscences of Yankton's Early Days," *The Monthly South Dakotan*, I (May, 1898), 12–16.

Hough, Emerson. "Pawning the Heirlooms," *Saturday Evening Post*, CXCIII (September 25, 1920), 12–13, 90, 95–96, 98, 102.

Howard, W. W. "The Rush to Oklahoma," *Harper's Weekly*, XXXIII (May 18, 1889), 391.

Hunter, W. H. "The Pathfinders of Jefferson County." *Ohio Archeological and Historical Publications*, VI (1898), 95–313.

Ingalls, John J., to His Father, October 5, 1858, *Collections* of the Kansas State Historical Society, XIV (1918), 99–101.

James, Marquis, and Harold Ickes. "The National Domain and the New Deal," *Saturday Evening Post*, CCVI (December 23, 1933), 10–11, 55.

Knight, Oliver. "Correcting Nature's Error: The Colorado-Big Thompson Project," *Agricultural History*, XXX (October, 1956), 157–169.

Lee, Lawrence B. "The Homestead Act: Vision and Reality," *Utah Historical Quarterly*, XXX (September, 1962), 215–234.

Libby, Owen G. (ed.). "Bonanza Farms and the One Crop System of Agriculture," *Collections* of the State Historical Society of North Dakota, III (Bismarck, 1910), 569–596.

Mattison, Ray H. "Homestead National Monument," *Nebraska History*, XLIII (March, 1962), 1–27.

Merrill, O. C. "A Hundred Million Horse Power Waiting to Be Used," *The Independent*, CIII (August 14, 1920), 172, 195–196.

Mesnard, Erie. "Surveys," *Firelands Pioneer* (Sandusky, Ohio), V (June, 1864), 94.

Michelson, Charles. "The War for the Range," *Munsey's Magazine*, XXVIII (December, 1902), 380–382.

"Middle Park Claim Club, 1861," *The Colorado Magazine*, X (September, 1933), 190–192.

Middleton, James. "The New West," *World's Work*, XXXI (April, 1916), 669–680.

Murray, Fred J. "Paul Bunyan's Rival," *Review of Reviews*, XCV (June, 1937), 44–45.

Pack, Arthur Newton. "Look Out for the Greased Pig," *Nature*, XXXI (January, 1938), 45–46.

Page, Arthur W. "Running a River Through a Mountain," *World's Work*, XIV (September, 1907), 9322–9330.

Parke, Hervey. "Reminiscences," *Michigan Pioneer Collections*, III (1881), 572–590.

Pinchot, Gifford. "How Conservation Began in the United States," *Agricultural History*, XI (October, 1937), 255–265.

Potter, Albert F. "How the Forest Service Has Helped the Stockmen," *American Forestry*, XXIV (March, 1918), 165–169.

Power, James B. "Bits of History Connected with the Early Days of the Northern Pacific Railway," *Collections* of the State Historical Society of North Dakota, III (1911), 337–349.

Reynolds, Arthur R. "The Kinkaid Act and Its Effects," *Agricultural History*, XXIII (January, 1949), 20–29.

———. "Land Frauds and Illegal Fencing in Western Nebraska," *Agricultural History*, XXIII (July, 1949), 173–179.

Ritchey, Charles J. "Claim Associations and Pioneer Democracy in Early Minnesota," *Minnesota History*, IX (June, 1928), 85–95.

Robbins, L. H. "Training Youth the CCC Way," *The New York Times Magazine* (August 11, 1940), pp. 8–9, 17.

Robeson, George F. "Justice in Early Iowa," *Palimpsest*, V (March, 1924), 102–113.

Rodolf, Theodore. "Pioneering in the Wisconsin Lead Region," *Collections* of the State Historical Society of Wisconsin, XV (1900), 338–389.

Rollins, George W. "Land Policies of the United States as Applied to Utah to 1910," *Utah Historical Quarterly*, XX (July, 1952), 239–251.

Sawyer, Alvah L. "The Forests of the Upper Peninsula and their Place in History," *Michigan History Magazine*, III (July, 1919), 367–383.

Sayre, Edward L. "Early Days in and about Bellevue," *Collections* of the Nebraska State Historical Society, XVI (1911), 66–114.

Silcox, F. A. "Our Adventure in Conservation—the CCC," *Atlantic Monthly*, CLX (December, 1937), 714–722.

Smith, Henry Nash. "Clarence King, John Wesley Powell, and the Establishment of the United States Geological Survey," *Mississippi Valley Historical Review*, XXXIV (June, 1947), 37–58.

Snow, E. P. Letter to the Editor, *Outlook*, LXXIII (April 4, 1903), 839–840.

Sterling, Everett W. "The Powell Irrigation Survey, 1888–1893," *Mississippi Valley Historical Review*, XXVII (December, 1940), 421–434.

Trimble, William J. "The Influence of the Passing of the Public Lands," *Atlantic Monthly*, CXIII (June, 1914), 755–767.

Tugwell, Rexford G. "Our New National Domain," *Scribner's Magazine*, XCIX (March, 1936), 164–168.

Van der Zee, Jacob. "The Opening of the Des Moines Valley," *Iowa Journal of History and Politics*, XIV (October, 1916), 479–558.

Victor, Frances F. "Our Public Land System and Its Relation to Education in the United States," *The Quarterly of the Oregon Historical Society*, I (June, 1900), 132–157.

Walker, William. "Governor Walker's Notes on the Early History of Nebraska," *Collections* of the Nebraska State Historical Society, III (1899), 58–60.

Ware, Eugene F. "History of Sun-Gold Section," *Kansas Historical Quarterly*, VI (August, 1937), 295–314.

———. "The Neutral Lands," *Transactions* of the Kansas State Historical Society, VI (1900), 147–169.

White, Charles A. "The Early Homes and Homemakers of Iowa," *Annals of Iowa*, 3d series, IV (October, 1899), 179–195.

Wicks, Hamilton S. "The Opening of Oklahoma," *Cosmopolitan*, VII (September, 1889), 460–470.

Widney, S. W. "Pioneer Sketches of DeKalb County," *Indiana Magazine of History*, XXV (June, 1929), 104–166.

Wilbur, Ray Lyman. "What About Our Public Lands," *Review of Reviews*, LXXX (December, 1929), 56–58.

Willey, Day Allen. "What Conservation Means to the Nation's Progress," *Putnam's Magazine*, VII (December, 1909), 259–270.

Wood, A. B. "The Coad Brothers, Panhandle Cattle Kings," *Nebraska History*, XIX (January–March, 1938), 28–43.

8. County and Local Histories

Angel, Myron (comp.). *A Memorial and Biographical History of the Counties of Fresno, Tulare, and Kern, California.* Chicago: Lewis Publishing Co., 1892.

Antrobus, Augustine M. *History of Des Moines County* [Iowa]. 2 vols. Chicago: S. J. Clarke Publishing Co., 1915.

Armor, Samuel (ed.). *History of Orange County, California.* Los Angeles: Historic Record Company, 1911.

Bagley, Clarence. *History of King County, Washington.* Chicago: S. J. Clarke Publishing Co., 1929.

———. *Pioneer Seattle and Its Founders.* Seattle: Argus Print, 1925.

Baldwin, Elmer. *History of La Salle County, Illinois.* Chicago: Rand McNally, 1877.

Barce, Elmore, and Robert A. Swan. *History of Benton County, Indiana.* Fowler, Indiana: Benton Review Shop, 1930.

Besson, J. A. B. *History of Eufaula, Alabama, the Bluff City of the Chattahoochee.* Atlanta, Georgia, 1875.

Betts, Edward Chambers. *Early History of Huntsville, Alabama.* Montgomery: The Brown Printing Company, 1916.

Black, Samuel T. *San Diego County, California.* Chicago: S. J. Clarke Publishing Company, 1913.

Boies, Henry Lamson. *History of DeKalb County, Illinois.* Chicago, 1868.

Butcher, S. D. *Pioneer History of Custer County.* Broken Bow, Nebraska: The Merchants Publishing Company, 1910.

Chamberlain, William Henry, and Harry Laurenz Wells. *History of Sutter County, California.* Oakland: Thompson & West, 1879.

———. *History of Yuba County, California.* Oakland, 1879.

Child, A. L. *Centennial History of Plattsmouth City and Cass County, Nebraska.* Plattsmouth City, Nebraska: Herald Book and Job Printing House, 1877.

Clark, Robert C. *History of the Willamette Valley, Oregon.* Chicago: S. J. Clarke Publishing Company, 1927.

Coles County, Illinois, History of. (No author given.) Chicago, 1879.

Daily News Journal History of Buchanan County [Missouri]. St. Joseph, 1898.

Davis, Winfield. *An Illustrated History of Sacramento County* [California]. Chicago: Lewis Publishing Company, 1890.

De Milt, A. P. *Story of an Old Town.* Omaha: Douglas Printing Co., 1902.

Dodge, Orvil. *Pioneer History of Coos and Curry Counties.* Salem, Oregon, 1898.

Duncan, L. Wallace, and Charles F. Scott. *History of Allen and Woodson Counties* [Kansas]. Iola, Kansas: The Iola Register, 1901.

Fagan, David. *History of Benton County, Oregon.* Portland, 1885.

Field, David D. *A History of the County of Berkshire, Massachusetts.* Pittsfield, 1829.

Franklin County, Pennsylvania, History of. (Author not given.) Chicago, 1887.

Gaston, W. L. and A. R. Humphrey. *History of Custer County, Nebraska.* Lincoln: Western Publishing and Engraving Company, 1919.

Goodrich, Albert. *History of Anoka County, Minnesota.* Minneapolis: Hennepin Publishing Company, 1905.

Grant County, Wisconsin, History of. (Author not given.) Chicago: Western Publishing Company, 1881.

Gregory, Tom. *History of Sonoma County.* Los Angeles: Historic Record Co., 1911.

Heilbron, Carl H. *History of San Diego County.* San Diego: San Diego Press Club, 1936.

Henderson, John G. *Early History of the "Sangamon Country"* [Illinois]. Davenport, Iowa, 1873.

History of Boone County, Iowa. Des Moines: Union Historical Company, 1880.

Holcombe, R. I. *Compendium of History and Biography of Minneapolis and Hennepin County.* Chicago: H. Taylor, 1914.

Holley, William. *Centennial Book of Alameda County* [California]. Oakland, 1876.

Holmes, Elmer W., and others. *History of Riverside County, California.* Los Angeles: Historic Record Company, 1912.

Hulaniski, Frederick J. *Contra Costa County.* Berkeley: The Elms Publishing Company Inc., 1917.

Humboldt County, California, History of. (Author not given.) San Francisco: W. W. Elliott & Co., 1882.

Illustrated History of Plumas, Lassen, and Sierra Counties. San Francisco: Ferris and Smith, 1882.

Kanaga, Mrs. Tillie. *History of Napa County, California.* Oakland: Enquirer Print, 1901.

Keffer, Frank M. *History of San Fernando Valley.* Glendale: Stillman Printing Co., 1934.

Kennedy, Robert P. *The Historical Review of Logan County, Ohio.* Chicago, 1903.

Leftwich, Nina. *Two Hundred Years at Muscle Shoals.* Tuscumbia, Alabama: Press of Multigraphic Advertising Co., 1935.

Little, John Buckner. *History of Butler County, Alabama, 1815–1885.* Cincinnati, 1895.

Martin, Edward. *History of Santa Cruz County, California.* Los Angeles: Historic Record Company, 1911.

Martin, John Bartlow. *Call it North Country: The Story of Upper Michigan.* New York: Knopf, 1944.

Mason, J. D. *History of Amador County.* Oakland, California, 1881.

Meginness, John F. (ed.). *Proceedings of the Centennial Anniversary of Lycoming County, Pennsylvania.* Williamsport, Pennsylvania, 1896.

Menefee, Eugene L., and Fred A. Dodge. *History of Tulare and King Counties.* Los Angeles: Historic Record Co., 1913.

Mokler, Alfred J. *History of Natrona County, Wyoming, 1888–1922.* Chicago: R. R. Donnelley and Sons, 1923.

Morgan, Wallace M. *History of Kern County, California.* Los Angeles: Historic Record Company, 1914.

Munro-Fraser, J. P. *History of Alameda County.* Oakland, 1883.

Neill, Edward D. *History of Ramsey County and the City of St. Paul.* Minneapolis: North Star Pub. Co., 1881.

Nodaway County, History of. (Author not given.) St. Joseph, Missouri, 1882.

Oliver, David D. *Centennial History of Alpena County, Michigan.* Alpena: Argus Printing House, 1903.

Olsen, Charles Oluf (ed.). *Writers' Program W.P.A., History of Linn County, Oregon.* MS, Library of Congress.

Orange County History Series. Vol. 3. Santa Anna, California: Orange County Historical Society, 1939.

Page, Oliver J. *History of Massac County, Illinois.* Metropolis, Illinois, 1900.

Palmer, Friend. *Early Days in Detroit.* Detroit: Hunt and June, 1906.

Palmer, Lyman L. *History of Napa and Lake Counties, California.* San Francisco, 1881.

Placer County, California, History of. (No author given.) Oakland, California: Thompson & West, 1882.

Powers, Perry F. *A History of Northern Michigan.* Chicago: Lewis Publishing Co., 1912.

Randall, T. E. *History of the Chippewa Valley.* Eau Claire, Wisconsin, 1875.

Rathbun, J. C. *History of Thurston County.* Olympia, Washington, 1895.

Riley, Benjamin Franklin. *History of Conecuh County* [Alabama]. Columbus, Georgia, 1881.

Roenigk, Adolph. *Pioneer History of Kansas.* Lincoln, Kansas: Adolph Roenigk, 1933.

Rupp, Daniel. *The History and Topography of Dauphin, Cumberland, Franklin, Bedford, Adams, and Perry Counties, Pennsylvania.* Lancaster, Pennsylvania, 1846.

San Joaquin County, History of [California]. (Author not given.) Chicago, 1890.

San Luis Obispo County, California, History of. (Author not given.) Oakland, California: Thompson & West, 1883.

Saunders, James Edmond. *Early Settlers of Alabama.* New Orleans, 1899.

Shaver, F. A. *An Illustrated History of Central Oregon.* Spokane, 1905.

Shrader, Forest B. *History of Washington County, Nebraska.* Omaha: Magic City Printing Co., 1937.

Shumway, Grant Lee. *History of Western Nebraska and Its People.* 3 vols., Vols. I–III. Lincoln, Nebraska: Western Publishing and Engraving Company, 1921.

Smiley, Jerome C. *Semi-Centennial History of the State of Colorado.* 2 vols., Vol. I. Chicago and New York: Lewis Publishing Co., 1913.

Smith, Nelson F. *History of Pickens County, Alabama.* Carrollton, Alabama, 1856.

Sorenson, Alfred. *The Story of Omaha.* Omaha: National Printing Company, 1923.

Stanger, Frank M. *History of San Mateo County.* San Mateo, California: San Mateo Times, 1938.

Steele, Richard F. *An Illustrated History of the Big Bend Country* [Washington]. Place of publication not given: Western Historical Publishing Company, 1904.

Stoddard, W. H. *Turner County Pioneer History.* Sioux Falls, South Dakota: Press of Brown and Saenger, 1931.

Towne, Arthur. *Old Prairie Days.* Otsego, Michigan: Otsego Union Press, 1941.

Wakeley, Arthur C. *Omaha and Douglas County.* 2 vols., Vol. I. Chicago: Western Publishing and Engraving Company, 1917.

Walling, Albert G. *History of Lane County, Oregon.* Place of publication not given, 1884.

Wells, Harry L. *History of Butte County, California.* San Francisco, 1882.

———. *History of Siskiyou County, California.* Oakland, 1881.

Welsh, Wm. D. *A Brief History of Oregon City and West Linn.* (Pamphlet) Oregon City: Oregon City Chamber of Commerce, 1941.

Whittlesey, Charles. *Early History of Cleveland, Ohio.* Cleveland, 1867.

Who's Who in Nebraska, 1940. Lincoln: Nebraska Press Association, 1940.

Williams, Harry Lee. *History of Craighead County, Arkansas.* Little Rock: Parke-Harper Company, 1930.

Williams, Irene Dunn. *Reminiscences of Early Eugene and Lane County, Oregon.* (Pamphlet) Eugene: Published by the author, 1941.

Woolridge, Jesse Walton. *History of the Sacramento Valley, California.* 3 vols., Vol. I. Chicago: Pioneer Historical Publishing Company, 1931.

9. GENERAL HISTORIES

Abernethy, Thomas Perkins. *The Formative Period in Alabama, 1815–1828.* Montgomery, Alabama: Brown Printing Company, 1922.

Andreas, Alfred Theodore. *History of the State of Kansas.* 2 vols., Vol. I, Chicago, 1883.

Bagley, Clarence. *The Acquisition and Pioneering of Old Oregon.* Seattle: Argus Print, 1924.

Bancroft, Hubert H. *The Works of Hubert H. Bancroft.* 39 vols., Vol. XXXIV. San Francisco, 1888.

Blackmar, Frank W. *The Life of Charles Robinson.* Topeka: Crane Printers, 1902.

Boggess, Arthur Clinton. *The Settlement of Illinois.* Chicago: The Chicago Historical Society, 1908.

Bond, Beverly W. *The Foundations of Ohio.* Columbus: The Ohio Archeological and Historical Society, 1941.

Briggs, Harold E. *Frontiers of the Northwest.* New York: D. Appleton-Century Company, 1940.

Brunken, Ernest. *North American Forests and Forestry.* New York, 1900.

Burlingame, Merrill G. *The Montana Frontier.* Helena: State Publishing Company, 1942.

Butler, Mann. *A History of the Commonwealth of Kentucky.* Louisville, 1834.

Carey, Charles Henry. *A General History of Oregon.* 2 vols., Vols. I–II. Portland, Oregon: Metropolitan Press, 1935–1936.

Carhart, Arthur H. *The National Forests.* New York: Knopf, 1959.

Clepper, Henry, and Arthur B. Meyer (eds.). *American Forestry: Six Decades of Growth.* Washington, D.C.: Society of American Foresters, 1960.

Cockrum, William M. *Pioneer History of Indiana.* Oakland City, Indiana: Press of *Oakland City Journal,* 1907.

Cole, Cyrenus. *Iowa Through the Years.* Iowa City, Iowa: The State Historical Society of Iowa, 1940.

Cotterill, R. S. *The Old South.* Glendale, California: Arthur H. Clark, 1937.

Cralle, Richard. *Speeches of John C. Calhoun.* New York: D. Appleton, 1883.

Crawford, Lewis F. (ed.). *Rekindling Camp Fires.* Bismarck, North Dakota: Capital Book Company, 1926.

Dale, Everett Edward, and Jesse Lee Roder. *Readings in Oklahoma History.* Evanston, Illinois: Row, Peterson and Company, 1930.

David, Robert B. *Malcolm Campbell, Sheriff.* Casper, Wyoming: Wyomingana, Inc., 1932.

Davis, Charles Shepard. *The Cotton Kingdom in Alabama.* Montgomery, Alabama: Auburn Printing Company, 1939.

Day, Sherman. *Historical Collections of Pennsylvania.* New Haven, 1843.

Dick, Everett. *The Dixie Frontier.* New York: Knopf, 1948.

———. *The Sod-House Frontier.* New York: D. Appleton-Century, 1937.

———. *Vanguards of the Frontier.* New York: D. Appleton-Century, 1941.

Ellison, Joseph. *California and the Nation.* Berkeley: University of California Press, 1927.

Esarey, Logan. *History of Indiana.* Indianapolis: W. K. Stewart Company, 1915.

Flandreau, Charles E. *The History of Minnesota and Tales of the Frontier.* St. Paul: E. W. Porter, 1900.

Folwell, William Watts. *A History of Minnesota.* 4 vols., Vol. I. St. Paul: Minnesota Historical Society, 1921.

Foss, Phillip A. *Politics and Grass.* Seattle: University of Washington Press, 1960.

Gates, Paul. *The Farmers Age, Agriculture 1815–1860.* New York: Holt, Rinehart & Winston, 1960.

Gettinger, Roy. *The Formation of the State of Oklahoma.* Berkeley, California: University of California Press, 1917.

Hafen, LeRoy. *Colorado and Its People*. 4 vols., Vol. II. New York: Lewis Historical Publishing Company, 1948.

Hanna, Charles A. *The Scotch-Irish*. New York: G. P. Putnam's Sons, 1902.

Hinsdale, Burke Aaron. *The Old Northwest*. New York, 1888.

Holbrook, Stewart H. *Holy Old Mackinaw*. New York: Macmillan & Company, 1938.

Howe, Henry. *Historical Collections of Ohio*. Cincinnati, 1875.

Hulbert, Archer Butler (ed.). *Ohio in the Time of the Confederation*. Marietta, Ohio: Marietta Historical Commission, 1918.

Humphrey, Seth K. *Following the Prairie Frontier*. Minneapolis: University of Minnesota Press, 1931.

Ise, John. *The United States Forest Policy*. New Haven, Connecticut: Yale University Press, 1920.

Kellar, Herbert Anthony (ed.). *Solon Robinson, Pioneer and Agriculturist*, I, 1825–1845, in *Indiana Historical Collections*, XXI. Indianapolis: Indiana Historical Bureau, 1936.

King, Judson. *The Great Conservation Fight*. Washington, D.C.: Public Affairs Press, 1959.

Kingsbury, George. *History of Dakota Territory*. 2 vols., Vol. I. Chicago: S. J. Clarke Company, 1915.

Kohl, Edith Eudora. *Land of the Burnt Thigh*. New York: Funk and Wagnalls, 1938.

Kraenzel, Carl F. *The Northern Plains in a World of Change*. Toronto: Gregory-Cartwright, Ltd., 1942.

Lamar, Howard Roberts. *Dakota Territory 1861–1889*. New Haven: Yale University Publications, 1956.

Levering, Julia Henderson. *Historic Indiana*. New York: Arthur H. Clark, 1909.

Lillard, Richard G. *The Great Forest*. New York: Knopf, 1947.

Linford, Velma. *Wyoming Frontier State*. Denver: Old West Publishing Company, 1947.

Lyman, George D. *John Marsh, Pioneer; The Life Story of a Trail Blazer*. New York: Scribners, 1930.

McCoy, Joseph G. *Historic Sketches of the Cattle Trade of the West*. Kansas City, Mo., 1874.

McDonald, John. *Biographical Sketches of General Nathaniel Massie*. Cincinnati, 1838.

MacMinn, Edwin. *On the Frontier with Colonel Antes*. Camden, New Jersey: S. Chew & Sons, Printers, 1900.

McNamara, John. *Three Years on the Kansas Border*. New York, 1856.

McNeal, T. A. *When Kansas Was Young*. New York: Macmillan and Company, 1922.

Macy, Jesse. *Institutional Beginnings in a Western State* [Iowa]. Baltimore: The Johns Hopkins Press, 1884.

Marshall, Robert. *The People's Forests*. New York: H. Smith, 1933.

Masterson, Vincent Victor. *The Katy Railroad and the Last Frontier*. Norman, Oklahoma: University of Oklahoma Press, 1952.

Meany, Edmond S. *History of the State of Washington*. New York: Macmillan and Company, 1924.

Moore, Albert B. *History of Alabama and Her People*. New York: American Historical Society, 1927.

Morton, J. Sterling, and Albert Watkins. *Illustrated History of Nebraska*. 3 vols., Vol. I. Lincoln: J. North and Co., 1906.

Mowry, George E. *Theodore Roosevelt and the Progressive Movement*. Madison: University of Wisconsin Press, 1946.

Nelligan, John Emmett. *The Life of a Lumberman*. Place of publication and publisher not given, 1929.

Nelson, Bruce. *Land of the Dakotahs*. Minneapolis: University of Minnesota Press, 1946.

Nevins, Allan. *Fremont, the West's Greatest Adventurer*. 2 vols., Vol. II. New York: Harper and Brothers, 1928.

Nixon, Edgar B. (ed.). *Franklin D. Roosevelt and Conservation*. Hyde Park, New York: Administration, National Archives and Records Service, Franklin D. Roosevelt Library, 1957.

Osgood, Ernest S. *The Day of the Cattleman*. Minneapolis: University of Minnesota Press, 1929.

Overton, Richard C. *Burlington West, A Colonization History of the Burlington Railroad*. Cambridge: Harvard University Press, 1941.

Parish, John C. *The Life of George W. Jones*. Iowa City, Iowa: State Historical Society of Iowa, 1912.

Parker, George F. *Pioneer Foundations* (Iowa). 2 vols., Vol. I. Iowa City: The State Historical Society of Iowa, 1940.

Pelzer, Louis. *The Cattlemen's Frontier*. Glendale, California: Arthur H. Clark Company, 1936.

Pinchot, Gifford. *Breaking New Ground*. New York: Harcourt, 1947.

Pooley, Vipond. *The Settlement of Illinois from 1830–1850*. Madison, Wisconsin: *Bulletin of the University of Wisconsin*, No. 220, 1908.

Prosch, Thomas W. *David S. Maynard, and Catherine I. Maynard*. Seattle: Lowman and Hanford Stationery and Printing Co., 1906.

Raine, Wm. MacLeod, and Will C. Barnes. *Cattle*. Garden City, New York: Grosset and Dunlap, 1930.

Richardson, Albert D. *Beyond the Mississippi*. Hartford, Connecticut, 1869.

Roosevelt, Theodore. *Winning of the West*. 4 vols., Vol. III. New York, 1889–1896.

Royce, Charles C. *John Bidwell, Pioneer, Statesman, Philanthropist*. Chico, California: C. C. Royce, 1906.

Russell, Charles Edward. *A-Raftin' on the Mississip'*. New York: The Century Company, 1928.

Sandoz, Mari. *Old Jules*. Boston: Little, Brown and Company, 1935.

———. *The Cattlemen*. New York: Hastings House, 1958.

Scherer, James A. B. *The First Forty-Niner*. New York: Minton, Balch and Company, 1925.

Shannon, Fred A. *The Farmers' Last Frontier*. New York: Farrar and Rinehart, Inc., 1945.

Shinn, Josiah H. *Pioneers and Makers of Arkansas*. Little Rock: Genealogical and Historical Publishing Company, 1908.

Spring, Agnes Wright. *Pioneers of the Black Hills*. Glendale: Arthur H. Clark Company, 1957.

Stuart, Granville. *Forty Years on the Frontier*. 2 vols., Vol. II. Cleveland: Arthur H. Clark Company, 1925.

Taber, Clarence Wilbur. *Breaking Sod on the Prairies*. Yonkers, New York: World Book Company, 1924.

Thwaites, Reuben Gold, and Louise P. Kellogg (eds.). *Documentary History of Lord Dunmore's War*. Madison, Wisconsin: Wisconsin State Historical Society, 1905.

Tilghman, Zoe A. *Marshal of the Last Frontier; Life and Services of William (Bill) Matthew Tilghman*. Glendale, California: Arthur H. Clark Company, 1949.

Trottman, Nelson. *History of the Union Pacific*. New York: Ronald Press Company, 1923.

Turner, Frederick Jackson. *Significance of the Frontier in American History*. New York: Henry Holt, 1920.

Upton, Charles E. *Pioneers of El Dorado*. Placerville: Published by the author, 1906.

Vancil, Frank M. *Frontier Days*. Oliver G. Swan (ed.). Philadelphia: Macrae Smith and Company, 1928.

Walker, Tacetta B. *Stories of Early Days in Wyoming*. Casper, Wyoming: Prairie Publishing Company, 1936.

Warren, George Henry. *The Pioneer Woodsman*. Minneapolis: Press of Hahn and Harmon Company, 1914.

Webb, Walter Prescott. *The Great Plains*. Boston: Ginn and Company, 1931.

Wentworth, Edward N. *America's Sheep Trails*. Ames, Iowa: State College Press, 1948.

Wheeler, Colonel Homer W. *Buffalo Days*. Indianapolis: Bobbs-Merrill Co., 1925.

10. BOOKS ON LAND

Brown, Lulu Lemmon. *Cherokee Neutral Lands Controversy*. Girard, Kansas: Privately printed, 1931.

Buffum, B. C. *Arid Agriculture*. Privately printed, 1909.

Campbell, Hardy W. *Campbell's Soil Culture Manual*. Privately printed, 1902.

Chandler, Alfred N. *Land Title Origins*. New York: Robert Schalkenbach Foundation, 1928.

Clawson, Marion, and Burnell Held. *The Federal Lands: Their Use and Management*. Baltimore: The Johns Hopkins Press, 1957.

Clawson, Marion. *Land for the Future*. Baltimore: The Johns Hopkins Press, 1960.

———. *Uncle Sam's Acres*. New York: Dodd, Mead and Company, 1951.

Donaldson, Thomas C. *The Public Domain*. Washington, D.C.: Govt. Printing Office, 1884.

Dunham, Harold H. *Government Handout*. New York: Edwards Brothers, Inc., 1941.

Egleston, Melville. *The Land System of the New England Colonies*. New York, 1880.

Ford, Amelia C. *Colonial Precedents of our National Land System. Bulletin of the University of Wisconsin*, History Series, II, No. 2. Madison: University of Wisconsin, 1910.

Gates, Paul. *Fifty Million Acres*. Ithaca, New York: Cornell University Press, 1954.

———. *The Wisconsin Pine Lands of Cornell University*. Ithaca, New York: Cornell University Press, 1943.

Gustafson, A. F., and others. *Conservation in the United States*. Ithaca, New York: Comstock Publishing Company, 1944.

Hibbard, Benjamin. *A History of the Public Land Policies*. New York: Macmillan and Company, 1924.

Hill, Robert Tudor. *The Public Domain and Democracy, Studies in History, Economics and Public Law*. Vol. XXXVIII. New York: Columbia University Press, 1910.

Huffman, Roy E. *Irrigation Development*. New York: Ronald Press, 1953.

James, George Wharton. *Reclaiming the Arid West*. New York: Dodd, Mead and Company, 1917.

Lampen, Dorothy. *Economic and Social Aspects of Federal Reclamation*. Baltimore: The Johns Hopkins Press, 1930.

Lester, William W. *Decisions of the Interior Department in Public Land Cases*. Philadelphia, 1860.

Lokken, Roscoe L. *Iowa Public Land Disposal*. Iowa City: The State Historical Society of Iowa, 1942.

Mumey, Nolie (ed.). *Westerners' Brand Book for 1951*. Denver: The Westerners, 1952.

Neuhoff, Dorothy. *The Platte Purchase*. Washington University Studies, Vol. XI. St. Louis, 1924.

Parkins, A. E., and J. R. Whitaker (eds.). *Our National Resources*. New York: John Wiley and Sons, 1939.

Peffer, Louise E. *The Closing of the Public Domain*. Palo Alto: Stanford University Press, 1951.

Price, Charles R. *Irrigated Lands of the United States*. Los Angeles: Pan Pacific Press, 1909.

Puter, S. A. D., and Horace Stevens. *Looters of the Public Domain*. Portland: Portland Printing House, 1908.

Rister, Carl Coke. *Land Hunger*. Norman, Oklahoma: University of Oklahoma Press, 1942.

Robbins, Roy M. *Our Landed Heritage*. Lincoln, Nebraska: University of Nebraska Press, 1962.

Robinson, William W. *Land in California*. Berkeley, California: University of California Press, 1948.

Sakolski, Aaron M. *The Great American Land Bubble*. New York: Harper and Brothers, 1932.

Schafer, Joseph. *The Wisconsin Lead Region*. Madison, Wisconsin: State Historical Society of Wisconsin, 1932.

Sheldon, Addison E. *Land Systems and Land Policies in Nebraska*. Lincoln, Nebraska: Nebraska State Historical Society, 1936.

Shinn, Charles Howard. *Mining Camps, A Study in American Government*. New York: Knopf, 1948.

Smith, Guy Harold. *Conservation of Natural Resources*. New York: J. Wiley and Sons, 1950.

Smith, Henry Nash. *Virgin Land*. Cambridge: Harvard University Press, 1950.

Smythe, William E. *The Conquest of Arid America*. New York: Harper and Brothers, 1905.

Stegner, Wallace. *Beyond the Hundredth Meridian*. Boston: Houghton Mifflin, 1954.

Stephenson, George M. *The Political History of the Public Lands from 1840 to 1862*. Boston: R. G. Badger, 1917.

Stewart, Lowell O. *Public Land Surveys*. Ames, Iowa: Collegiate Press, 1935.

Treat, Payson J. *The National Land System, 1785–1820*. New York: E. B. Treat & Co., 1910.

11. MANUSCRIPT THESES AND DISSERTATIONS

Agnew, Dwight. "The Government Surveyor as a Pioneer." Master's thesis, University of Iowa, 1938.

Albrecht, Abraham. "Mennonite Settlement in Kansas." Master's thesis, University of Kansas, 1925.

Allison, May. "Conditions in the Illinois Country, 1787–1800." Master's thesis, University of Illinois, 1907.

Fries, Robert F. "A History of the Lumber Industry in Wisconsin." Doctor's thesis, University of Wisconsin, 1939.

Kershaw, Mary Catherine. "Early History of Shawneetown, Illinois." Master's thesis, University of Illinois, 1941.

Lichty, Kathryne. "A History of the Settlement of the Nebraska Sand Hills." Master's thesis, University of Wyoming, 1960.

Mellberg, Russell. "The Public Career of Moses P. Kinkaid." Master's thesis, University of Nebraska, 1933.

Morril, Jennie Hughes. "The Settlement of Alabama." Master's thesis, University of Wisconsin, 1905.

Robbins, Roy M. "A History of the Pre-emption of Public Lands." Doctor's thesis, University of Wisconsin, 1928.

Smith, George Winston. "Problems in the Economic Development of Dixon, Illinois." Bachelor's thesis, University of Illinois, 1934.

Index

Abel, Edward, of Cherry County, Nebr., 246
Aberdeen, So. Dak., 303
Abilene, Kans., 220, 221, 243
Absentee landlords, 144
Absentee owners, 213
Absentee ownership, 205, 217
Absentee speculator, 213
Act for the Armed Occupation and Settlement of East Florida, 128
Adams County, Wash., 167
Agents: sent from General Land Office, 47; immigration, 158; of railroads sent to Europe, 175; to preserve forest resources, 193–194; of General Land Office, 193; trap set for, 197; sent by government to Sand Hills, 253
Akin, C. C., tarred and feathered, 148
Alabama, 11, 123, 162, 180, 192, 193, 195, 199, 208; worst hit by installment buying, 11; land relinquished, 12
Alameda County, Calif., 76
Alaska, 364
Alcalde, 83, 95
Aliens, required to begin naturalization process before registering for land, 295
Allard, Mont., 222
Allegheny River, 182
Alternate sections, 161–162, 175
Alva, Okla., 294
Alvarado, Juan B., 74
American Sheep Breeder, 344, 345
Anadarko, Okla., 294
Anderson, Ranger, of Kooskia, Ida., 335
Anderson, Mary, 43
Anglo-American Cattle Company, 250
Anticonservation, 338
Anti-Leaguers, 163, 164
Appalachian Mountains, 2, 5, 50
Appropriation: doctrine of, 310, 311; right of, 311
Arapahoe County Claim Club, 111
Arbor Day, 224
Ard, Newt, 163

Arizona, 30, 70, 80, 83, 84, 223, 257, 308, 313, 342
Arkansas, 121, 126, 181, 184; fraudulent claims sold in, 17; donation bill, 126–127
Arkansas City, Kans., 271, 284
Arkansas River, 231, 243, 244, 246, 316
Arkansas Valley Land Company, 246
Armijo, Manuel, 81
Armstrong, Ensign John, 50
Arnold, Ben, 224
Articles of Confederation, 19, 356
Ashland, Wisc., 197
Assignment of claims, 229, 230
Atchison, Kans., 111
Attorney, contesting, 148. *See also* Lawyers
Attorney General, 82, 119, 181, 205, 331, 343
Auction: public, 6, 12, 36; law provided for, 6, 7; feature of Harrison Land Law, 9; of relinquished lands, 12, 13; free, 13, 57; description of, 37–38, 64, 65; practices, 38; private, 39, 200; a sham, 47; fraud, 57, 200; law to assure fair dealing, 58; speculators bid against squatters, 59; land covered by, 64, at Dubuque, Ia., 64; mock, 65; of mineral lands, 86, 91, 357; ordered held at Kaskaskia, Ill., 86; at Mineral Point, 92; difficult to hold land after, 108; culled land, 123; at Osage, Ia., 132; of logs rigged, 184; collusion at, 186, 200; held only in special cases, 189; of state school lands, 190; collusion at private ones, 190; competition eliminated at, 190; not fair, 199; at Chocchuma, Miss., 200; government, 200; price sometimes above minimum, 212; of town lots, 266; largely a farce, 356–357
Auctioneer, 37, 64, 200, 201
Aughey, Samuel, 300
Austin, Moses, 17, 205
Australia, 213
Axmen, 23

389